Lecture Notes in Computer Science

Vol. 1: GI-Gesellschaft für Informatik e.V. 3. Jahrestagung, Hamburg, 8.–10. Oktober 1973. Herausgegeben im Auftrag der Gesellschaft für Informatik von W. Brauer. XI, 508 Seiten. 1973.

Vol. 2: GI-Gesellschaft für Informatik e.V. 1. Fachtagung über Automatentheorie und Formale Sprachen, Bonn, 9.–12. Juli 1973. Herausgegeben im Auftrag der Gesellschaft für Informatik von K.-H. Böhling und K. Indermark. VII, 322 Seiten. 1973.

Vol. 3: 5th Conference on Optimization Techniques, Part I. (Series: I.F.I.P. TC7 Optimization Conferences.) Edited by R. Conti and A. Ruberti. XIII, 565 pages. 1973.

Vol. 4: 5th Conference on Optimization Techniques, Part II. (Series: I.F.I.P. TC7 Optimization Conferences.) Edited by R. Conti and A. Ruberti. XIII, 389 pages. 1973.

Vol. 5: International Symposium on Theoretical Programming. Edited by A. Ershov and V. A. Nepomniaschy. VI, 407 pages. 1974.

Vol. 6: B. T. Smith, J. M. Boyle, J. J. Dongarra, B. S. Garbow, Y. Ikebe, V. C. Klema, and C. B. Moler, Matrix Eigensystem Routines – EISPACK Guide. XI, 551 pages. 2nd Edition 1974. 1976.

Vol. 7: 3. Fachtagung über Programmiersprachen, Kiel, 5.–7. März 1974. Herausgegeben von B. Schlender und W. Frielinghaus. VI, 225 Seiten. 1974.

Vol. 8: GI-NTG Fachtagung über Struktur und Betrieb von Rechensystemen, Braunschweig, 20.–22. März 1974. Herausgegeben im Auftrag der GI und der NTG von H.-O. Leilich. VI, 340 Seiten. 1974.

Vol. 9: GI-BIFOA Internationale Fachtagung: Informationszentren in Wirtschaft und Verwaltung. Köln, 17./18. Sept. 1973. Herausgegeben im Auftrag der GI und dem BIFOA von P. Schmitz. VI, 259 Seiten. 1974.

Vol. 10: Computing Methods in Applied Sciences and Engineering, Part 1. International Symposium, Versailles, December 17–21, 1973. Edited by R. Glowinski and J. L. Lions. X, 497 pages. 1974.

Vol. 11: Computing Methods in Applied Sciences and Engineering, Part 2. International Symposium, Versailles, December 17–21, 1973. Edited by R. Glowinski and J. L. Lions. X, 434 pages. 1974.

Vol. 12: GFK-GI-GMR Fachtagung Prozessrechner 1974. Karlsruhe, 10.–11. Juni 1974. Herausgegeben von G. Krüger und R. Friehmelt. XI, 620 Seiten. 1974.

Vol. 13: Rechnerstrukturen und Betriebsprogrammierung, Erlangen, 1970. (GI-Gesellschaft für Informatik e.V.) Herausgegeben von W. Händler und P. P. Spies. VII, 333 Seiten. 1974.

Vol. 14: Automata, Languages and Programming – 2nd Colloquium, University of Saarbrücken, July 29–August 2, 1974. Edited by J. Loeckx. VIII, 611 pages. 1974.

Vol. 15: L Systems. Edited by A. Salomaa and G. Rozenberg. VI, 338 pages. 1974.

Vol. 16: Operating Systems, International Symposium, Rocquencourt 1974. Edited by E. Gelenbe and C. Kaiser. VIII, 310 pages. 1974.

Vol. 17: Rechner-Gestützter Unterricht RGU '74, Fachtagung, Hamburg, 12.–14. August 1974, ACU-Arbeitskreis Computer-Unterstützter Unterricht. Herausgegeben im Auftrag der GI von K. Brunnstein, K. Haefner und W. Händler. X, 417 Seiten. 1974.

Vol. 18: K. Jensen and N. E. Wirth, PASCAL – User Manual and Report. VII, 170 pages. Corrected Reprint of the 2nd Edition 1976.

Vol. 19: Programming Symposium. Proceedings 1974. V, 425 pages. 1974.

Vol. 20: J. Engelfriet, Simple Program Schemes and Formal Languages. VII, 254 pages. 1974.

Vol. 21: Compiler Construction, An Advanced Course. Edited by F. L. Bauer and J. Eickel. XIV. 621 pages. 1974.

Vol. 22: Formal Aspects of Cognitive Processes. Proceedings 1972. Edited by T. Storer and D. Winter. V, 214 pages. 1975.

Vol. 23: Programming Methodology. 4th Informatik Symposium, IBM Germany Wildbad, September 25–27, 1974. Edited by C. E. Hackl. VI, 501 pages. 1975.

Vol. 24: Parallel Processing. Proceedings 1974. Edited by T. Feng. VI, 433 pages. 1975.

Vol. 25: Category Theory Applied to Computation and Control. Proceedings 1974. Edited by E. G. Manes. X, 245 pages. 1975.

Vol. 26: GI-4. Jahrestagung, Berlin, 9.–12. Oktober 1974. Herausgegeben im Auftrag der GI von D. Siefkes. IX, 748 Seiten. 1975.

Vol. 27: Optimization Techniques. IFIP Technical Conference. Novosibirsk, July 1–7, 1974. (Series: I.F.I.P. TC7 Optimization Conferences.) Edited by G. I. Marchuk. VIII, 507 pages. 1975.

Vol. 28: Mathematical Foundations of Computer Science. 3rd Symposium at Jadwisin near Warsaw, June 17–22, 1974. Edited by A. Blikle. VII, 484 pages. 1975.

Vol. 29: Interval Mathematics. Procedings 1975. Edited by K. Nickel. VI, 331 pages. 1975.

Vol. 30: Software Engineering. An Advanced Course. Edited by F. L. Bauer. (Formerly published 1973 as Lecture Notes in Economics and Mathematical Systems, Vol. 81) XII, 545 pages. 1975.

Vol. 31: S. H. Fuller, Analysis of Drum and Disk Storage Units. IX, 283 pages. 1975.

Vol. 32: Mathematical Foundations of Computer Science 1975. Proceedings 1975. Edited by J. Bečvář. X, 476 pages. 1975.

Vol. 33: Automata Theory and Formal Languages, Kaiserslautern, May 20–23, 1975. Edited by H. Brakhage on behalf of GI. VIII, 292 Seiten. 1975.

Vol. 34: GI – 5. Jahrestagung, Dortmund 8.–10. Oktober 1975. Herausgegeben im Auftrag der GI von J. Mühlbacher. X, 755 Seiten. 1975.

Vol. 35: W. Everling, Exercises in Computer Systems Analysis. (Formerly published 1972 as Lecture Notes in Economics and Mathematical Systems, Vol. 65) VIII, 184 pages. 1975.

Vol. 36: S. A. Greibach, Theory of Program Structures: Schemes, Semantics, Verification. XV, 364 pages. 1975.

Vol. 37: C. Böhm, λ-Calculus and Computer Science Theory. Proceedings 1975. XII, 370 pages. 1975.

Vol. 38: P. Branquart, J.-P. Cardinael, J. Lewi, J.-P. Delescaille, M. Vanbegin. An Optimized Translation Process and Its Application to ALGOL 68. IX, 334 pages. 1976.

Vol. 39: Data Base Systems. Proceedings 1975. Edited by H. Hasselmeier and W. Spruth. VI, 386 pages. 1976.

Vol. 40: Optimization Techniques. Modeling and Optimization in the Service of Man. Part 1. Proceedings 1975. Edited by J. Cea. XIV, 854 pages. 1976.

Vol. 41: Optimization Techniques. Modeling and Optimization in the Service of Man. Part 2. Proceedings 1975. Edited by J. Cea. XIII, 852 pages. 1976.

Vol. 42: James E. Donahue, Complementary Definitions of Programming Language Semantics. VII, 172 pages. 1976.

Vol. 43: E. Specker und V. Strassen, Komplexität von Entscheidungsproblemen. Ein Seminar. V, 217 Seiten. 1976.

Vol. 44: ECI Conference 1976. Proceedings 1976. Edited by K. Samelson. VIII, 322 pages. 1976.

Vol. 45: Mathematical Foundations of Computer Science 1976. Proceedings 1976. Edited by A. Mazurkiewicz. XI, 601 pages. 1976.

Vol. 46: Language Hierarchies and Interfaces. Edited by F. L. Bauer and K. Samelson. X, 428 pages. 1976.

Vol. 47: Methods of Algorithmic Language Implementation. Edited by A. Ershov and C. H. A. Koster. VIII, 351 pages. 1977.

Vol. 48: Theoretical Computer Science, Darmstadt, March 1977. Edited by H. Tzschach, H. Waldschmidt and H. K.-G. Walter on behalf of GI. VIII, 418 pages. 1977.

Lecture Notes in Computer Science

Edited by G. Goos and J. Hartmanis

76

Codes for Boundary-Value Problems in Ordinary Differential Equations

Proceedings of a Working Conference
May 14–17, 1978

Edited by
B. Childs, M. Scott, J. W. Daniel,
E. Denman and P. Nelson

Springer-Verlag
Berlin Heidelberg New York 1979

Editors

Prof. Bart Childs
Department of Industrial Engineering
Texas A & M University
College Station, Texas 77843/USA

Dr. Melvin Scott
Department of Applied Mathematics
Sandia Laboratories
Albuquerque, NM 87115/USA

Dr. Jim W. Daniel
Department of Mathematics
University of Texas at Austin
Austin, Texas 78712/USA

Dr. Eugene Denman
Department of Electrical Engineering
University of Houston
Houston, Texas 77004/USA

Dr. Paul Nelson
School of Mathematics
Georgia Tech
Atlanta, GA 30332/USA

AMS Subject Classifications (1970): 34 BXX, 56 LXX, 65 DXX, 65 KXX,
CR Subject Classifications (1974): 34 A10, 34 A34, 34 A50

ISBN 3-540-09554-3 Springer-Verlag Berlin Heidelberg New York
ISBN 0-387-09554-3 Springer-Verlag New York Heidelberg Berlin

Library of Congress Cataloging in Publication Data
Working Conference on Codes for Boundary-Value Problems in Ordinary Differential Equation, University of Houston, 1978.
Codes for boundary-value problems in ordinary differential equations.
(Lecture notes in computer science; v. 76)
Bibliography: p.
Includes index.
1. Differential equations--Numerical solutions-- Data processing--Congresses. 2. Boundary value problems--Numerical solutions--Data processing--Congresses. 3. Coding theory--Congresses. I. Childs, Bart, 1938- II. Title. III. Series.
QA372.W76 1978 519.4 79-21694
ISBN 0-387-09554-3

Printing and binding: Beltz Offsetdruck, Hemsbach/Bergstr.
2145/3140-543210

FOREWORD

I met Melvin Scott at the SIAM meeting in San Francisco, December 1975. In discussing the beauty of the host city and other finer points, we reached a mutual decision that there was need for a conference, workshop, and/or meeting with a central theme of Working Codes for Boundary-Value Problems in ODEs. Persuant to this conversation and some prodding telephone calls from Mel, we selected the organizing committee, we all agreed to serve, and we all worked to perform the many tasks necessary. The organizing committee of:

Jim Daniel - University of Texas at Austin
Gene Denman - University of Houston
Paul Nelson - Texas Tech University
(Paul was at Georgia Tech 1977-78)
Melvin Scott - Sandia Laboratories

was not selected because we felt that all knowledge springs from the Southwest, but because we had no budget for planning and we were close, geographically. We gratefully acknowledge our employing institutions for the individual assistance given during the planning.

We met in Austin, Texas to outline the proposals for support, identify codes for demonstration and to be the subject of expository papers, identify possible conference dates, compile mailing lists for solicition of participants, and discuss guidelines of selecting the final participants giving papers. I am especially pleased that the conference was well received and believe that this was largely due to the open-minded professional attitudes of the organizing committee at this meeting and through their subsequent efforts.

Our primary motivation came from appreciation of the advanced state of codes in the area, the fact that papers describing codes are often not publishable in the usual journals, that much was to be gained by having code authors, users, and potential users together in a pleasant surroundings, and that prompt publication of a proceedings would be proper.

We are grateful to Editors Juris Hartmanis and Cleve Moler for accepting this Proceedings into their outstanding series. The Proceedings contain many valuable papers and we express our appreciation to the authors for their efforts and also thank the participants who were not authors for their excellent participation.

The Working Conference on Codes for Boundary-Value Problems in Ordinary Differential Equation was held May 14-17, 1978 at the University of Houston. This meeting was jointly supported by the National Science Foundation, Grant No. MCS 77-22818 and the Department of Energy, Grant No. ER-78-G-05-5885. We are especially grateful for their support.

These proceedings contain the invited papers and the contributed papers presented at the Conference. Various workshops to discuss working codes, algorithms utilized in the codes and benchmark problems were held, and workshop reports are given in these Proceedings.

The first three papers in the Proceedings are invited survey papers on numerical methods for two-point boundary-value problems, initial value integrators, and nonlinear equation solvers. Three additional surveys are interspersed in the Proceedings, two on methods that are not as widely understood as finite difference and shooting methods, namely projection methods and invariant imbedding. The third survey paper describes various approaches in finite-difference and collocation codes for mesh selection.

Invited papers on working codes that are available for problem-solving are given in these proceedings. The codes presented at the conference were a) a shooting code for Sturm-Liouville problems (Bailey-Shampine), b) a finite-difference code for first-order systems (Pereyra), c) a multiple shooting code for first-order systems (Bulirsch), d) a multiple shooting code with orthogonalization (Scott), e) a spline-collocation code for mixed-order systems (Asher, Christiansen and Russell), and f) a shooting code for multipoint boundary-value problems arising in system identification (Childs-Porter). All of the above codes were demonstrated in some manner at the meeting and information on the codes is available from the authors or other sources.

The set of codes available from the NAG Library in England was described by Gladwell but were not demonstrated at the conference.

Numerous contributed papers were presented and the papers are published in these Proceedings. These papers describe particular aspects of solving boundary-value problems or discuss results of a numerical experiment in which boundary-value problems are encountered.

The code demonstration workshop at the conference was a valuable part of the meeting in that the workshop acted as a stimulus for active discussion of codes. Information gained from implementation of codes in a "conference environment" should be of value for future conferences. Code transportability did not prove to be a major problem, although considerable pre-conference effort is required for successful implementation.

We did exercise editorial license as a committee. Some worthwhile papers were not accepted for presentation at the conference. We have made some minor changes in some manuscripts to enhance clarity and have requested rewriting of others to meet the conference goals. I accept the responsibility for any errors we have made in these efforts. The statements and claims of the individual authors are their own and do not necessarily reflect the views of the committee, our institutions, or the sponsoring agencies NSF and DOE.

Finally, I wish to express my most sincere appreciation to Gene and Norma Denman and the University of Houston for the excellent facilities and hospitality they provided. As several participants have written, I owe the success and pleasant atmosphere of the conference to my wife Shirley for her many hours of work in making reservations, calling taxis, being a pleasant guide, being a stern camp director, and being herself. Other than the thanks I have spoken, the auditors will let me thank her only by dedicating this work to her and our wonderful daughter, Meredith.

S. Bart Childs
August 1978
College Station, Texas

Those interested in obtaining a code should write the code authors directly. See the Workshop Summary beginning on page 370.

Several of the papers do not have individual bibliography. A combined bibliography of 290 entries is at the end of these Proceedings. I intend to update this bibliography and distribute it on some logical basis. Interested parties are encouraged to send relevant entries to me for inclusion in the next release of the bibliography.

Table of Contents

A ROAD MAP OF METHODS FOR APPROXIMATING SOLUTIONS OF TWO-POINT BOUNDARY-VALUE PROBLEMS

by

James W. Daniel*

1. INTRODUCTION

I intentionally avoided calling this paper a "survey" because, having once worked as a surveyor, I know that a survey of a city gives an extremely detailed description of the precise layout of the property in that city and is not very helpful to someone trying to find his or her way around town. Analogously, presenting all the details of various implemented methods for solving boundary-value problems can obscure the concepts. It is also true, however, that a coarse aerial photograph of a city is a poor guide for the lost traveler, and, analogously, a very abstract model representing all methods for boundary-value problems is too general to impart much information. What both the traveler and the student of numerical methods need is a useful roadmap with not only enough detail to show the various points of interest but also enough perspective to show where these sites lie in relation to one another. Here I present my own such roadmap of what some numerical methods for boundary-value problems are, of how they relate to one another, and of what areas need development in order to improve methods. (My use of "I" as the first word of this paper is also intentional: the reader is to be warned that this is the personal view of one individual.)

Now, what kinds of boundary-value problems are we to consider? In the spirit of the first paragraph I want to present neither a single abstract problem including all cases nor a vast list of specific special problems. I will discuss instead a couple of model problems for which the solution methods will share many features with methods for the panorama of distinct problem types: eigenvalues, non-linear boundary conditions, m-th order equations, systems of equations for vector-valued functions, mixed-order systems, infinite-intervals for the independent variable, singular problems, singular-perturbation problems, multi-point boundary conditions, et cetera. I will consider both the first-order system for the $n \times 1$ vector valued function $\underline{y}$:

$$\underline{y}'(t) = \underline{f}(t,\underline{y}(t)) \quad \text{for} \quad 0 < t < 1 \tag{1.1}$$

and the second-order scalar equation:

$$y''(t) = f(t,y(t),y'(t)) \quad \text{for } 0 < t < 1 \tag{1.2}$$

since numerical methods on the first-order system equivalent to (1.2) usually are

* Departments of Mathematics and of Computer Sciences and Center for Numerical Analysis at The University of Texas at Austin. Research supported in part by the U. S. Office of Naval Research under Contract N00014-76-C-0275;

dramatically less efficient than methods directly intended for second-order problems. Boundary conditions for (1.1) are given by n nonlinear equations involving $\underline{y}(0)$ and $\underline{y}(1)$:

(1.3) $$\underline{b}(\underline{y}(0),\underline{y}(1)) = \underline{0}$$

in vector notation. For (1.2) we give two nonlinear equations relating y(0), y'(0), y(1), and y'(1), which we can express in vector notation:

(1.4) $$\underline{c}(y(0),y'(0),y(1),y'(1)) = \underline{0}.$$

In many cases the boundary conditions will in fact be linear, in which case we replace (1.3) with

(1.5) $$\underline{B}_0\underline{y}(0) + \underline{B}_1\underline{y}(1) = \underline{e}$$

where $\underline{B}_0$ and $\underline{B}_1$ are $n \times n$ and $\underline{e}$ is $n \times 1$, while we replace (1.4) with

(1.6) $$\underline{c}_0 y(0) + \underline{d}_0 y'(0) + \underline{c}_1 y(1) + \underline{d}_1 y'(1) = \underline{a}$$

where $\underline{c}_0$, $\underline{d}_0$, $\underline{c}_1$, $\underline{d}_1$, and $\underline{a}$ are all 2×1; these special forms can be useful computationally. Another common and computationally advantageous situation is that in which the boundary conditions are separated, so that conditions at $t = 0$ and at $t = 1$ do not interact. In this case we can write (1.2) and (1.5) as

(1.7) $$\tilde{\underline{B}}_0\underline{y}(0) = \underline{e}_0, \quad \tilde{\underline{B}}_1\underline{y}(1) = \underline{e}_1$$

where $\tilde{\underline{B}}_0$ is $q \times n$, $\tilde{\underline{B}}_1$ is $(n-q) \times n$, $\underline{e}_0$ is $q \times 1$, and $\underline{e}_1$ is $(n-q) \times 1$, for some integer q with $1 < q < n$. Similarly (1.4) and (1.6) become in the separated case

(1.8) $$c_0 y(0) + d_0 y'(0) = a_0, \quad c_1 y(1) + d_1 y'(1) = a_1.$$

Thus we will be considering either (1.1) with one of the boundary conditions (1.3), (1.5), (1.7), or (1.2) with one of the boundary conditions (1.4), (1.6), (1.8). In the interest of time and space we often will discuss a method as applied to either the first-order or the second-order problem when the analogous use of the idea of the method for the other standard problem is fairly straightforward.

The next task and the main task of this paper is to describe how to classify various methods. I view a complete method as having three aspects:

(1) a Transformed Problem,

(2) a Discrete Model of the Transformed Problem, and

(3) a Solution Technique for the Discrete Model.

In the next sections I will describe methods from this viewpoint and will comment briefly on some challenging research areas. I give only a brief set of references, since extensive references may be found in [Keller (1975), Aktas-Stetter (1977)]. An expanded version of this talk is available as a report, CNA-130, Center for Numerical Analysis, University of Texas, Austin.

2. TRANSFORMED PROBLEMS

The basic notion of this paper is that a complete method can be viewed as the straightforward application of a fairly standard discretization process to a Transformed Problem that is equivalent to the original boundary-value problem. In this section we examine several Transformed Problems.

2.1 No transformation. For completeness we mention the trivial case of applying no transformation, so that the Transformed Problem and the original problem coincide.

2.2 Variational problems. Many boundary-value problems arise in the physical sciences as the variational or Euler-Lagrange equations for problems in the calculus of variations. For example, consider the problem of minimizing

$$J[y] = \int_0^1 \{\tfrac{1}{2}(y'(t))^2 + F(t,y(t))\}\,dt \tag{2.1}$$

for all sufficiently smooth functions y satisfying the linear and separated boundary conditions

$$y(0) = a, \quad y(1) = b. \tag{2.2}$$

Then the theory of the calculus of variations shows that

$$y''(t) = f(t,y(t)) \quad \text{for} \quad 0<t<1, \quad y(0) = a, \quad y(1) = b \tag{2.3}$$

where $f(t,y) = \frac{\partial}{\partial y} F(t,y)$. In this case, we change the original boundary-value problem to the Transformed Problem: find a function y minimizing $J[y]$ in (2.1) subject to conditions (2.2).

2.3 Shooting and its variants. We consider first here the simplest form of shooting applied to the first-order system (1.1) with boundary conditions (1.3), that is,

$$\underline{\underline{y}}' = \underline{\underline{f}}(t,\underline{\underline{y}}), \quad \text{for } 0 < t < 1, \quad \underline{\underline{b}}(\underline{\underline{y}}(0),\underline{\underline{y}}(1)) = \underline{\underline{0}}.$$

We choose an initial-value vector $\underline{\underline{z}}$ that is $n \times 1$ and let $\underline{\underline{y}}(t;\underline{\underline{z}})$ solve (1.1) subject to the initial condition

$$\underline{\underline{y}}(0;\underline{\underline{z}}) = \underline{\underline{z}}.$$

The original problem now can be restated as the Transformed Problem: find an $n \times 1$ vector $\underline{\underline{z}}$ so that $\underline{\underline{b}}(\underline{\underline{z}},\underline{\underline{y}}(1;\underline{\underline{z}})) = \underline{\underline{0}}$. It is easy to see one of the potential difficulties in using simple shooting (independent of the numerical technique used to compute $\underline{\underline{y}}(1;\underline{\underline{z}})$) by examining a variant of shooting called superposition [Scott-Watts (1977)].

Suppose that our first-order system (1.1) is linear with linear boundary conditions (1.5) so that

$$(2.4) \qquad \underline{\underline{y}}'(t) = \underline{\underline{A}}(t)\underline{\underline{y}}(t) + \underline{\underline{g}}(t) \quad \text{for} \quad 0 < t < 1, \ \underline{\underline{B}}_0\underline{\underline{y}}(0) + \underline{\underline{B}}_1\underline{\underline{y}}(1) = \underline{\underline{e}}$$

where $\underline{\underline{A}}$ is n x n. We let $\underline{\underline{Y}}(t)$ be the n x n fundamental solution matrix satisfying

$$\underline{\underline{Y}}'(t) = \underline{\underline{A}}(t)\underline{\underline{Y}}(t) \quad \text{for} \quad 0 < t < 1, \quad \underline{\underline{Y}}(0) = \underline{\underline{I}}$$

and let the n x 1 vector $\underline{\underline{p}}$ be any particular solution to

$$\underline{\underline{p}}'(t) = \underline{\underline{A}}(t)\underline{\underline{p}}(t) + \underline{\underline{g}}(t) \quad \text{for} \quad 0 < t < 1.$$

Then every solution $\underline{\underline{y}}$ to (2.4) is of the form

$$(2.5) \qquad \underline{\underline{y}}(t) = \underline{\underline{p}}(t) + \underline{\underline{Y}}(t)\underline{\underline{x}} \quad \text{for} \quad 0 < t < 1$$

for some n x 1 vector $\underline{\underline{x}}$ independent of t. The boundary conditions now merely become the linear algebraic equations for $\underline{\underline{x}}$:

$$[\underline{\underline{B}}_0 + \underline{\underline{B}}_1\underline{\underline{Y}}(1)]\underline{\underline{x}} = \underline{\underline{e}} - \underline{\underline{B}}_0\underline{\underline{p}}(0) - \underline{\underline{B}}_1\underline{\underline{p}}(1).$$

To determine $\underline{\underline{x}}$ it is essential of course that $\underline{\underline{B}}_0 + \underline{\underline{B}}_1\underline{\underline{Y}}(1)$ be nonsingular; the difficulty can be that the numerical computation of $\underline{\underline{Y}}$ causes the crucial matrix to become singular. Thus simple superposition can have difficulties; since from (2.5) we see that $\underline{\underline{y}}(0) = \underline{\underline{p}}(0) + \underline{\underline{x}}$, the coefficients $\underline{\underline{x}}$ are nearly the initial values $\underline{\underline{z}}$ of shooting, and indeed $\underline{\underline{x}} = \underline{\underline{z}}$ if $\underline{\underline{p}}(0) = \underline{\underline{0}}$, so we see that the same potential difficulty is inherent in shooting.

From the shooting viewpoint, a way out of this problem is multiple shooting in which we simultaneously shoot from k distinct t values $0 = T_1 < \ldots < T_k < 1$. That is, for arbitrary n x 1 vectors $\underline{\underline{z}}_1, \ldots, \underline{\underline{z}}_k$ we let $\underline{\underline{y}}_i(t;\underline{\underline{z}}_i)$ for $1 \le i \le k$ solve $\underline{\underline{y}}_i'(t) = \underline{\underline{f}}(t,\underline{\underline{y}}_i(t))$ for $T_i < t < T_{i+1}$ (with $T_{k+1} \equiv 1$) subject to the initial conditions $\underline{\underline{y}}_i(\underline{\underline{T}}_i;\underline{\underline{z}}_i) = \underline{\underline{z}}_i$. The original problem now can be restated as the Transformed Problem: find k n x 1 vectors $\underline{\underline{z}}_1, \ldots, \underline{\underline{z}}_k$ so that $\underline{\underline{b}}(\underline{\underline{z}}_1, \underline{\underline{y}}_k(1;\underline{\underline{z}}_k)) = 0$, $\underline{\underline{y}}_i(T_{i+1};\underline{\underline{z}}_i) = \underline{\underline{z}}_{i+1}$ for $1 \le i \le k-1$, a system of k n equations for the k n unknown components of $\underline{\underline{z}}_1, \ldots, \underline{\underline{z}}_k$. The hope is, of course, that the $\underline{\underline{z}}_i$ and T_i can be chosen so shrewdly that the numerically singular matrices mentioned in the preceding paragraph do not arise.

From the superposition viewpoint we can use multiple starting points $T_1 = 0 < T_2 < \ldots < T_k < 1$ as well. We merely represent $\underline{\underline{y}}$ for $T_i \le t \le T_{i+1}$ by $\underline{\underline{y}}(t) = \underline{\underline{Y}}_i(t)\underline{\underline{x}}_i + \underline{\underline{p}}_i(t)$ where $\underline{\underline{p}}_i$ is a particular solution of the inhomogeneous equation on $T_i < t < T_{i+1}$ and $\underline{\underline{Y}}_i$ is a fundamental solution there solving $\underline{\underline{Y}}_i' = \underline{\underline{A}}(t)\underline{\underline{Y}}_i$ with $\underline{\underline{Y}}_i(\underline{\underline{T}}_i) = \underline{\underline{Y}}_{i,0}$ for some given nonsingular matrix $\underline{\underline{Y}}_{i,0}$. Recalling that we need to satisfy the linear boundary conditions $\underline{\underline{B}}_0\underline{\underline{y}}(0) + \underline{\underline{B}}_1\underline{\underline{y}}(1) = \underline{\underline{e}}$ and the continuity conditions for $\underline{\underline{y}}(T_i)$, we see that we again have kn (linear) equations for the kn unknown components of $\underline{\underline{x}}_1, \ldots, \underline{\underline{x}}_k$. Since $\underline{\underline{x}}_{i-1}$ and $\underline{\underline{x}}_i$ are the unknowns in the continuity equation we see that the system of linear equations we must solve is essentially block bi-diagonal with $Y_{i-1}(T_i)$ and $Y_{i,0}$ appearing as the blocks. Just as for simple shooting and simple superposition, if we choose $Y_{i,0} = I$ and $p_i(T_i) = 0$ then the coordinates x_i in multiple superposition equal the initial values z_i in multiple shooting. Other choices of $Y_{i,0}$ and $p_i(T_i)$ are possible, however. In the so-called re-orthogonalization method [Scott-Watts (1977)], $Y_{1,0} = I$, and each subsequent $Y_{i,0}$ is chosen as the Gram-Schmidt orthogonalized version of $Y_{i-1}(T_i)$. In the case of the re-orthogonalization method the nearly block bi-diagonal matrix describing the equations for $x_1,\ldots,x_k$ has very simple blocks consisting of I and right triangular matrices R_i, making solution of the system quite simple. These methods are discussed in detail by R. Bulirsch, by I. Gladwell, and by M. Scott in their talks at this conference.

2.4 Quasi-linearization. Mathematicians are well known as people who, when they cannot solve a certain difficult problem, instead solve some easy problem in the hope that this will somehow be profitable. Quasi-linearization, often known as Newton's method, is the application of this ploy to create Transformed Problems simpler than an original difficult nonlinear boundary-value problem. The idea is that, given one approximate solution $y_i(t)$ to the first-order system (1.1), with general boundary conditions (1.3), we approximate the differential equation (1.1) for y near y_i by the linear (in y_{i+1}) differential equation

$$(2.6)\qquad y'_{i+1}(t) = f(t,y_i(t)) + \frac{\partial f}{\partial y}(t,y_i(t))(y_{i+1}(t) - y_i(t)),$$

where $\frac{\partial f}{\partial y}$ is the n x n Jacobian matrix of f with respect to y. Similarly, we approximate the boundary conditions (1.3) by linearized boundary conditions. The linearized equations comprise a linear boundary-value problem for y_{i+1} of the same form as (2.4). As usual with Newton's method, the hope is that the sequence of functions $y_0, y_1, \ldots$ converges to y solving (1.1), (1.3). Thus we have reduced the original nonlinear boundary-value problem to the Transformed Problem: solve a sequence of linear boundary-value problems for $y_0, y_1, \ldots$ converging to y.

At this point notice that we can easily speak of Transformed^2 Problems whenever the Transformed Problem is transformed again; this occurs, for example, if we use shooting or superposition as in subsection 2.3 to solve each of the linearized boundary-value problems. Some methods designed only for linear problems can thus be used with quasilinearization on nonlinear problems [for example, see Scott (1975), Scott-Watts (1977)].

2.5 Continuation and embedding. In many real problems the differential equation (and perhaps the boundary conditions) depends on certain physical parameters, and solutions are desired over a range of values of these parameters. We suppose that we have a family of differential equations

$$\underline{y}' = \underline{f}(t,\underline{y};\lambda) \tag{2.7}$$

whose solution $\underline{y}(y;\lambda)$ is especially desired for $\lambda = \lambda_F$ and perhaps for many other values of λ as well.

In the continuation method we assume that (2.7) can be solved easily for some value λ_0 of the parameter. Assuming $\lambda_0 < \lambda_F$ for convenience, we then set out to solve (2.7) for a sequence of k values of λ, say $\lambda_1 = \lambda_0 < \lambda_2 < \ldots < \lambda_k = \lambda_F$. If λ_{i+1} is "near" λ_i, the hope is that (2.7) for $\lambda = \lambda_{i+1}$ can be solved fairly easily by making use of the already obtained solution $\underline{y}(t;\lambda_i)$ at $\lambda = \lambda_i$. Thus we have replaced the original boundary-value problem (1.1) by the Transformed Problem: solve (2.7) for a sequence $\lambda_0,\lambda_1,\ldots,\lambda_k$ of values of the parameter λ. This is a useful device whenever one can use $\underline{y}_i$ to advantage in obtaining $\underline{y}_{i+1}$.

Another approach to solving (2.7) for $\lambda = \lambda_F$ is to use the embedding method [Scott (1973)] which derives differential equations for the dependence of $\underline{y}(t;\lambda)$ on λ. While this usually results in nonlinear partial differential equations for $\underline{y}$ as a function of t and λ, the side conditions often can be chosen to be initial conditions since we assumed the problem to be easily solved initially at $\lambda = \lambda_0$. Thus the original ordinary differential equation boundary-value problem is replaced by the Transformed Problem: solve an initial-value problem for a partial differential equation involving $\underline{y}$ as a function of t and λ.

A wide variety of these embedding methods have been used depending on precisely how λ enters the differential equation. A very common practice is to use the interval length over which t varies as the embedding parameter; it is for this case that I will restrict the use of the broad term invariant embedding. Thus we think of the family of problems defined for $0 < t < \lambda$ and we let λ range from zero to unity. When the original differential equation (or boundary condition) is nonlinear, invariant embedding yields a nonlinear partial differential equation. To avoid this difficulty the computationally most successful approach appears to be to develop invariant embedding for linear problems (which turn out to lead to ordinary differential equations when invariant embedding is used) and then to use quasi-linearization as a device for replacing nonlinear problems by a sequence of linear problems, each of which is transformed and solved by invariant embedding. For the rest of this section we restrict ourselves to a consideration of the linear second-order equation

$$y''(t) + p(t)y'(t) + q(t)y(t) = g(t) \quad \text{for } 0 < t < \lambda \tag{2.8}$$

subject to separated linear boundary conditions

$$(2.9) \qquad c_0 y(0) + d_0 y'(0) = a_0, \quad c_1 y(\lambda) + d_1 y'(\lambda) = a_1$$

as in (1.8); the solution to (2.8), (2.9) is $y(t;\lambda)$ and it is desired for $0 \leq \lambda \leq 1$. General linear boundary conditions can be handled as well.

The simplest invariant embedding method for (2.8), (2.9) is the sweep or factorization method in which we introduce two auxiliary functions $\alpha(t)$ and $\beta(t)$ for $0 \leq t \leq 1$ and set $y' = \alpha y + \beta$; it turns out that α and β must satisfy

$$(2.10) \qquad \begin{cases} \alpha'(t) = -q(t) - p(t)\alpha(t) - \alpha^2(t) & \text{for } 0 < t < 1, \ \alpha(0) = \dfrac{-c_0}{d_0} \\ \beta'(t) = g(t) - (p(t) + \alpha(t)\beta(t) & \text{for } 0 < t < 1, \ \beta(0) = \dfrac{a_0}{d_0} . \end{cases}$$

(If $d_0 = 0$, a slightly different method is used.) Having computed α and β from (2.14), applying $y' = \alpha y + \beta$ at $t = \lambda$ along with the boundary condition $c_1 y(\lambda) + d_1 y'(\lambda) = a_1$ gives us two linear equations which we solve for the unknowns $y(\lambda;\lambda)$ and $y'(\lambda;\lambda)$. Having found $y(\lambda;\lambda)$ and $\alpha(t), \beta(t)$ for $0 \leq t \leq \lambda \leq 1$ we finally solve

$$(2.11) \qquad y'(t;\lambda) = \alpha(t) y(t;\lambda) + \beta(t) \qquad \text{for } 0 < t < \lambda$$

in the backward direction starting from the recently found value $y(\lambda;\lambda)$ for $y(t;\lambda)$ at $t = \lambda$. This gives the desired solution $y(t;\lambda)$ for $0 \leq t \leq \lambda$. Note that the initial-value problems for α and β need only be solved once. Thereafter, to find $y(t;\lambda)$ for any λ only requires the solution of the two linear algebraic equations for $y(\lambda;\lambda)$ and then integration of one backwards initial-value problem (2.11) for y.

Experience has indicated that a somewhat more complex invariant embedding method is better than the sweep method above. The sweep method, however, serves to illustrate the nature of the invariant embedding approach. General methods are described and references are given by E. Denman in his talk at this conference.

In all cases, we replace the original boundary-value problem by the Transformed Problem: solve some initial-value problems (for ordinary differential equations) and one small linear system of algebraic equations.

2.6 Integral equations. By using an appropriate Green's function we can transform our original boundary-value problem into an integral equation. As an illustration, consider the second-order problem (1.2) subject to linear boundary conditions. Usually, by subtracting from $\underline{y}$ an appropriate linear function, we can force the boundary conditions to be homogeneous. We therefore consider

$$(2.12) \qquad y''(t) = f(t, y(t), y'(t)) \qquad \text{for } 0 < t < 1$$

subject to the homogeneous version of (1.6), namely

$$(2.13) \qquad \underline{\underline{c}}_0 y(0) + \underline{\underline{d}}_0 y'(0) + \underline{\underline{c}}_1 (1) + \underline{\underline{d}}_1 y'(1) = \underline{\underline{0}} .$$

If $y = 0$ is the only solution to $y'' = 0$ subject to (2.13), then we can use the Green's function $G(t,\tau)$ to show that y solves (2.12), (2.13) if and only if y solves

$$y(t) = \int_0^1 G(t,\tau)f(\tau,y(\tau),y'(\tau))d\tau \quad \text{for } 0 \le t \le 1 . \tag{2.14}$$

In this generality we have replaced (2.12), (2.13) by an integro-differential equation. Thus we replace the original boundary-value problem by a Transformed Problem: solve for y in the integro-differential equation (2.14).

3. DISCRETE MODELS OF TRANSFORMED PROBLEMS

We have seen a few of the many ways in which our original boundary-value problem can be transformed into an equivalent problem; now we want to discuss methods for launching a frontal assault on the Transformed Problem. Although there are other methods available [Aktas-Stetter (1977)], I will restrict myself to the most successful methods, namely finite differences and projections, as approaches to discrete modeling.

3.1 Finite differences. The basic idea here is to represent desired functions $g(t)$ for $0 \le t \le 1$ by the values of g at some finite set of points $0 \le t_1 < t_2 < \dots < t_N \le 1$. We approximate $g(t_i)$ by some number G_i and generate relationships among the values G_i intended to model what the (transformed) problem tells us about g. Such modeling methods are, of course, very well known: we generally replace derivatives by divided differences, integrals by quadrature sums, et cetera. We look briefly at the models that result when finite differences are used with the Transformed Problems of section 2.

Finite differences for the original problem: Basic finite differences for the original boundary-value problem are, of course, very well known. For the first-order system (1.1), for example, we discretize by letting $t_1 = 0 < t_2 < \dots < t_N = 1$ and letting the $n \times 1$ vector $\underline{\underline{Z}}_i$ approximate $\underline{y}(t_i)$. A simple, natural, and effective scheme is to model the differential equation (1.1) by

$$(\underline{\underline{Z}}_{i+1}-\underline{\underline{Z}}_i)/(t_{i+1}-t_i) = \underline{\underline{f}}(\tfrac{1}{2}t_i + \tfrac{1}{2}t_{i+1}, \tfrac{1}{2}\underline{\underline{Z}}_i + \tfrac{1}{2}\underline{\underline{Z}}_{i+1}), \quad \text{for } 1 \le i \le N-1 \tag{3.1}$$

and to model the nonlinear boundary conditions $\underline{\underline{b}}(\underline{y}(0), \underline{y}(1)) = \underline{\underline{0}}$ in (1.3) by

$$\underline{\underline{b}}(\underline{\underline{Z}}_1, \underline{\underline{Z}}_N) = \underline{\underline{0}}. \tag{3.2}$$

Under reasonable hypotheses, of course, this is a second-order method, that is,

$$\|\underline{\underline{Z}}_i - \underline{y}(t_i)\|_\infty \le ch^2 \quad \text{for } 1 \le i \le n, \quad c \text{ independent of } N, \tag{3.3}$$

where throughout this paper we use h to denote

(3.4) $$h = \max \{|t_{i+1} - t_i|;\quad 1 \le i \le N-1\}.$$

Since the nonlinear equations (3.1), (3.2) are often solved by some linearization process and, since linear problems also arise naturally, it is instructive to look briefly at the structure of (3.1) and (3.2) when the problem is linear. We therefore consider again (2.4), namely

$$\underline{y}'(t) = \underline{\underline{A}}(t)\underline{y}(t) + \underline{g}(t), \quad \underline{\underline{B}}_0\underline{y}(0) + \underline{\underline{B}}_1\underline{y}(1) = \underline{e}\ .$$

Writing $h_i = t_{i+1} - t_i$, $\underline{\underline{A}}_i = \frac{1}{2}\underline{\underline{A}}(t_i+h_i/2)$, and $\underline{g}_i = \underline{g}(t_i+h_i/2)$, equations (3.1), (3.2) take the form

$$(\underline{\underline{I}}-h_i\underline{\underline{A}}_i)\underline{Z}_{i+1} = (\underline{\underline{I}}+h_i\underline{\underline{A}}_i)\underline{Z}_i + h_i\underline{g}_i \quad \text{for } 1 \le i \le N-1$$

$$\underline{\underline{B}}_0\underline{Z}_1 + \underline{\underline{B}}_1\underline{Z}_N = \underline{e}.$$

In block matrix notation, this is

(3.5) $$\begin{bmatrix} \underline{\underline{B}}_0 & \underline{\underline{0}} & \underline{\underline{0}} & & \cdots & \underline{\underline{B}}_1 \\ -\underline{\underline{P}}_1 & \underline{\underline{M}}_1 & \underline{\underline{0}} & & \cdots & \underline{\underline{0}} \\ \underline{\underline{0}} & -\underline{\underline{P}}_2 & \underline{\underline{M}}_2 & \underline{\underline{0}} & \cdots & \underline{\underline{0}} \\ & & & & & \\ \underline{\underline{0}} & \cdots & & \underline{\underline{0}} & -\underline{\underline{P}}_{N-1} & \underline{\underline{M}}_{N-1} \end{bmatrix} \begin{bmatrix} \underline{Z}_1 \\ \underline{Z}_2 \\ \underline{Z}_3 \\ \vdots \\ \underline{Z}_N \end{bmatrix} = \begin{bmatrix} \underline{e} \\ h_1\underline{g}_1 \\ h_2\underline{g}_2 \\ \\ h_{N-1}\underline{g}_{N-1} \end{bmatrix}$$

involving an almost (except for the first block row) bi-diagonal matrix, where $\underline{\underline{P}}_i = \underline{\underline{I}} + h_i\underline{\underline{A}}_i$, $\underline{\underline{M}}_i = \underline{\underline{I}} - h_i\underline{\underline{A}}_i$. Although N may be quite large in order to obtain much accuracy, the special structure of the $Nn \times Nn$ matrix in (3.5) allows the system to be solved efficiently.

<u>Finite differences for variational problems</u>: We saw in subsection 2.2 that second-order problems (1.2) subject to separated linear boundary conditions (2.2) and not involving y' explicitly in the differential equation are often equivalent to minimizing J[y] in (2.1). Since J involves an integral and a derivative, the natural finite difference approach is to use a quadrature sum for the integral and a divided difference for the derivative and then to minimize the resulting function of the $n \times 1$ vectors $\underline{Z}_i$ approximating $\underline{y}(t_i)$.

<u>Finite differences for shooting and its variants</u>: All of the variants of shooting described in subsection 2.3 involve solving some initial-value problems for ordinary differential equations as an intermediate step on the way to solving a set of algebraic equations. Finite differences can come into play by providing a way to solve these initial-value problems approximately. Any of the high-quality initial-value codes such as those for variable-order Adams methods or Runge-Kutta-Fehlberg methods can be used to solve the initial-value problem; many of these are

described by H. A. Watts in his talk at this conference.

Finite differences for quasilinearization: Quasilinearization discussed in subsection 2.4 merely transformed the original nonlinear problem to a sequence of linear boundary-value problems. We can therefore use finite differences, for example as in (3.5), to solve each of these linear problems.

Finite differences for continuation and embedding: Finite differences can be used on the continuation problem just as it was on the original (untransformed) problem. On the other hand, for the embedding methods we needed to solve initial-value problems like (2.10), (2.11). High-quality finite difference methods for initial-value problems can therefore be applied to solve these just as for shooting methods.

Finite differences for integral equations: We saw in subsection 2.6 how we could transform, for example, (2.12)-(2.13) with f independent of y' into an integral equation, namely,

$$y(t) = \int_0^1 G(t,\tau)\, f(\tau, y(\tau))\, d\tau .$$

Letting $t_1 = 0 < t_2 < \ldots < t_N = 1$ and approximating $y(t_i)$ by Z_i as usual, we can replace the integral in the equation with a quadrature sum, obtaining a system of nonlinear equations to solve for the Z_i.

3.2 Projections. As we saw in subsection 3.1, various discrete problems result from using finite differences on the various Transformed Problems. We will see in this subsection that the projection approach to discrete modeling gives different models in the same ways. First we sketch the projection idea itself.

The projection approach can be viewed as a way to approximate the solution to an equation

$$(3.6) \qquad Dx = F(x)$$

where D is a linear operator from some linear vector space X into some linear vector space Y and F is a possibly nonlinear operator from X into Y. We choose X_h to be some finite dimensional subspace of X and we let Y_h be the finite-dimensional subspace of Y defined by $Y_h = DX_h$. Finally, let P_h be some linear projection of Y into Y_h, so that P_h is a linear operator for which $P_h y_h = y_h$ for all y_h in Y_h. The main idea is to seek an approximate solution x_h to (3.6) in X_h rather than in X; if x_h is in X_h, however, than Dx_h is in Y_h while generally $F(x_h)$ is not in Y_h so that (3.6) cannot be solved in X_h. Instead, we modify $F(x_h)$ to $P_hF(x_h)$ to get it into Y_h. Thus we approximate x solving (3.6) by x_h solving

$$(3.7) \qquad Dx_h = P_hF(x_h),$$

a finite-dimensional problem. General theorems are known on the existence of x_h and on the error $x-x_h$; these theorems involve the approximation properties of the subspaces X_h and Y_h and the precise nature of the projection P_h.

For our problems, X and Y are spaces of functions defined on $0 \leq t \leq 1$, and elements y_h of Y_h are usually represented as linear combinations

$$y_h = a_1\sigma_1 + a_2\sigma_2 + \ldots + a_L\sigma_L$$

of simple basis functions $\sigma_1,\ldots,\sigma_L$ for Y_h of dimension L, so that (3.7) defines a set of equations in the unknowns $a_1,\ldots,a_L$. Important choices for the subspaces X_h and Y_h are the <u>spline</u> spaces $S(\Pi,k,r)$. Here Π is a set of break points $\xi_0 = 0 < \xi_1 < \xi_2 < \ldots < \xi_\ell = 0$, and k and r are integers with $k \geq 0$, $r \geq -1$. An element of $S(\Pi,k,r)$ is an r times continuously differentiable (often vector-valued) function on $0 \leq t \leq 1$ which is defined by a (different) polynomial of degree at most k-1 on each interval $\xi_i < t < \xi_{i+1}$. A sufficiently smooth function f on $0 \leq t \leq 1$ can usually be approximated by some spline σ in $S(\Pi,k,r)$ to order k in the sense that $\max_{0\leq t\leq 1} |f(t) - \sigma(t)| = \mathcal{O}(|\Pi|^k)$ where $|\Pi| = \max_{0\leq i\leq \ell-1} |\xi_{i+1}-\xi_i|$. An important fact is that every element of $S(\Pi,k,r)$ can be written as a linear combination of special basis splines (<u>B-splines</u>) each of which vanishes identically on all but a few adjacent intervals $\xi_\ell < t < \xi_{i+1}$. Such a basis is called a <u>local</u> B-spline basis. In practice the projection P_h into Y_h is usually defined by (i) collocation conditions, (ii) orthogonality (or Galerkin) conditions, or (iii) a mixture of collocation and orthogonality conditions. <u>Collocation</u> conditions are of the form $(P_h y)(\eta) = y(\eta)$ for certain values η; <u>orthogonality</u> (or <u>Galerkin</u>) conditions are of the form $\langle P_h y-y,\psi\rangle = 0$ where ψ is some function and $\langle\cdot,\cdot\rangle$ denotes some inner product (usually involving integrals) on our function spaces. We proceed now to describe briefly some projection methods; many more are explained by G. Reddien in his talk at this conference.

<u>Projection for the original problem, for quasilinearization, and for continuation</u>: As we saw in subsection 3.1, the Transformed Problems in these three cases all are still explicitly described as two-point boundary-value problems; to be specific, consider

$$\underline{y}'(t) = \underline{f}(t,\underline{y}(t)) \quad \text{for} \quad 0 < t < 1, \ \underline{\underline{B}}_0\underline{y}(0) + \underline{\underline{B}}_1\underline{y}(1) = \underline{0},$$

where we assume homogeneous boundary conditions for convenience. Here we can think of the space X as, say $C^1[0,1]$, Y as $C[0,1]$, the operator D as d/dt, and the operator F as taking $\underline{y}$ into $\underline{f}(t,\underline{y}(t))$. If we take X_h to be the spline subspace $S(\Pi,k,r)$ subject to our homogeneous boundary conditions above, then $Y_h = DX_h$ is essentially

$S(\Pi,k-1,r-1)$ (subject to some boundary conditions). Therefore, if P_h denotes some projection into this modified $S(\Pi,k-1,r-1)$, our projection reduces to finding $\underline{\underline{\sigma}}$ in $S(\Pi,k,r)$ satisfying

$$\underline{\underline{\sigma}}' = P_h \underline{\underline{f}}(t,\underline{\underline{\sigma}}), \; \underline{\underline{B}}_0 \underline{\underline{\sigma}}(0) + \underline{\underline{B}}_1 \underline{\underline{\sigma}}(1) = \underline{\underline{0}}.$$

If, for example, P_h is defined by some collocation conditions $(P_h y)(\eta) = y(\eta)$, then we impose

$$\underline{\underline{\sigma}}'(\eta) = \underline{\underline{f}}(\eta, \underline{\underline{\sigma}}(\eta)). \tag{3.8}$$

Note that if $\underline{\underline{\sigma}}$ is expressed as a linear combination of local basis elements (B-splines),

$$\underline{\underline{\sigma}} = a_1 \underline{\underline{\sigma}}_1 + \dots + a_L \underline{\underline{\sigma}}_L,$$

then (3.8), for example, becomes

$$a_1 \underline{\underline{\sigma}}_1'(\eta) + \dots + a_L \underline{\underline{\sigma}}'_L(\eta) = \underline{\underline{f}}(\eta, a_1 \underline{\underline{\sigma}}_1(\eta) + \dots + a_L \underline{\underline{\sigma}}_L(\eta)). \tag{3.9}$$

Since $\underline{\underline{\sigma}}_i'(\eta) = \underline{\underline{\sigma}}_i(\eta) = 0$ except for only a few subscripts i because the $\underline{\underline{\sigma}}$'s form a <u>local</u> basis, only a very few of the coefficients a_i are explicitly involved in each collocation equation. This implies that each equation in the system (3.8) for $a_1,\dots,a_L$, in fact, only involves a few a_i; this <u>sparsity</u> is what makes local bases important.

<u>Projection for shooting and for embedding</u>: The important feature of the Transformed Problems produced by shooting or embedding is that they are initial-value problems. The only effect this has on the discussion just completed is to change the side conditions on the splines to initial rather than boundary conditions.

<u>Projection for integral equations</u>: If the Green's function is used to transform our original problem, say of second-order, we end up with an integral equation. In this case we can take X and Y to be $C[0,1]$, $D = I$, and F as the mapping from y to $\int_0^1 G(t,\tau) f(\tau, y(\tau))\, d\tau$. Using splines σ to approximate y and collocation, for example, again gives us a system of equations for our basis coefficients $a_1,\dots,a_L$. Note in this case that even if we represent σ in terms of local basis functions σ_i the resulting problem is <u>not</u> sparse.

<u>Projection for variational problems</u>: Although projection as I have described it does not strictly apply to variational problems, the spirit of projection does apply. Recall from subsection 2.2 that we are considering the problem of minimizing $J[y]$. One of the ideas behind projection was to seek an approximate solution in a finite-dimensional subspace. Applying the same idea here we replace y by $Y = a_1\sigma_1 + \dots + a_L\sigma_L$ for some chosen function $\sigma_1,\dots,\sigma_L$ and then choose $a_1,\dots,a_L$ to

minimize $\tilde{J}(a_1,\ldots,a_L) = J[Y]$. This is commonly called the Rayleigh-Ritz method. It is in fact strongly related to a projection method since extremizing J is strongly related to making $\nabla\tilde{J} = \underline{\underline{0}}$; this is the same as using projection with orthogonality conditions determined by σ_i and the inner product $\langle\sigma_i, g\rangle = \int_0^1 \sigma_i(t)g(t)dt$.

4. SOLUTION TECHNIQUES FOR DISCRETE MODELS

This section contains much less detail than its predecessors. Primarily, I want to emphasize the fact that transforming a problem (as in Section 2) and then developing a finite-dimensional discrete model of the Transformed Problem (as in Section 3) do not a method make! There still remains the formidable task of solving for the solution of the discrete problem, and there are usually very many computational techniques for doing this; only when the solution technique is known is the complete algorithm for the boundary-value problem finally specified. Each of our discrete models produced either a finite-dimensional minimization problem, or a finite system of nonlinear algebraic equations, or a finite system of linear algebraic equations.

Quite a number of distinct methods are available for minimizing a function of several variables [Murray (1972)], the problem which results from discrete models of the variational version of boundary-value problems; conjugate direction and variable metric methods are among the most powerful. Because our problems often have special structure, such as having many variables and a sparse Hessian, techniques should be used which are designed to make use of such structure.

Similarly, many methods are available [Ortega-Rheinboldt (1970)] for solving the finite systems of nonlinear algebraic equations which result from the original problem, the shooting, and the integral equation approaches to boundary-value problems; among the most popular are the quasi-Newton update methods which essentially use Newton's method only with rough approximations to the Jacobian matrix of the nonlinear system. The systems arising from the original problem and from the integral equation approaches usually have many more unknowns than in the shooting systems. Systems for the original problem are usually sparse while those for the integral equation are usually dense. Again special methods should be used depending on the system's structure, as emphasized by P. Deuflhard in his talk at this conference.

Since systems of linear algebraic equations often arise from methods to solve nonlinear equations as well as from linear differential equations with linear boundary conditions, methods for solving linear algebraic systems are fundamental to solution techniques for our discrete models. Again, although we often think only of straightforward Gauss elimination, there are many techniques available for solving linear systems.

5. RELATIONSHIPS AMONG COMPLETE ALGORITHMS

We have indicated that a complete algorithm is specified by three "coordinates": a Transformed Problem, a Discrete Model, and a Solution Technique. Unfortunately, different sets of coordinates can describe identical (or very similar) complete algorithms. In this section I want to indicate a few relationships among such algorithms.

It has been shown that certain spline collocation procedures are identical to finite-difference procedures when both are applied to the original problem. For example, using the spline space $S(\Pi,2,0)$ of continuous piecewise linear functions on the first-order problem (1.1) with collocation at the middle of the interval between break points yields precisely the finite-difference equations (3.1) if the points t_i are the break points and $\underline{Z}_i$ denotes the value of the spline at t_i.

At present it seems to be generally believed that the most competitive methods for boundary-value problems are based on projection for the original problem, finite differences for the original problem, finite differences for shooting and its variants, and finite differences for embedding; I therefore want to look briefly at the relationships among these procedures. We have already seen a relationship between finite differences and projection for the original problem, so I want to examine finite differences for the original problem, for shooting, and for embedding. For linear problems the relationships are very striking, since the overall methods can be identical! For nonlinear problems the same methods are not necessarily identical but are very similar. Simply to convey the idea here we look at linear first-order problems.

Consider first simple shooting for the linear scalar problem

$$y' = A(t)y + g(t), \quad B_0y(0) + B_1y(1) = e$$

where we implement shooting by the simple finite-difference method (3.1); letting Z_i approximate $y(t_i)$, and taking just six points $t_1 = 0 < t_2 < t_3 < t_4 < t_5 < t_6 = 1$ for illustration, then for simple shooting we try to find z so that

$$Z_1 = z, \quad M_iZ_{i+1} = P_iZ_i + h_ig_i \quad \text{for} \quad 1 \leq i \leq 5, \quad B_0z + B_1Z_6 = e$$

is satisfied. In shooting, we solve the above recursion for Z_6 in terms of z and then use this plus the boundary condition $B_0z + B_1Z_6 = e$ to select z correctly. If we write the above recursion and boundary condition in matrix notation, we obtain (5.1), which is precisely (3.5), the equations we solved for finite differences applied to the original problem. Thus finite differences for simple shooting and for the original problem give the same answers. Moreover, we can interpret the way in which shooting solves for Z_6 in terms of $z = Z_1$ in the language of an elimination method for solving (3.5) or (5.1) for finite differences on the original problem.

$$(5.1)\qquad \begin{bmatrix} B_0 & 0 & 0 & 0 & 0 & B_1 \\ -P_1 & M_1 & 0 & 0 & 0 & 0 \\ 0 & -P_2 & M_2 & 0 & 0 & 0 \\ 0 & 0 & -P_3 & M_3 & 0 & 0 \\ 0 & 0 & 0 & -P_4 & M_4 & 0 \\ 0 & 0 & 0 & 0 & -P_5 & M_5 \end{bmatrix} \begin{bmatrix} Z_1 \\ Z_2 \\ Z_3 \\ Z_4 \\ Z_5 \\ Z_6 \end{bmatrix} = \begin{bmatrix} e \\ h_1 g_1 \\ h_2 g_2 \\ h_3 g_3 \\ h_4 g_4 \\ h_5 g_5 \end{bmatrix}.$$

In (5.1), use the (2,2)-element M_1 to eliminate the (3,2)-element P_2 and divide the second row by the (2,2)-element. Next, use the (3,3)-element to eliminate the (4,3)-element and divide row three by the (3,3)-element. Keeping this up we eventually transform the matrix in (5.1) into

$$(5.2)\qquad \begin{bmatrix} B_0 & 0 & 0 & 0 & 0 & B_1 \\ X & I & 0 & 0 & 0 & 0 \\ X & 0 & I & 0 & 0 & 0 \\ X & 0 & 0 & I & 0 & 0 \\ X & 0 & 0 & 0 & I & 0 \\ X & 0 & 0 & 0 & 0 & I \end{bmatrix}$$

where X denotes the presence of some nonzero element. The last row of (5.2) expresses Z_6 in terms of Z_1, as in shooting. If we now solve for Z_1 between the first and last rows in (5.2) and substitute the computed Z_1 into the equations (5.2), we obtain all the values Z_i, precisely as in shooting. Therefore, not only do we produce the same solutions by the two procedures, but also <u>finite differences for simple shooting on linear problems is computationally step-by-step equivalent with a particular elimination method for solving the linear system resulting from the same finite difference method for the original problem</u>. It is important to note above that we had to use the <u>same</u> finite difference grid points t_i for both methods. For the boundary-value approach, these points must be chosen <u>in advance</u>; in shooting, initial-value codes usually select the grid points <u>automatically</u>. Thus the two methods are identical <u>if</u> we can somehow determine the appropriate grid points in the shooting approach. This illustrates the importance of selecting good grid points for finite differences applied to the boundary-value problems.

By a slight generalization on the preceding argument, we can show that finite differences for multiple shooting is identical step-by-step with an elimination method for the finite-difference method for the boundary-value problem. Likewise, both simple and multiple superposition are identical with an elimination process. Somewhat more complex is the fact that the re-orthogonalization process implemented with finite differences is identical step-by-step with a solution technique for the finite difference equations (3.5) for the original problem. Also, it can be shown that finite differences on the sweep method of embedding is essentially just standard Gauss elimination in (3.5).

Thus finite differences for the original problem, for shooting and its variants and for embedding only differ by being different solution techniques for the same set of equations (3.5). This does not mean that the methods are not very different; different solution techniques can have drastically different results in the presence of rounding error. What our statement does mean is that it is reasonable to concentrate on alternatives to Gauss elimination in order to solve (3.5). Again I observe also that finite-difference methods for shooting and embedding have the ability to select grid points dynamically, while the finite-difference method for the original problem selects grid points in advance.

6. ACCELERATING CONVERGENCE AND ESTIMATING ERRORS

For simplicity we begin the discussion of this topic in a simpler setting than differential equations. Suppose that there is some marvelous number Y_0 that we wish to compute, and that as some positive parameter h tends to zero we are instead able to compute some approximation $Y(h)$ to Y_0. The problem of error estimation is obviously that of estimating the size of the error $Y(h) - Y_0$; the problem of acceleration is that of generating another scheme $\tilde{Y}(h)$ for which its error $\tilde{Y}(h) - Y_0$ is "much" smaller than $Y(h) - Y_0$. The two problems are closely related: if $e(h)$ is an accurate estimate of $Y(h) - Y_0$ then surely $\tilde{Y}(h) \equiv Y(h) - e(h)$ is an accelerated estimate of $Y_0 = Y(h) - (Y(h) - Y_0)$, while if some $\tilde{Y}(h)$ is "much" nearer Y_0 than is $Y(h)$, then surely $\tilde{e}(h) \equiv Y(h) - \tilde{Y}(h)$ is very near $Y(h) - Y_0$ which is the true error. I will first phrase my discussion in terms of accelerating convergence.

Three convergence-acceleration devices which have been used for boundary-value problems are Richardson extrapolation [Joyce (1971)], iterated deferred correction [Pereyra (1967)], and iterated defect correction [Frank (1976)]. Richardson extrapolation computes both $Y(h)$ and $Y(rh)$ for some $r < 1$ and uses some theoretical information on behavior of $Y(h) - Y_0$ in order to compute an improved $\tilde{Y}(h)$; for differential equations this involves computations on two discretizations in order to improve the accuracy on the less accurate of the two solutions (the one with the more crude discretization). Both deferred correction and defect correction are much more complicated than Richardson extrapolation but have the advantage of avoiding computations on a refined discretization. Experiments indicate that deferred correction and defect correction are more efficient than Richardson extrapolation, but the methods are too complex to explain here. There are a number of other methods for estimating errors $Y(h) - Y_0$; these are discussed in detail by R. D. Russell in his talk and in the workshop run by V. Pereyra at this conference.

Returning to the discussion of differential equations, what we really want is an estimate of the error in approximating a solution $y(t)$ at each t; several of the estimation schemes suggested above have been used to do just that for discrete models of the original boundary-value problem. In shooting and embedding we are solving initial-value problems, and most codes for such problems estimate the local or one-step error rather than the global or total error we desire. Clearly, the two errors are related, but it is not fair to say, as some have, that error estimation is easier for initial-value problems; the fallacy of the statement comes from measuring two different errors.

7. ERROR CONTROL AND PARAMETER SELECTION

What we usually want is to control the error, in the sense that we want to make the error less than some tolerance provided by a user of our method at as low a cost as possible. In the real methods we discussed in Sections 2, 3, and 4, there are many parameters at our disposal. The first, of course, are the Transformed Problem, the Discrete Model, and the Solution Technique we choose to use. After choosing these, we still face many parameters. For example: with finite differences, how many points t_i to use and where to place them, and what difference approximations to use; for spline collocation, how many break points to use and where to place them, where to place collocation points, what degree and how smooth splines to use; for shooting, how many shooting points to use and where to place them; et cetera. While the user of a computer code can sometimes wisely select parameters, in many cases a good choice of parameters depends on properties of the solution about which the user has no ideas. For this reason an important trend in code development is the inclusion of procedures which automatically select parameters in an attempt to attain the desired error efficiently. More detail on this is presented in the talk by R. D. Russell and in the workshops led by F. Krogh, by R. Sincovec, and by A. White at this conference.

8. CONCLUSIONS

My aim in this paper has been to explain briefly what each of a variety of methods is, how methods relate to one another, and where are the difficulties today that stimulate interesting research problems. To describe what the methods are and how they relate we viewed each method as a Solution Technique for some Discrete Model of a Transformed Problem. Those areas which in my opinion deserve much more study and development include: numerical effects and efficiency of different methods of solving the linear algebraic systems that arise; methods for solving the special nonlinear algebraic systems that arise; comparative performance of codes implementing various methods on carefully chosen classes of test problems; and methods for estimating and controlling global errors by automatic selection of parameters of the method.

9. REFERENCES

1. Aktas, Z., and H. J. Stetter (1977), "A classification and survey of numerical methods for boundary-value problems in ordering differential equations," Int. J. Num. Meth. Eng., vol. 11, 771-796.

2. Frank, R. (1976), "The method of iterated defect correction and its application to two-point boundary-value problems, I," Numer. Math., vol. 25, 409-418.

3. Joyce, C. C. (1971), "Survey of extrapolation processes in numerical analysis," SIAM Rev., vol. 13, 435-590.

4. Keller, H. B. (1975), "Numerical methods for boundary-value problems in ordinary differential equations: Survey and some recent results on difference methods," in Numerical Solutions of Boundary-value Problems in Ordinary Differential Equations (A. K. Aziz, ed.), Academic Press, New York, 27-88.

5. Murray, W. (ed.) (1972), Numerical Methods for Unconstrained Optimization Problems, Academic Press, London.

6. Ortega, J. M., and W. C. Rheinboldt (1970), Iterative Solution of Nonlinear Equations in Several Variables, Academic Press, New York.

7. Pereyra, V. (1967), "Iterated deferred corrections for nonlinear boundary-value problems," Numer. Math., vol. 10, 316-323.

8. Scott, M. R. (1973), Invariant Imbedding and Its Applications to Ordinary Differential Equations, Addison-Wesley, Reading, Mass.

9. Scott, M. R., and H. A. Watts (1977), "Computational solution of linear two-point boundary-value problems via orthonormalization," SIAM J. Numer. Anal., vol. 14, 40-70.

INITIAL VALUE INTEGRATORS IN BVP CODES*

H. A. Watts

1. Introduction

For several years now, we have been studying methods and codes to solve the two-point boundary value problem in ordinary differential equations [238-241]. Our goal has been to develop software of the highest quality. To this end our efforts have paralleled (and were a natural extension of) the earlier (and ongoing) work on initial value problems at Sandia Laboratories [245,248-250]. That is, we have been interested in boundary value problem procedures which utilize initial value methods--commonly referred to as shooting procedures in much of the literature, although we do not consider this to be an adequate identifier. We shall refer to these procedures as initial value techniques and shooting will merely denote a particular initial value procedure.

Popularity for using initial value methods in solving boundary value problems stems from two principal reasons. First, the present state-of-the-art in solving initial value problems is quite good. Theoretical and practical aspects of numerical methods are well developed and understood at least for non-stiff differential equations. Good software is available and is (or has become) a standard part of mathematical subroutine libraries everywhere. Second, there is a basic simplicity in understanding and writing an elementary program which uses initial value methods in attempting to solve a boundary value problem. Thus the initial value procedures are among the best known and most universally applicable methods for the numerical solution of boundary value problems.

In this survey paper we shall look at initial value integrators and their role in boundary value problem codes. In particular, we shall examine initial value methods, describe algorithmic matters which are important for the design of

*This work supported by U.S. Department of Energy.

quality software, mention some available codes which have been well tested and documented, and look at some recent developments and future areas of study. We then discuss some boundary value codes which are based on initial value methods. Lastly, we look at the applicability of standard integrators to boundary value problems (with special classes of equations in mind) and to certain boundary value techniques. Should there be special consideration given to future software development for the initial value problem which would aid its utility in boundary value codes?

2. Initial Value Methods

The history of activities in the numerical solution of the initial value problem for ordinary differential equations can be traced through the following references. These are the books of Milne (1953), Henrici (1962), Ceschino and Kuntzmann (1966), Lapidus and Seinfeld (1971), Gear (1971), Lambert (1973), Stetter (1973), Shampine and Gordon (1975), Hall and Watt (1976), and Van der Houwen (1977). In this section we shall describe numerical methods (of most interest) which solve the equation $y'(x) = f(x,y(x))$ on the interval $[a,b]$ with initial value $y(a) = \eta$. For a system of equations we view this problem in vector notation. A numerical solution is an approximation $y_{n+1} \doteq y(x_{n+1})$ which is generated by advancing y_n over the step h_n, where $x_{n+1} = x_n + h_n$.

2.1 Non-stiff methods

The best methods being used today to solve non-stiff equations are generally agreed to be the Runge-Kutta, Adams, and extrapolation methods. Although there are other possibilities which might be kept in mind, such as a scheme based on Taylor series, none have achieved the level of usage with real problem solving as with those mentioned above.

An explicit Runge-Kutta method with s stages or evaluations computes an approximation to the solution of an initial value problem with the formulas

$$f_o = f(x_n,y_n)$$

$$f_i = f(x_n + \alpha_i h_n, y_n + h_n \sum_{j=0}^{i-1} \beta_{ij} f_j) \text{ , } i=1,\dots,s$$

$$y_{n+1} = y_n + h_n \sum_{i=0}^{s} c_i f_i \quad .$$

We shall be interested only in methods which have a companion error estimation formula of the form [250]

$$est = h_n \sum_{i=0}^{s} e_i f_i \quad .$$

The Adams methods are based on the identity

$$y(x) = y(x_n) + \int_{x_n}^{x} f(t,y(t))dt$$

and integration of an interpolating polynominal P(t) which interpolates to values $f_{n-j} = f(x_{n-j}, y_{n-j})$. The Adams-Bashforth formula of order k takes the form

$$y_{n+1} = y_n + h \sum_{i=1}^{k} \beta_{ki} f_{n-i+1} \quad .$$

This is an explicit formula which is generally used as a predictor equation for the implicit Adams-Moulton formula of order k + 1,

$$y_{n+1} = y_n + h \sum_{i=1}^{k} \beta_{ki}^* f_{n-i+1} + h\beta_{ko}^* f(x_{n+1},y_{n+1}) \quad .$$

The more common and effective approach used by current Adams integration codes is to define a predictor-corrector scheme, usually referred to as a PECE method. That is, predict p_{n+1} from the Adams-Bashforth formula, evaluate $f(x_{n+1},p_{n+1})$, use in the Adams-Moulton equation to compute a corrected value y_{n+1}, and follow with another derivative evaluation $f_{n+1} = f(x_{n+1},y_{n+1})$. The extra evaluation is for better stability properties. Using the corrector formula of order k+1 (instead of k) is frequently referred to as local extrapolation. Reference [245] contains an excellent treatment of the Adams method.

Extrapolation methods use a simple formula without memory to step to x_{n+1} repeatedly, using a step size sequence whose values decrease fairly rapidly. By suitably combining these results of low accuracy, one can obtain highly accurate approximations to $y(x_{n+1})$. The modified midpoint rule is the formula which has received most attention. Like the Runge-Kutta schemes, these methods have little overhead computations.

2.2 Stiff methods

We shall say that the differential equation is stiff in an interval about x if $Re(\lambda_i) < 0$ and $\max Re(-\lambda_i) >> \min Re(-\lambda_i)$, where the λ_i are the eigenvalues of of the Jacobian $\frac{\partial f}{\partial y}$ evaluated along the solution curve at x. Stiff problems are are those with very stable integral curves and which involve quantities changing on very different time scales. This is an important class of problems which are extremely expensive to solve by classical methods. The basic problem is that of numerical stability which causes a rather severe limitation to be imposed on the step size. Whereas for most problems the accuracy requirement dictates the choice of step size, for stiff problems the stability requirement does. The essence of stiffness, then, is that one wishes to compute the slowly changing solution very efficiently. Reference [246] gives an excellent discussion and a user's viewpoint on solving stiff equations.

The most widely used and successful methods are based on the backward differentiation formulas. These are linear multi-step methods of the form

$$y_{n+1} = \sum_{i=1}^{k} \alpha_{ki}\, y_{n-i+1} + h\, \beta_{ko} f(x_{n+1}, y_{n+1}) \; .$$

As the name suggests, the derivative at x_{n+1} is approximated (implicitly) by a linear combination of solution values taken from the backward direction. These formulas satisfy a concept of stability which makes them useful on many stiff problems. Their principal limitation is on problems having complex eigenvalues lying very near to the imaginary axis. See [115] for more details.

Solution of implicit equations, applied to stiff problems, requires Jacobian evaluations for a Newton-like iteration. Enright [284] explored the use of the Jacobian matrix in calculating second derivatives for a multi-step formula. By requiring desirable stability characteristics, this class of formulas take the form

$$y_{n+1} = y_n + h \sum_{i=0}^{k} \beta_{ki}\, f_{n+1-i} + h^2 \gamma_{ko}\, y''_{n+1} \; .$$

Other possibilities which show some promise are various implicit Runge-Kutta methods (which include block implicit one-step methods) and composite multi-step formulas. The latter also generate a block or set of solution points simultaneously. Specialized formulas derived through exponential fitting have also proved useful.

3. Algorithmic Matters

In this section we shall briefly mention some of the most important factors which bear on the design of a computer program worthy of general use. Reference [247] discusses these matters in depth in the context of Runge-Kutta methods.

3.1 Error tolerance criteria

Popular choices are absolute, relative or a mixed error test. Also in wide use is the test made relative to the maximum absolute value of the solution component seen so far in the integration. Other more general choices are reasonable for special circumstances but the above choices appear to be completely satisfactory for most problems. In the context of boundary value codes, superposition techniques typically require that the components defining the superposition coefficients be computed with a certain amount of relative accuracy. In this case the error tolerance criteria can play an important role, and we would recommend against using the last of the above choices.

We must also consider whether the tolerance information should be specified by a scalar or if a vector (relating to the different components) is needed. For stiff problems an error tolerance vector seems more appropriate. A point worth emphasizing is that the integration scheme will attempt to control the error in the worst behaving component. If the system of equations comes from redefining a higher order equation as a first order system, the higher derivative components are usually more difficult to control than the solution component. In this case, using a scalar error tolerance will generally lead to more accuracy in the solution than requested. For a boundary value problem, we believe it is relatively rare that anyone is interested in more than the solution component and perhaps the first derivative. Hence, more efficient integration can be achieved through appropriate use of an error tolerance vector for boundary value techniques requiring first order systems of equations.

3.2 Error control

Present codes adjust the step size so as to control the local error (ℓ.e.) although the global error is the item of interest to the user. However, good software delivers an error which is rather uniformly proportional to the tolerance ε and is approximately the accuracy requested for routine problems. There are two principal criteria in use for accepting or rejecting a step. Error per step is to require $|\ell.e.| \leq \varepsilon$ whereas error per unit step is to require $|\ell.e.| \leq h\varepsilon$. Differences resulting from the two ways are most pronounced at low orders, at limiting precision, and at discontinuities. In our experience, error per step has been more effective.

3.3 Locally optimal step size

For a method of order p we assume that the local error has the form

$$\ell.e. = h_n^{p+1}\phi(x_n,y_n) + O(h_n^{p+2}) \quad ,$$

with a smooth principal error function ϕ, and that the integration method has an effective error estimator which computes

$$|est| = |h_n^{p+1} \, \phi\,(x_n,y_n)| \quad .$$

By a "locally optimal step size" we mean to choose the next step size from

$$h_{n+1} \doteq h_n \left|\frac{\varepsilon}{est}\right|^{\frac{1}{p+1}}$$

which is derived from aiming at $|\ell.e.| \doteq \varepsilon$ on the next step. In practice, one is not so bold and actually chooses a fraction, say 0.9, of the locally optimal step size. This is to protect against poor error estimates due to ϕ changing too rapidly, the equations not being sufficiently smooth, or the inability to neglect higher order terms. Using nearly optimal step sizes produces good error behavior (uniformly proportional to the tolerance).

3.4 External limits on the step size

It is necessary to limit the rate of increase and decrease of the step size. Prediction of a large change nearly always signals a failure of the validity of the assumptions. Appropriate factors are somewhat method-dependent but values of 1/10 and 1/2 are common for the limit on step size decreases whereas factors of 2 and 5 are quite common for increases. Placing such external limits on the step size greatly damps chattering on problems with a severe lack of smoothness.

3.5 Selecting an initial step size

Several ways of selecting an initial step size can be found. One way is to require the user to supply a guess. This is at least an annoyance since it is rather unlikely that the user can provide a reasonably good value. Another way is to take a fixed fraction of the interval length. However, since an appropriate initial step size depends only on the initial solution behavior it seems unnatural for the choice to depend on the interval of integration. A better way is to utilize the initial slope in estimating the starting step size automatically [245,247]. A rule of thumb which seems to work well in practice is to hypothesize that the error in starting off a method of order p is h^p times the error, $hy'(x_o)$, of a constant approximation. Boundary value procedures using multiple shooting, orthonormalization techniques, or quasilinearization [239] require restarting the initial value solution process at the breakpoints. Much of the time behavior of the integral curves does not vary greatly across these points. In such circumstances, using the current step length to the breakpoint for the initial step size in restarting the integration seems advantageous for Runge-Kutta methods. Variable order Adams procedures require further consideration.

3.6 Output considerations

Adams methods which use interpolation for output are very insensitive to the frequency of output requests. Runge-Kutta algorithms, on the other hand, must be carefully designed to avoid a severe impact on the natural step size sequence. Taking exceedingly small steps to obtain output causes complications. Two devices which are used to prevent unusually small steps are features called "stretching" and "looking ahead" [247].

3.7 Scale of the problem

The necessity of providing some measure of the scale of the problem seems clear; without it important phenomena may be skipped. This is more likely to be a serious problem with Runge-Kutta methods than with Adams methods. Three schemes have received some attention. A traditional approach is for the user to supply a maximum step size. This is easy to understand but it is not, in general, easy to select a good value. Another approach is to have the user supply a scale parameter which is roughly the size of a Lipschitz constant which is related to the problem. A maximum allowable step size is then appropriately calculated. A different viewpoint is to note that users are likely to scale their problem in a reasonable way without even giving any special thought to it. In particular, (in the context of Runge-Kutta methods) their choice of output will ordinarily limit the step size in an appropriate way. Furthermore, scaling difficulties are most likely to occur on the first step. With this in mind, appropriate selection of the initial step size plus a safety factor of frequency of output appears to be a satisfactory solution to most scaling difficulties. However for boundary value procedures using superposition techniques, the intermediate integrations (solutions) may have little in common with the solution of the boundary value problem. Hence, output should not be relied upon as a satisfactory device for maximum step size control.

3.8 Minimum step size considerations

In the past a minimum step size has been supplied by the user to detect trouble spots or to control the amount of work. In addition, it was not uncommon to accept steps at a minimum allowable level, regardless of the status of the error test, in order that the integration might proceed to the end of the interval. There is little justification for doing any of these. Rather, an appropriate minimum step size corresponding to limiting precision is readily computable and should be used for that purpose only.

3.9 Effects of computer arithmetic

As one attempts more and more accuracy there comes a point when it is no longer possible to achieve better results because of working with a limited number of digits available with the computer. Thus it is important to detect limiting precision and take appropriate action.

4. Quality Software

In recent years, codes for solving the initial value problem in ordinary differential equations have been greatly improved. The most significant advances have been in the areas of overall efficiency, reliability, robustness (safety features and the ability to diagnose or handle mistakes and misuse of the code), and convenience (ease of use). Furthermore, there has been a great amount of interest in testing, comparing and certifying the ODE programs. All this gives the casual user of such codes considerable assurance that his scientific problem can be solved satisfactorily and effectively.

4.1 Some codes

In this section we shall mention some codes which are readily available, portable (easy to implement at different computing installations), and which are among the most efficient codes known to us. We shall first list those which are appropriate for non-stiff equations.

We mention three Runge-Kutta codes. The first is RKF45, a fourth order Fehlberg method which uses local extrapolation to achieve fifth order. This code was written by Watts and Shampine and can be found in references [247,112]. The code DVERK is based on Verner's fifth and sixth order pair of formulas. It was written by Hull, Enright, and Jackson and can be found in reference [136] as well as in the IMSL library [141]. The GERK code uses the basic Runge-Kutta-Fehlberg formulas as in RKF45 to produce an estimate of the global error. This code is available from the authors or through the TOMS algorithms service [248].

The first Adams code we mention is the well-documented DE/STEP,INTRP suite of Shampine and Gordon [245]. This is a variable order procedure which uses formulas through order twelve. It is also available from the Argonne Code Center [12]. Another variable order Adams code which has seen wide use is DVDQ (more recent versions are SODE,DODE), written by Krogh [162]. These are extremely flexible routines, having a number of unique features. The GEAR package, developed by Hindmarsh [130], is yet a different implementation of the Adams formulas. GEAR is also available via [12].

Other codes which should be mentioned are DIFSY1 [140], an improved-version of the extrapolation procedure developed by Bulirsch and Stoer, and DIFSUB, the well-known program written by Gear [115]. A number of good codes are also being developed at the University of Toronto by Hull and others. Still other codes can be found in the IMSL library, NAG library, and the proprietary Bell Labs library.

The state of development for codes appropriate for stiff systems lags further behind. The GEAR and DIFSUB routines also include the backward differentiation formulas and probably represent the most successful and widely used codes for solving stiff equations. Further development is contained in the code EPISODE, written by Byrne and Hindmarsh [39]. It embodies a completely variable step formulation and can be obtained via [12]. The second derivative formulas were implemented in the code SDBASIC by Enright [284]. Hulme has implemented a family of implicit Runge-Kutta methods in COLODE at Sandia Laboratories, also available through [12]. Extrapolation has also been used for stiff problems; an example is the IMPEX2 code written by Lindberg [284]. Useful codes implementing block-implicit one-step and multi-step methods have been developed at Syracuse University by Bickart and others. Still other stiff codes can be found in the IMSL library and Harwell library (e.g., the very elaborate FACSIMILE code).

4.2 Solving a differential equation

We shall now examine some of the important factors in choosing an integration procedure. First, what do we mean about solving a differential equation numerically? There are several possibilities. We may be interested in getting a solution approximation only at a single point, say y(b). More often a solution approximation is requested on a set of output points so as to generate a table or smooth curve of the solution. Sometimes one wants essentially a continuous approximation to the solution. This latter situation can be handled effectively only by global techniques such as provided by the Adams methods. Thus frequency of output is an important consideration. In the context of boundary value procedures, all of the above possibilities are likely to arise. Perhaps the most important factors, in general, are the accuracy being requested and the cost of evaluating the derivative function. Typically, methods that require relatively few derivative evaluations (such as the Adams Methods) have a rather large amount of overhead whereas those methods requiring more evaluations for the same tasks (Runge-Kutta methods) have relatively low overhead costs. In choosing a program one should be guided by the relative cost of evaluating the derivative while keeping in mind that the low overhead methods are usually more efficient for the crude tolerance range.

Still other important factors to consider are the size of the system of equations, stiffness, and presence of discontinuities. The larger the size of the system, the smaller is the relative effect of overhead costs. If the equations are just mildly stiff, using a Runge-Kutta code such as RKF45 or an Adams code such as DE works well. In fact, in such instances where the derivative cost is inexpensive, these codes are often more efficient than the stiff solvers. While it is better to avoid integrating through integrable singularities and discontinuities, one may not know the exact location of such difficulties in advance. Runge-Kutta codes such as RKF45 are better able to cope with such problems though DE, DVDQ and GEAR solve them quite effectively.

Linearity and sparseness are also factors which may determine the choice of integrator. Most large systems of stiff equations are sparse and it is essential that the method take advantage of the structure if it is to be efficient. Advantage can easily be taken of the linearity of a problem with Adams and backward differentiation codes. By saving some information in the derivative subroutine the user can avoid recomputing expressions when the independent variable remains unchanged. For standard predictor-corrector schemes a substantial savings can be achieved. This same kind of device does not lead to any savings with the Runge-Kutta codes mentioned. There are, however, other Runge-Kutta formulas which can take special advantage of the linear problem. Lastly, but certainly not least important in the present context, we must decide on the applicability of the integrator to the boundary value problem or technique for solving the boundary value problem. We shall return to this matter.

4.3 Comparisons and guidelines

A recent survey and comparison of the best software for non-stiff problems can be found in reference [249]. The aim in that paper was to describe the characteristics and capabilities of some good software in order to assist the person who wants to install a high quality initial value code at his computer center. Further valuable comparisons have been performed by Hull and others from the University of Toronto, references [135,103] for the non-stiff methods and reference [104] for stiff methods. In their work the aim has been to compare methods and not codes. Unfortunately, their objectives have been widely misunderstood. It has been our experience that how a method is implemented may be more important than the choice of method.

The conclusions of these and other studies are rather uniform. If the equations are not expensive and moderate accuracy is required, one should use a Runge-Kutta code such as RKF45 or DVERK. If the equations are not expensive and a lot of accuracy is needed, an extrapolation code such as DIFSY1 is appropriate. (We should point out that the software development of extrapolation codes is relatively primitive.) If the equations are rather expensive to evaluate, one should use a variable order Adams code of which DE represents the highest level of development. If one needs answers at a great many output points, the Adams methods are best. Extrapolation procedures should be avoided but Runge-Kutta codes such as RKF45 will usually be satisfactory, at least if the one-step integration mode of supplying answers after each natural step size can be used. If the equations lack smoothness or there is some stiffness present, avoid extrapolation. For stiff problems try GEAR initially. Of course, the context of solving initial value equations for a particular boundary value technique adds further information for the choice of appropriate integrator to be used. For example, boundary problem procedures which allow or require frequent restarting of the integration process favor the use of Runge-Kutta methods. This is because the Adams schemes start at order one, building up the order and step size as quickly as possible. Thus the starting phase for an Adams algorithm is not as efficient when compared to the progress achieved by a Runge-Kutta algorithm. For instance, we find that an Adams procedure is rather severely impacted when an excessive number of orthonormalization points is used [63].

The best codes are extremely easy to use. Furthermore they furnish a great deal of protection as well as convenience to the user. By comparison with software for the non-stiff problem, codes for stiff equations are somewhat primitive and unreliable and the cost of solving such problems is high. At this time many stiff methods are being extensively developed but rather few of them are represented by more than experimental codes.

5. Recent Developments

We shall now mention very briefly some of the newer developments in the area of solving initial value problems numerically. We wish to emphasize that although the present state-of-the-art is quite good, this area of study is still extremely active.

5.1 Blended multi-step formulas

Skeel [254] examines the possibility of blending an Adams formula and a backward differentiation formula together. The idea is to retain the order of accuracy of the Adams methods when accuracy considerations are important and to retain the stability properties of the backward differentiation formulas when stiffness is a factor. These formulas take the form

$$\left\{\text{Adams}\right\} - ch\,\frac{\partial f}{\partial y}\,\left\{\text{Backward Differentiation}\right\}$$

for some constant c.

5.2 Second order equations

Horn [132] developed moderately high order Runge-Kutta-Nystrom formulas to solve systems of second order initial value equations in which the first derivative is absent; that is, equations of the form $y''(x) = f(x,y)$. Coefficients are determined which yield algorithms having minimal truncation error terms and large stability regions. Also ideas are proposed for improving the efficiency of Runge-Kutta algorithms when dealing with rejected steps and with frequency of output.

5.3 Oscillatory problems

Petzold and Gear [208], Miranker and Wahba [188], and Amdursky and Ziv [10] study problems with highly oscillatory solutions. Such problems have been called stiff oscillatory problems because they usually have large eigenvalues although this terminology can be misleading. Usually one wants to follow the actual solution accurately over a cycle of the oscillation from time to time and to be able to find the long-term behavior of the solution without following all oscillations closely. In [208] the authors define a quasi-envelope of the solution and discuss a numerical procedure.

5.4 Variable formula Runge-Kutta

Imbedded Runge-Kutta formulas of a wide range in order are being investigated independently by Bettis (University of Texas), Shampine (Sandia Laboratories) and Verner (Queens University). The objective is to develop a variable order Runge-Kutta method which will partially compete with the variable order Adams methods at stringent tolerances and which will rival the extrapolation methods.

5.5 Global error estimates

All the codes we have examined attempt to control the local errors. However, GERK does provide the user with an estimate of the global error and use of these estimates to aid in selecting an appropriate step size is currently being considered. Recent work has been performed by Stetter (see [284] for a discussion of the technique) on economical global error estimation in ODE solvers and, in particular, in relation to Adams predictor-corrector codes. He has put the scheme, due to Zadunaisky [this proceedings], on firmer theoretical support. Another interesting technique is described in [182].

5.6 Stiff problems

The subject of classifying stiff problems and developing numerical procedures for effective solution of them is one of the most important and active areas of study at present. We shall briefly make reference to some of the activities. Skelboe [255] discusses improvements in the control of order and steplength for the backward differentiation formulas. Substantial improvements are reported for problems having eigenvalues near the complex axis. Implicit Runge-Kutta methods, with emphasis on the efficient implementation of the computational process, are receiving a great deal of attention; e.g., see Butcher [38], Bickart [26], and Epton [106]. Diagonally implicit Runge-Kutta schemes have been considered by Norsett [193], Alt [9], and Alexander [4]. Better handling of matrix computations such as with the Jacobian formulation and LU decompositions have been studied by Enright [105] and others. Use of structural information and exponential approximation schemes are also being investigated.

5.7 Testing, program verification and validation

One of the main purposes for testing a program is to help determine if the program does what it is supposed to do. That is, we are interested in establishing the correctness or validity of the program tasks. Testing a program also enables us to draw some conclusions about the efficiency of the procedure. Naturally, exhaustive testing will never completely verify that a program is correct and it would be helpful to have on hand some theoretical evidence to reinforce such claims. Work in this important area is being done by Hull, Enright, and others; e.g., see [142].

5.8 Program design and standards

We must keep up with the continuing development of software as programming standards are still changing. One need only take notice of the many conferences devoted to various aspects of mathematical software during the past couple of years. A current endeavor of some DOE laboratories is to attempt systematization of initial value software. In particular, standards for the design of user interface are being considered. We also want to call attention to FORTRAN callable assembly language modules. In the future, we may see more use made of these, especially for large problems.

6. Boundary Value Software Using Initial Value Methods

Here we mention some boundary value codes (known to us) which utilize initial value methods. We divide them into four categories.

6.1 Superposition techniques (applied to original problem)

The SUPORT code [238] uses superposition principles coupled with an orthonormalization procedure for solving linear two-point boundary value problems. Several choices are available to the user for the integration scheme. These are the Runge-Kutta procedures RKF45 and GERK and the Adams package of STEP,INTRP.

The SUPOR Q code [239] combines the techniques used by SUPORT with a linearization process (quasilinearization) to form a solver for nonlinear boundary value problems. The present working version of this code contains the RKF45 and GERK codes. The Adams integrator will be made available in the near future and a stiff integrator may also be provided.

The QUASII code [50] has been designed to solve nonlinear multi-point problems. The method of particular solutions is used along with a fixed step classical fourth order Runge-Kutta method. This is a superposition procedure which combines solutions of the linearized inhomogeneous equation.

The textbook code of Beltrami [25] is another orthonormalization code which uses quasilinearization on nonlinear problems. The integration method consists of an Adams predictor-corrector scheme which goes up to eighth order.

QSLIN/ORTNRM [253] was developed by Conte and Silverston at Purdue University a number of years ago. It used orthonormalization along with quasilinearization for nonlinear problems. The integration method was a fixed step classical Runge-Kutta scheme.

6.2 Superposition techniques (applied to transformed problem)

The INVIMB code [270] uses invariant imbedding techniques (Ricatti transformations) to transform the original boundary value problem into an initial value problem, using superposition principles to achieve a solution to the boundary problem. The present version of the code solves linear systems with the choice of using a Runge-Kutta, Adams or stiff integrator (RKF45, DE and a variant of GEAR).

Other research oriented invariant imbedding codes have been written by Scott [236] which have used all of the integrators available at Sandia Laboratories.

6.3 Shooting for general nonlinear problems

The BOUNDSOL code, developed by Bulirsch, Stoer, and Deufelhard [35] implements a multiple shooting algorithm. It works with the DIFSY1 extrapolation integrator though other one-step oriented integrators having the same argument list could be easily used.

The Harwell code DD03AD [102] is another multiple shooting procedure. Shooting points can be provided by the user or determined automatically by a first pass integration using the variational equations. The integration process is a fourth order Runge-Kutta scheme due to England.

SBVP is a multiple shooting code being developed at JPL [146]. Shooting points are chosen automatically and adjusted dynamically as the solution process proceeds. The integrator used is the Adams package of Krogh.

A collection of multiple shooting codes (of varying levels of sophistication) have been developed by Gladwell for the NAG library over the past several years. The most recent version is DO2SAF [see this proceedings].

Several general shooting codes [241] have also been written at Sandia Laboratories and all allow the user a choice of a Runge-Kutta, Adams or stiff integrator. These codes include MSHOOT, SHOOT1, and SHOOT2 of which MSHOOT is a multiple shooting code. They are not yet developed to the level which has been planned for.

6.4 Shooting for Sturm-Liouville problems

The code SLEIGN [18] solves the second order linear Sturm-Liouville problem using Prufer transformations to modify the original equation. The global error estimation code GERK is used for the integrations.

7. Matters Concerning Use of IVP Codes in BVP Solvers

When appropriate, an existing software routine (well tested and documented) should be used, and if possible, it should be used without change. Unfortunately, this is not always possible nor desirable as it may be necessary for some tailoring to specific applications. If one is fortunate enough to be working with the initial value code developer, making such modifications can be achieved without serious concern. In addition, it is likely that future changes and improvements will need to be incorporated in the integrator and this also leads to implementation difficulties. It is often the case that when too many modifications are made, quality software fails to retain its quality.

We recognize the need for both general flexibility and efficiency in the integrators. However, these are in obvious conflict. Too much flexibility could make the routine hopelessly inefficient for some classes of problems which a particular boundary value technique is aimed at solving.

7.1 Problems in using library integrators

The following difficulty occurs when the initial value code requires a derivative evaluation routine in the form F(x,y,y'). Let us consider a boundary value technique which solves the linear problem $y'(x) = M(x)y + g(x) \equiv f(x,y)$. It is not currently possible to construct an algorithm which allows the matrix M to be defined with variable dimensions unless the required derivative subroutine form for the initial value code is altered.

Another situation which arises is the need for both one-step oriented and interval oriented integrators. One or the other mode of integration will be applicable to various boundary value techniques. With the orthonormalization procedure in SUPORT, for example, it is necessary to monitor the solutions frequently so that the integrator must have the feature of returning answers after each integration step. Some integration packages that allow both features do so with different subroutine modules. While this is more efficient (avoiding extra subroutine linkage), it is certainly not the most convenient. We have had experience in implementing the Adams single step module STEP in the SUPORT code. This was no easy matter.

7.2 Advantages to special integration schemes

Some of the boundary value techniques are aimed at solving linear equations. Advantage should be taken of linearity by using appropriate integration schemes.

In some cases, careful programming can yield substantial savings [278]. For example, the cost of solving an expensive linear differential equation by an Adams code can effectively be cut in half. This is because the predictor-corrector scheme evaluates the derivative (of the form $y' = M(x)\ y + g(x)$) successively at the same value of the independent variable. One need only save the computations from $M(x)$, $g(x)$ to avoid the wasted expense of re-evaluating them on the subsequent entry in which x is unchanged. The Runge-Kutta methods used in RKF45 and DVERK do not present any such savings as there are no consecutive multiple nodes appearing in the algorithm. Other possibilities are currently being investigated and it is our belief that special integration methods, directed at the efficient solution of linear differential equations, should be used by the corresponding boundary value techniques.

It would not be efficient to install a stiff integrator off the shelf into the SUPORT code. This is because the superposition solutions are being solved simultaneously from one large system. However, this large system actually consists of uncoupled smaller systems. To use a stiff solver effectively, the stiff code must be modified to work with the smaller systems, noting that they have the same Jacobians.

Another item which deserves comment is the solution of the invariant imbedding equations obtained by applying a Ricatti transformation to the original problem. In this approach unstable equations are transformed to stable initial value equations, sometimes ultra stable or stiff. Thus a stiff integrator would be an essential feature of boundary value codes using the invariant imbedding principle. Because of the form of the equations special integrators may be advantageous; implicit Runge-Kutta schemes have been used in some work.

7.3 Backward differentiation methods on unstable equations

Integration of a mathematically unstable system of differential equations seems more likely to arise in connection with the attempt to solve a boundary value problem than purely from an initial value problem arising physically. Unstable equations which have large eigenvalues are also referred to by many as stiff systems. However, this is not in unison with our earlier definition of stiff. The trouble comes from unsuspecting users applying the backward differentiation codes such as DIFSUB to this type of problem. These methods are applicable to stiff equations (that is, highly stable) but also have a somewhat dangerous property associated with the stability regions. Namely, the unstable region is a connected region which protrudes into a small portion of the right half plane near the origin, leaving a stable region which extends throughout the remainder of the right half plane. This means that growing solution components will actually be damped if the step size is taken sufficiently large. The single step code DIFSUB has been used with a rather alarming frequency for exactly this purpose. The error status flags (reporting the inability of the code to achieve the requested accuracy) are overridden until the necessary damping effect occurs, which is to say until the step size is able to work its way out of the unstable region corresponding to the numerical method. Although it may be possible to do this successfully on some problems, it is at best dangerous and unsuspecting users must be warned about the distinction between large positive and large negative eigenvalues and the applicability of methods such as the backward differentiation formulas.

7.4 Global errors in the solution of boundary value problems

The boundary value codes we have mentioned do not guarantee to deliver the specified level of accuracy requested by the user. Rather, their approach is similar to that taken by the initial value codes. The aim is to deliver global errors which are proportional to the error tolerances in general, while for routine problems the accuracy delivered is approximately that which is requested. Clearly there are other factors than just the integration errors which affect the global errors of the boundary value techniques. This is an area which deserves further attention. Perhaps integration with the global error estimation schemes, such as in the GERK code or the procedures used by Zadunaisky, can be utilized more extensively.

7.5 Conclusions

We have mentioned some items relating to the appropriate choice of integration scheme and to the aspect of structuring and designing initial value codes for better applicability in solving boundary value problems. The capabilities needed for the various boundary problem techniques seem to be sufficiently different so as to warrant treatment on an individual basis. The best available software for the initial value problem should be utilized to the extent for which it is appropriate. In some instances, modifications or different methods will be necessary or else some inefficiency will result. (See also Anderson's paper [this proceedings].)

NONLINEAR EQUATION SOLVERS IN BOUNDARY VALUE PROBLEM CODES

Peter Deuflhard

0. INTRODUCTION

In recent years, the development of general purpose routines for the solution of *nonlinear two-point boundary value problems (BVPs)* has reached some level of sophistication. In all the various approaches, certain *systems of nonlinear equations (NLEQs)* arise. This class of NLEQs has turned out to be far more challenging than the standard set of (often artificial) test examples spread in the literature and usually taken as a basis for comparisons of different NLEQ solvers. This situation justifies a separate survey of NLEQ methods in connection with BVP algorithms. Moreover, most of the NLEQs arising in this context have some common *cyclic* structure as shown in chapter 1 of the present paper. These cyclic NLEQs cover e.g. the systems arising in the different multiple shooting codes (both the one due to Bulirsch/ Stoer/Deuflhard [35] and the one due to England [102] and Reid [216]), a Taylor series method (due to Rentrop [218]), certain collocation codes (such as the B-spline method due to Ascher/Christiansen/Russell [13] or the third order Hermite interpolation method due to Dickmanns/ Well [88]), and the deferred correction code (due to Lentini/Pereyra [170]). The common cyclic structure of these NLEQs permits a unified presentation of Newton's method in the form suggested by Deuflhard [77, 78, 79] and its combination with continuation methods (cf. [80, 81]). These methods were selected, since they have proved to be both efficient and reliable in connection with several BVP codes (such as [35], [218], [13]). Other methods have been omitted here, partly for lack of space and partly for reasons that will emerge in the course of the presentation.

1. CONNECTIONS NLEQ - BVP

Consider the BVP (in general nonlinear)

$$(1.1)\quad \begin{aligned} &y' = f(t,y) \qquad t \in [a,b] \\ &r(y(a),y(b)) = 0 \end{aligned}$$

with n first-order differential equations and n boundary conditions. Let (1.1) have a solution $y^* : [a,b] \to \mathbb{R}^n$. For convenience of the subsequent presentation, the following notation is introduced: for any $t_0, t_1 \in [a,b]$ let

$$(1.2)\quad W^*(t_1,t_0) = \exp\left[\int_{t_0}^{t_1} f_y(t,y^*(t))\, dt\right]$$

denote the *Wronskian (n,n)-matrix* (of the variational equation associated with (1.1)) in terms of an exponential of the Fréchet matrix f_y. (If *any* trajectory $y \neq y^*$ is inserted, then the asterisk will be dropped.) Whenever a smooth trajectory y on $[a,b]$ is inserted into (1.2), these matrices define a *continuous group* which implies e.g. the following properties

$$(1.3)\quad \begin{aligned} &a)\ W(t_2,t_1)W(t_1,t_0) = W(t_2,t_0) \\ &b)\ W(t_1,t_0)^{-1} = W(t_0,t_1) \end{aligned}$$

These properties will be used extensively throughout the paper.

LEMMA 1. Let the BVP (1.1) have at least one solution y^*. Then y^* is locally unique, if and only if the (n,n)-matrix

$$(1.4)\quad E^* := A^* + B^* W^*(b,a)$$

with $A^* := \left.\frac{\partial r}{\partial y_a}\right|_{y^*}, \quad B^* := \left.\frac{\partial r}{\partial y_b}\right|_{y^*}$

is nonsingular.

Interpretation. From the definitions of $A^*, B^*, W^*(b,a)$, the matrix E^* may be denoted as a *sensitivity matrix* (with respect to $t = a$), since

$$(1.5)\quad E^* = \frac{\partial r}{\partial y_a^*} + \frac{\partial r}{\partial y_b^*} \cdot \frac{\partial y_b^*}{\partial y_a^*}\ .$$

Of course, an analogous matrix is associated with any $t \in [a,b]$.

In real life applications, the above uniqueness condition can rarely be tested, since it requires the solution y^* to be available in closed analytic form. On the other hand, an efficient realization of a BVP algorithm will anyway involve some (implicit) test on the local uniqueness of the solution y^* to be approximated. Let y_h^* denote some *approximation* of y^* obtained from a BVP code by some *discretization* or *projection* technique. y_h^* is usually defined only on some (suitably selected) *grid* G_h, where the subscript h (for mesh size) characterizes the discretization (or projection) process. For an efficient BVP code, a *one-to-one correspondence* between each solution y^* of (1.1) and each discrete solution y_h^* obtained from the algorithm will be reasonably required: for a corresponding pair (y^*, y_h^*), a relation of the following type will hold (in some norm):

(1.6) $\|y_h^* - y^*\| = O(h^p)$,

$p > 0$, h "sufficiently small".

Remark. Interesting counter-examples for higher order difference methods have been presented by Spreuer/Adams [256].

In order to determine y_h^*, a *system of N nonlinear equations* (NLEQs), say

(1.7) $F(x) = 0$,

must be solved in each BVP code. Each solution $x^* \in \mathbb{R}^N$ of (1.7) determines some y_h^* which, in turn, is associated with some y^* by virtue of (1.6).

LEMMA 2. Let the NLEQ (1.7) have at least one solution x^*. Then x^* is locally unique, if and only if the Jacobian (N,N)-matrix $J(x^*)$ is nonsingular.

As the NLEQ (1.7) arises from the BVP (1.1), one will expect a connection between Lemma 1 and Lemma 2. Such a connection will be given below in a unified presentation covering most of the BVP algorithms.

Cyclic NLEQs. Upon partitioning $[a,b]$ according to

$$a = t_1 < t_2 < \cdots < t_m = b \qquad (m > 1)$$

and setting

$$x_j = y_h(t_j) \in \mathbb{R}^n \qquad \text{for} \quad j = 1,\dots,m ,$$

this type of NLEQ is characterized by the following system:

(1.8) a) matching conditions $(j = 1,\dots,m-1)$:

$$F_j(x_j, x_{j+1}) = 0,$$

b) boundary conditions:

$$r(x_1, x_m) = 0,$$

which, by comparison with (1.7), can be written as

$$F(x) = \begin{bmatrix} F_1(x_1,x_2) \\ \vdots \\ F_{m-1}(x_{m-1},x_m) \\ r(x_1,x_m) \end{bmatrix} = 0 \quad \text{with} \quad x = \begin{bmatrix} x_1 \\ \vdots \\ x_m \end{bmatrix} \quad \text{and} \quad N = n \cdot m .$$

The associated Jacobian (N,N)-matrix J has the following block cyclic structure

$$\text{c)}\ J = \begin{bmatrix} G_1 & -\bar{G}_2 & & & \\ & G_2 & -\bar{G}_3 & & \\ & & \ddots & \ddots & \\ & & & G_{m-1} & -\bar{G}_m \\ A & & & & B \end{bmatrix},$$

where

$$G_j := \frac{\partial F_j}{\partial x_j}, \quad \bar{G}_{j+1} := -\frac{\partial F_j}{\partial x_{j+1}}, \qquad j = 1,\dots,m-1$$

and A,B as in Lemma 1.

LEMMA 3. Assume that

(1.9) $\bar{G}_j$ nonsingular for $j = 2,\dots,m$

Let C_i^l and E_h denote the (n,n)-matrices

$$C_i^l := \bar{G}_i^{-1} G_{i-1} \cdot \ldots \cdot G_{l+1}^{-1} G_l \quad \text{for} \quad 1 \le l < i \le m$$

$$E_h := A + BC_m^1 = A + B\bar{G}_m^{-1} G_{m-1} \cdot \ldots \cdot \bar{G}_2^{-1} G_1 .$$

Then the following relations hold:

(1.10) a) $\bar{G}LJR = S$

with (N,N)-matrices $\bar{G}, L, R, S$ defined by

$$\bar{G} := \begin{bmatrix} \bar{G}_2 & & & \\ & \ddots & & \\ & & \bar{G}_m & \\ & & & I \end{bmatrix}, \qquad S := \begin{bmatrix} E_h & & & \\ & I & & \\ & & \ddots & \\ & & & I \end{bmatrix},$$

$$L := \begin{bmatrix} BC_m^2 & \cdots & BC_m^{m-1} & I \\ -I & & & \\ & \ddots & & \\ & & -I & \end{bmatrix}, \qquad R^{-1} := \begin{bmatrix} I & & & \\ -C_2^1 & \ddots & & \\ & \ddots & \ddots & \\ & & -C_m^{m-1} & I \end{bmatrix},$$

b) $$\det(J) = \frac{\det(E_h)}{\det(\bar{G}_2) \cdot \ldots \cdot \det(\bar{G}_m)}$$

Proof. Extension of Lemma 5.1 in [78].

Upon summarizing the results of Lemma 2 and Lemma 3, one obtains

LEMMA 4. Let x^* denote a solution of a cyclic NLEQ (1.8). Then, under the assumption (1.9), x^* is locally unique, if and only if the (n,n)-matrix E_h^* is nonsingular.

For the rest of this chapter, examples of BVP algorithms will be given that involve cyclic NLEQs. In these examples, assumption (1.9) is shown to be a natural assumption and E_h^* is an approximation of E^* (as already expressed by the suggestive notation).

(I) *Multiple shooting* as described by Keller [147], Osborne [197], Bulirsch [34], Stoer/Bulirsch [258], and realized in the code [35]. A sequence of initial value problems (IVPs)

$$(1.11)\quad \begin{aligned} y' &= f(t,y) \\ y(t_j) &= x_j \end{aligned}$$

is solved yielding $(m-1)$ subarcs (see Fig. 1)

$$y(t;t_j,x_j) \quad \text{for} \quad t \in [t_j,t_{j+1}]$$

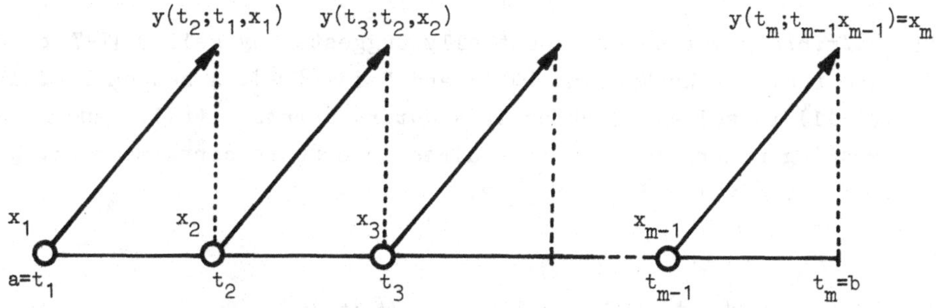

Fig. 1. Schematic representation of Multiple Shooting Method I

Matching conditions (= continuity conditions):

$$(1.12)\ \text{a)}\quad F_j(x_j,x_{j+1}) := y(t_{j+1};t_j,x_j) - x_{j+1} = 0$$

Jacobian matrix block elements (analytic expressions)

$$\text{b)}\quad G_j = \frac{\partial y(t_{j+1};t_j,x_j)}{\partial x_j} \equiv W(t_{j+1},t_j),\ \bar{G}_{j+1} = I$$

Assumption (1.9) holds trivially. Instead of the analytic expression for G_j, a numerical integrator will supply an approximation

$$(1.13)\ \text{a)}\quad G_j = W_h(t_{j+1},t_j)$$

which yields

$$\text{b) } E_h = A + BW_h(t_m,t_{m-1}) \cdot \ldots \cdot W_h(t_2,t_1).$$

Hence, in view of the continuous group property (1.3), E_h^* is an approximation of E^* with

$$(1.14)\quad \|E_h^* - E^*\| \doteq \|y_h^* - y^*\|,$$

where the relation (1.14) just means that the approximation errors of y_h^* and of E_h^* are of the same order in h. Of course, if finite differences are used in lieu of the differentials in E^*, then the finite difference error has to be added.

(II) *Multiple shooting* as essentially suggested by Keller [147 ,p. 67] and realized by England [102] and Reid [216]. A sequence of IVPs (1.11) is solved starting at *shooting points*, $\{t_j\}$, and integrating numerically in *both* directions up to certain *matching points*, $\{\bar{t}_j\}$ - see Fig. 2.

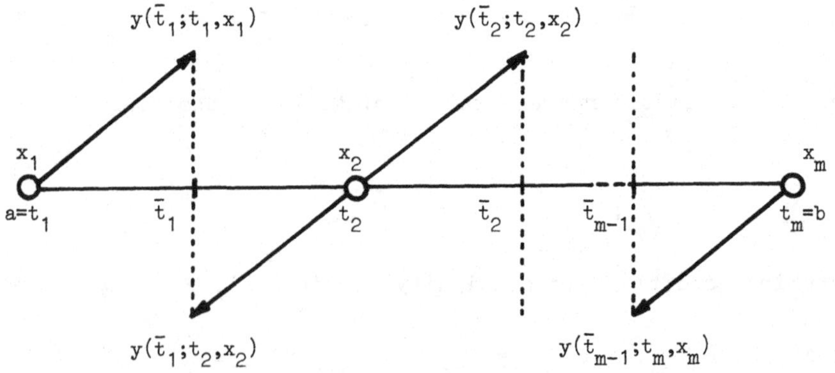

Fig. 2. Schematic representation of Multiple Shooting Method II

Matching conditions (= continuity conditions):

$$(1.15)\ \text{a) } F_j(x_j,x_{j+1}) := y(\bar{t}_j;t_j,x_j) - y(\bar{t}_j;t_{j+1},x_{j+1}) = 0$$

Jacobian matrix block elements:

$$\text{b)}\quad G_j := \frac{\partial y(\bar{t}_j;t_j,x_j)}{\partial x_j}, \quad \bar{G}_{j+1} := \frac{\partial y(\bar{t}_j;t_{j+1},x_{j+1})}{\partial x_{j+1}}$$

As in (1.13) a), one may formally write

$$(1.16)\quad \text{a)}\quad G_j = W_h(\bar{t}_j,t_j), \quad \bar{G}_{j+1} = W_h(\bar{t}_j,t_{j+1}).$$

Since $W(\bar{t}_j,t_{j+1}) = W(t_{j+1},\bar{t}_j)^{-1}$, one may naturally assume that $\bar{G}_{j+1}$ is nonsingular, if an efficient numerical integrator is used. This is just assumption (1.9). Then one obtains

$$\text{b)}\quad E_h = A + BW_h(\bar{t}_{m-1},t_m)^{-1}W_h(\bar{t}_{m-1},t_{m-1}) \cdot \ldots$$
$$\ldots \cdot W_h(\bar{t}_1,t_2)^{-1}W_h(\bar{t}_1,t_1).$$

Once more, in view of the continuous group property (1.3), E_h^* is an approximation of E^* satisfying (1.14).

(III) *Taylor series method* (see Rentrop [218]). The NLEQ to be solved has essentially the same structure as under (II) differing slightly in subinterval $[\bar{t}_{m-1},t_m]$. The main difference is that, instead of using a numerical integrator, certain *nested truncated Taylor series* are evaluated to solve the IVPs. The accuracy of y_h^* is guaranteed by checking the convergence behavior of the truncated Taylor series (mesh selection!). Thus E_h^* is an approximation of E^* as in (1.16) b) and satisfies (1.14).

(IV) *Iterated deferred corrections* as proposed by Pereyra [201] and worked out by Lentini/Pereyra [170]. Let

$$h_j := t_{j+1} - t_j \qquad j = 1,\ldots,m-1.$$

Matching conditions (based on the implicit trapezoidal rule):

$$(1.17)\quad \text{a)}\quad F_j(x_j,x_{j+1}) := x_j - x_{j+1} + \frac{h_j}{2}[f(t_j,x_j)+f(t_{j+1},x_{j+1})]-\Phi_j=0$$

Jacobian matrix block elements

$$\text{b)}\quad G_j = I + \frac{h_j}{2}\, f_y(t_j,x_j), \quad \bar{G}_{j+1} = I - \frac{h_j}{2}\, f_y(t_{j+1},x_{j+1}).$$

Assumption (1.9) requiring the $\bar{G}_{j+1}$ to be nonsingular implies a *restriction on the stepsizes* h_j. This very restriction, however, is necessary for an *asymptotic* h^2*-expansion* to hold, which is the theoretical basis of the whole deferred correction approach. Hence, assumption (1.9) reflects a *basic feature of the algorithm.*

In order to understand the type of approximation that occurs here, recall (1.2) which - by truncation of the matrix exponential series - yields

$$(1.18)\ \text{a)}\ W(t_{j+1},t_j) \doteq I + \int_{t_j}^{t_{j+1}} f_y(t,y(t))\,dt + \ldots$$

On the other hand, note that

$$\text{b)}\ \bar{G}_{j+1}^{-1}G_j \doteq I + \frac{h_j}{2}[f_y(t_j,x_j) + f_y(t_{j+1},x_{j+1})] + \ldots$$

which, in comparison with (1.18) a), indicates that

$$(1.19)\ \text{a)}\ \bar{G}_{j+1}^{-1}G_j = W_h(t_{j+1},t_j),$$

where W_h denotes some kind of *(1,1)-Padé approximation* of W. Hence, as before, the (n,n)-matrix

$$\text{b)}\ E_h^* = A^* + B^*W_h^*(t_m,t_{m-1}) \cdot \ldots \cdot W_h^*(t_2,t_1)$$

is an approximation of the sensitivity matrix E^*. In contrast to relation (1.14) for methods (I, II, III), one obtains here

$$(1.20)\ \|E_h^* - E^*\| = O(h^2)$$

(V) *Certain collocation methods.* For ease of presentation the method due to Dickmanns/Well [88] is described. Same partition as in (II). The solution of (1.1) is approximated by the polynomial

$$(1.21)\ \text{a)}\ p_j(t) := a_j + b_j(t-t_j) + c_j(t-t_j)^2 + d_j(t-t_j)^3$$

where, for given x_j, $j = 1,\ldots,m$, the coefficients a_j,b_j,c_j,d_j are uniquely determined by the *Hermite interpolation conditions*

$$\text{b)}\ p_j(t_j) = x_j, \qquad p_j(t_{j+1}) = x_{j+1}$$
$$p_j'(t_j) = f(t_j,x_j), \qquad p_j'(t_{j+1}) = f(t_{j+1},x_{j+1}).$$

One obtains subarcs

$$p_j(t;t_j,x_j;t_{j+1},x_{j+1}) \qquad t \in [t_j,t_{j+1}]$$

Matching conditions $(\bar{t}_j := \frac{1}{2}(t_j+t_{j+1}))$:

$$(1.22)\ F_j(x_j,x_{j+1}) := p_j'(\bar{t}_j) - f(\bar{t}_j,p_j(\bar{t}_j)) = 0.$$

Once more, the standard *cyclic* structure is encountered. The space consuming derivation of G_j, $\bar{G}_{j+1}$, and E_h is omitted here. As in (III), the quality of the approximation E_h^* depends on the efficiency of the mesh selection. Note that other collocation methods also fit into the given framework (cf. de Boor/Weiss [73] and Ascher/Christiansen/Russell [13]).

2. EFFICIENT REALIZATION OF NEWTON'S METHOD

In order to solve the NLEQ (1.7), one may apply Newton's method - approximating the Jacobian (N,N)-matrix J by finite differences. Assume that J is nonsingular for the time being. Then, for given starting point x^0, the Newton iterates x^k are defined by

$$(2.1)\ a) \quad x^{k+1} := x^k + \Delta x^k \qquad k = 0,1,...$$

where the *Newton correction* Δx^k is the solution of the *large, sparse* linear system

$$b) \quad J(x^k)\Delta x^k = -F(x^k).$$

In section 2.1, special algorithms for *cyclic linear systems* (2.1) b) are discussed under the assumption that J is nonsingular. However, in applications, the Jacobian matrix may turn out to be *ill-conditioned* at some iterate. Then (2.1) b) may be "solved" in a least squares sense by applying some generalized inverse. A specific generalized inverse reflecting the structure of the underlying BVP, is treated in section 2.2. For nonsingular Jacobian $J(x^*)$, the above *ordinary* Newton method (2.1) is known to converge *quadratically*, if x^0 was chosen to be "sufficiently close" to x^*. In order to expand the domain of convergence, (2.1) a) is usually replaced by the *modified* Newton interation

c) $x^{k+1} := x^k + \lambda_k \Delta x^k$

where the *relaxation factor* λ_k varies in the range

$$0 < \lambda_k \leq 1.$$

Section 2.3 deals with the determination of λ_k at each iterative step. Moreover, in order to save computing time, the *alternative use of quasi-Newton corrections at selected iterates* is suggested. Finally, for highly nonlinear systems (1.7), the additional use of continuation methods is discussed (see section 2.4). All of the techniques presented below have been extensively tested in real life applications (see e.g. Diekhoff et al. [89]).

2.1. Solution of cyclic linear systems

In this special case, (2.1) b) has the following form (dropping the index k):

$$(2.2)\qquad \begin{aligned} G_j\Delta x_j - \bar{G}_{j+1}\Delta x_{j+1} &= -F_j, \qquad j = 1,\dots,m-1 \\ A\ \Delta x_1 + B\quad \Delta x_m &= -r \end{aligned}$$

Under the natural assumptions that the (n,n)-matrices $\bar{G}_{j+1}$ and the (n,n)-matrix E_h are nonsingular (see Lemma 3/4), the following informal algorithm is defined (setting $E = E_h$):

(2.3) a) $\Delta x_1 := -E^{-1}u$

where $\quad E := A + B\bar{G}_m^{-1}G_{m-1} \cdot \ldots \cdot \bar{G}_2^{-1}G_1$

$\qquad\quad u := r + B\bar{G}_m^{-1}F_{m-1} + \ldots + B\bar{G}_m^{-1} \cdot \ldots \cdot \bar{G}_2^{-1}F_1$

b) $\Delta x_{j+1} := \bar{G}_{j+1}^{-1}(G_j\Delta x_j + F_j) \qquad j = 1,\dots,m-1$

For $\bar{G}_{j+1} = I$, this algorithm seems to have first been suggested by Stoer/Bulirsch [258] in connection with multiple shooting techniques. For $\bar{G}_{j+1} \neq I$, Rentrop [218] seems to have been the first to realize (2.3). In his realization, however, the inverses $\bar{G}_{j+1}^{-1}$ are explicitly computed by means of a Gauss-Jordan algorithm which may be tolerable for small n. For arbitrary n, one may prefer to apply orthogonal transformations, Q_j, due to Businger/Golub [37] generating certain upper triangular matrices, R_j:

$$(2.4)\ \text{a)}\ \bar{G}_j =: Q_j R_j \quad (\text{for } \bar{G}_j \neq I)\quad j = 2,\dots,m,$$

$$\text{b)}\ E =: Q_1 R_1 \quad .$$

The advantage of this realization is that several useful *estimates* are supplied as a by-product (let $r_{ii}^{(j)}$ denote the diagonal entries of R_j):

$$(2.5)\ \text{a)}\ \bar{c}_j := \left|\frac{r_{11}^{(j)}}{r_{nn}^{(j)}}\right| \leq \text{cond}_2(\bar{G}_j), \qquad j = 2,\dots,m,$$

$$\text{b)}\ c_1 := \left|\frac{r_{11}^{(1)}}{r_{nn}^{(1)}}\right| \leq \text{cond}_2(E)$$

$$c_0 := \left|r_{11}^{(1)}\right| =: \|E\|$$

In view of the interpretation of E^* as a sensitivity matrix (see (1.5)), c_0^*(at x^*) is called the *sensitivity* of the BVP.

Remark. For actual coding, two modifications are recommended. First, in the case of *linear separate boundary conditions*, certain components of x_1 can be fixed: as a consequence, part of E and G_1 can be dropped. Then c_0, c_1 refer to the remaining part of E. Second, the matrices $E, \bar{G}_2, \dots, \bar{G}_m$ should be *scaled* using diagonal weighting marices, D_j, and *normalizing the boundary conditions* (a-priori). Without such a scaling, the quantities $c_0, \dots, \bar{c}_m$ may be meaningless!

The above quantities are most helpful for the construction of a BVP algorithm.

(I) *Check of assumption (1.9) of Lemma 3:* Should any of the $\bar{c}_2, \dots, \bar{c}_m$ exceed some permitted maximum value (internal parameter of a code), then the *partition* should be changed (or $a \leftrightarrow b$).

(II) *Information on the underlying BVP:* For strictly singular E^*, one would (theoretically) obtain $c_1 = \infty$ (or $c_0 = 0$, if $E^* = 0$). In applications, difficulties already arise for c_1 "too large" or c_0 "too small". The following possibilities might be indicated: a) there are locally multiple solutions (at x^*), b) one should turn to higher precision, c) one should use a rank reduction device (see section 2.2).

The numerical examples to be given below shall illustrate the use of the key numbers c_0, c_1 in analyzing the underlying BVP. All computations were performed by means of the multiple shooting code [35] i.e. one had $\bar{c}_2 = \dots = \bar{c}_m = 1$.

Example 1. "Plasma Confinement" Problem (due to Troesch [264])

$$(2.6)\quad y'' = \tau \sinh(\tau y), \quad \tau > 0 \qquad t \in [0,1]$$
$$y(0) = 0, \quad y(1) = 1.$$

This popular test problem is usually solved for increasing values of τ. The first component of x_1 can be fixed to be $y(0) = 0$. Thus E is reduced to one element which implies $c_1 = 1$. In Table 1, the sensitivity $c_0(\tau)$ as obtained by the integrator DIFSY1 (notation see [89]) is listed for several τ. The table indicates that for $\tau > 17.5$ higher precision should be used (rel. mach. prec. was 1.E - 11 here).

Table 1. Sensitivity of Ex. 1 (due to [81, 89])

τ	$c_0(\tau)$
1	1. E 0
7	0.5 E 2
10	0.8 E 3
16	2. E 8
17.5	1. E 9

Example 2. Artificial Boundary Layer Problem (cf. [170])

$$(2.7)\qquad y'' = -\frac{3\tau y}{(\tau+t^2)^2}, \quad t \in [-0.1,0.1], \ \tau > 0$$

$$y(0.1) = -y(-0.1) = \frac{0.1}{\sqrt{\tau+0.01}}$$

One easily verifies that the solution y^* must be *odd*, i.e.

$$(2.8)\ \text{a)}\quad y^*(-t) = -y^*(t)$$

which readily implies

$$\text{b)}\quad y^*(0) = 0.$$

Hence, problem (2.7) can be reduced to $t \in [0,0.1]$ with boundary condition (2.8) b). On the other hand, (2.8) is well suited to test any BVP code. Upon using the multiple shooting code [35] for the solution of (2.7), the expected agreement with (2.8) was found, *unless* $\tau = 0.01$. In Fig. 3, the final trajectories obtained for $\tau = 0.01$ from forward shooting (graph II) and backward shooting (graph III) are compared with the solution of the *reduced* BVP computed on [0,0.1] and completed to [-0.1,0.1] by virtue of (2.b) a) (graph I). Fig. 3 seems to indicate a significant failure of the BVP code [35].

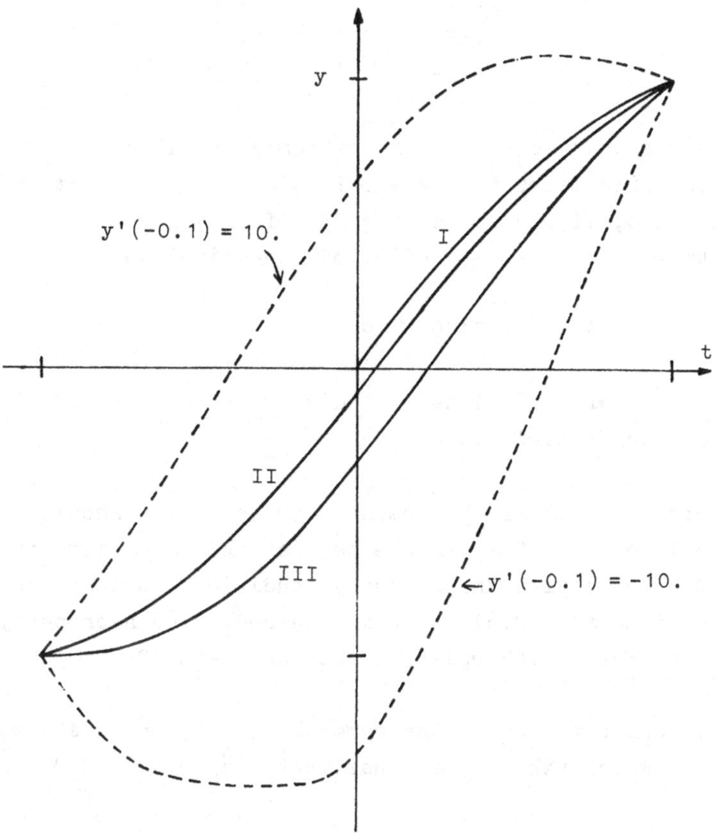

Fig. 3

However, this surprising phenomenon can be explained by examining Table 2 where $c_0(\tau)$ is listed for several τ (integator RKF7, see [89], used here).

Table 2. Sensitivity of Ex. 2

τ	$c_0(\tau)$
1. E 0	2. E-1
1. E-1	2. E-1
1. E-2	4. E-9
1. E-3	1. E+1
1. E-4	4. E+1
1. E-5	1. E+2
1. E-8	2. E+3

One observes that $c_0(0.01)$ is extremely small compared with the other values which means that the BVP for $\tau = 0.01$ is *extremely insensitive.* In fact, if one solves the IVPs for $y'(-0.1) \in [-10.,+10.]$ (see dotted trajectory graphs in Fig. 3), the final value

$$y(0.1) = 0.70710678119$$

is obtained nearly to 11 decimal digits *independent of the above choice of the initial value!*

Interpretation. All of the computed trajectories should be accepted as "numerical solutions" in the sense that they are (discrete) solutions of the ODE satisfying the boundary conditions to a prescribed relative accuracy. Symmetry (2.8) is thus regarded to be a property of the solution associated with relative accuracy $eps = 0$.

Hence, in order to assure the *symmetry* (2.8), one must solve the *reduced* BVP - which exhibits a sensitivity $\hat{c}_0(0.01) = 0.2$ (shooting backward).

Example 3. Superconductivity Problem (cf. Rentrop [217]).

The example arises in the quantum theory of superconductivity (see [217] for details and further references). As before, the BVP is solved for increasing values of a parameter τ. In Fig. 4, the values $c_1(\tau)$ are represented on a logarithmic scale (due to [80]). One readily observes a sharp change of c_1 at $\tau \approx 5$. In fact, near that point, a *bifurcation* occurs (merging of two solution branches) which implies E^* to be singular due to Lemma 1.

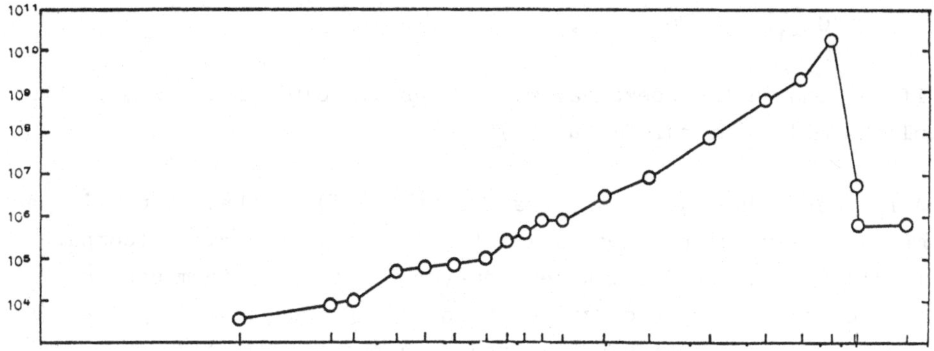

Fig. 4

Obviously, this phenomenon is significantly indicated.

In all of the above examples, certain difficulties arise which can be clearly analyzed in terms of the key numbers c_0, c_1 obtained as a by-product when using algorithm (2.3) together with the decomposition (2.4). The author is well aware of the fact that an algorithm of the type (2.3) is not realized in the present version of a deferred correction method [170] (where a linear equation solver due to Varah [272] is used) and in the collocation method [13] (where the linear equation solver due to de Boor/Weiss [73] is used). The traditional argument against (2.3) in this connection is that the computation of the matrix E will cause exponential overflow (or at least an untolerable blow up of numbers). However, in view of the interpretation of E, such an unwanted effect will only occur for ill-conditioned $\bar{G}_{j+1}$. Just this case, however, is expected to be ruled out by limiting the quantities $\bar{c}_2, \ldots, \bar{c}_m$ as described before. Moreover, this limitation might help to choose an *initial mesh*. To the author's knowledge, the realization of (2.3) in the form (2.4) with (2.5) has not been tried yet for $\bar{G}_{j+1} \neq I$.

Remark. In a possible application of (2.3)/(2.4)/(2.5) to a deferred correction algorithm one can, in addition, exploit the relation

$$G_{j+1}\bar{G}_{j+1}^{-1} = 2\bar{G}_{j+1}^{-1} - I,$$

if the implicit trapezoidal rule is used. (Similar device, if the implicit mid-point rule is used.)

A further advantage of the realization (2.3) is that it permits an immediate easy extension to a least squares BVP algorithm (compare (1.1') in section 2.2). Note, however, that apart from section 2.2, the techniques to be described below apply *independent of the linear equation solver* that was selected in a special BVP code.

2.2. Treatment of ill-conditioning in cyclic NLEQ

Assume that the cyclic linear Newton system (2.2) is attacked by means of the algorithm (2.3)/(2.4). Recall that ill-conditioning of $\bar{G}_j$ can be avoided by suitable adaptation of the partitioning. Thus, only the case of an *ill-conditioned matrix* E in (2.3) a) remains to be discussed. Let this ill-conditioning have been detected by an increase of c_1 beyond a prescribed permitted upper bound (say, the reciprocal of the relative machine precision).

In this situation, the following property of the upper triangular matrix $R_1 = (r_{ij})$ is most helpful:

(2.9) $|r_{ij}| \le |r_{ii}|$ for $j \ge i$

$|r_{jj}| \le |r_{ii}|$ for $j \ge i$

This type of order relation is represented schematically in Fig. 5 (for $n = 6$).

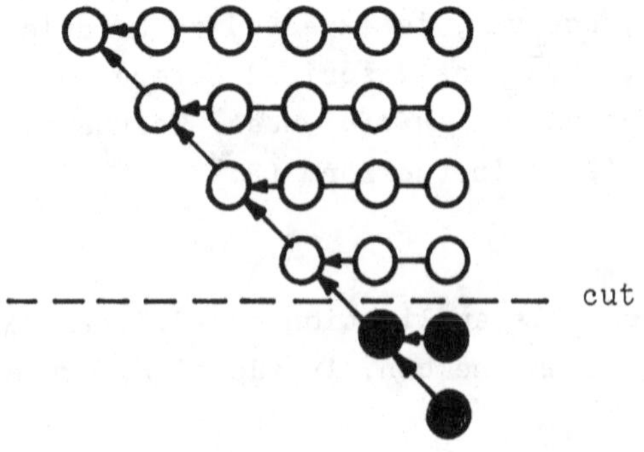

Fig. 5

If c_1 is "too large", then part of R_1 is cut off, dropping the filled-circle elements of Fig. 5. This cut-off procedure induces the following

DEFINITION. Pseudo-rank p

$$\begin{aligned} (2.10) \qquad & |r_{pp}| \geq |r_{11}| \cdot \varepsilon_{cut} \\ & |r_{p+1,p+1}| < |r_{11}| \cdot \varepsilon_{cut} \qquad \text{(if } p<n) \\ & \text{for some } \varepsilon_{cut} \geq \text{epmach (rel. mach. prec.)} \end{aligned}$$

Note that $p<n$ occurs, if and only if

$$c_1 \cdot \varepsilon_{cut} > 1.$$

Let $\bar{R}_1$ denote the remaining part of R_1. Then, by the cut-off procedure, E is replaced by some

$$(2.11) \text{ a) } \bar{E} := Q_1\bar{R}_1$$

of (exact) rank p. Hence, the linear n-system (2.3) a) can only be "solved" in a least-squares sense which means to replace the inverse by the *Penrose pseudo-inverse*

$$\text{b) } \bar{E}^+ = (Q_1\bar{R}_1)^+ = \bar{R}_1^+ Q_1^T .$$

For the realization of this rank-deficient pseudo-inverse, one may either choose the algorithm due to Peters/Wilkinson [206] or the algorithm given by the author in [77]. In the case

$$\frac{n}{2} < p < n$$

the second algorithm is slightly faster than the first one.

Remark. A more time consuming realization is possible by means of the singular value decomposition as worked out by Golub/Reinsch [119]. Note, however, that discretization and rounding errors induce an uncertainty in the choice of ε_{cut} in (2.10) which implies that a precise rank determination (in the pure sense of Linear Algebra) is impossible. Thus the additional computing time necessary for singular value decomposition does not pay out in the class of problems discussed here.

Formally, the use of $\bar{E}^+$ implies the use of some generalized inverse J^- defined by virtue of the decomposition (1.10) a):

$$(2.12)\quad J^- := R\bar{S}^+\bar{G}L$$

with $\bar{E}$ contained in $\bar{S}$. In the associated Newton step, the Newton correction in terms of the Jacobian inverse is replaced by

$$(2.1')\ \text{b)}\quad \Delta x^k := -J(x^k)^- F(x^k).$$

Repeated application of (2.1) c) and (2.1') b) defines a *generalized Gauss-Newton method* for the solution of the least squares BVP

$$(1.1')\quad y' = f(t,y) \qquad t \in [a,b]$$
$$\|r(y(a),y(b))\|_2 = \min$$

Under mild assumptions, convergence of this Gauss-Newton procedure can be shown (cf. Deuflhard/Heindl [83], Theorem 4) requiring essentially

$$(2.13)\quad J(x^k)^- J(x^k)\Delta x^k = \Delta x^k$$

which is an immediate consequence of the definition (2.12).

Remark. For general *nonlinear least squares BVPs,* the matrix E will just have $\bar{n}$ rows and n columns with $\bar{n} > n$. Then (2.11) b) will be replaced by the proper Penrose pseudo-inverse for that $(\bar{n},n)$-matrix E.

Case of locally multiple solutions. In this case, E^* is singular (see Lemma 1) which may induce that its approximation E_h^* is ill-conditioned. Then pseudo-rank reduction will be activated yielding a solution of (1.1'). (Note that, in this case, the solution obtained will depend on the starting point chosen.) Since the residual is expected to vanish, some type of "small residual" decision criterion will be required in the BVP code.

Finally, in view of (2.10), note that the pseudo-rank p depends on the number of available digits, if ε_{cut} = epmach. Thus, ill-conditioning caused by a "too large" value of c_1 can (in most examples) be avoided, if a sufficiently high precision is used. However, ε_{cut} may be much larger than epmach due to rounding and discretization errors (see also (2.19)).

2.3. Affine invariant modifications

Affine invariance. Note that the original NLEQ problem (2.1) is just one problem out of the following class:

$$(2.14)\quad G(x) := MF(x) = 0$$
$$M \text{ nonsingular } (N,N)\text{-matrix.}$$

The point x^* is a common solution point of all problems contained in the class (2.14). Moreover, for given starting point x^0, the ordinary Newton iterates (with $\lambda_k = 1$) are also invariant under *affine transformation*

$$F \rightarrow G := MF,$$

since $G'(x^k)^{-1}G(x) = F'(x^k)^{-1}F(x^k)$.

Hence, one will require the modifications of Newton's method to be also affine invariant. A detailed theoretical discussion of this principle is given in the paper by Deuflhard/Heindl [83]. However, apart from any purely theoretical interest, affine invariance has appeared to be most important for the numerical solution of real life NLEQs.

Monotonicity test. Until now, standard textbooks advise to determine the relaxation factors λ_k in such a way that

$$(2.15)\quad \|F(x^k+\lambda_k\Delta x^k)\|_2 \leq \|F(x^k)\|_2.$$

The existence of a *positive* λ_k in (2.15) is theoretically guaranteed. This type of test, however, is unsatisfactory in several respects. First, the above test is not even invariant under multiplication of the components of F by *different* scalar factors. This consideration led earlier to the use of *diagonal scaling* by testing

$$(2.15')\quad \|D_k^{-1}F(x^k+\lambda_k\Delta x^k)\|_2 \leq \|D_k^{-1}F(x^k)\|_2,$$

where D_k is a diagonal scaling matrix (containing certain weights at x^k). However, (2.15') is still not affine invariant. This latter requirement led to the so-called *natural scaling* by testing (cf. [77, 78])

(2.16) $\|\overline{\Delta x}^{k+1}\|_2 \le \|\Delta x^k\|_2$

where $\overline{\Delta x}^{k+1} := -J(x^k)^{-1}F(x^k+\lambda_k\Delta x^k)$

denotes the *simplified* Newton correction. Note that the additional computing costs of (2.16) - compared with (2.15) - are tolerable, since a decomposition of the Jacobian is already available from the computation of Δx^k. Finally, in order to assure the monotonicity test to be also invariant under re-gauging of the components of x, (2.16) is actually realized in the form

(2.16') $\|D_k^{-1}\overline{\Delta x}^{k+1}\|_2 \le \|D_k^{-1}\Delta x^k\|_2$.

Remark. If $J(x^k)$ is extremely ill-conditioned requiring a rank reduction as described in section 2.2, then the Jacobian inverse has to be replaced by the generalized inverse in both sides of (2.16'). In this case, affine invariance is restricted to hold in some subspace of $\mathbb{R}^N$.

In [78, 83], the above natural scaling was shown to be optimal in a well-defined theoretical sense. In order to illustrate its importance in actual computation, consider the example below.

Example 4. Satellite Orbit Change Problem (due to Dickmanns [85])

The underlying technical problem is the optimal orbit plane change of a satellite in dense atmosphere (such as Mars). Results of extensive computations (using multiple shooting with natural scaling in the solution of the arising NLEQs) can be found in the diploma thesis of Zimmermann [289]. Some details were also given in [77, 78]. For a selected computer run, Fig. 6 demonstrates the behavior of the various level functions that are evaluated in the tests (2.15), (2.15'), and (2.16').

One clearly observes that the old tests (2.15) and (2.15') are of nearly no help in this example. This type of phenomenon is typical for a wide class of problems, especially when (as in the present example) continuation methods are used (see section 2.4).

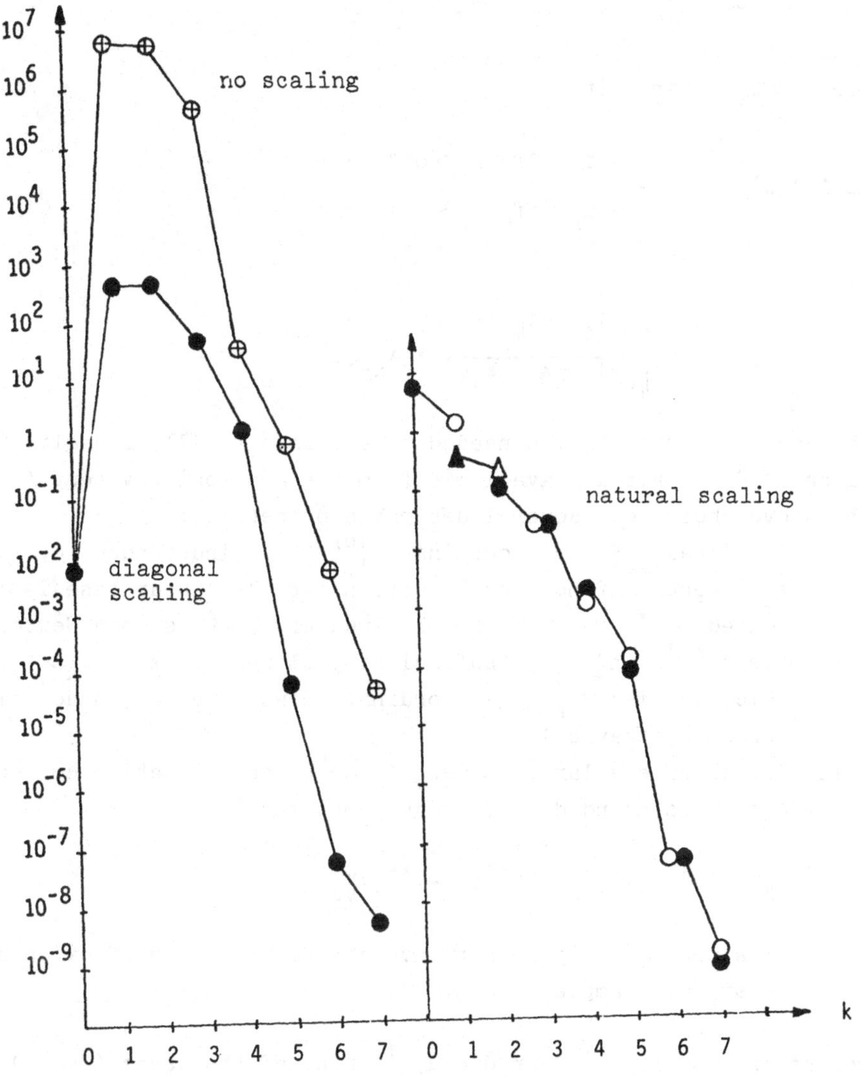

Fig. 6

Relaxation strategy. In example 4, a so-called *empirical* relaxation strategy was used with

$$\lambda_k \in \left\{1, \frac{1}{2}, \frac{1}{4}, \ldots, \frac{1}{64}\right\}.$$

For sufficiently sensitive and highly nonlinear problems, the following strategy (based on theoretical considerations in [79]) has proved to be both more flexible and robust. Let $\lambda_k^{(i)}$ denote the ith *trial value* of the relaxation factor. For $k = 0$, choose a small value of λ_0, say

$\lambda_0^{(0)} := 0.0.1.$

For $k > 0$, start with

(2.17) a) $\lambda_k^{(0)} := \begin{cases} 1 & \text{if } \mu_k > 0.7 \\ \mu_k & \text{if } \mu_k \le 0.7 \end{cases}$

with

$$\text{b) } \mu_k := \frac{\|D_k^{-1}\Delta x^{k-1}\|_2}{\|D_k^{-1}(\overline{\Delta x}^k - \Delta x^k)\|_2} \cdot \lambda_{k-1}.$$

The amount of computation needed to evaluate (2.17) is negligible, since $\overline{\Delta x}^k$ is already available from the monotonicity test (2.16'). The above choice has several desirable properties:

(I) For *linear* F, one obtains $\lambda_1^{(0)} = 1$ - independent of x^0 and λ_0. Hence, if no special option for the linear case is implemented, x^* is at least obtained after the second Newton step.

(II) For x^{k-1} and x^k "sufficiently close" to x^*, $\mu_k > 1$ occurs which implies $\lambda_k^{(0)} = 1$ (ordinary Newton method, quadratic convergence behavior!).

(III) For extremely large values of Δx^k, the effective correction $\lambda_k \Delta x^k$ is bounded. One roughly obtains

$$\|D_k^{-1}(x^{k+1} - x^k)\|_2 \approx \|D_k^{-1}(x^k - x^{k-1})\|_2.$$

This property may help to avoid exponential overflow in highly sensitive examples.

The relaxation factor is reduced, if none of the tests (2.16') or (2.15') holds which implies that

$$\text{(2.18) a) } \Theta_k := \frac{\|D_k^{-1}J(x^k)^{-1}F(x^k + \lambda_k \Delta x^k)\|_2}{\|D_k^{-1}\Delta x^k\|_2} > 1.$$

This information is exploited in the following reduction formula (cf. [80]):

$$\text{b) } \lambda_k^{(i+1)} := \lambda_k^{(i)} \cdot \left[-1 + \sqrt{1 + \frac{8(\Theta_k + \lambda_k^{(i)} - 1)}{\lambda_k^{(i)}}}\right]^{-1}, \quad i = 0,1,\ldots$$

One easily verifies that

$$\lambda_k^{(i+1)} < 0.5 \cdot \lambda_k^{(i)} .$$

Rank strategy. In extremely critical examples, Δx^k may be disturbed (due to rounding and discretization errors) to such an extent that

$$(2.19)\quad \lambda_k < \lambda_{min}$$

is obtained for some input parameter λ_{min} (say $\lambda_{min} = 0.01$ as in [35]). In this case, a rank reduction device should be applied - such as the one described in section 2.2 for cyclic NLEQ. Then, together with the replacement of Δx^k, μ_k in (2.17) b) has to be replaced by

$$(2.17')\ \text{b)}\quad \mu_k := \frac{\|D_k^{-1}\Delta x^{k-1}\|_2}{[\|D_k^{-1}(\overline{\Delta x}^k - \Delta x^k)\|_2^2 - \delta_k^2]^{\frac{1}{2}}} \cdot \lambda_{k-1}$$

with

$$\Delta x^k = -J(x^k)^- F(x^k)$$

$$\delta_k := \|D_k^{-1}(I - J(x^k)^- J(x^k))\overline{\Delta x}^k\|_2 .$$

If necessary, repeated reduction of the pseudo-rank p may be applied. The theoretical justification of this rank strategy was discussed in [79]. Incidentally, in Fig. 6 rank reduction was used at $k = 1$.

Intermediate quasi-Newton steps. In NLEQs arising in BVP codes, the main bulk of computing costs will usually be spent in evaluating the Jacobian matrix by finite difference approximation. Hence, in order to speed up the computations, the alternative use of rank-1 approximations (due to Broyden [33] or Schubert [231]) is recommended. In connection with multiple shooting techniques, certain specifications have been worked out that might be useful for cyclic NLEQs in general.

(I) Let $\hat{J}_{k+1}$ denote the quasi-Newton update in lieu of $J(x^{k+1})$. In order to achieve invariance under re-gauging of the components of x, the rank-1 approximation for $(J(x^{k+1})D_k)$ is applied yielding some *scaled* rank-1 approximation for $J(x^{k+1})$ (cf.[77]).

(II) For *cyclic* systems, certain rank-1 approximations $\hat{G}_j, \hat{A}, \hat{B}$ are chosen in such a way that the Davidon-Fletcher-Powell condition holds for both the total Jacobian and the block matrix entries (see [77] for the special case $\overline{G}_j = I$, and [218] for $\overline{G}_j \neq I$). Thus one obtains

$$1 \leq \mathrm{rank}(\hat{E}-E) \leq \min(n,m-1)$$

For actual application of these approximations, the following has appeared to be a most helpful *selection criterion* (cf. [79]): these approximations are only used, if

(2.20) $\hat{\mu}_k \geq \sigma \cdot \lambda_{k-1}$

for some safety factor $\sigma \in [3.,10.]$,

where $\hat{\mu}_k$ denotes the analogon of μ_k as defined in (2.17) b), but with the quasi-Newton correction, $\widehat{\Delta x}^k$, inserted instead of the Newton correction Δx^k. A thorough theoretical justification of (2.20) is still lacking. However, numerical experience confirms that, with the above selection criterion, a total reduction of 30% up to 70% of computing time is usually achieved - even though the number of iterations is usually increased by the use of quasi-Newton steps.

Example 5. Space Shuttle Problem (due to Dickmanns/Pesch [87])

The underlying technical problem is the optimal descent of a Space Shuttle subject to heating constraints. A detailed description of the problem can be found in a NASA report by Dickmanns [86]. Progress in the computation of this problem is reported in [78, 81, 80]. In this example, the tentative use of rank-1 approximations (in connection with former empirical selection criteria) used to cause exponential overflow in the course of the iteration. Hence, rank-1 approximations were generally avoided. With the relaxation strategy and the selection criterion as presented here, the use of rank-1 approximations could be permitted. In a selected computer run (presented in [80]) the amount of computation decreased from 340 trajectory evaluations to 114 trajectory evaluations - which roughly makes a 70% reduction. Incidentally, the estimates c_0, c_1 in this run were $c_0 \approx 10^{15}$, $c_1 \approx 10^{19}$.

2.4. Combination with continuation methods

In highly sensitive BVPs, the above iterative techniques (as well as any other general purpose NLEQ solver) will tend to be inefficient or even fail to supply a solution. For instance, the preceding examples 3,4,5 are of this kind. In these examples, the additional use of continuation methods has proved to be extremely helpful.

A continuation method can be expected to be successfully applied whenever a natural one-parameter imbedding of the BVP can be found inducing an imbedded NLEQ, say

(2.21) $F(x;\tau) = 0 \qquad \tau \in [\tau_0, \tau^*]$.

Let $x^*(\tau_0)$ denote a solution of (2.21) for $\tau = \tau_0$ which is already given or easily available. Then a *homotopy chain* of subproblems

(2.22) $F(x;\tau_\nu) = 0 \qquad \nu = 1,2,\ldots,M$

is solved for the partition

$$\tau_0 < \tau_1 < \ldots < \tau_M = \tau^* .$$

In the *classical* continuation method (cf. e.g. Keller [147], Roberts/ Shipman [221]), the solutions $x^*(\tau_\nu)$ are used as starting points for Newton's method when solving (2.22) for $\tau = \tau_{\nu+1}$. In the *modified* continuation method, a trivial differential equation ($\tau' = 0$) and a further boundary condition of the form

(2.23) $h(\tau) := \tau - \tau_\nu$

are added to the original BVP yielding an extended NLEQ (2.22)/(2.23) - compare e.g. Deuflhard/Pesch/Rentrop [81]. With this method, the preceding Space Shuttle problem (Ex. 5) has been solved for the first time. As pointed out in [81], the latter method is similar to the so-called *Euler* c.m. (or c.m. *with incremental load*) which is implemented as an option e.g. in the deferred correction code due to Lentini/ Pereyra [170] and in a special homotopy version (due to Deuflhard [80]) of the multiple shooting code [35]. In [80], an affine invariant *control of the homotopy stepsizes*

$$\Delta\tau_\nu := \tau_{\nu+1} - \tau_\nu$$

has been proposed on a theoretical basis. Details of implementation and numerical examples demonstrating the efficiency of that technique can be found there.

At the present state-of-the-art, the *choice of the imbedding* remains the essential task. Generally speaking, the selected parameter should have a natural interpretation in terms of the BVP, in order to assure the existence of solutions for all values of $\tau \in [\tau_0, \tau^*]$. Thus the success of continuation methods mainly depends on the user's skill and insight into the problem that he wants to solve.

Example 6. Kidney Model Problem
(due to Stephenson/Tewarson/Meija [257])

In the underlying physiological problem, the renal counterflow system of the mammalian kidney is quantitatively described in terms of a six-tube model. The arising mathematical problem (for the steady state of the system) can be formulated as a BVP with $n = 13$ (equivalent to the BVP with $n = 17$ as treated by Farahzad/Tewarson [107]). In [175], Lory obtained the solution of this BVP by means of the multiple shooting code [35] using the homotopy version with automatic stepsize control as proposed in [80].

The three water permeability coefficients were chosen as natural homotopy parameters. The problem was solved in 31 (classical) homotopy steps from permeabilities (0.,0.,0.) up to (10.,1.,10.). In the course of the computations, the estimates c_0, c_1 (due to (2.5.b)) for the sensitivity matrix of the BVP increased from $(10^7, 10^8)$ to $(10^{13}, 10^{18})$. The homotopy stepsizes were spread by a factor of about 550. The prescribed relative accuracy was $eps = 10^{-5}$ for the intermediate subproblems and $eps = 10^{-12}$ for the final problem (CDC Cyber, double precision). An important check is the conservation of mass which was computed by Lory to hold to a relative accuracy of 10^{-19} for his final results. With the above information at hand, one easily understands the difficulties that other authors had in their attempts to find a solution of this challenging BVP.

CONCLUSION

In this paper, the state-of-the-art of solving NLEQs arising in BVP codes has been surveyed. One of the essentials was to point out that the structure of the underlying BVP should be transparent in the selected realization of the NLEQ algorithm. A second point was to emphasize the importance of affine invariant techniques in the numerical treatment of highly nonlinear real life problems. For this reason and for lack of space, NLEQ solvers different from Newton's method were omitted in this presentation. However, a thorough comparison of different NLEQ algorithms implemented in each BVP code is still lacking. Such a comparison, which would have been beyond the scope of this paper, should be based on a set of real life BVPs, in order to permit a comparative judgment of the different NLEQ solvers in BVP codes.

PASVA3: AN ADAPTIVE FINITE DIFFERENCE FORTRAN PROGRAM FOR FIRST ORDER NONLINEAR, ORDINARY BOUNDARY PROBLEMS

V. Pereyra*
Applied Mathematics
California Institute of Technology

1. INTRODUCTION

During the past few years M. Lentini and I have been involved in the development of usable software for the numerical solution of two point boundary value problems of the form

$$\omega' = f(t, \omega) \quad , \quad t \in (a, b) \ ,$$

$$g(\omega(a), \omega(b)) = 0 \quad .$$

Here the functions ω, f, g take values in $\mathbb{R}^d$; f and g are assumed to be sufficiently smooth, and we also assume that problem (1.1) has an isolated solution $\omega^*(t)$.

In this paper we will present the latest version of our variable order, variable step, finite difference code for problem (1.1). Only those features which have not hitherto been published will be discussed in any detail.

2. SOME HISTORICAL REMARKS

This seems to be a suitable place to do some recapitulation about the history of our present day techniques. I do not intend to give an exhaustive survey of all the developments leading to the present state, but rather a documentation of my personal involvement.

This long saga started with some programs for solving boundary value problems for scalar second order equations (Pereyra [1965, 1968]). Those early efforts culminated in a Report, Pereyra [1973], in which the first

---

*On leave from Escuela de Computación, Univ. Central de Venezuela, Caracas. This work was supported by Contract No. 14-08-0001-1677 with the U.S. Geological Survey (Earthquake Hazards Reduction Program).

generation of the present methods appeared. That program implemented already a variable order finite difference method based on deferred corrections, had global error estimation and automatic uniform mesh refinements.

Later on, Lentini and Pereyra [1974] presented PASUNI, a program for first order systems, tailored around the ideas of Pereyra [1973]. These developments were made possible by coupling the already well established theory for some basic global methods as the trapezoidal and mid-point rules (Keller [1968, 1974]), with our a posteriori error estimation and order improvement via deferred corrections (Pereyra [1968]). As it is now widely acknowledged (I hope), the deferred corrections approach showed marked superiority over Richardson extrapolation type techniques, and it has by now superseded it in this area of application.

It became immediately clear that uniform step algorithms have limited applicability, since they become very expensive as soon as some type of irregularity is present in the solution to the problem, such as boundary layers, steep gradients, and so on. Since those difficulties seem to occur fairly frequently in the applications, we rapidly came upon the analog of stiffness for initial value problems, and to the necessity of developing a dynamical non uniform mesh adaptation procedure.

At the time of my first interest in this problem there was not much in the literature about it, and I benefitted greatly from a conversation in early 1974 with H. B. Keller who generously informed me about his personal experience in the matter.

The first positive results were published in Pereyra and Sewell [1975], and the actual implementation of those ideas for problem (1.1) was discussed in Lentini and Pereyra [1975a, 1978]. The resulting program, PASVAR, incorporated for the first time (as far as we know) automatic variable order and variable step capabilities into global finite difference techniques for problem (1.1). The key idea in its automatic mesh refinement procedure was the equidistribution of a norm of the local truncation error. This idea was borrowed from Burchard [1974], who had developed it in the context of the approximation of functions by splines with variable knots. Sewell and deBoor (see Pereyra and Sewell [1975]) employed this concept in the spline solution of elliptic boundary value problems and scalar two-point boundary value problems respectively.

So, although the idea is not exactly new, we believe to have been the first to introduce it into the present context, and we are certain of having baptized it with the name that has now been officially adopted, i.e. "equidistribution".

The next generation, program PASVA2 (Lentini and Pereyra [1975b]), represents the first attempt to produce a more professional library type program, fully documented and written in fairly transportable FORTRAN. This is the program that has been more widely used in the past three years and is in operation in a number of installations around the world. It incorporates some very significant improvements over its predecessors, which will be discussed in the body of this paper since they have not been published earlier.

The present version PASVA3 incorporates still some more changes and improvements derived from user's feedback and our own experience in employing PASVA2 in a variety of applications (Concus and Pereyra [1978], Pereyra, Lee and Keller [1978], Lentini [1978]).

A version similar to PASVA3 is now available for distribution from Harwell, Computer Science and System Division, AERE, Oxfordshire, Ox 11 ORA, England. That code is named DD04AD [1978], and it has passed the scrutiny of the PFORT verifier. This is the most professional version in existence at the present time and it has benefited from Dr. I. Duff's careful inspection and also from some earlier suggestions made by Dr. J. Bolstad.

This work is dedicated to L. Fox (Oxford) and H. B. Keller (Caltech), pioneers and unselfish friends.

3. THE NUMERICAL METHOD

The numerical method used to solve equations (1.1) is based on a very simple finite difference approximation to $\frac{d\omega}{dt}$ on a mesh with $(J+1)$ points in the interval $[a, b]$. Let us then consider a mesh π of points $\{t_j\}_{j=1,\dots,J+1}$ satisfying

$$a = t_1 < t_2 < \dots < t_{J+1} = b \ , \tag{3.1}$$

and the trapezoidal rule approximation

$$\frac{W_{j+1} - W_j}{h_j} = \tfrac{1}{2} \left[f(t_j, W_j) + f(t_{j+1}, W_{j+1}) \right] \ , \quad j=1, \dots, J \ , \tag{3.2a}$$

with the boundary conditions

$$g(W_1, W_J) = 0 \ . \tag{3.2b}$$

Here the d-vectors W_j are meant to approximate $\omega^*(t_j)$, and $h_j = t_{j+1} - t_j$ is the mesh spacing which we do not assume to be uniform. This can be of importance if some component of the solution $\omega^*(t)$ has a steep gradient in some subregion, since then the mesh can be made locally finer in order to resolve this anomalous behavior in an efficient manner.

Equations (3.2) form a system of $(J+1) \times d$ nonlinear algebraic equations in the same number of unknowns $\{W_{ij}\}_{\substack{i=1,\dots,d \\ j=1,\dots,J+1}}$.

Using further vector notation we will refer to (3.2) as the discrete system and write it as:

$$F_\pi (W) = 0 \ , \tag{3.3}$$

where

$$W \equiv \begin{bmatrix} W_{11} \\ W_{21} \\ \cdot \\ \cdot \\ \cdot \\ W_{d1} \\ W_{12} \\ \cdot \\ \cdot \\ \cdot \\ W_{dJ} \end{bmatrix} , \quad F_{\pi i}(W) \equiv \begin{pmatrix} g^{(1)}(W_1) \\ W_2 - W_1 - \frac{h_1}{2}(f_1 + f_2) \\ \cdot \\ \cdot \\ \cdot \\ W_{J+1} - W_J - \frac{h_J}{2}(f_{J+1} + f_J) \\ g^{(2)}(W_1, W_{J+1}) \\ g^{(3)}(W_{J+1}) \end{pmatrix} \leftarrow \text{d-vectors} \quad .$$

with $f_j \equiv f(t_j, W_j)$, and $g = (g^{(1)}, g^{(2)}, g^{(3)})^T$.

Under mild assumptions system (3.3) will have an isolated solution $W*$ near $\{\omega*(t_j)\}$, provided $h = \max_{j=1,\ldots,J} h_j$ is sufficiently small. Moreover, this discrete approximation will be accurate to order h^2, i.e.

(3.4)
$$\|W*-w*\| \equiv \max_{\substack{i=1,\ldots,d \\ j=1,\ldots,J+1}} | W^*_{ij} - \omega^*_i(t_j)| \le c\ h^2 \quad .$$

and it can be computed by a quadratically convergent Newton iteration if a sufficiently accurate starting trajectory W^o is given (cf. Keller [1974]).

If we call $F_W(W)$ to the Jacobian matrix of F_π , we have that in $d \times d$ block form

(3.5)
$$F_W(W) = \left(\frac{\partial F_{\pi i}}{\partial W_j}\right)_{i,j=1,\ldots,J+1} \cdot$$

More specifically, $F_W(W)$ has the following block structure

(3.6)
$$F_W(W) = \begin{bmatrix} A_1 & C_1 & O & \cdot & \cdot & O \\ B_2 & A_2 & C_2 & O & \cdot & \cdot \\ \cdot & \cdot & \cdot & \cdot & & \cdot \\ \cdot & & \cdot & \cdot & \cdot & \cdot \\ \cdot & & \cdot & B_J & A_J & C_J \\ D_1 & O & \cdot & \cdot & B_{J+1} & A_{J+1} \end{bmatrix}$$

where the $d \times d$ subblocks C_j, B_j have the further sparseness indicated below

$B_j =$ 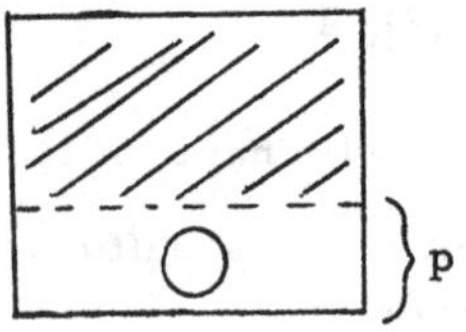

$C_j =$ 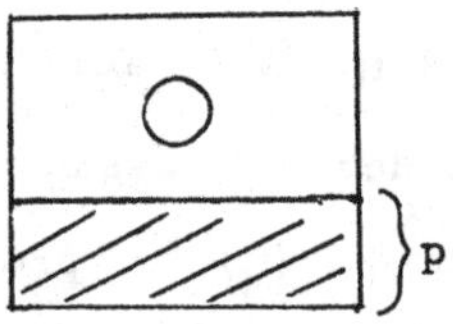

The shaded regions indicate possible non zero elements. Finally

$D_1 =$ 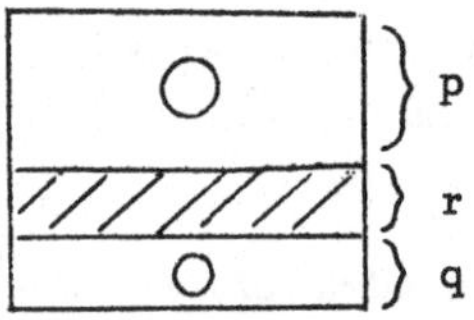

.

In order to construct this Jacobian matrix the program will require of the user the Jacobian matrix of the vector function $f(t,\omega)$ with respect to the variables ω, evaluated at all the grid points of the mesh π, and also those corresponding to the boundary conditions. Let us then define the $d \times d$ matrices of partial derivatives

(3.7a)
$$f_{wj} = \left(\frac{\partial f_i}{\partial w_s}(t_j, W_j)\right)_{i,\, s=1,\dots,d}, \quad j = 1, \dots, J+1,$$

and the ones corresponding to the boundary conditions

$$g^{(1)}_{W_1} = \left(\frac{\partial g_i^{(1)}}{\partial W_s(a)}(W_1)\right)_{\substack{i=1,\dots,p\\ s=1,\dots,d}} ,$$

$$g^{(2)}_{W_1} = \left(\frac{\partial g_i^{(2)}(W_1, W_{J+1})}{\partial W_s(a)}\right)_{\substack{i=1,\dots,r\\ s=1,\dots,d}} ,$$

(3.7b)

$$g^{(2)}_{W_{J+1}} = \left(\frac{\partial g_i^{(2)}(W_1, W_{J+1})}{\partial W_s(b)}\right)_{\substack{i=1,\dots,r\\ s=1,\dots,d}} ,$$

$$g^{(3)}_{W_{J+1}} = \left(\frac{\partial g_i^{(3)}(W_{J+1})}{\partial W_s(b)}\right)_{\substack{i=1,\dots,q\\ s=1,\dots,d}} .$$

Then we have that the first p rows of A_1 are $g^{(1)}_{W_1}$, $D_1 \equiv g^{(2)}_{W_1}$, and the last $(r+q)$ rows of A_{J+1} are $(g^{(2)}_{W_{J+1}}, g^{(3)}_{W_{J+1}})^T$.

An easy way of visualizing the rest of the matrix F_W is to think that block columns correspond to mesh points, while block rows correspond to equations. There is a little complication in the fact that the p initial conditions induce a shift of p rows on the whole matrix, and thus the partial derivatives corresponding to the jth difference equation appear as the last p rows of block rwo j and the first $(r+q)$ rows of block row $(j+1)$.

This ordering has been chosen because it puts F_W in almost block tridiagonal form; the only departure from this form is caused by D_1.

4. SOLUTION OF THE NONLINEAR DISCRETE EQUATIONS

The solution of (3.3) by Newton's method requires an initial approximation W^o and is then given by the iteration for $\nu = 0,1,\dots$

a) solve the system of linear equations:

(4.1a) $$F_W(W^\nu)\,\Delta W^\nu = -F_\pi(W^\nu)$$

b) Correct to obtain a new iterate

(4.1b) $$W^{\nu+1} = W^{\nu} + \Delta W^{\nu} .$$

As we said before, if W^{o} is a sufficiently good initial estimate, this process will have the property

(4.2) $$\|W^{\nu+1} - W*\| \leq k\|W^{\nu} - W*\|^{2} ,$$

where $\|\cdot\|$ stands for the infinity vector norm defined in (3.4); i.e. the convergence of the sequence $\{W^{\nu}\}$ to the solution $W*$ of $F_{\pi}(W) = 0$ will be quadratic. It turns out that the norm of the error at the νth iteration is bounded by the norm of the residual

(4.3) $$\|W^{\nu} - W*\| \leq k'\|F_{\pi}(W^{\nu})\| ,$$

so it is enough to monitor this residual in order to obtain a satisfactory stopping criteriom. Recalling that, after all, $W*$ is only an order h^2 approximation to the discretization of $w*(t)$ in the mesh π (see(3.4)), then it will only be necessary to approximate $W*$ to a level compatible with this truncation error. Thus a reasonable criterium for the Newton iteration is to stop when the following inequality is satisfied:

(4.4) $$\|F_{\pi}(W^{\nu})\| \leq \tilde{k}\, h^{2} ,$$

where $\tilde{k}$ is a small constant.

A simple minded Newton iteration as indicated above may not be sufficient for difficult nonlinear problems for which a good initial estimate is not readily available. Our program incorporates some additional features which make the iterative process more robust and give the user some options which may be of help in difficult cases. In the present volume, P. Deuflhard discusses some additional possibilities.

Many times a problem contains a physically meaningful parameter so that for some values of this parameter the problem is easily solvable, while for the value of interest the problem is very difficult. If no such natural parameter is present an artificial one can be introduced. An embedding or continuation option is available in our program. It assumes that the problem is now of the form $G(W;\lambda) = 0$ where λ is the parameter mentioned before, and that the problem $G(W;0) = 0$ is easily solvable while, $G(W;1) \equiv F_\pi(W)$.

The continuation procedure solves a set of intermediary problems $G(W;\lambda_i) = 0$, $\lambda_i = \lambda_{i-1} + \Delta\lambda_i$, $i = 1,\ldots,n$, $\sum_{i=1}^{n} \Delta\lambda_i = 1$, by Newton's method using as a starting vector for the ith problem the final iterate of problem (i-1) extrapolated by Euler's method. The parameter step $\Delta\lambda_i$ is chosen dynamically by the program. For more theoretical details on this technique see Ortega and Rheinboldt [1970] and also Deuflhard (loc. cit.) and [1976].

Another way of enhancing the global convergence properties of Newton's method is by insisting that the iteration have the property of descent with respect to an appropriate functional. We have borrowed for this purpose some techniques which are common in the unconstrained minimization of nonlinear functionals (see for instance Kowalik and Osborne [1968], pp. 66-67).

We consider instead of (4.1b) the following step controlled correction procedure

(4.1b') $$W^{\nu+1} = W^{\nu} + \mu_\nu \Delta W^{\nu},$$

where $0 < \mu_\nu \leq 1$ modifies the length of the Newton correction ΔW^ν. Of course, $\mu_\nu = 1$ gives the quadratically convergent Newton iteration, but again, if we are not in the zone of attraction of the desired solution W^*, that may produce a divergent iteration.

In order to choose μ_ν so that convergence is induced in difficult cases we consider the auxiliary functional

(4.5) $$r(W) = \tfrac{1}{2} \|F_\pi(W)\|_2^2$$

where $\|\cdot\|_2^2$ stands for the Euclidean norm of the vector $F_\pi(W)$, i.e. the sum of squares of its components. The gradient of $r(W)$ is given by

(4.6) $$\nabla r(W) = F_\pi^T F_W,$$

where the upperscript T means transpose.

We shall say that the iteration (4.1a), (4.1b') has the property of descent if

(4.7) $$r(W^{\nu+1}) \leq c_\nu r(W^\nu) ,$$

where $0 < c_\nu < 1$ will be specified later.

It is well known that the direction $-\nabla r(W)$ is such that the function $r(W)$ decreases the most rapidly along it, at least in a neighborhood of W. This is the so called direction of steepest descent. However, any direction p that forms an acute angle with $-\nabla r(W)$ will also be of descent. This condition is expressed by saying that the functional $r(W)$ will decrease locally along any direction p satisfying

(4.8) $$< -\nabla r(W), p > \quad > 0$$

where $<,>$ denotes vector inner product. In fact, $<-\nabla r(W), p>$ is a positive multiple of the cosine of the angle formed by the vectors $-\nabla r(W)$ and p, and therefore (4.8) guarantees that this angle lies within $(-\frac{\pi}{2}, \frac{\pi}{2})$.

It turns out that the Newton direction $\Delta W = -F_W^{-1}(W)\ F_\pi(W)$ is always of descent for the functional $r(W)$, since

(4.9) $$< -\nabla r(W), \Delta W > = F_\pi^T(W)\ F_W(W) F_W^{-1} F_\pi(W)$$
$$= \|F_\pi(W)\|_2^2 = 2r(W) \geq 0 ,$$

and $r(W) = 0$ only if $F_\pi(W) = 0$. This means that by choosing the step size μ_ν appropriately in the modified correction (4.1b') it is always possible to satisfy a condition like (4.7). In fact, general results on iterative methods for unconstrained minimization guarantee that the following procedure due to Armijo (see Ortega and Rheinboldt [1970]) will always produce a convergent iteration under appropriate assumptions.

Armijo's step control

Choose as μ_ν the first value of μ in the sequence $\{1, \frac{1}{2}, 1/4, \ldots\}$ for which

$$r(W^\nu) - r(W^\nu + \mu\, \Delta W^\nu) \geq \mu\ r(W^\nu) .$$

From (4.1b') and (4.7) we see then that $c_\nu = 1 - \mu$, and that in fact such a μ can always be found.

One difficulty with this procedure is that in some instances it may produce a very slowly convergent sequence by using very small steps, but that in turn, is a sure indication that the problem is very difficult (or that there are user errors either in the function f or its Jacobian matrix), and that continuation or some other auxiliary technique is called for.

Observing that the two sides of identity (4.9) are computed independently we can use (4.9) to check the accuracy of the linear equation solver. In fact, the correction ΔW is obtained by solving the system of linear equations (4.1a), and although we use a very stable algorithm, of which we will talk more below, it is possible for the large matrix $F_W(W)$ to be ill conditioned. In such a case, the Newton correction may be very badly computed, up to the point that the identity (4.9) is not even nearly verified.

Therefore we check both the descent property and the approximate verfication of (4.9) and if either fails, we use the negative gradient direction $-\nabla r(W^{\nu})$ instead of ΔW^{ν} in (4.1b').

An unhappy choice of embedding may produce continuation paths which can be interrupted by turning or bifurcation points (Jacobian becomes singular). If the embedding is artificial and it is only being used in order to produce good starting values for solving $F_{\pi}(W) = 0$, then that is a very annoying situation (cf. Deulfhard [1976]). Recently, Keller [1977a, b] has developed new techniques for avoiding most such problems. A modified version of PASVA3, incorporating some of these ideas and named PASSIN has been written by Lentini [1978] and applied to some fairly hard problems (cf. the article by Keller and Lentini in this volume).

Solution of the linearized equations

In performing step (4.1a) of the Newton iteration and also, as we shall see later, in computing global error estimates, it is necessary to solve linear systems of equations with a block quasitridiagonal matrix of coefficients of the form (3.6). Let us call for short $\mathbb{A} \equiv F_W(W)$.

A stable $\mathbb{L}\,\mathbb{U}$ factorization for this type of matrices is described in

Keller [1974]. An alternating partial pivoting strategy guarantees the stable construction of this decomposition with practically no fill-in, i.e. the sparse structure of $\mathbb{A}$ is inherited by the triangular factors $\mathbb{L}\mathbb{U}$ with the exception of the rows corresponding to D_1 (see(3.6)) in $\mathbb{L}$ which get filled. The block structure of $\mathbb{L}$ and $\mathbb{U}$ is then

$$(4.10a) \qquad \mathbb{L} = \begin{bmatrix} I & 0 & \cdot & \cdot & \cdot & \cdot & 0 \\ \beta_2 & I & 0 & \cdot & \cdot & \cdot & \cdot \\ 0 & \cdot & \cdot & \cdot & \cdot & & \cdot \\ \cdot & \cdot & \cdot & \cdot & \cdot & O & \cdot \\ \cdot & \cdot & \cdot & \cdot & \cdot & & \cdot \\ \cdot & 0 & \cdot & \cdot & \beta_J & I & \cdot \\ \delta_1 & \delta_2 & \cdot & \cdot & \delta_{J+1} & \beta_{J+1} & I \end{bmatrix},$$

$$(4.10b) \qquad \mathbb{U} = \begin{bmatrix} \alpha_1 & \gamma_1 & 0 & \cdot & \cdot & \cdot & 0 \\ 0 & \alpha_2 & \gamma_2 & & & & \cdot \\ & & \cdot & & & & \\ & & & \cdot & & & \\ & & & & \cdot & & \\ & O & & & & \cdot & \\ & & & & & \alpha_J & \gamma_J \\ & & & & & 0 & \alpha_{J+1} \end{bmatrix}$$

where all the blocks are $d \times d$ dimensional and I is the identity matrix. The matrices β_j, γ_j have the same distribution of zero elements as their counterparts in $\mathbb{A}$, B_j, C_j, while the δ_j have that of D_1.

5. ERROR ESTIMATION, ADAPTIVE MESHES, AND VARIABLE ORDER OF ACCURACY

As we pointed out in §3, the discretization (3.2) has order of accuracy h^2, even if a nonuniform mesh is used. Whenever there is a priori information on regions in which the solution $\omega^*(t)$ might have rapid variations it should be used by considering an appropriate mesh π.

Rather than have the user to worry about what is "appropriate" we have incorporated in our program an automatic mesh selection procedure which, in the course of the computation will try to find a good mesh for the problem. This is similar, although more complicated, to what current state of the art programs do in adaptive quadratures and in the solution of initial value problems.

The order of accuracy of the basic method (3.2) will usually be too low and higher efficiency can be achieved by considering higher order methods. On the other hand, if we make a direct approach to obtain this higher order the simple structure of (3.2) will be most surely lost.

Our approach to this problem is in spirit also similar to the one used in the adaptive techniques mentioned above. We have developed and implemented a variable order method based on deferred corrections (cf. Pereyra [1967, 1968]) which, coupled with the variable mesh capabilities provides a fully adaptive tool for solving a wide variety of nonlinear two point boundary value problems.

If we write (3.2) with W_j replaced by $\omega^*(t_j)$ and expand in Taylor's series around $t_j + h_j/2$, recalling that $f(t_j, \omega^*_j) \equiv \omega^{*\prime}(t_j)$, we obtain the so called <u>local truncation error</u> of the method:

(5.1)
$$\begin{aligned}\tau_j &\equiv \frac{\omega^*_{j+1} - \omega^*_j}{h_j} - \tfrac{1}{2}\left[f(t_j, \omega_j^*) + f(t_{j+1}, \omega^*_{j+1})\right] \\ &= \frac{h_j^2}{12}\,\omega^{*\prime\prime\prime}(t_j + h_j/2) + O(h^4)\,.\end{aligned}$$

Of course, further terms can be obtained by assuming sufficient smoothness in the data and taking more terms in the Taylor expansion, but this will suffice for our present purposes.

We shall call a mesh π <u>equidistributing</u> if τ_j is constant for $j = 1, \ldots, J$. Thus we see that, roughly speaking, an equidistributing mesh will have small step sizes where the third derivative of the solution is large. A justification for the use of equidistributing meshes and an explanation on how to actually construct them can be found in Pereyra and Sewell [1975], and Lentini and Pereyra [1977]. Here let us only say that we need in that process to approximate the leading term of the truncation error to order h^2, and that can be done by using the $\mathcal{O}(h^2)$ approximation W_j. Obviously this will lead to a two pass algorithm in which an initial mesh π^o is given and a discrete solution W_{π^o} is computed. Then τ_j is estimated and the mesh is corrected in an attempt to achieve equidistribution, and so on, until some stopping criterium is satisfied.

We have been able to produce a fairly satisfactory implementation of this procedure which is incorporated in our program. In the average, no more than 2 or 3 passes are necessary to achieve an adequate level of equidistribution, and the resulting non-uniform meshes have enlarged considerably the classes of problems that the finite difference method can solve. A different, although very related technique has been proposed recently by A. White [1976]. See also Russell and Christiansen [1978], and Russell's article in this volume.

Clearly, the extra computation required for the above procedure adds to the total cost of the computation. However, it turns out that we have at least two additional, very important uses for that information.

Let us call W^o to the computed $\mathcal{O}(h^2)$ solution of $F_\pi(W) = 0$, and $S_1(W^o)$ to the $\mathcal{O}(h^2)$ approximation to the local truncation error . Then, by solving the <u>linear</u> problem

$$F_W(W^o)\,\Delta = -S_1(W^o) \tag{5.2}$$

we will obtain an $\mathcal{O}(h^2)$ approximation to the global error $W_j^* - \omega^*(t_j)$, i.e.

$$\Delta_j = W_j^* - \omega^*(t_j) + \mathcal{O}(h^2) \ .$$

Observe that (5.2) actually costs very little since we can use the last available $\mathbb{L}$ $\mathbb{U}$ decomposition of the Jacobian. If the mesh is adequate, this will usually be a very precise error estimate which is a feature that is surely lacking in most available present day software. But this is not all. It also turns out, that by solving the nonlinear problem

(5.3) $$F_{\pi}(W) = S_1(W^o)$$

one obtains an $\mathcal{O}(h^4)$ approximate solution, i.e. if W^1 is the computed solution of (5.3) then

$$W_j^1 - \omega^*(t_j) = \mathcal{O}(h^4) .$$

This is the first step in the deferred correction method. As a matter of fact, this process can be continued as long as the solution ω^* is sufficiently regular and as long as the mesh is adequate. Further terms in the expansion of τ must be approximated to increasing orders and then the kth correction will be accurate to order h^{2k+2}.

Observe that all the systems to be solved will be of the form (5.3), i.e. like the original simple systems for the trapezoidal rule with a nonzero right hand side of the form $S_k(W^{k-1})$, which is a known vector. Thus the procedure we explained in detail in § 4 is applicable to all the corrections:

(5.4) $$F_{\pi}(W) = S_k(W^{k-1})$$

where W^{k-1} is the $\mathcal{O}(h^{2k})$ approximate solution after (k-1) correction steps, and $S_k(W^{k-1})$ is a finite difference approximation to the first k terms in the local truncation error expansion. For more details on the implementation of this method, theoretical justification and applications to other problems see Pereyra [1967, 1968, 1973], Lentini and Pereyra [1974, 1978].

These various techniques are arranged in a somewhat complex intertwined structure with a master control program that makes automatic decisions based on currently available information. It is assumed that the user request a discrete solution on a given mesh π^o with absolute accuracy in all its components of size ϵ. Of course, a relative error tolerance, or a weighted error tolerance can be incorporated if that seems more suitable. Thus, the program will attempt to obtain $\tilde{W}$ satisfying

$$(5.5) \qquad \max |\tilde{W}_{ij} - \omega_i^*(t_j)| \leq \epsilon$$

on a mesh π^f containing the original mesh π^o, i.e. mesh refinements may occur.

After an initial check on the mesh to see if it requires refining, the basic strategy consists of trying to achieve (5.5) just by increasing the order of the method. There are several reasons for this strategy:

i) The computational work involved in solving a nonlinear system like (5.4) is proportional to the number of mesh points J.

ii) Once the first system $F_{\pi^o}(W) = 0$ is solved, all the remaining problems are small perturbations of it, and therefore we can save considerable computational effort by keeping Jacobians and therefore their $\mathbb{L}$ $\mathbb{U}$ decompositions fixed all the time. Of course, after a mesh refinement the Jacobian must be recomputed.

Although this procedure will produce a linearly convergent iteration (a quasi or modified Newton iteration), the rate of convergence is so high, due to the accuracy of the approximated Jacobian and initial guess, that there is practically no increase in the number of iterations required to achieve an accuracy in W^k compatible with the expected global error for that correction level.

Unfortunately, unless the mesh π^o is sufficiently fine to start with (with respect to the difficulty of the problem and the desired final accuracy ϵ), in general it won't be possible to achieve this goal by correcting only. After each correction the global error is estimated and compared with the error for the preceeding correction. If no substantial improvement has occurred then a mesh refinement is requested.

A number of error conditions guarantee that this process will always terminate, either with a solution purportedly accurate to level ϵ, or with an indication of failure. Possible reasons for failure are:

a) Error in some of the input parameters;

b) Divergence of Newton's method; this could occur if, for instance the Jacobian matrix is very ill conditioned and the safeguard mechanisms are not enough to steer the iteration away from this situation.

c) Not enough mesh points available; this condition is of course computer dependent, i.e. the more storage is available, the more mesh points can be used.

d) Too much accuracy is requested, incompatible with the computer word length and the problem variations in scale.

6. FINAL REMARKS

In this final section we would like to collect a hodgepodge of comments and information about the code, its use and performance, limitations and extensions.

In previous publications we have exhibited some comparisons between earlier versions of PASVA3 and other existing codes. Those comparisons have been in our opinion, and perhaps for other reasons, in that of the authors of other codes involved, fairly unsatisfactory. Mainly we experienced the standard difficulty of comparing different methods on what at first sight looks like a fairly well defined problem, but which on further analysis turns out to be multifaceted.

We hope that this conference will produce some kind of agreement on how codes are to be compared. In particular, we need a finer subclassification of our problem domain, and a clear definition of the objectives of any given computation.

Therefore, at this time we do not offer any further numerical examples or comparisons, since we feel they will only be redundant. As a matter of fact, we think that ideally, after some standards are set, and if every code author tries to achieve those standards, an "independent agency", probably in close contact with the authors, should carry out these comparisons.

In any case we do not feel that the field has already reached a sufficient state of maturity that final decisions must be made, but we are getting closer to that point all the time.

With respect to our code, we would like to point out some of the fuzzy boundaries of applicability. We expect to be able to solve most smooth problems of moderate size $(d \leq 20)$. We also expect to resolve moderate boundary layers (say up to 10^{-4} width in $[0,1]$) and other irregularities of similar strength.

The effect of nonlinearity is harder to gauge, since very innocent looking problems may be very hard to solve, and vice-versa. In any case, this is part of the more general lack of globally convergent iterative methods for solving systems of nonlinear equations. Progress in that area is being achieved daily.

Global methods, as opposite to marching techniques, are fairly space consuming. Our program uses roughly $3d \cdot J \cdot (d+2)$ words of working storage for solving a problem with d equations and J mesh points. The program itself has about 1500 fortran statements. "Dynamic" dimensioning provides an efficient use of the storage. On the positive side, the fact that we have present the whole discrete solution at all times gives us considerable freedom for many tasks which are much harder otherwise. To mention just a few: global error estimation and control, automatic detail in rough regions for plotting, lack of difficulties in Newton like iterations, etc.

Although it is well known to practitioners that many problems can be brought to the form (1.1) and therefore are susceptible of solution by codes like ours, I would like to give a short list of some such problems and also some hints on how the reduction can be effected.

a) High order systems are easily reduced to first order by introducing lower order derivatives as new unknowns. As the paper by Ascher in this volume indicates (and also the work of Keller and Pereyra [1978]), it may not be such a good idea to effect this reduction, unless you only have available a first order solver.

b) Nonlinear eigenvalue problems can be solved by introducing the trivial differential equation $\lambda' = 0$ and an appropriate normalization for the eigenfunction. This avoids having to introduce ad hoc iterations to determine the eigenparameter. This class of problems includes characteristic interval problems (where the length of the interval of integration is unknown), or what is the same, one dimensional free boundary problems, and many other problems as well (see Concus and Pereyra [1978], Pereyra, Lee and Keller [1978], and Keller [1976] for some applications and more theoretical details).

c) Piecewise smooth problems can be dealt with, despite the apparent restriction of our code to totally smooth data. Both fixed and movable discontinuities can be considered by a "multiplexing" approach in which the problem is solved independently in each smooth subinterval. Coupling between the different pieces is provided by the interface conditions. (See Keller [1969] for the case of fixed, known, discontinuities). The case of jump discontinuities at unknown locations is treated by a combination of multiplexing and the free boundary technique of (b). This provides a tool for solving bang-bang control problems, where the moving interfaces are given by switching functions. We have successfully employed this technique in solving two-point seismic ray tracing problems in a piecewise smooth inhomogeneous medium (see Pereyra, Lee and Keller [1978]).

This again does not represent an efficient solution to the present class of problems, and we are working on a variant of PASVA3 that will handle discontinuities more gracefully and efficiently.

d) End point singularities and infinite intervals. Recently Lentini [1978] has extended the applicability of our code to the problems of this subsection. The major point to be made here is that no change in the code is necessary to compute bounded, continuous solutions of problems with regular or irregular singular points, or in semi-infinite intervals. All that is necessary is a "preprocessing" of the equations which is clearly specified by the theory.

e) Partial differential equations can be solved with this package by using either the method of lines or Fourier expansions for some of the independe variables. Traditionally similar techniques have been used on time depend problems to reduce them to initial value problems for (large, generally stif systems of ODE's.

We propose here to reverse this by semi-discretizing stably in the time direction, while solving the resulting BVP's very accurately on space PASVA3. The systems stemming from this approach may be fairly large but they will also exhibit additional sparseness. At Harwell, I. Duff has pr duced a -so far informal- version of PASVA3 with our linear equation solve replaced by their general sparse solver package MA28. This program has yet been extensively tested, but as expected, does <u>not</u> perform more efficie than PASVA3 on small problems. We hope that gains will be shown when problems like the one mentioned above are tried. A very interesting paper by G. H. Meyer [1978] exploiting some of these ideas but with different techniques has just appeared.

f) <u>Multipoint boundary conditions</u> appear naturally in some applications. T can be dealt with the multiplexing technique of (c), but a more efficient approach can be implemented with a minor change in PASVA3. This change amounts to having in (3.6) some extra non-zero blocks in the same rows as D_1. Our linear equations solver is already prepared to solve such problem without alterations. Sometimes integral constraints are to be considered. simplest way to handle them -when possible- is via transformation into diffe ential equations.

g) <u>Nonlinear parameter identification</u> problems are of great importance in applications. Our code can handle such problems when the differential mod is of the form (1.1). One important feature of our approach is that derivatives of the objective functional with respect to the model parameters are very easily and cheaply computed. We have obtained excellent results using small variant of PASVA3 on some inverse problems in seismology which ca be stated as parameter identification problems.

REFERENCES

1. Burchard, H.G. [1974]. Splines (with optimal knots) are better. J. App. Anal. 3, 309-319.

2. Concus, P. and V. Pereyra [1978]. A software package for meniscus calculations. In preparation.

3. DD04AD [1978]. Program documentation. Harwell, AERE, Oxfordshire England.

4. Deuflhard, P. [1976]. A stepsize control for continuation methods with special application to multiple shooting techniques. Tum. Math. 7627, Techn. Univ. München.

5. Fox, L. [1957]. The Numerical Solution of Two Point Boundary Problems in Ordinary Differential Equations. Clarendon Press, Oxford.

6. Keller, H. B. [1968]. Numerical Methods for Two-Point Boundary Value Problems, Blaisdell, London.

7. Keller, H. B. [1969]. Accurate difference methods for linear ordinary differential systems subject to linear constraints. SIAM J. Numer. Anal. 6, 8-30.

8. Keller, H. B. [1974]. Accurate difference methods for nonlinear two point boundary value problems, SIAM J. Numer. Anal. 11, 305-320.

9. Keller, H. B. [1976]. Numerical Solution of Two Point Boundary Value Problems. Reg. Conf. Series in App. Math. No. 24. 61 p. SIAM, Philadelphia, Penn. 19103.

10. Keller, H. B. [1977a]. Numerical solution of bifurcation and nonlinear eigenvalue problems. In Applications of Bifurcation Theory (Ed. P. Rabinowitz), p. 359-384. Academic Press, New York.

11. Keller, H. B. [1977b]. Constructive methods for bifurcation and nonlinear eigenvalue problems. In Proc. 3rd Int. Symp. on Comp. Methods in Applied Sc. and Engineering. Versailles, France.

12. Keller, H. B. and V. Pereyra [1978]. Difference methods and deferred corrections for ordinary boundary value problems. To appear in SIAM J. Numer. Anal.

13. Kowalik, J. and M.R. Osborne [1968]. Methods for Unconstrained Optimization Problems. A. Elsevier Pub., New York.

14. Lentini, M. [1973]. Correcciones diferidas para problemas de contorno en sistemas de ecuaciones diferenciales de primer orden. Pub. 73-04, Depto. de Comp. Fac. Ciencias, Univ. Central de Venezuela, Caracas.

15. Lentini, M. [1978]. Boundary Value Problems over Semi-Infinite Intervals. Ph.D. Thesis, Cal. Inst. of Technology, 123 pp.

16. Lentini, M. and V. Pereyra [1974]. A variable order finite difference method for nonlinear multipoint boundary value problems, Math. Comp. 28, 981-1004.

17. Lentini, M. and V. Pereyra [1975b]. PASVA2-Two point boundary valu problem solver for nonlinear first order systems. Lawrenc Berkeley Lab. program documentation Rep.

18. Lentini, M. and V. Pereyra [1978]. An adaptive finite difference solve for nonlinear two point boundary problems with mild boundary layers, SIAM J. Numer. Anal. 14 pp. 91-111. (Also STAN-CS-75-530 [1975a], Comp. Sc. Dept., Stanford Univ.).

19. Meyer, G. H. [1978]. The method of lines for Poisson's equation with nonlinear or free boundary conditions. Numer. Math. 29, pp. 329-344.

20. Ortega, J. M. and W. C. Rheinboldt [1970]. Iterative Solution of Nonlin Equations in Several Variables, Academic Press, New York.

21. Pereyra, V. [1965]. The difference correction method for nonlinear tv point boundary value problems of class M. Rev. Union Mat. Argentina 22, 184-201.

22. Pereyra, V., W. H. K. Lee and H. B. Keller [1978]. Solving two-poi seismic ray-tracing problems in a heterogeneous medium. Part I. A general numerical method based on adaptive finite differences. In preparation.

23. Pereyra, V . [1967]. Iterated deferred corrections for nonlinear operat equations, Numer. Math 10, 316-323.

24. Pereyra, V. [1968]. Iterated deferred corrections for nonlinear bounda value problems, Numer, Math. 11, 111-125.

25. Pereyra, V. [1973]. High order finite difference solution of differentia equations, Comp. Sci. Dept. Stanford Univ. Report STAN-CA-73-348.

26. Pereyra, V. and G. Sewell [1975]. Mesh selection for discrete solutio of boundary problems in ordinary differential equations. Num Math., 23, 261-268.

27. Russell, R. D. and J. Christiansen [1978]. Adaptive mesh selection strategies for solving boundary value problems.

28. White, A. [1976]. On selection of equidistributing meshes for two-poin boundary value problems. CNA-112, Center for Numer. Anal The Univ. of Texas, Austin. Submitted for publication in SIAM J. Numer. Anal.

COMPUTATION OF KÁRMÁN SWIRLING FLOWS

M. Lentini[+] and H. B. Keller[*]

Applied Mathematics

California Institute of Technology

1. INTRODUCTION.

The steady flow of a viscous incompressible fluid above an infinite rotating disk has been of considerable interest since von Kármán [2] showed in 1921 that the Navier-Stokes equations reduce in this case to a system of nonlinear ordinary differential equations. A standard dimensionless form of these equations is:

$$\text{(1.1)}\quad \begin{aligned} &\text{a)}\quad \frac{d^3 f}{d\zeta^3} + 2f\frac{d^2 f}{d\zeta^2} = \left(\frac{df}{d\zeta}\right)^2 + \gamma^2 - g^2 , \\ &\text{b)}\quad \frac{d^2 g}{d\zeta^2} + 2f\frac{dg}{d\zeta} = 2g\frac{df}{d\zeta} , \end{aligned}$$

The boundary conditions are

$$\text{(1.2)}\quad \begin{aligned} &\text{a)}\quad \zeta = 0:\quad f = \frac{dg}{d\zeta} = 0,\quad g = 1 , \\ &\text{b)}\quad \zeta = \infty:\quad \frac{df}{d\zeta} = 0,\quad g = \gamma . \end{aligned}$$

In terms of these variables the velocity components in cylindrical coordinates (r, θ, z) are, respectively:

$$\text{(1.3)}\quad \text{a)}\ u = r\Omega\, df(\zeta)/d\zeta , \quad \text{b)}\ v = r\Omega g(\zeta) , \quad \text{c)}\ w = -2(\nu\Omega)^{1/2} f(\zeta);$$

where $\zeta = (\Omega/\nu)^{1/2} z$. The constant γ, called the Rossby number, is the ratio of the angular velocity of the fluid at ∞ to that of the disk. We seek the detailed nature of the solutions and their multiplicity as γ varies;

+ On leave from Universidad Central de Venezuela. The work of this author was supported by CONICIT (Caracas, Venezuela).

* This work was partially supported under ARO contract No. DAAG 29-78-C-0011 and DOE contract EY-76-S-03-0767, Project Agreement No. 12.

in particular solutions for $\gamma = 0$ are the Kármán swirling flows and they are of special interest.

There is a continually growing list of computational attacks on this problem, starting with that of von Kármán [2]. Our current computations are more complete than any of the others, clearly indicate that there are in fact infinitely many Kármán swirling flows, and our techniques are capable of computing any reasonable number of them. We have obtained four of them and saw no reason to continue as the general pattern became clear after three had been determined. As fas as we know only Dijkstra and Zandbergen [1] and White [8] have computed more than one Karman swirling flow. They each computed the "second" such flow and were essentially forced to stop at or before reaching the second critical Rossby number, which we describe below.

There are several causes for numerical difficulties in this problem. The semi-infinite interval is always a problem and in this case the point at infinity is an irregular singular point. In fact the linearized problem about $f \equiv$ const, $g \equiv \gamma \neq 0$ has two exponentially growing solutions, two decaying solutions and one constant solution. Thus shooting methods would not seem to be advisable although they are often used on this problem [1]. The fact that we seek multiple solutions and possibly bifurcations means that nonisolated solutions must also be computed.

We circumvent these difficulties by adapting two new techniques [4, 5] within the framework of a production code PASVA3 [7] for computing isolated solutions of two point boundary value problems on finite intervals. We note that this code is based on the trapezoidal rule applied to nonlinear first order systems subject to nonlinear boundary conditions. It employs deferred corrections for accuracy and efficiency which is also enhanced by automatic net selection. Newton's method and the modified Newton (i.e. chord) method are used to solve the nonlinear difference equations.

The new techniques are based on a general theory for boundary conditions at infinity to insure bounded solutions [5] and a continuation procedure which easily computes near limit points where solutions become nonunique [4].

2. BOUNDARY CONDITIONS AT ∞.

To derive the correct boundary conditions at ∞ we introduce the new variables

$$(2.1)\qquad \begin{aligned} \underset{\sim}{y}(\zeta) &\equiv [y_1(\zeta),\ y_2(\zeta),\ y_3(\zeta),\ y_4(\zeta),\ y_5(\zeta)]^T, \\ &\equiv [f(\zeta)-f_\infty,\ f'(\zeta),\ f''(\zeta),\ g(\zeta)-\gamma,\ g'(\zeta)]^T; \end{aligned}$$

where $f_\infty = \lim_{\zeta\to\infty} f(\zeta)$ is unknown. Then (1.1) can be written as:

$$(2.2)\qquad \underset{\sim}{y}'(\zeta) = A(f_\infty,\gamma)\,\underset{\sim}{y}(\zeta) + \underset{\sim}{Q}(\underset{\sim}{y})$$

where:

$$(2.3)\qquad A(f_\infty,\gamma) \equiv \begin{pmatrix} 0 & 1 & 0 & 0 & 0 \\ 0 & 0 & 1 & 0 & 0 \\ 0 & 1 & -2f_\infty & -2\gamma & 0 \\ 0 & 0 & 0 & 0 & 1 \\ 0 & 2\gamma & 0 & 0 & -2f_\infty \end{pmatrix},\quad Q(y) \equiv \begin{pmatrix} 0 \\ 0 \\ y_2^2 - 2y_1y_3 - y_4^2 \\ 0 \\ 2y_2y_4 - 2y_1y_5 \end{pmatrix}$$

Our general theory shows, [5], that bounded solutions of (2.2) on $[0,\infty)$ can be insured if the corresponding linearized problem about

$\underset{\sim}{y}(\zeta) \equiv 0$, has bounded solutions on $[0, \infty)$. This linearized problem is obtained by setting $\underset{\sim}{Q} \equiv \underset{\sim}{0}$ in (2.2) and has the fundamental solution matrix.

$$Y(\zeta) = \exp[A(f_\infty, \gamma)\zeta] .$$

It easily follows that any solution, $Y(\zeta)\underset{\sim}{\xi}$, will be bounded as $\zeta \to \infty$ iff we require the vanishing of the projection of that solution into the union of: i) the invariant subspace of $A(f_\infty, \gamma)$ belonging to eigenvalues with real part positive; and ii) the complement of the eigenspace in any invariant subspace of $A(f_\infty, \gamma)$ belonging to eigenvalues with real part zero. From the eigenvalues and eigenvectors of $A(f_\infty, \gamma)$, which can be found explicitely, our projection conditions at ∞ are determined. In terms of the new variables:

$$\begin{aligned} \underset{\sim}{v}(\zeta) &\equiv [v_1(\zeta),\ v_2(\zeta),\ v_3(\zeta),\ v_4(\zeta),\ v_5(\zeta)]^T, \\ (2.4) \qquad &= [f(\zeta),\ f'(\zeta),\ f''(\zeta),\ g(\zeta)-\gamma,\ g'(\zeta)]^T ; \end{aligned}$$

the boundary conditions at ∞ are:

$$\begin{aligned} &\lim_{\zeta \to \infty} [(a(f_\infty, \gamma) + f_\infty) v_2(\zeta) + v_3(\zeta) - \frac{\gamma}{a(f_\infty, \gamma)} v_4(\zeta)] = 0 \\ (2.5) \qquad & \\ &\lim_{\zeta \to \infty} [\frac{b^2(f_\infty, \gamma)}{\gamma} a(f_\infty, \gamma) v_2(\zeta) + (a(f_\infty, \gamma) + f_\infty) v_4(\zeta) + v_5(\zeta)] = 0 \end{aligned}$$

Here we have introduced:

$$\left.\begin{aligned} a(f_\infty, \gamma) \\ \\ b(f_\infty, \gamma) \end{aligned}\right\} \equiv \frac{1}{\sqrt{2}}[(f_\infty^4 + 4\gamma^2)^{1/2} \pm f_\infty^2]^{1/2}$$

and we recall that $f_\infty = \lim_{\zeta \to \infty} v_1(\zeta)$ is unknown so that the boundary conditions (2.5) are highly nonlinear. The system (2.2) becomes in terms of the variables (2.4):

(2.6) $\quad \underset{\sim}{v}'(\zeta) = A(\gamma)\,\underset{\sim}{v}(\zeta) + \underset{\sim}{Q}(\underset{\sim}{v}(\zeta))$

where $A(\gamma) \equiv A(0,\gamma)$ from (2.3). The conditions (1.2a) become

(2.7) $\quad v_1(0) = 0, \quad v_2(0) = 0, \quad v_4(0) = 1-\gamma$

Of course in the numerical work we approximate (2.6) on some finite interval $[0, \zeta_\infty]$ and impose (2.5) at $\zeta = \zeta_\infty$. During the course of the calculations ζ_∞ is increased till the computed results stabilize to at least four significant digits. Other tests were also used, see [5, 6].

3. CONTINUATION PROCEDURES.

On some nonuniform net $\{\zeta_j\}_0^J$ placed on $[0, \zeta_\infty]$ with $\zeta_0 = 0$, $\zeta_J = \zeta_\infty$ the difference approximations to (2.5), (2.6) and (2.7) can be represented as the nonlinear algebraic system of $5(J+1)$ equations

(3.1) $\quad G(V;\gamma) = 0 .$

The unknowns $\underset{\sim}{v}_j$, $0 \leq j \leq J$ are represented by the $5(J+1)$ vector V. These equations are solved by Newton's method, or variants of it, say:

(3.2)

a) $V^0(\gamma) \equiv$ initial guess,

b) $\dfrac{\partial G}{\partial V}(V^\nu;\gamma)\,\delta V^\nu = -G(V^\nu;\gamma)$,

c) $V^{\nu+1}(\gamma) = V^\nu(\gamma) + \delta V^\nu(\gamma)$.

(Occasionally we use the special Newton or chord method in which the Jacobian matrix $\partial G/\partial V$ is frozen at some previous iterate. But all this and more, including mesh refinement is done automatically by the code, see [7].)

For $\gamma = 1$ the solution is a rigid body rotation and so our calculations easily start there. To continue from a known solution $V(\gamma)$ we use as the estimate at $\gamma + \delta\gamma$:

(3.3) a) $$V^0(\gamma+\delta\gamma) = V(\gamma) + \delta\gamma \frac{\partial V(\gamma)}{\partial\gamma} .$$

Here $V_\gamma \equiv \partial V/\partial\gamma$ is the solution of the variational problem about $V(\gamma)$:

(3.3) b) $$\frac{\partial G}{\partial V}(V;\gamma)\, V_\gamma = -\frac{\partial G}{\partial\gamma}(V;\gamma) .$$

Of course the coefficient matrix in (3.3b) is known, in LU-factored form, from the last iterate in (3.2b) and so the computation of V_γ is not expensive. This procedure is quite effective for large γ-intervals but becomes difficult and inefficient as $\partial G/\partial V$ approaches singularity. However we switch over, at the first sign of difficulty, to the pseudoarclength continuation procedure of Keller [4].

In this new procedure we introduce a parameter, σ, and seek $V = V(\sigma)$ and $\gamma = \gamma(\sigma)$ to satisfy:

(3.4)

a) $$G(V;\gamma) = 0 ;$$

b) $$N(V,\gamma;\sigma) \equiv \dot{V}_0^T[V(\sigma)-V_0] + \dot{\gamma}_0[\gamma(\sigma)-\gamma_0] - (\sigma-\sigma_0) = 0 .$$

Here we have assumed known, say at $\sigma = \sigma_0$, the quantities $V_0, \gamma_0, \dot{V}_0, \dot{\gamma}_0$ which satisfy:

(3.5)

a) $$G(V_0;\gamma_0) = 0 ;$$

b) $$\frac{\partial G}{\partial V}(V_0;\gamma_0)\,\dot{V}_0 + \frac{\partial G}{\partial\gamma}(V_0;\gamma_0)\,\dot{\gamma}_0 = 0 ;$$

c) $$\|\dot{V}_0\|^2 + |\dot{\gamma}_0|^2 = 1 .$$

Our continuation step is now $(\sigma - \sigma_0)$ and it automatically determines the change in γ, perhaps even reversing its sign. The steplength is monotored to insure convergence of Newton's method for solving (3.4) for (V, γ). Even though $\partial G / \partial V$ may be singular this procedure is quite effective. After $(V(\sigma), \gamma(\sigma))$ are computed we easily compute $(\dot{V}(\sigma), \dot{\gamma}(\sigma))$ satisfying (3.5b, c) with σ_0 replaced by σ. A crucial element here is to choose the sign such that

$$\dot{V}_0^T \dot{V}(\sigma) + \dot{\gamma}_0 \dot{\gamma}(\sigma) > 0 .$$

This insures continuation in the same orientation and not simply recomputing a solution arc previously determined.

This procedure is continued by simply replacing σ_0 by σ and repeating the procedure. As soon as $|\gamma(\sigma) - \gamma(\sigma_0)|$ is sufficiently large we can return to direct continuation in γ.

4. RESULTS.

Starting at $\gamma = 1$ our procedures generate solutions over the intervals: $1 \geqslant \gamma \geqslant \gamma_1 = -0.16057$; $\gamma_1 \leqslant \gamma \leqslant \gamma_2 = 0.07452$; $\gamma_2 \geqslant \gamma \geqslant \gamma_3 = -0.0574$ and $\gamma_3 \leqslant \gamma \leqslant 0$. This last interval was terminated at $\gamma = 0$ intentionally. Near each of the limit points γ_1, γ_2, γ_3 the pseudo-arclength procedure simply continued the branch of solutions around the limit point to the next branch. A graph of $f_\infty(\gamma)$ vs γ is given in Figure 1 to indicate the behavior. In the previous work [1, 8] their techniques could not continue up to or beyond γ_2. We conjecture that there are an infinite sequence of limit points, γ_j, forming an alternating sequence about $\gamma = 0$ and converging to that value. Thus we also conjecture an infinite number of Karman swirling flows.

We show in Figures 2a, b, c the four such flows we have computed. Asymptotic expansions confirming our conjecture and giving good agreement with the computations have recently been given by R. Rosales (private communication). In the limit, of higher mode solutions, they yield $f(M_j)/f(M_{j-1}) \to 4$, $f(m_j)/f(m_{j-1}) \to \sqrt{2}/8$, $(m_{j+1}-m_j)/(m_j-m_{j-1}) \to 2$ where M_j and m_j are the locations of the local maxima and minima of $-f(\zeta)$. More details are contained in [6].

REFERENCES

[1] D. Dijkstra and P. J. Zandbergen: Non Unique Solutions of the Navier-Stokes Equations for the Karman Swirling Flow. Technische Hogeschool Twente, Report No. 155, November 1976.

[2] T. von Karman: Über laminare und turbulente Reibung; ZAMM 1 (1921) 232-252.

[3] H. B. Keller: Numerical Solution of Two Point Boundary Value Problems. Regional Conference Series in Applied Mathematics. SIAM, Philadelphia, Pa. 1976 (61 pages).

[4] H. B. Keller: Numerical Solution of Bifurcation and Nonlinear Eigenvalue Problems, in Applications of Bifurcation Theory; Academic Press, New York, (1977) 359-384.

[5] M. Lentini: Boundary value problems over semi-infinite intervals; Ph.D. Thesis, California Institute of Technology, May 1978.

[6] M. Lentini and H. B. Keller: The von Karman swirling flows, submitted to J. Fluid Mech.

[7] M. Lentini and V. Pereyra: An adaptive Finite Difference Solver for Nonlinear Two Point Boundary Value Problems with Mild Boundary Layers. SINUM 13 (1).

[8] A. B. White: Multiple solutions for rotationally symmetric incompressible, viscous flow; Ctr. for Num. Anal., University of Texas, Austin; CNA-132, 1978.

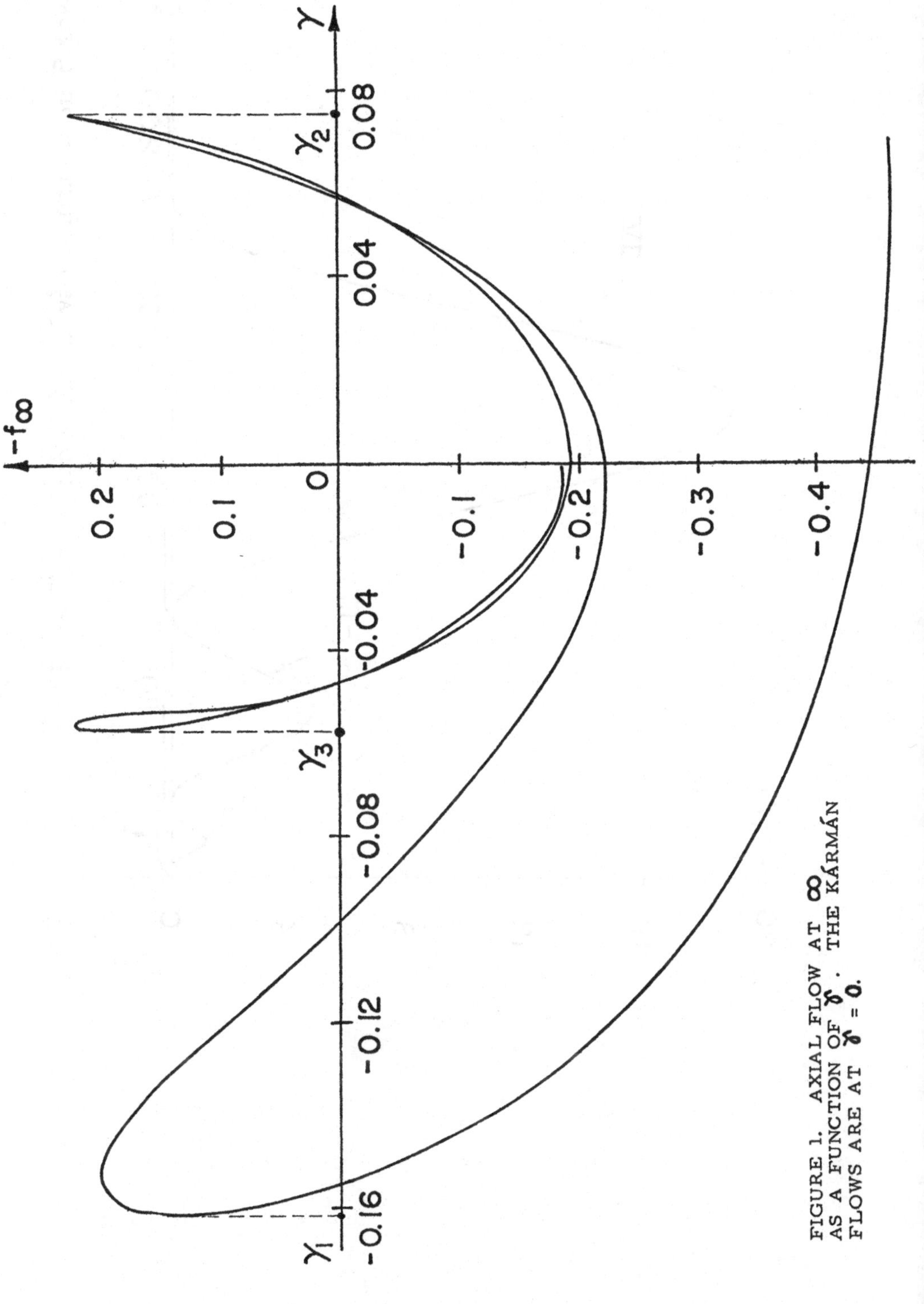

FIGURE 1. AXIAL FLOW AT ∞ AS A FUNCTION OF γ. THE KÁRMÁN FLOWS ARE AT $\gamma = 0$.

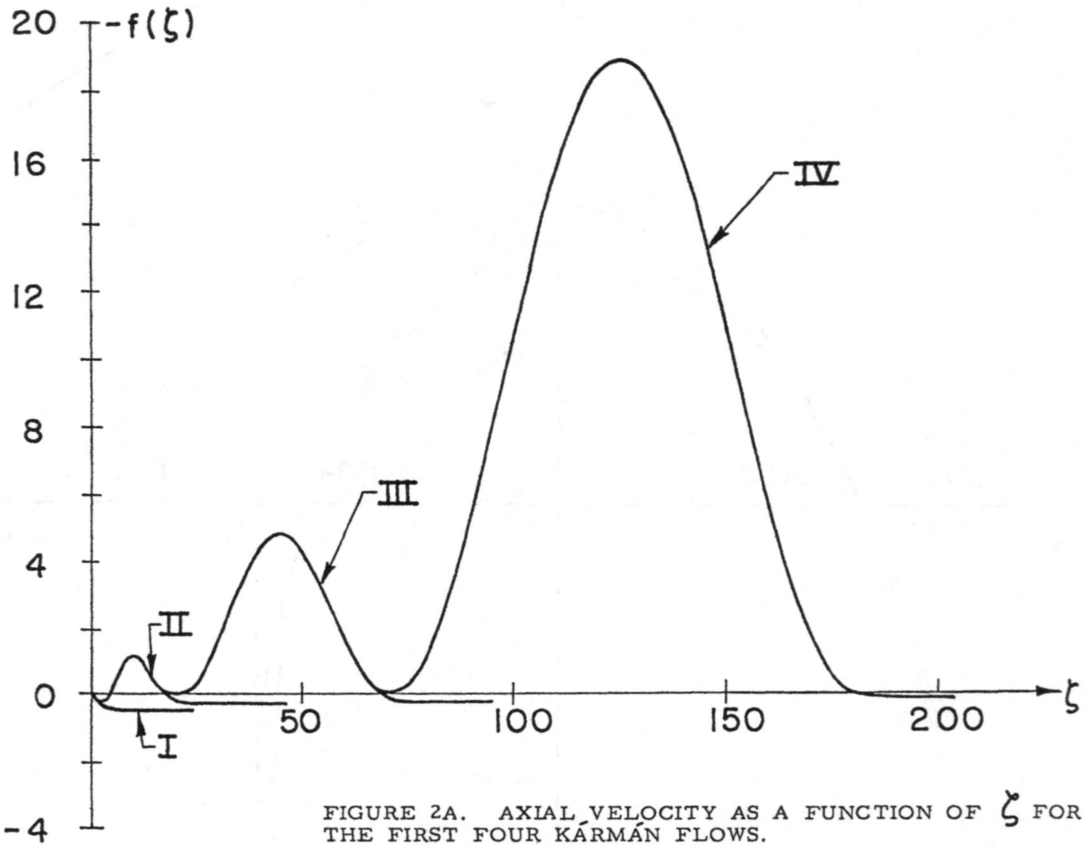

FIGURE 2A. AXIAL VELOCITY AS A FUNCTION OF ζ FOR THE FIRST FOUR KÁRMÁN FLOWS.

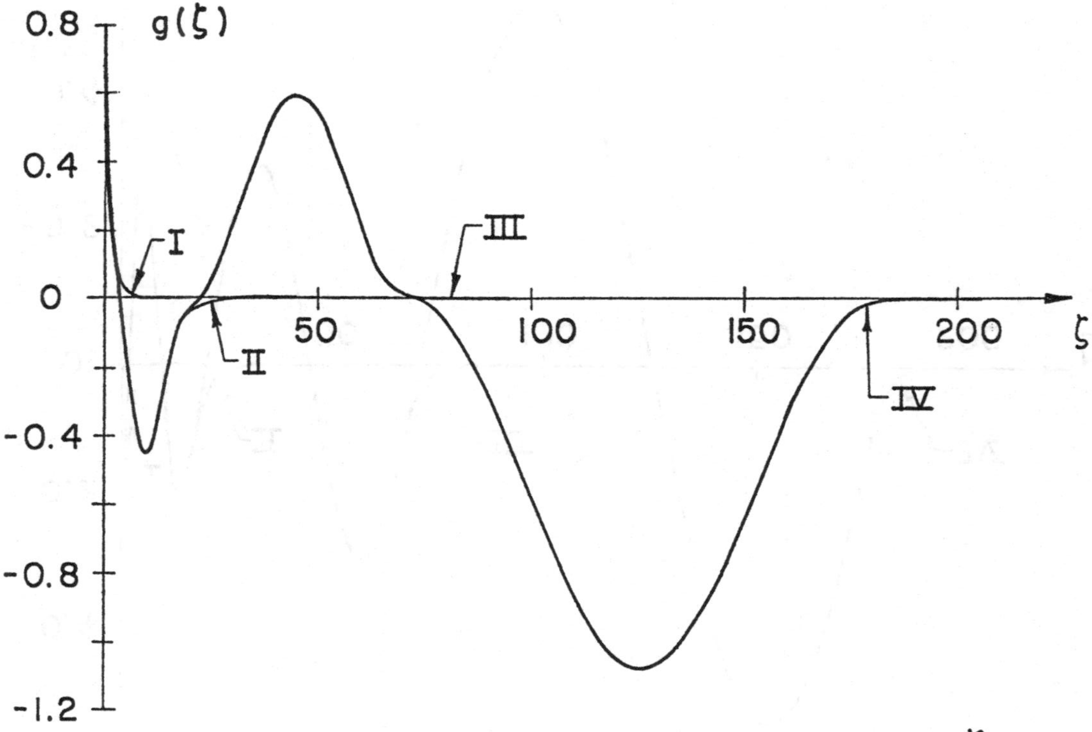

FIGURE 2B. ANGULAR VELOCITY AS A FUNCTION OF ζ FOR THE FIRST FOUR KÁRMÁN FLOWS.

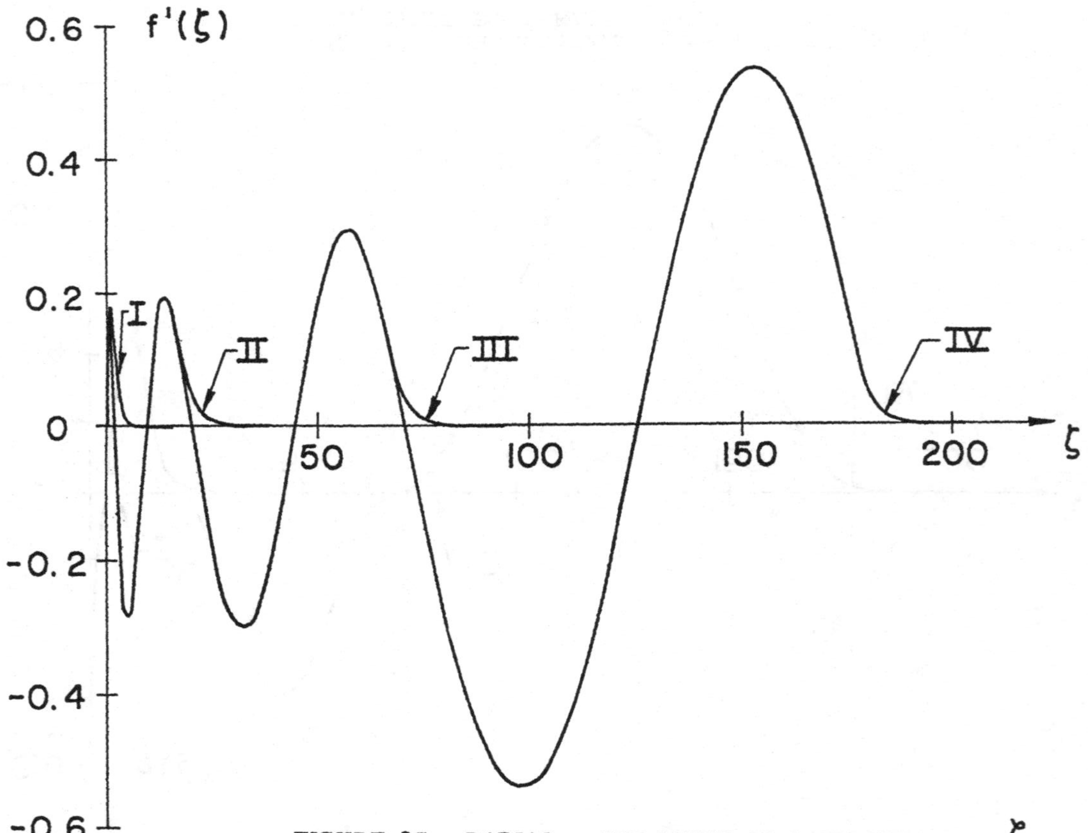

FIGURE 2C. RADIAL VELOCITY AS A FUNCTION OF ζ FOR THE FIRST FOUR KÁRMÁN FLOWS.

THE SOLUTION OF SECOND ORDER PROBLEMS WITH A SYMBOLIC-NUMERIC METHOD

A.M. Olson

Advances in special purpose compilers and mathematical processors such as FORMAC, REDUCE, MACSYMA, and others have spurred the development of computational methods that employ on a computer both symbolic and numerical computations to obtain a solution to a problem. The particular symbolic-numeric algorithm that we will consider here is a series method for solving two-point boundary value problems which was proposed in [3]. We will discuss only the case of the so called "first boundary value problem":

(1.) $$y''(x) = f(x,y,y') \qquad y(a) = A, \quad y(b) = B.$$

Our purpose in the present article is to discuss various aspects of implementing the method on a computer, show its application to the concrete situation of (1.) and present data that illustrates the method's flexibility, its limits of applicability and its error characteristics.

The method assumes that the solution of (1.) can be represented by a convergent, two-point series

(2.i) $$y(x) = \sum_{i=1}^{\infty} a_j b_j(x), \qquad \text{where for} \quad j = 0, 1, 2, \ldots,$$

(2.ii) $$b_{2j+1}(x) = (x-a)^j (x-b)^j, \qquad b_{2j+2}(x) = (x-a) b_{2j+1}(x)$$

Substituting (2.) into (1.) and equating the coefficients of like terms, we obtain an ordinary system of equations in the coefficients of y. Then we solve each equation in this for the coefficient of highest index to obtain the general system

(3.) $$a_j = g_j(a_{j-1}, a_{j-2}, f_{j-4}), \qquad j = 5, 6, 7, \ldots,$$

in which the functions f_j are the two-point series coefficients of the function $f(x, y'(x), y(x))$ expressed in terms of those of y. From (1.),

(4.) $$a_1 = A, \qquad a_2 = (B-A)/(b-a).$$

This work was supported in part by the National Science Foundation under Grant SER 77-04546.

By employing the integral equation that is equivalent to (1.), we obtain the following expressions for the two missing coefficients

$$(5.i) \qquad a_3 = (b-a)^{-2} \int_a^b (s-b)\, f(s, y'(s), y(s))\, ds$$

$$(5.ii) \qquad a_4 = (b-a)^{-3} \int_a^b (b+a-2s)\, f(x, y'(s), y(s))\, ds\ .$$

When we replace f in (5.) by a series, (5.) reduces to

$$(6.i) \qquad a_3 = w - \frac{1}{b-a} \sum_{i=1}^{\infty} c_i f_i\ , \qquad a_4 = -(a_3+w)/(b-a)\ ,$$

in which

$$(6.ii) \qquad w = \sum_{n=0}^{\infty} [\, c_{2n+1} f_{2n} + c_{2n+2} (f_{2n+1} + [b-a]\, f_{2n+2})] \ .$$

Here the coefficients $\{f_i\}$ are those appearing in (3.) with $f_o = 0$ and the constants $\{c_i\}$ are defined by $c_i = \int b_i$, $i = 1, 2, 3, \ldots$.

(1.) is now represented by the system of equations (4.), (3.) and (6.), which will be abbreviated S(4, 3, 6). This represents a fixed-point problem, $z = h(z)$, that $z = (a_3, a_4)$ satisfies. The symbolic phase corresponds to the generation on a computer of the symbolic expressions $f_i(a_{i+2}, \ldots, a_1)$, $i = 1, 2, 3, \ldots$, These are then incorporated into (3.), which is coded (usually by the computer) in the working language and inserted in to a partially precoded subroutine whose purpose is the evaluation of the system S(4, 3, 6). This is called during the numerical phase by a main program designed to solve fixed-point problems numerically.

As conceived here, the symbolic phase is divorced from the numerical phase so that it is executed only once for a given differential equation. If we include symbolic parameters in the differential equation, the output of this phase can be made to correspond to a family of boundary value problems. Consequently, its cost, although significant in absolute terms, may be prorated over many different executions of the numerical phase, thus reducing the cost per problem to an insignificant level. This separation even permits the two phases to be executed at different computer installations, say a large one with capacity for a large mathematical processor and another, more restricted one with only arithmetic capabilities.

The desire to achieve the independence of the two phases imposes certain restrictions on their formulation. If we wish to leave the specification of the degree of approximation free to be assigned during the numerical phase, then the expressions in (3.) must be exact for all j. Happily two-point series are sufficiently nice algebraically to enable us to find convenient ways to obtain the exact expressions for rational f in (1.) and for most of the common transcendental functions [4].

The symbolic phase consists of two basic steps: the reduction step in which the expressions in (3.) are derived, and the translation step in which they are coded and integrated into the partially precoded subroutine and the result compiled. The present version of the reduction step is coded in PL/1-FORMAC. In retrospect, it seems to the author that the automatic simplification facilities in FORMAC are of little use in the code, except perhaps for the calculation of the numerous indices in the expressions generated. Simplification is important, but the nature of the expressions to be simplified is so general that it presents a difficult problem requiring special treatment. Nevertheless, the performance of the program does not seem to be unduly affected. It seems that the inclusion of a powerful, special purpose simplifier would reduce the memory and time demands of the resulting code by no more then several percent. More crucial is the optimal organization of the input data. That is, f in (1.) should be carefully simplified manually before being supplied to the program.

The first step of the numerical phase is the obvious iteration,

$$(7.) \qquad z_{k+1} = h(z_k) \qquad k = 0, 1, 2, \ldots, \qquad \text{where} \quad z = (a_3, a_4).$$

The iterates from this usually progress quite rapidly (although linearly), allowing the program to distinguish convergence or divergence at an early stage.

To accelerate the convergence, a higher order method is employed. Because of the complexity of h, a method requiring derivatives such as Newton's clearly presents difficulties in implementation. Therefore a Secant method [5] was incorporated into the code. This and (7.) are coupled in such a way that the first serves to accelerate the convergence of the latter. When one method fails, the other takes over again, etc.. That is, the program is designed so that it continues until both methods fail to improve the best point found. In this way, the algorithm converges for a greater range of starting values than with any given one of the component methods.

The combined method's convergence is rapid. Accumulation of computational error does not seem to be a problem; the reinversion of the approximate Jacobian matrix rarely has been of any use in the computations performed in the study reported here. The reputed instability of the Secant method due to the movement of the iterates out of "general position" has not been of any practical significance, although it was observed earlier when the Secant method was initiated manually.

Although the definitive answer must wait until the algorithm has matured to the production stage, some indication can be obtained now of whether it has hope of being competitive with the currently available codes, some of which have a considerable history of progressive improvement behind them. To this end, we compare it here with one of the more reliable methods presently available - the Newton-like algorithm [2] sometimes referred to as "quasilinearization". The particular code employed is that documented in [1].

The execution times of these two codes are compared in Table II. at the end of the article. The problem references there are to the boundary value problems listed in Table I.. In solving these problems, the two methods were initiated at the same starting values and the CPU times at completion were measured. The data tabulated in Table II. are typical values of the ratio of the series code CPU time to that of the Newton code. When comparing these times, the reader should bear in mind the following differences in the codes, which tend to make the comparisons suggestive rather that absolute: The Newton algorithm is coded in FORTRAN and the series algorithm is coded in PL/1, which probably produces the slower machine language code. The series code is restricted to problem (1.), whereas the Newton code can handle first-order autonomous systems, and therefore will have a significantly higher overhead. Neither code can be considered optimally tuned by the standards of present day production codes, but the Newton code is undoubtedly much closer to this than the series code. The series code is written in single precision, except for the double precision accumulation of long sums, such as in (6.), while the Newton code is written in double precision.

Now we turn to the calculation of the approximation error of the method. The approximation occurs during the numerical phase when it is necessary to truncate the infinite series in (6.) in order to evaluate a_3 and a_4. If a function u is holomorphic in the interior of a lemniscate $L_r(a,b) = \{z \text{ in } \mathbb{C} / |z-a||z-b| \le r\}$, then it possesses a two-point series there. The error e_m in truncating this series at degree $m = 2n+1$ can be written

$$e_{2n+1}(z) = [u_{2n+3} + (z-a)u_{2n+4}]\, b_{2n+3}(z) + e_{2n+3}(z)$$

If the series converges quickly for the point z (i.e., $|e_{2n+3}(z)| \ll |e_{2n+1}(z)|$), then an approximation to the truncation error $e_{2n+1}(z)$ is provided by the next two terms of the series. For the case in which a, b, u are real, the sum of these is bounded on the lemniscate $L_p(a, b)$, where $p = |b-a|/2$, by

$$p^{2n+2}[\,|u_{2n+3}| + |b-a|\,|u_{2n+4}|\,(\sqrt{2} + \mathrm{sgn}(q))/2\,], \text{ where } q = u_{2n+4}u_{2n+3}(b-a). \tag{8.}$$

$L_p(a, b)$ is the smallest lemniscate that contains the interval joining a and b.

When the convergence is not quick, (8.) still gives an estimate of how much e_m would change on increasing m from 2n+1 to 2n+3. This can be useful in deciding whether to change the degree of approximation m.

Note that if $u = y$, (8.) gives a bound on the truncation error of y, while if $u = f$, then it gives one for the error in y''.

If we have two different functions for f in (6.), say $h^{(1)}$, $h^{(2)}$, giving rise to two different values of the coefficients in (6.), say $a^{(1)}$, $a^{(2)}$, and if $|h^{(1)}(s) - h^{(2)}(s)| \le E$ on the interval of integration, then from (6.) we obtain the bounds

$$|a_3^{(1)} - a_3^{(2)}| \le E/2 \quad \text{and} \quad |a_4^{(1)} - a_4^{(2)}| \le E/2\,|b-a|\,. \tag{9.}$$

A practical estimate of the error in a_3 and a_4 can be obtained from (9.) with E given by (8.) in which $u = f$. In this case, $h^{(1)}$ is the series of f truncated at 2n+3, while $h^{(2)}$ is that truncated at 2n+1, both evaluated at the same pair of values (a_3, a_4). When this pair is relatively close to its final value, we can use this estimate to decide whether to increase the degree of approximation or not. It does not seem to be a sufficiently accurate indicator of the real error to be used in deciding how much the degree should be modified.

If $h^{(2)}$ is as above but with the f_1 evaluated at the fixed point $(a_3^{(2)}, a_4^{(2)})$ of $S(4, 3, 6)$ modified by replacing f by $h^{(2)}$, if $h^{(1)} = f$ evaluated at $(a_3^{(2)}, a_4^{(2)})$, and the series converge quickly, then (8.), (9.) provide a relatively good criterion for judging the accuracy of a computed solution of $S(4, 3, 6)$ before accepting it as the final solution. Experience suggests that the code could use this estimate to maintain the error within an acceptable interval.

We can assess the susceptibility of the algorithm to computational error by comparing the correct value of (a_3, a_4) with the computed value when the degree of approximation is high enough so that the truncation error is below the roundoff error level. Some typical values are listed in Table IV. It is to be expected that the last digit shown is unreliable because of the convergence tolerance level and possible binary-decimal conversion error. From this data, we note that it is frequently possible to achieve the maximum accuracy possible with the given computer word (24 bit mantissa).

To obtain an idea of the size of the convergence region for a moderately easy problem, we refer to Problems 1.1 to 1.9. The correct value of (a_3, a_4) is (.5, .5). With the degree of approximation at $m = 15$, the region of convergence extends in the plane to somewhere around 12 units from the exact solution, except for a sector that roughly covers the third quadrant. The nature of this region improves as the degree of approximation increases. At $m = 27$, convergence occurs from points in this sector as far out as 15 units.

The rough sector exemplifies a phenomenon observed in other problems too. It contains another solution to S(4, 3, 6) at degree 15. Such extraneous solutions are usually relatively easy to distinguish from the correct solution because they have large error bounds from (8.), (9.). For example, see Table III.. Moreover, they are much more sensitive to changes in degree than the computed values that closely approximate the exact solution. For example, in Problem 1.2, the code started from the same point as Problem 1.3, but increased the degree to find the right solution. The precise origin of these extraneous solutions is not clear. Are they nebulous aberrations of the approximating problem that appear at one degree and disappear at the next, or are they true approximations of alternate solutions of the boundary value problem?

The Newton method also had difficulty in this sector. Of particular interest is the fact that it failed for the starting point of Problems 1.2 and 1.3.

Problem 2.4 is a moderately difficult problem because of the longer interval. At degree 61, the precision obtained from the code is satisfactory, but the region of convergence extends not much beyond .01 unit about the exact solution (-.25, 0.). The situation becomes even worse in Problem 2.8, in which the singularities are slightly closer to the minimal lemniscate. With the same degree, the radius is less than about .0004 units about the correct solution (4/9, 0.). For the Newton method, the convergence region seems to be even smaller for this problem. On the other hand, it seems less affected by the singularity of Equation 3 than the series code.

Although they have no singularities, Problems 5.2 and 5.1 present moderately difficult problems. The convergence radii are less than about .5 units about the correct solution (3.24975, -1.7899) at degree 15 and 1 unit about (114.6938, -81.65525) at degree 41, respectively.

Equation 1	Equation 2	Equation 3	Equation 4	Equation 5
$f = y'y$ $y = 2/(2-x)$	$f = 2((y')^2/y - y^2)$ interval $[-1, 1]$	$f = -(y')^2/y$ interval $[0, 1]$	$f = 2x + (x^2 - y')^2$ $y = x^3/3 - \ln(2-x)$	$f = (y')^2/y - y' - y$ $y = \exp(e^{-x} - x)$
on $[0, 1]$	2.1, $y = 1/(x^2+144)$	$y = \sqrt{a-x}$ with	4.1 on $[0, 1]$	5.1 on $[-1, 0]$
Prob. 1.1 to 1.9	2.2, $y = 1/(x^2+9)$	$a = 2, 1.8, 1.5$	intervals	5.2 on $[0, 1]$
1.10 on $[.5, 1.5]$	$y = 1/(x^2+1)$	1.3, 1.21,	$[.25, 1.25]$,	5.3 on $[1, 2]$
1.11, $[.75, 1.75]$	2.3 to 2.7	$(\sqrt{2}+1)/2$,	$[.5, 1.5]$	5.4 on $[3, 4]$
1.12, $[.78, 1.78]$		1.20	$[.75, 1.75]$	
	2.8, $y = 1/(x^2 + \frac{1}{2})$		$[.78, 1.78]$	

Example Boundary Value Problems

TABLE I.

Prob.	CPU Ratio	Prob.	CPU Ratio
1.1	.0129	2.1	.0673
1.2	1.63 */†	2.2	.0782
1.4	.0423	2.4	.1108
1.5	.0308	2.5	.1403
1.6	.1070	2.6	.1845
1.7	.0297	2.8	10.6 */†
1.10	.3153		
1.11	1.481		
1.12	1.632		

† Newton Failure
* Time in Seconds IBM 370/148

Series/Newton Execution Time Ratios

TABLE II

	Degree 15	Degree 21
	Problem 1.9	Problem 2.7
Exact a_3	.5	-.25
Computed a_3	.5000584	-.2463822
Error Bound	.0027	.050899
Exact a_4	.5	.0
Computed a_4	.4993931	4.0127E-8
Error Bound	.0027	.0254
	Problem 1.3	Problem 2.3
Extraneous a_3	-.6907396	.4392238
Error Bound	38.16	.53
Extraneous a_4	-23.68968	-9.079E-8
Error Bound	38.16	.27

Extraneous Solutions

TABLE III

Prob.	Dg.	a_3	Error Bound ×E5	a_4	Error Bound ×E5
1.8	23	.5000001*	.185	.4999993	.185
1.2	27	.5000001	.00367	.4999990	.00637
1.6	27	.4999995	.0133	.4999986	.0133
1.12	91	1.777771	.0813	3.555559	.0813
2.4	61	-.2500000	.0779	2.5 E-8 †	.0389
2.5	61	-.2499999	.0861	-5.1 E-8 †	.0430
2.2	19	-.01000000	.00983	1.8 E-9 †	.00983
4.1	17	.5264801	2.13	.4470421	2.13
5.4	15	.02125942	.00483	-6.580933 E-3	.000483
5.3	15	.3504608	.425	-.1498639	.425

* Incorrect digits are underlined.

† Exact value is 0.

Some Computed Solutions of S(4, 3, 6)

TABLE IV

In its ability to vary the precision of the calculated solution, the series algorithm compares favorably with all well known methods. The limiting factors are usually only execution time and computer word length. There are demands for additional memory as the precision increases, but these are not critical and are considerably less than those of the methods based on stepsize.

This facility suggests varying the degree automatically with, say (8.), (9.). One of the strategies for achieving high precision efficiently that first suggests itself is to begin the search for the solution with a very low degree, say, 5. Once the solution to this approximate problem is found, the degree is increased, say by 2, and the new problem is solved, starting from the solution just found. This process is repeated until the desired precision is obtained. This strategy has not been implemented in the present code because it has been discovered that it frequently does not work unless the degree of approximation is already rather high. The problem is that the distance separating the solutions for two consecutive degrees frequently is so large that the two solutions lie outside of each other's convergence region. Despite this negative experience, the author remains confident that more work on this problem will yield a practical solution, allowing some form of the strategy described above to be implemented.

REFERENCES

[1] E.J. Beltrami, An Algorithmic Approach to Nonlinear Analysis and Optimization, Academic Press, New York, 1970.

[2] R. McGill and P. Kenneth, "Solution of Variational Problems by Means of a Generalized Newton-Raphson Operator," AIAA J., 2, pp. 1761-1766.

[3] A.M. Olson, "A Two-Point Series Method for Two-Point Boundary Value Problems: Theoretical Foundation," SIAM J. Numer. Anal., 14 (1977) pp. 2-18.

[4] __________, "Computable Series Representations of Nonlinear Operators," Mathematics Department, University of Puerto Rico, May, 1978.

[5] P. Wolfe, "The Secant Method for Simultaneous Nonlinear Equations", Comm. ACM, 2 (1959) pp. 12-14.

Superposition, Orthonormalization, Quasilinearization and Two-Point Boundary-Value Problems*

M. R. Scott and H. A. Watts
Applied Mathematics Division
Sandia Laboratories
Albuquerque, New Mexico 87185

1. Introduction

Over the past few years, we have devoted a considerable amount of effort to the development of high-quality mathematical software. One of the major goals has been to produce a suite of codes for the computational solution of two-point boundary-value problems. We have considered a number of algorithms including orthonormalization, multiple shooting, and invariant imbedding. Although quality codes can and have been developed using all of these algorithms, we chose to devote most of our time in developing a code utilizing the orthonormalization process.

In Section 2, we shall give a brief presentation of the superposition-orthonormalization procedure for solving linear two-point boundary-value problems which forms the basis of the computer code SUPORT [238,240]. In recent months, we have made a number of modifications to the SUPORT code and these are discussed in Section 3. Section 4 is devoted to the idea of converting the SUPORT code to solving eigenvalue-eigenfunction problems. Although superposition is a linear concept, it can be combined with a linearization process to solve nonlinear problems. This is discussed in Section 5. In Section 6 we discuss some of the algorithmic details of code development.

2. Superposition and Orthonormalization

We shall begin our discussion with a brief description of the methods of superposition and orthonormalization as implemented in the SUPORT code. The same ideas are imbedded in the SUPORQ code and the code for solving eigenvalues. We consider linear boundary-value problems of the form

*This work was supported by the U.S. Department of Energy.

$$y'(x) = F(x)\, y(x) + g(x) \quad , \tag{1}$$

$$Ay(a) = \alpha \, , \tag{2}$$

$$By(b) = \beta \, , \tag{3}$$

where y and g are vector functions with n components; F is an n x n matrix; A is an (n - k) x n matrix of rank n - k; B is a k x n matrix of rank k; α is a vector with n - k components; and β is a vector with k components.

The method of superposition is conceptually very simple. Any solution of (1) can be written as a linear combination of n linearly independent solutions $u_1(x),\ldots,u_n(x)$ of the homogeneous equation

$$u'(x) = F(x)\, u(x) \tag{4}$$

and a particular solution v(x) of the inhomogeneous equation

$$v'(x) = F(x)\, v(x) + g(x) \quad . \tag{5}$$

Because the boundary conditions are separated, we need examine only a subspace of dimension k or n - k for the homogeneous solutions. This is possible by suitably choosing initial values for these solutions at one or the other end point. In this paper we shall assume the initial point to be a, so the integration proceeds from a to b. In practice, the choice of the initial point is made by the user of the code. This can be important in achieving an efficient solution. Thus, instead of the classical superposition approach, we use the reduced algorithm allowed by separated boundary conditions and compute

$$y(x) = v(x) + U(x)c \quad , \tag{6}$$

where c is a k-dimensional vector and U is a matrix consisting of k-independent solutions to (4). The initial conditions for the $u_i(x)$ and v(x) are chosen to satisfy

$$AU(a) = 0 \quad , \tag{7}$$

$$Av(a) = \alpha \quad ,$$

so that (6) satisfies (2). In [240] we discuss how these initial conditions are computed by the code. In order to specify the constant vector c, we evaluate (6) at x = b and substitute into (3), thus obtaining

$$By(b) = BU(b)c + Bv(b) = \beta \quad . \tag{9}$$

This represents a system of k linear equations for the k unknowns defining c. The solution of the original boundary-value problem (1-3) is now completely specified. Notice that all of the equations to be integrated, namely (4) and (5), along with (7) and (8), can now be treated as initial-value problems. Thus, we can put to good use the sophisticated integrators already developed for the initial-value problems [249].

Although the superposition method is conceptually simple and works in many instances, it has some major drawbacks. In order for the method to yield accurate results, it is important that v(x) and the columns of U(x) be linearly independent for all x. The initial conditions, as given by (7) and (8) theoretically ensure that v(x) and the columns of U(x) are linearly independent. However, due to the finite word length used by computers, the solutions may lose their numerical independence. When this happens, the resulting matrix in (9) may be so poorly conditioned that c cannot be determined accurately. Another problem, also related to the finite word length of the computer, is a loss of significance and can occur even if the linear combination vector c has been computed accurately. This will occur if the base vectors are large compared to the desired solution; that is, accuracy is lost in the recombination of (6). For this reason we want to keep v(x) independent of the columns of U(x).

There is another less apparent difficulty which is closely associated with the cancellation difficulty and occurs with certain types of problems. The principle of superposition requires the accurate determination of the various solution components which enter into the matrix BU(b) in (9). For problems where some of these components rapidly become negligible relative to others present in the solution, it may be difficult to achieve the desired accuracy for all components. Typically, it will be important to ensure that the components defining the superposition coefficients are sufficiently accurate in a relative sense.

The orthonormalization procedure is designed to overcome the above difficulties. Each time the linearly independent solutions of the homogeneous and inhomogeneous equations "start to lose their numerical independence," the solution vectors are reorthonormalized before integration proceeds. Thus, if z_i represents an orthonormalization point, the superposition solution becomes

$$y(x) = v_m(x) + U_m(x)c_m \quad , \qquad \text{for } x\ [z_m, z_{m+1}] \quad . \tag{10}$$

At $x = z_m$, a new orthonormal set of vectors is formed and becomes the initial conditions on the integration interval $[z_m, z_{m+1}]$;

$$U_{m-1} = U_m P_m \quad , \text{and} \tag{11}$$

$$v_m = v_{m-1} - U_m \omega_m \, , \qquad v_m = \tilde{v}_m / ||\tilde{v}_m|| \quad , \tag{12}$$

where P_m and ω_m contain the Gram-Schmidt information. Continuity of y is achieved by matching the solutions over successive orthonormalization subintervals. This leads to the basic recursion relation

$$P_m c_{m-1} = c_m - \omega_m \quad . \tag{13}$$

The process is, therefore, a two-pass affair. The first constitutes the integration sweep from a to b while storing the orthogonalization information at the points of orthonormalization and homogeneous and particular solution values at all the designated output points. The second involves the computation of the c_m vectors from the boundary conditions at b and use of the recursion equation so that the solution values y may be determined at the output points.

It is important that the test for determining when to reorthonormalize be as efficient as possible. Since we are using variable-step integrators, there is a definite trade-off between integration and orthonormalization. For example, if we fail to orthonormalize often enough, the integrator has to track components which are growing very rapidly; and, in order to maintain the input tolerance, it must reduce the stepsize. It normally will require only a few extra integration steps to override the cost of performing the orthonormalization. On those problems requiring orthonormalizations, we have observed excessive cost and accuracy deterioration for too few orthonormalizations but only a gradual change when above the "optimal" number of orthonormalizations. On the other hand, we do not want to use an excessive number of orthonormalizations because of the resulting inefficiency in storage. Also, as the number of orthonormalizations approaches the number of integration steps, the computational effort increases and, ultimately, the accuracy severely deteriorates because of the extensive operations required. Hence, we have attempted to design the orthonormalization tests so as to give a balance between efficiency, accuracy, and orthonormalizations--typically awarding a slight bias in favor of more orthornormalizations rather than too few.

The details of the algorithm for choosing the orthonormalization points are given in [240] . Basically, we use the modified Gram-Schmidt procedure to monitor the solutions of the homogeneous and inhomogeneous equations. During the process of the Gram-Schmidt procedure, we compare the norms of the new orthogonal set to the corresponding norms of the old "independent" set. If the base vectors are becoming linearly dependent, then the norms of one or more of the new vectors are becoming quite small in comparison to the norms of the corresponding old set. When a loss of independence is detected, the orthonormalization process is then completed.

3. Recent Modifications to the SUPORT Code

In this section we shall discuss a number of modifications to the SUPORT code which have been incorporated recently. Quality mathematical software normally evolves over a period of time. Since the original code was announced in 1975 [240], it has been disseminated to over 50 users all over the world. Consequently, we have had the opportunity to receive excellent feedback from our users. Many of the changes discussed in this section are a direct result of this feedback.

3.1 Preselected Orthonormalization Points

The success of the algorithm for solving general boundary-value problems hinges on the ability to determine when reorthonormalizations should take place. In the default (or normal) execution of SUPORT, the orthonormalization points are determined automatically.

While our test for deciding when reorthonormalization should be performed has worked extremely well in practice, it can be expensive when the test is performed after each integration step.

In many applications the user has a good knowledge of where to place the orthonormalization points. Hence, we have modified the code to allow the user to choose a preselected set of orthonormalization points. In this case, testing is not performed, but reorthonormalizations are done at the specified points. Clearly, this can be a useful mode of operation--the obvious gain in efficiency is undeniable. However, the burden of code reliability is now placed squarely in the user's hands. If the orthonormalization points are not assigned with sufficient frequency, the intermediate initial-value solutions will lose their linear independence numerically, and the resulting boundary value solution will be inaccurate. Still, there are circumstances when the pre-assignment of orthonormalization points can be made and is justified. For more details, see [63].

3.2 Testing Linear Dependence Less Frequently

In the original version of SUPORT, a check for the solution becoming nearly linearly dependent was performed after each integration step. For problems of large dimension, this results in a considerable effort being expended by the orthogonalization process. We shall now discuss a scheme for performing the "linear dependence" test less frequently. Essentially, we put a counter on the number of integration steps from the last checkpoint and compute an extrapolated value of the independent variable where reorthonormalization is expected to be needed. Then, when either the allowable number of steps is exceeded or when the integration variable steps over the extrapolation value, the modified Gram-Schmidt procedure is called and a test for linear dependence is performed. For more details see [174].

3.3 Auxiliary Storage of Intermediate Computations

Recall that in the algorithm description, it is necessary to store the v and U solutions at all the designated output points of interest as well as the transformation information at all the orthonormalization points. The first consists of $n \cdot (k+1) \cdot p$ items of data, where n is the number of differential equations, k is the number of final boundary conditions, and p represents the number of output points. The other storage mainly consists of $\frac{1}{2} \cdot k(k + 5) \cdot m$ items of data, where m represents the number of orthonormalizations required. For most physical problems, k will be n/2 (or close to it) and so it is easy to see that for large, difficult problems (n, p and m not small) machine core storage rapidly becomes a problem. Even if the large problem does fit into the available memory requirements, the user will pay for the big core requirements not only in extra dollars but, perhaps more irritating, by a slow turnaround time for the job.

It turns out that the structure of the algorithm makes it fairly easy to use some auxiliary storage space such as disk or tape. Naturally we are now paying more for transmitting the data to and from auxiliary storage as compared to the in-core storing facility. See [63] for some comparisons of cost.

3.4 Auxiliary Initial-Value Problem

Frequently we are interested in problems prescribed by

$$y'(x) = F(x,u(x))\, y(x) + g(x,u(x)) \quad , \tag{14}$$

$$Ay(a) = \alpha \quad , \qquad By(b) = \beta \quad , \tag{15}$$

and

$$u'(x) = f(x,u(x)) \tag{16}$$

$$u(a) = \eta \quad . \tag{17}$$

Several approaches are possible. If f and g are linear in u and F does not actually depend on u, the linear boundary-value problem could be enlarged to include u. Clearly, this is undesirable when avoidable. Another possibility (for the general problem) is to compute u separately as the solution of the prescribed initial-value problem, storing values on an appropriate mesh which then lends itself to accurate interpolation for u at any arbitrary choice of x. A better approach which is both more efficient and more convenient to the user is to integrate the u equation simultaneously with the v and U integrations in the superposition algorithm.

The SUPORT code has been modified to include this latter approach [63]. The algorithm for solving the boundary-value problem is unchanged. We merely append another initial-value system to those already being integrated; i.e., equations defining v and U. Solving all equations simultaneously provides the continuous representation of u(x) as needed in the boundary-value problem. For this approach to be successful, the differential equation governing u(x) should be neutrally stable in the direction of integration from a to b. We assume this to be the case in order to achieve accurate integration of u. See [63] for some examples.

3.5 Adams' Integrator

We have incorporated a variable order Adams' integration procedure to complement the presently available Runge-Kutta integrator. These powerful methods include formulas from order one through order twelve in contrast to the fixed fourth-order Runge-Kutta. Thus, the Adams' process is able to adapt the most appropriate formula to the behavior of the problem at hand, as well as choose the optimal step size for efficient and accurate computation. Furthermore, fewer derivative evaluations are required since past history is relied upon. For these reasons, whenever the differential equation is expensive to evaluate or high accuracy is desired, the Adams' integrator will generally provide the most efficient integration process. See [64] for some comparisons using the Runge-Kutta and the Adams' processes.

4. Eigenvalues and Eigenfunctions

A new capability which is being incorporated into the SUPORT family of codes is the ability to solve for eigenvalue problems. This particular version of the code is still under development at this time. However, we shall present a few preliminary results.

The technique is iterative on the eigenvalue parameter and requires a nonlinear equation solver as a driver routine. Two such root finders are being investigated--a quasi-Newton technique and a combination secant and interval-halving method.

When solving eigenvalue problems by means of an initial-value technique, the nonlinear function which is evaluated by the root finder is dependent on the boundary conditions at the final end point. Several choices for this function are being investigated and tested. The iteration schemes proceed by adjusting the eigenvalue parameter until a certain boundary-condition matrix is singular. One choice defines the function as the determinant of the final-boundary-condition matrix. Another method involves computing the minimum singular value of the boundary-condition matrix. Other choices involve satisfying certain boundary equations exactly and driving the remaining boundary equations to zero.

A number of other items must be resolved before the code can be classified as a productive code. Some of these are the following: Two-error tolerances arise naturally in our technique for solving the eigenvalue problem. One tolerance involves the convergence test in the nonlinear equation solver; that is, the error tolerance in the iteration on the eigenvalue parameter. The other error tolerance to be specified is that used in the initial-value solver. The relationship between these error tolerances is currently being investigated. Other investigations center around the effects of the orthonormalization process on the iterative scheme and will be published elsewhere.

5. Quasilinearization

Except for some of the shooting techniques, most methods for solving nonlinear boundary-value problems involve linearization at some stage in the process. For example, in many finite difference codes [168] the nonlinear problem is discretized and the resulting set of nonlinear equations are solved by Newton's method (discretization followed by linearization). In the quasilinearization process, the nonlinear operator is linearized by Newton's method which results in a sequence of linear boundary-value problems that are solved by discrete variable integration methods (linearization followed by discretization). In this section we shall discuss the solution of the nonlinear problem by combining quasilinearization with the superposition and orthonormalization process as implemented in the SUPORQ code.

We shall consider nonlinear boundary-value problems of the form

$$y'(x) = f(x,y) \tag{18}$$

$$\phi(y(a)) = 0 \quad , \quad \varphi(y(b)) = 0 \quad . \tag{19}$$

The sequence of linear boundary-value problems obtained by using the quasilinearization process can be written as

$$y'_{i+1}(x) = F(x)\, y_{i+1}(x) + g(x) \quad , \tag{20}$$

$$Ay_{i+1}(a) = \alpha \quad , \qquad By_{i+1}(b) = \beta \quad , \tag{21}$$

where

$$F(x) = \frac{\partial f}{\partial y}\,(x,y_i(x)) \quad , \tag{22}$$

$$g(x) = f(x,y_i(x)) - \frac{\partial f}{\partial y}\,(x,y_i)\, y_i(x) \quad , \tag{23}$$

$$A = \frac{\partial \phi}{\partial y}\,(y_i(a)) \quad , \qquad B = \frac{\partial \psi}{\partial y}\,(y_i(b)) \quad , \tag{24}$$

$$\alpha = \frac{\partial \phi}{\partial y}\,(y_i(a))\, y_i(a) - \phi\,(y_i(a)) \quad , \tag{25}$$

$$\beta = \frac{\partial \psi}{\partial y}\,(y_i(b))\, y_i(b) - \psi\,(y_i(b)) \quad . \tag{26}$$

Here, $\frac{\partial f}{\partial y}$, $\frac{\partial \phi}{\partial y}$, and $\frac{\partial \psi}{\partial y}$ represent the corresponding Jacobian matrices. Notice that (20) and (21) are in the form of the linear problems discussed in Section 2.

For a significant class of problems, the sequence of functions $y_i(x)$ converges to the solution of (18), provided the initial approximation $y_0(x)$ is appropriately chosen. The choice of $y_0(x)$ which will ensure convergence is left open. Partial knowledge of the solution $y(x)$ or some of its properties may be helpful in selecting $y_0(x)$. Indeed, such knowledge may be vital in obtaining convergence.

In discussions of the use of iterative processes for solving nonlinear problems, one of the most overlooked sources of difficulty is the necessity of providing the solution of the previous iteration everywhere it is needed. For example, in the quasilinearization process, the functions $F(x)$ and $g(x)$ are actually functions of the solution at the previous iteration. Normally, $y_i(x)$ is stored only at a few points and not at the natural integration points provided by the integrator. Moreover, even if we stored $y_i(x)$ at every integration point, the integration points would still differ from iteration to iteration. Hence, the function $y_i(x)$ must be provided by some auxiliary means when solving at the (i + 1)-st iteration. Obviously, this difficulty is not present if the method of integration is restricted to using the same mesh from one iteration to the next. The limitation of such a choice precludes the effective use of variable step integrators.

As is normally the case when solving differential equations, the function and its first derivative are readily available. Hence, Hermite interpolation is one method of providing $y_i(x)$. This has been used in some test cases in [241]. However, it should be stressed that it is important for the interpolation process to produce very smooth results (continuous derivatives of sufficiently high order throughout the interval [a,b]). Otherwise, the efficiency of the integration scheme will be seriously impaired.

Another method of providing $y_i(x)$ which we feel is superior to the interpolation approach is to integrate the original nonlinear equation using as initial conditions the solution of the previous iteration. Thus, we assume that we have on tap the i-th iterative solution approximation $y_i(x)$ at certain designated points x_k, which we refer to as output points. On the interval $[x_k, x_{k+1}]$, $y_i(x)$ is provided as the solution to

$$u'(x) = f(x,u) \tag{27}$$

$$u(x_k) = y_i(x_k) \quad . \tag{28}$$

We shall loosely refer to the $y_i(x)$ and $u(x)$ so generated between successive output points as the nonlinear solution approximation. Because this process introduces discontinuities in $F(x)$ and $g(x)$ at each x_k (at least in the early iterations when poor guesses have been provided), the integration scheme is restarted at all the output points.

6. Other Considerations

Arguments frequently given in favor of shooting codes over the linearization procedure just described are the conveniences of not having to provide analytical partial derivatives for the Jacobian and of not having to provide initial solution guesses at more than one point. While these arguments are valid for simple problems, they become weaker in the cases of problems exhibiting strong unstable components or sensitivities with respect to the initial conditions. If multiple shooting procedures are necessary, then initial guesses must be supplied at each shooting point and this obviously is equivalent to providing a rough initial profile for all solution components. Furthermore, some forms of the shooting do require analytical partial derivatives while others use numerical approximations.

Another point worth mentioning is that the multiple shooting codes with which we are familiar either require the user to input the shooting points or they are chosen automatically by an essentially preprocessing phase. In either case these points remain fixed for all the iterations used by the procedure. Without discussing the pros and cons for such a technique, we remark that the orthonormalization points (as well as other points to be described below) are selected dynamically in the SUPORQ code. That is, they may change from one iteration to the next, adapting to the current solution approximation available and the improved approximation being computed.

On each iteration, the SUPORQ code computes $k + 1$ independent solutions: a particular solution to the inhomogeneous problem and k solutions which are sufficient to form the basis of the homogeneous problem space. Since all equations are integrated simultaneously, a considerable savings can be achieved whenever $F(x)$, the Jacobian, is expensive to evaluate; that is, only one evaluaton of $F(x)$ will suffice for the $k + 1$ solutions. The importance of this observation is seen whenever function evaluations are used as a measure of the efficiency of codes.

Typically the code will compute the solution of the boundary-value problem at a predetermined set of output points. However, since it will usually be of interest to locate the places where the solution varies most rapidly and since we generally do not know the precise behavior of the solution a priori, we have included provisions for adding or deleting output points from one iteration to the next. This is particularly important for problems having a lot of structure in the solution, such as boundary layers. Our aim has been to provide this information in a way that adequately describes the solution character without undue penalties on the computational cost and storage.

Another reason for bringing in additional points is to allow the solutions of the linearized boundary-value problems to proceed. That is, integration of sensitive problems may require shorter subintervals for the integration process, particularly when we are attempting to overcome bad starting guesses. In this same vein, we must remember that Newton's method is guaranteed to converge only if we are sufficiently close to the solution. Thus, in practice, we must exert additional constraints or controls on the iterative process to enhance the overall convergence possibilities. Insertion of other points and controlling the growth of the nonlinear solution approximation between output points does this.

We shall distinguish between an output point and a breakpoint. An output point is a point where the solution of the linearized problem is computed by the superposition and orthonormalization procedure. A breakpoint results from interruption of the initial-value process due to unacceptable growth of the nonlinear solution approximation between current output points. Generally, a breakpoint becomes an output point or causes a new output point to be added to the set. This new point set is then processed to determine if some of the points can be deleted so that from one iteration to the next, output points may be added or deleted. An output point is removed if in adjoining subintervals the solution is monotonic, or nearly so, and the variation per subinterval of the solution changes little (i.e., the derivative remains about the same). An output point is added when the nonlinear solution approximation varies substantially between current output points. The details of the algorithm will be published elsewhere.

The Development of the Boundary-Value Codes in the Ordinary Differential Equations Chapter of the NAG Library

Ian Gladwell

University of Manchester

Abstract

We discuss the historical development of the ordinary differential equations chapter of the Numerical Algorithms Groups Library with special emphasis on boundary-value codes. Much of this development has been motivated by the need to solve practical problems. We give six examples of problems which have influenced us and we consider in some detail how these problems can be solved using the shooting and matching codes in the NAG library. We also briefly describe other boundary-value codes in the NAG library and discuss future plans. In an appendix we give a classified list of the current NAG library boundary-value codes.

1. Introduction

1.1 Historical Background

The Numerical Algorithms Group library of Fortran subroutines and Algol procedures was started in the late 1960's. In the first "marks" of the library a number of codes for solving initial-value problems were included. These first codes were based on Runge-Kutta-Merson methods and Adams codes were included soon after. At the time, methods for boundary-value problems were poorly documented (other than for a few special cases) and no attempt was made to include codes in the NAG library. The initial-value codes had been developed through the 1960's in response to user demand. They formed part of local libraries before the advent of the NAG library.

As the use of libraries such as NAG became more widespread, it became clear that many users were solving simple nonlinear boundary-value problems by using the initial-value codes in simple shooting and matching techniques. Of course, these users encountered difficulties (i) in achieving convergence in the simple functional iterations which they usually employed and (ii) with relative instability. It was these difficulties which the numerical analysts at Manchester (in particular Prof. J. E. Walsh and the author) encountered and attempted to overcome. Our first reaction was to write a simple shooting and matching routine based on integrating using the Runge-Kutta-Merson code, DO2ABF[†], in the NAG library and using a modified Newton iteration. This routine, in modified form, is still available in the NAG library and named DO2ADF (see NAG library manual, Mark 7). As far as local use was concerned, this routine was a great success and was instrumental in solving a large number of problems arising in fluid mechanics and other areas.

Encouraged by the success of DO2ADF, the author designed the more general routine DO2AGF. This routine also employs a shooting and matching technique using the same Runge-Kutta code and a similar Newton iteration. The main difference between the routines DO2ADF and DO2AGF is that DO2ADF solves for unknown boundary values whereas DO2AGF solves for unknown parameters which may be boundary values but will also be any other unknown parameters of the problem; see

---

† A full list of NAG library routines referred to in the text is given in the Appendix.

subsection 2.1 for further discussion. D02AGF also permits driving equations.

Recently the initial-value solvers in the NAG library have been updated and the author has designed a new boundary value code D02SAF based on a Runge-Kutta-Merson code D02PAF which has many more facilities than the old code D02ABF. In addition to the facilities of D02AGF, D02SAF permits solution of additional algebraic equations, description of constraints, a more flexible output system, the ability to split the range of integration to facilitate the integration of the differential system, and a more robust Newton iteration based on a singular-value decomposition.

At the same time as the code D02AGF was developed (about 1971), there was some demand for a code which would give closed form solutions for differential equations, and especially for linear equations. A National Physical Laboratory routine, ref. Picken (1970), was modified and included in the NAG library as D02AFF. Its use determines the solution of a general linear system of differential equations in Chebyshev series. E.L. Albasiny describes the original version of this code (see pages 280-286). The author has recently modified D02AFF and provided two driver routines for the modified version, see subsection 2.2.

Another area of boundary-value problems where we have found a demand for codes is in solving eigenvalue problems. The author has been interested in eigenvalue problems arising from stability analysis of fluid flow and we will return to problems of this type in the next subsection. A rather simpler problem (at least superficially) is the solution of a general (perhaps singular) Sturm-Liouville problem

$$(p(x)y')' + Q(x, \lambda)y = 0 \tag{1.1}$$

with general boundary conditions. Recently a code D02KDF written by J.D. Pryce of the University of Bristol has been included in the NAG library to solve (1.1). This code uses a shooting and matching technique based on a scaled Prüfer transformation and gives very accurate error estimates for the computed eigenvalues, λ, see subsection 2.3. A more general version of D02KDF for multi-parameter eigenvalue problems is described in Hargrave and Pryce (1977).

1.2 Some Boundary-Value Problems

As indicated in the previous subsection the motivation for the development of the shooting and matching methods codes in NAG has been the type of problem which has been met by the author and his colleagues. These problems arise in fluid mechanics, heat transfer, meteorology, magnetohydrodynamics and other related fields. In these areas, the problems usually arise from employing similarity-solution techniques or perturbation analysis to solve boundary-layer problems in partial differential equations. Many examples can be found in the literature, see for example issues of the Journal of Fluid Mechanics, Journal of Heat Transfer, Quarterly Journal of Mechanics and Applied Mathematics, Journal of Atmospheric Science, or see Watson (1976). Much of the applied mathematical postgraduate work in the Department of Mathematics, University of Manchester, is concerned with solving such problems and many of the problems have been solved using the code D02AGF, see Walton (1972), Walker (1972), Hatton (1973), Moss (1973) (which also contains problems which were not solvable using D02AGF) and Walsh and Wilson (1978).

We will briefly discuss a small selection of the boundary-value problems which we have solved in practice as an introduction to the following section.

(i) A Parameter Estimation Problem

The differential equations are

$$u''' = -v + 2u'^2/5 - uu'', \qquad (1.2)$$

$$v'' = - uv'/2,$$

and

$$y''' = -z + yu''(4\lambda/3 - 1) - uy'' - u'y'(4\lambda/3 - 4/5) \qquad (1.3)$$

$$z'' = -(uz' + 4\lambda(u'z - v'y)/3 + v'y)/2$$

with boundary conditions

$$u(0) = u'(0) = 0, \quad v(0) = 1, \qquad (1.4)$$

$$u'(\infty) = v'(\infty) = 0,$$

and

$$y(0) = y'(0) = z(0) = 0, \; y''(0) = 1, \qquad (1.5)$$

$$y'(\infty) = z(\infty) = 0.$$

Here the (eigenvalue) parameter λ is to be determined. Note that equations (1.2) can be solved first with boundary conditions (1.4). Then equations (1.3) with boundary conditions (1.5) constitute a linear eigenvalue problem with equations (1.2) with (1.4) as driving equations.

(ii) A Singular Problem

The differential equations are

$$3yy'' = 2(y' - z),\ z'' = -yz', \tag{1.6}$$

with boundary conditions

$$y(0) = 0,\ z(0) = 1,\ y'(\infty) = z'(\infty) = 0. \tag{1.7}$$

The differential equation is singular at $x = 0$ but we may use a power series

$$\begin{aligned} y &= x + p_1x^2 + p_2x^{7/3} + p_1^2x^3/3 + p_1p_2x^{10/3}/3 \\ &\quad + 7p_2^2x^{11/3}/66 + p_1x^4/60 + \ldots, \\ z &= 1 + p_1x - p_1x^3/5 - p_1^2x^4/12 + \ldots \end{aligned} \tag{1.8}$$

to shift the boundary conditions from $x = 0$ to some value $x > 0$.

(iii) A Free Boundary Problem

The differential equations are

$$\begin{aligned} y''' &= 2y'(y' + 2)/3 - y''(x + 2(y + z/2)/3), \\ z''' &= z'(z' + 2)/3 - z''(x + 2(y + z/2)/3), \end{aligned} \tag{1.9}$$

with boundary conditions

$$y \sim e^{-x^2/2},\ z \sim e^{-x^2/2} \quad \text{as} \quad x \to \infty, \tag{1.10}$$

and

$$y' = z' = 1,\ z = -2(3p/2 + y + 10\sqrt{3/2}), \tag{1.11}$$

to be applied at a point p to be determined (the last condition in (1.11) can be viewed as an equation for p). The conditions (1.10) can be replaced by the asymptotic expansion

$$y \sim rS(4/3),\ z \sim sS(2/3) \tag{1.12}$$

where r and s are unknown parameters to be determined and where

$$S(q) = x^{-q-2}(1 - (q+2)(q+3)/2x^2 + (q+2)(q+3)(q+4)(q+5)/8x^4 + \ldots)e^{-x^2/2} \tag{1.13}$$

(iv) A Perturbation Problem

The differential equations are

$$r''' = -s' - rr'' + r'^2/2,\ s'' = -rs', \tag{1.14}$$

with boundary conditions

$$r(0) = r'(0) = 0; \quad s(0) = 1, \tag{1.15}$$

$$r', \quad s \to 0 \quad \text{as} \quad x \to \infty;$$

$$t''' = -rt'' + 2't' - 2r''t + 4r'^2/3 - u, \tag{1.16}$$

$$u'' = -(ru' - r'u + 2ts'),$$

with boundary conditions

$$t(0) = t'(0) = u(0) = 0; \tag{1.17}$$

$$t', \quad u \to 0 \quad \text{as} \quad x \to \infty;$$

$$v''' = -w-(vr'' + v''r) + v'r' - 2s'r'' + s^2, \tag{1.18}$$

$$w'' = -(vs' + rw'),$$

with boundary conditions

$$v(0) = v'(0) = w(0) = 0, \tag{1.19}$$

$$v', \quad w \to 0 \quad \text{as} \quad x \to \infty;$$

and

$$y''' = - z - (2r''y - 2r'y' + ry'' + 2v''t - 8r'v'/3$$
$$- 2v't' + vt'' + 2s't'' + 2u'r'' - 2su), \tag{1.20}$$

$$z'' = -(z'r - zr' + 2ys' + u'v + 2tw' - uv'),$$

with boundary conditions

$$y(0) = y'(0) = z(0) = 0, \tag{1.21}$$

$$y', \quad z \to 0 \quad \text{as} \quad x \to \infty.$$

As with case (i), it is difficult to decide whether it is better to solve the four problems in turn or together. The author has favoured solving them in turn as this approach may provide additional insight into the properties of their solutions.

(v) A Multipoint Free Boundary Problem

The differential equations are

$$F''' = -FF'' + 2\beta(1 - F'^2), \tag{1.22}$$

$$\phi'' = -Pr_e \, F\phi',$$

and

$$f''' = -2\beta + A(2\beta f'^2 - ff''), \qquad (1.23)$$

$$\theta'' = - A\, Pr_v\, f\theta',$$

with boundary conditions

$$F(0) = Bf(\eta),\ f'(\eta) = CF'(0),$$

$$F''(0) = Df''(\eta),\ f(\eta) + \theta'(\eta) = E\phi'(0), \qquad (1.24)$$

$$\theta(\eta) = 0,\ \theta(0) = 1,\ f(0) = f'(0) = 0,\ \phi(0) = 1,$$

$$F'(\infty) = 1,\ \phi(\infty) = 0.$$

Here β is a parameter of the problem to be fixed by the user, $Pr_e \sim 1.74$ and $Pr_v \sim 0.996$ are Prandtl numbers for liquid and vapour respectively and A, B, C, D and E are constants given by

$$A = .00088\ \Delta_v,\ B = .0002\Delta_v^{3/4}, \qquad (1.25)$$

$$C = .7\Delta_v^{-1/2},\ D = .3\Delta_v^{1/4},\ E = 5.8\Delta_e/\Delta_v^{1/2},$$

where Δ_e and Δ_v are parameters which can be chosen, see Walsh and Wilson (1978), and η is the position of the liquid/vapour interface and is to be determined.

(vi) A Difficult Eigenvalue Problem

The differential equations are

$$v' = -u - \alpha w,\ w' = \Omega - \alpha v,$$

$$u'' = (\alpha^2 + \beta + 2F')u + F''v - Fu', \qquad (1.26)$$

$$\Omega'' = (\alpha^2 + \beta - F')\Omega - F\Omega',$$

with boundary conditions

$$u(0) = v(0) = w(0) = 0, \qquad (1.27)$$

and, as $x \to \infty$,

$$\Omega \sim AX^{-\alpha^2-\beta}\ e^{-X^2/2},$$

$$U \sim BX^{-\alpha^2-\beta-3}\ e^{-X^2/2}, \qquad (1.28)$$

$$v \sim Ce^{-\alpha X} - \alpha AX^{-\alpha^2-\beta-2}\ e^{-X^2/2},$$

$$w \sim Ce^{-\alpha X} - AX^{-\alpha^2-\beta-1}\ e^{-X^2/2},$$

where $X = x - 0.64790 \ldots$. Here F is the solution of

$$F''' = - FF'' + F'^2 - 1, \qquad (1.29)$$

with boundary conditions

$$F(0) = F'(0) = 0, \; F' \to 1 \text{ as } x \to \infty. \tag{1.30}$$

The author has treated this problem by solving equations (1.29) and (1.30), and then solving the nonlinear eigenvalue problem (1.26)-(1.28) for β for various choices of α, see Gladwell (1978).

The problems outlined above are quite typical of those produced by applied mathematicians, in the author's experience. It is worth noting that problems of certain types which appear in the literature have never arisen (as numerical problems) in the author's environment. In particular we note the considerable literature, in this context, on the second order problem

$$y'' = f(x, y), \tag{1.31}$$

and on the singular perturbation problem

$$\varepsilon y^{(n)} = f(x, y, y', \ldots, y^{(n-1)}). \tag{1.32}$$

2. The NAG Library Boundary-Value Solvers

In the following subsections we consider in detail the construction of and reasoning behind the parameter sequences of the NAG boundary-value solvers. This leads us into the final section where we discuss plans for the development of the NAG library chapter in the near future and finally we attempt to look a little further into the future.

2.1 Shooting Codes

In this section we consider the three shooting codes currently available or about to be made available soon in the NAG library, see NAG library manuals, Marks 7 and 8. We start by considering the most complicated of these subroutines (DO2SAF) and go on to discuss the others in the light of this description (DO2ADF and DO2AGF).

Subroutine DO2SAF is designed to solve the problem

$$\underline{y}' = \underline{f}(x, \underline{y}, \underline{z}, \underline{p}), \tag{2.1}$$

with driving equations

$$\underline{z}' = \underline{g}(x, \underline{z}). \tag{2.2}$$

The separated boundary conditions are applied at two points $x_1(\underline{p})$ and $x_n(\underline{p})$ and are of the form

$$\underline{y}(x_1(\underline{p})) = \underline{b}_1(\underline{p}),\ \underline{y}(x_n(\underline{p})) = \underline{b}_n(p), \tag{2.3}$$

and the initial conditions for (2.2) are

$$\underline{z}(x_1(\underline{p})) = \underline{c}(\underline{p}). \tag{2.4}$$

The differential equations (2.1) and (2.2) are defined by one subroutine which evaluates the vector $\left[\frac{\underline{g}}{\underline{f}}\right]$; note that the vector $\underline{g}$ is put first as this is normally helpful in practice (see Section 1.2). Similarly the boundary and initial conditions are also defined by one subroutine.

It is assumed in DO2SAF that the user wishes to solve m equations in m unknowns; that is, $\underline{p}$ has m components. It is also assumed (2.3) provides m_1 equations where $m_1 \leq m$; that is $\underline{y}$ has m_1 components. If $m_1 = m$ no other equations need be defined. If $m_1 < m$ then $m - m_1$ additional equations

$$\underline{e}(\underline{p}) = \underline{0} \tag{2.5}$$

must be defined using another subroutine which evaluates $\underline{e}(\underline{p})$.

The range of integration $x_1(\underline{p})$ to $x_n(\underline{p})$ is defined by a subroutine. The user is also permitted to define break-points $x_2(\underline{p}),\ x_3(\underline{p}),\ \ldots,\ x_{n-1}(\underline{p})$ where

$$x_1(\underline{p}) < x_2(\underline{p}) < \ldots < x_n(\underline{p}) \tag{2.6}$$

(or $x_1(\underline{p}) > x_2(\underline{p}) > \ldots > x_n(\underline{p})$). The direction of shooting is always from x_1 to x_n. The purpose of these breakpoints is twofold. First, since we permit the user to specify an initial and a maximum integration stepsize on each subinterval $[x_i, x_{i+1}]$, careful positioning of breakpoints can enable him to isolate parts of the integration range where the solution $\underline{y}$ and $\underline{z}$ are expected to be badly behaved and to take apropriate action. Secondly, this facility permits the user to describe discontinuous functions $\underline{f}$ and $\underline{g}$ in (2.1) and (2.2). Note that to facilitate the use of the breakpoints, the subroutine which specifies $\underline{f}$ and $\underline{g}$ contains a parameter which defines the subinterval $[x_i, x_{i+1}]$ in which the argument where $\underline{f}$ and $\underline{g}$ are to be evaluated.

Before describing further facilities of DO2SAF and the techniques used to perform the shooting and matching process, let us consider how the problems of Section 1.2 may be posed for solution by DO2SAF.

Problem (i), equations (1.2)-(1.5), can be solved as a whole or in two parts. Treated as a single problem equations (1.2) and (1.3) define $\underline{f}$ in (2.1) and equations (1.4) and (1.5) define $\underline{b}_1$ and $\underline{b}_n$ in (2.3). The boundary conditions at infinity can be imposed at a suitable large value of the independent variable x (though asymptotic expansions for u, v, y and z could be supplied) hence defining $\underline{b}_n$. The boundary conditions provide the ten equations for the unknowns

$$\begin{aligned} &p_1 = \lambda,\ p_2 = u''(0),\ p_3 = v'(0),\ p_4 = u(\infty),\ p_5 = u''(\infty), \\ &p_6 = v(\infty),\ p_7 = z'(0),\ p_8 = y(\infty),\ p_9 = y''(\infty),\ p_{10} = z(\infty). \end{aligned} \tag{2.7}$$

We will discuss splitting a system into more than one part when we come to problem (iv).

Problem (ii), equations (1.6) and (1.7), can be solved in a straightforward manner. Again a large value of x can be used as a position to apply the boundary conditions at infinity. The singularity at the origin can be treated by using the expansions (1.8) to give values for the components of $\underline{b}_1$ in (2.3). Our technique for dealing with boundary conditions permits such an expansion to be entered directly. Note that the unknown parameters p_1 and p_2 are determined, replacing the boundary values y'(0) and z'(0) as unknowns. The main difficulty with this approach is in deciding where to evaluate the series expansion. If the expansion is evaluated too far from x = 0, it may not be sufficiently accurate to determine the solution to the required accuracy; whereas if it applied too close to x = 0, the boundary values will be very accurate but the differential equation will be difficult to integrate initially due to heavy cancellation errors when evaluating $\underline{f}$. One must take sufficient terms in the expansion so that $\underline{f}$ need not be evaluated where heavy cancellation will result.

Problem (iii), equations (1.9), (1.10) and (1.11), can clearly be posed in a suitable form for solving by D02SAF. We set $x_1 = p$ and x_2 = XINF where XINF is a suitably chosen large value and where the asymptotic expansions (1.12) are used when setting $\underline{b}_n$. We attempt to choose XINF sufficiently large so that the asymptotic expansion is accurate, yet small enough so that no difficulty is experienced in integrating the differential equations across the range x_1 to x_n. This problem can quite sensibly be viewed as one with ten or eleven unknowns depending on how the boundary conditions are treated. If the moving boundary position, p, and y(p) and z(p) are all treated as unknown parameters then the third condition of (1.10) must be treated as an equation e(p) = 0 in (2.5). Otherwise one can consider just one of y(0) and z(0) as unknown and eliminate the other from the equation, then this boundary condition will appear in eliminated form in $\underline{b}_1$ in (2.3). Note that r and s in (1.12) are treated as components of the unknown parameter $\underline{p}$.

Problem (iv), equations (1.14)-(1.21), can be solved directly as with problem (i), or can be solved by breaking the problem into smaller parts. It is worth remembering that the smaller the system the less the work involved in approximating the Jacobian (and in the linear algebra in the modified Newton method). Also equations (1.14) and (1.15) are nonlinear whereas equations (1.16)-(1.21) are linear. Hence it would seem sensible to solve the problem (1.14) and (1.15) first and then the other problems either separately or as a whole using (1.14) and (1.15) as driving equations. The way that the differential equation and boundary conditions must be presented to D02SAF has been designed so as to permit this approach with the minimum of programming effort; no reprogramming is required as one moves on from one sub-problem to the next. Note that though equations (1.16)-(1.21) are linear, a Newton iteration to solve for $\underline{p}$ will not usually converge in one iteration, due to the errors from the numerical integrations. When solving problems such as (1.14)-(1.21) by splitting the problem into several subproblems, the argument x where the boundary conditions at infinity should be applied is often not the same from one subproblem to the next. Of course, this only becomes obvious if one computes the solution for a number of such values x. It is often the case that the solutions of the later problems decay more slowly than those of the initial problem. Lest it seem that all one need do is to choose the argument x to be very large, it must be remarked that since all the solutions of the equations have components which exponentially decay, too large a value for x may lead to an ill-conditioned Jacobian in Newton's method.

Problem (v), equations (1.22)-(1.24), differs from the earlier problems in that the boundary conditions are given at three points. Note however that they are not true multipoint conditions since each variable has boundary conditions defined at only two points. In fact, the systems (1.22) and (1.23) are connected only through the boundary conditions (1.24). Since the system (1.22) is defined on $[0, \infty)$ and (1.23) is defined on $[0, \eta]$ where η is to be determined, we can use the facilities of DO2SAF. We define

$$x_1(\underline{p}) = 0,\ x_2(\underline{p}) = p_1,\ x_3(\underline{p}) = \text{XINF} \tag{2.8}$$

where $p_1 = \eta$ is the first component of $\underline{p}$ and XINF is a large value. We then redefine the differential equations (1.23) as

$$f' = f'' = f''' = 0 = \theta' = \theta'' \tag{2.9}$$

on the range $[x_2, x_3]$. We can then apply the boundary conditions in the usual way, replacing η by ∞ in (1.24).

Problem (vi), equations (1.26)-(1.30), can be set up for solution by DO2SAF using techniques already described. However, equations (1.26) are unstable when integrated from $x = 0$. Though this difficulty can be overcome, we have not found solution of this problem tractable via simple shooting and matching. We will return briefly to more practical methods in Section 3.2.

Let us now return to a description of the facilities of subroutine DO2SAF. The aim of the shooting and matching technique is to solve an equation

$$\underline{f}(\underline{p}) = \underline{0} \tag{2.10}$$

for $\underline{p}$. The residual $\underline{f}$ may be split into two parts $\underline{f} = [\frac{\underline{r}}{\underline{e}}]$ where $\underline{e}$ is defined by equation (2.5), and $\underline{r}$ by

$$\underline{r}(\underline{p}) = \underline{b}_n(\underline{p}) - \underline{y}(\underline{p}) \tag{2.11}$$

where $\underline{y}(\underline{p})$ is the solution of the differential equations (2.1) and (2.2) with initial condition

$$\underline{y}(x_1(\underline{p})) = b_1(\underline{p})$$

evaluated at $x_n(\underline{p})$, and $\underline{b}_1$ and $\underline{b}_n$ are defined by (2.3). The shooting and matching equations are solved by a modified Newton method. At each iteration we choose

$$\underline{p}^{(n+1)} = \underline{p}^{(n)} - \lambda_t \tilde{J}^{-1}\underline{f}^{(n)}. \tag{2.12}$$

Here $\underline{p}^{(n)}$ is the n-th iterate for $\underline{p}$, $\underline{f}^{(n)} = f(\underline{p}^{(n)})$, $\tilde{J}$ is an approximation to J, and J is an approximation to the Jacobian

$$J \simeq (\partial f_i/\partial p_j)(\underline{p}^{(n)}). \tag{2.13}$$

In fact, J is calculated by numerical differentiation. The approximation is then modified if it is almost singular or if the iteration (2.12) is not converging sufficiently fast. Suitable modifications of J are discussed in Gay (1976). The modified matrix is $\tilde{J}$. The constant λ_t is chosen, if possible, from the sequence $1, \frac{1}{2}, \frac{1}{4}, \frac{1}{8}, \frac{1}{16}$ so that

$$||\tilde{J}^{-1}\underline{f}^{(n+1)}|| \leqslant 0.9\,||\tilde{J}^{-1}\underline{f}^{(n)}||, \tag{2.14}$$

see Deuflhard (1974) for details of a similar method. The Jacobian is only re-evaluated if necessary; we re-evaluate if

$$||\tilde{J}^{-1}\underline{f}^{(n+1)}|| > .0625(1 - \frac{1}{m+1})\ ||\tilde{J}^{-1}\underline{f}^{(n)}|| \tag{2.15}$$

Criterion (2.15) is chosen, in part, to reflect the extra cost of evaluating the Jacobian as it size, m, increases. The iteration is only terminated if it cannot be started, that is if $\underline{f}(\underline{p}^{(0)})$ or $J(\underline{p}^{(0)})$ cannot be evaluated, or if, whatever the choice of λ_t or the modification of J used, the criterion (2.14) cannot be satisfied.

The Jacobian (2.13) is evaluated by either forward, backward or central differences depending on the significance of the approximation obtained. We do not feel that the user should be expected to define the variational equations as they are rather complicated for the general problem which is treated here (there is a distinctly greater possibility of the user committing calculation or typographical errors when supplying the variational equations, than when defining the original problem). The user is asked to supply increments for use in the difference approximations, but, recognising how difficult this might be, default values are calculated in terms of the size of the parameters $\underline{p}$ and the square root of the machine precision.

The user is also required to supply error tolerances for use with the initial-value solver in the integration of equations (2.1) and (2.2). He is also required to supply error tolerances for testing for convergence in the iteration (2.12). It is unfortunate but unavoidable that these error tolerances cannot be combined in general. The user is, in any case, advised to check his results by varying the error tolerances in the integration.

When the boundary-value problem is ill-conditioned, even careful use of the singular-value decomposition in the Newton iteration (2.12), results in values $\underline{p}$ being generated which are a long distance from the solution and are much worse approximations to the solution than $\underline{p}^{(n)}$. Of course, such values $\underline{p}$ will be rejected when the test (2.14) is applied. However, it can easily happen that the user knows that certain values are physically unacceptable and may possibly lead to a difficult evaluation of $\underline{f}(\underline{p})$ or even one where the results of the integration overflow. Two facilities are provided to prevent these problems arising. First, the user is permitted to define constraints on the parameter values $\underline{p}$. These constraints are used statically, that is they are used to reject choices of $\underline{p}$ before evaluating $\underline{f}(\underline{p})$ but they are not used to alter the progress of the iteration in any other way. The other facility is defined via a parameter YMAX which is used as bound on the solution of equations (2.1) and (2.2) with initial values $\underline{b}_1(\underline{p})$ for each choice $\underline{p}$ arising in the Newton iteration. It is intended that YMAX be used to prevent overflows during evaluations of $\underline{f}(\underline{p})$ by stopping the integration if $\|\underline{y}(x)\|_\infty$ exceeds YMAX for any x in the range.

Finally, subroutine D02SAF has a facility to output the solution of equations (2.1)-(2.5) for the value of $\underline{p}$ accepted as the solution of these equations. The solution is output via a subroutine at a set of points of the user's choice in the range $[x_1(\underline{p}), x_n(\underline{p})]$.

We have found that to attract inexperienced users to a subroutine library it is necessary to provide routines with simple parameter sequences in each chapter. After using the simpler routines they can move on to the more complicated routines, if necessary, with some confidence. In the case of the boundary-value problem section, the simpler routines must, inevitably, have less facilities and solve a restricted class of problems. There are two such subroutines DO2AGF and DO2ADF (these names will probably change as the library is updated). The first, DO2AGF, has the same aim as DO2SAF, namely to solve a problem of the form (2.1)-(2.4). The difference between DO2AGF and DO2SAF is that the equations (2.5) are not permitted, there are no breakpoints (2.6), the solution is output on an equispaced mesh via an array, and the error control parameters are simplified. The residuals $\underline{f}$ are formed by matching the solutions obtained by integration from both end-points at a point of the user's choice. This additional facility over those of DO2SAF permits possible solution of the few problems where integration away from both boundary points is essential.

Subroutine DO2ADF has a much simpler parameter sequence. The parameters $\underline{p}$ are unknown boundary values and hence the range of integration and the differential equations have no explicit dependence on the parameter. Only one set of error tolerances is required and it is used in controlling the integrations, testing for convergence at the unknown boundary values and in the increments for numerical differentiation for the Jacobian. Clearly, only well-scaled problems will be solvable with these restrictions, but for such problems the user probably finds it easier to control the solution process. Again the residual $\underline{f}$ is formed by matching at a point chosen by the user and the solution is output at equispaced points in an array.

At the time of writing, DO2SAF, DO2AGF and DO2ADF are completely separate subroutines. However, as DO2AGF and DO2ADF are updated it is planned that they be linked to DO2SAF. It would clearly be possible to make DO2AGF as driver subroutine for DO2SAF and, with more difficulty, to make DO2ADF a driver for DO2AGF. However, we favour modularization here. The modules will be designed so that each of the subroutines DO2SAF, DO2AGF and DO2ADF calls a number of modules used in common (for example, the Newton iteration subroutine) and some separate (but similar) modules (for example, the residual calculation subroutine).

2.2. Chebyshev Series Solvers

Since the original subroutine on which the main NAG subroutine, DO2TGF, has been based is described by E.L. Albasiny in these proceedings, we will not discuss it in any detail. We remark only that the subroutine calculates a regular solution to a system of multipoint (singular) linear boundary-value problems in a Chebyshev series. The user must define the problem, the order of the Chebyshev series required and the number of collocation points to be used in a least squares solution. The user is expected to study the resulting Chebyshev series to determine its adequacy as a solution. Nonlinear problems may be treated by quasilinearisation (Newton's method).

The NAG library will also shortly contain two driver subroutines for the main routine outlined above (NAG library manual, Mark 8). One, DO2SAF, is designed to solve the regular problem

$$\sum_{i=0}^{n} a_i(x)\, y^{(i)}(x) = f(x), \tag{2.13}$$

and the other, DO2SBF, is designed to solve the regular problem

$$\underline{y}' = A(x)\underline{y} \tag{2.14}$$

both with two-point boundary conditions. Both driver subroutines are similar to the main routine in all other respects (the main difficulty in using DO2TGF is in specifying the differential equation and its multipoint conditions).

2.3 Sturm-Liouville Solvers

Again we do not discuss the NAG subroutines in detail since a similar, but quite distinct, routine is describe by P.B. Bailey and L.F. Shampine (see pages 274-279) and in Bailey (1978). In both Bailey and Shampine's routine and the NAG routine, DO2KDF, a scaled Prüfer transformation is used to solve the Sturm-Liouville problem (see (1.1))

$$(p(x)y')' + Q(x, \lambda)\, y = 0$$

with two-point boundary conditions sufficiently general to treat singular problems. The NAG routine, DO2KDF, integrates the scaled Prüfer equations from both ends to a matching point defined by the user. It rescales the Prüfer equations regularly during the integration (and breakpoints are permitted as in DO2SAF). The matching equations are solved for the eigenvalue λ by a NAG rootfinder which uses secant and bisection steps as appropriate; it is based on the procedure 'zeroin' of Bus and Dekker (1975). The routine DO2KDF returns an accurate error estimate with the computed eigenvalue (which is obtained to a user-specified accuracy under certain assumptions on the local error estimate of the initial value solver employed).

A driver subroutine, DO2KAF, for DO2KDF is also available. This is designed to solve regular Sturm-Liouville problems with regular boundary conditions (which are specified in a simple way).

3. Extensions to the NAG Library Chapter on Ordinary Differential Equations

Here we discuss briefly how we expect the NAG library chapter to develop over the next couple of Marks, as far as boundary-value codes are concerned.

3.1 Development of Existing Codes

The major extensions of and changes to the shooting codes which we envisage include:

(i) incorporation of additional code to permit the use of the variational equations in computing Jacobians where this is feasible;

(ii) possible use of the new NAG nonlinear least squares routines (NAG library manual, Mark 8) if these prove more effective than our modified Newton method;

(iii) inclusion of the new modularised NAG singular-value code (NAG library manual, Mark 8) in place of the current code;

(iv) a facility to permit integration using the NAG Adams and/or Gear codes (NAG library manual, Mark 7) instead of the Runge-Kutta code;

(v) use of the planned NAG graph-plotting routines to permit pictorial representation of the solution of boundary-value problems;

(vi) a driver routine for DO2SAF which performs continuation on a (physical) parameter identified by the user, probably performing simple extrapolation as a predictor for the continuation process and permitting pictorial representation of the variation of the components of $\underline{p}$ with the continuation parameter.

It is expected that these changes will take about two Marks (1 Mark = 1 year) to implement.

Extensions of the eigenvalue solver DO2KDF are also planned by Dr. J.D. Pryce. The main extension is to compute eigenfunctions corresponding to computed eigenvalues, probably in terms of the scaled Prüfer variables rather than the original variables of the problem. It is also hoped to provide for the computation of quantities which depend on the eigenfunctions, such as inner-products, and for the pictorial representations of eigenfunctions.

3.2 Incorporation of New Codes

Despite the plans to extend the existing library as outlined in the last subsection, it is envisaged that most of our future effort will be expended in modifying generally available codes so that they are suitable for the NAG library. In this context, most of the codes discussed in these proceedings would be candidates for inclusion. The difficulty is in deciding how many codes, and which, to include.

We can identify two main areas where new codes are required in the NAG library. First, there are those linear and nonlinear boundary-value problems for which simple shooting is inadequate, usually because of problems with instability (or relative instability). Secondly, there are eigenvalue problems, such as problem (vi) of Section 1.2, which are too general for the Sturm-Liouville solvers and are too difficult for the simple shooting subroutines.

For the first of these classes of problems, there are a number of codes described in these proceedings (see the contributions by Melvin Scott, V. Pererya and U. Ascher) which could be used, and there are a number of others in existence. One possibility is to include all these codes in the library. This is, at least to some extent, against the philosophy of the NAG library, which is to include only a few (one or two) codes for each problem and so a choice seems necessary. Since the codes are based on different techniques it is very difficult to compare them. Indeed, as far as the author is aware, there has been no thorough comparison of codes for boundary-value problems as there has been for initial-value codes. Indeed such comparisons may not be possible until a finer classification of nonlinear boundary-value problems becomes clearer.

As an interim measure, it is the author's intention to include at least one multiple-shooting method and at least one global method in the NAG library in the near future and then to await developments in comparison techniques.

For eigenvalue problems, the situation is rather simpler. The SUPORT orthonormalisation code (see Melvin Scott's contribution in these proceedings) has the ability to solve problems as general as problem (vi) of Section 1.2. Other techniques are available for solving such eigenvalue problems, see J.S. Bramley's contribution in these proceedings and Davey (1978), both of which use Riccati transformations. These techniques may well prove less expensive than using an orthonormalisation code but they are difficult to automate and so are not obvious candidates for a library.

Acknowledgements

I wish to thank my colleagues Christopher Baker and Len Freeman for their advice on and helpful criticism of this manuscript. My thanks go also to my colleagues Joan Walsh and George Hall for their advice and help in the development of this chapter of the NAG library.

Appendix

NAG Library Routines referred to in the text.

Shooting Codes

DO2SAF - very general shooting and matching code

DO2AGF - shooting and matching code with a selection of the facilities of DO2SAF

DO2ADF - simple shooting and matching code

Chebyshev Series Solvers

DO2AFF - general linear multipoint boundary-value solver

DO2TGF - revamped DO2AFF

DO2JAF, DO2JBF driver routines for DO2TGF

Sturm-Liouville Codes

DO2KDF - general Sturm-Liouville solver

DO2KAF - simple driver for DO2KDF

Initial Value Solvers

DO2ABF - Runge-Kutta-Merson code (vintage 1970)

DO2PAF - Runge-Kutta-Merson code (vintage 1977).

References

Albansiny, E.L. (1978). A Subroutine for Solving a System of Differential Equations in Chebyshev Series, pages 280-286 of these proceedings.

Ascher, U., Christiansen, J. & Russell, R.D. (1978). COLSYS--A Collocation Code for Boundary-Value Problems, pages 164-185 of these proceedings.

Bailey, P.B. (1978). An Eigenvalue-Eigenfunction Code for Sturm-Liouville Problems. Report SAND77-2044. Sandia Laboratories, Alburquerque, New Mexico.

Bailey, P.B. & Shampine, L.F. (1978). Automatic Solution of Sturm-Liouville Eigenvalue Problems, pages 274-279 of these proceedings.

Bramley, J.S. (1978). Calculation of Eigenvalues of Systems of ODE's Using the Riccati Transformation, pages 319-324 of these proceedings.

Bus, J.C.P. & Dekker, T.J. (1975). Two Efficient Algorithms with Guaranteed Convergence for Finding a Zero of a Function. TOMS, 1, pp.330-345.

Davey, A. (1978). On the Removal of the Singularities from the Riccati method. J. Comp. Phys. To appear.

Deuflhard, P. (1974). A Modified Newton Method for the Solution of Ill-Conditioned Systems of Nonlinear Equations with Application to Multiple Shooting. Num. Math. 22, pp.289-315.

Gay, D. (1976). On Modifying Singular Values to Solve Possibly Singular Systems of Nonlinear Equations. Working Paper No.125. Computer Research Center for Economics and Management Science. NBER. Cambridge, Mass.

Gladwell, I. (1978). On the Numerical Solution of a Differential Nonlinear Eigenvalue Problem on an Infinite Range. App. Math. and Comp. To appear.

Hargrave, B. & Pryce, J.D. (1977). NPARAM: Report on a Program to Solve Multi-parameter Sturm-Liouville Problem. Bristol U. Computer Science Dept.

Hatton, L. (1973). On the Dynamics of Concentrated Atmospheric Vortices. Ph.D. Thesis. University of Manchester.

Moss, D.M. (1973. Stars in Radiative Equilibrium Containing Multiple Magnetic Fields. Mon. Not. R. astr. Soc. 164, pp. 33-51.

Numerical Algorithms Group Manual. Mark 7 (1978). NAG, 7 Banbury Rd., Oxford.

Numerical Algorithms Group Manual. Mark 8 To appear. NAG, 7 Banbury Rd., Oxford.

Pereyra, V. (1978). An Adaptive Finite Difference Fortran Program for First Order Nonlinear, Ordinary Boundary Problems, pages 67-88 of these proceedings.

Picken, S.M. (1970). Algorithms for the Solution of Differential Equations in Chebyshev Series by the Selected Points Method. Report Math. 94. NPL, Teddington, Middlesex.

Scott, M.R. & Watts, H.A. (1978). Superposition, Orthonormalization, Quasi-linearization and Two-Point Boundary-Value Problems, pages 109-121 of these proceedings.

Walker, R.S. (1972). Boundary Layers in Rotating Bodies. Ph.D. Thesis. University of Manchester.

Walton, I.C. (1972). Problems in Laminar Boundary Layer Flow. Ph.D. Thesis. University of Manchester.

Walsh, S.K. & Wilson, S.D.R. (1978). Boundary Layer Flow in Forced-Convection Film-Boiling on a Wedge. Submitted for Publication.

Watson, E.J. (1976). Similarity Solutions in Fluid Dynamics. Paper given at a conference on "Partial Differential Equations in Industry, University of Manchester, 1976".

Wilson, S.D.R. and Gladwell, I. (1978). The Stability of a Two-Dimensional Stagnation Flow to Three-Dimensional Disturbances. J. Fluid Mech. 84, pp. 517-527.

AN ANALYSIS OF THE STABILIZED MARCH

M. R. Osborne

1. INTRODUCTION

The main subject of this paper is the numerical solution by superposition methods of the boundary-value problem for the first order system of ordinary differential equations

$$\frac{d\underset{\sim}{z}}{dt} = A(t)\,\underset{\sim}{x} + \underset{\sim}{f}(t) \tag{1.1}$$

subject to the boundary conditions

$$B^0\underset{\sim}{x}(0) + B^1\underset{\sim}{\chi}(1) = \underset{\sim}{b} \tag{1.2}$$

where $\underset{\sim}{x}$, $\underset{\sim}{b}$, $\underset{\sim}{f}(t)$ are of dimension n, and A, B^0, B^1 are $n \times n$ matrices. It is assumed that the matrix A is such that the initial-value problem for (1.1) is unstable, but that the solution of the boundary-value problem (1.1), (1.2) is well determined in the sense that the solution can be bounded a priori in terms of the data $\underset{\sim}{f}(t)$ and $\underset{\sim}{b}$. The key point is that the constants which occur in this bound must be of the order of the quantities in the problem statement and not of the size of the rapidly growing solutions to (1.1). This implies an inequality expressing the dependence on the data in the form (assuming the use of the maximum norms)

$$||\underset{\sim}{x}||_{C[0,1]^n} \leq \max\{k_1||\underset{\sim}{f}||_{C[0,1]^n},\ k_2||\underset{\sim}{b}||_{R_n}\} \tag{1.3}$$

where k_1 and k_2 are quantities limited in the manner explained above.

Before considering superposition methods it is convenient to define the fundamental matrix $X(t,\xi)$ by

$$\frac{dX}{dt} = A(t)X,\quad X(\xi,\xi) = 1 \tag{1.4}$$

and the particular integral $\underset{\sim}{v}(t,\xi)$ by

$$\frac{d\underset{\sim}{v}}{dt} = A(t)\underset{\sim}{v} + \underset{\sim}{f}(t) \ , \ \underset{\sim}{v}(\xi,\xi) = 0 \tag{1.5}$$

The basic simple shooting method follows by noting that any solution to (1.1) can be written in the form

$$\underset{\sim}{x}(t) = X(t,0)\,\underset{\sim}{x}(0) + \underset{\sim}{v}(t,0) \tag{1.6}$$

and that this satisfies the boundary conditions provided

$$M_0\,\underset{\sim}{x}(0) = [B^0 + B^1\,X(1,0)]\,\underset{\sim}{x}(0) = \underset{\sim}{b} - B^1\underset{\sim}{v}(1,0) \tag{1.7}$$

It is well known that (1.7) can be difficult to solve when (1.1) is unstable. This is because the rapidly growing solutions force $||M_0||$ to be large, and hence the condition number $\kappa(M_0)$ to be large, despite the fact that, setting $\underset{\sim}{f}(t) = 0$,

$$||M_0^{-1}|| = \max_{\underset{\sim}{b},||\underset{\sim}{b}||=1} ||\underset{\sim}{x}(0)|| \leq \max_{\underset{\sim}{b},||\underset{\sim}{b}||=1} ||\underset{\sim}{x}(t)|| \leq k_2 \tag{1.8}$$

To overcome this problem the method of multiple shooting was introduced [1]. In this case the interval [0,1] is partitioned so that $0 = t_0 < t_1 < \ldots.$ $< t_m = 1$. On each subinterval we write $\underset{\sim}{x}(t)$ as

$$\underset{\sim}{x}(t) = X(t,t_i)\underset{\sim}{x}(t_i) + \underset{\sim}{v}(t,t_i). \tag{1.9}$$

Denoting $X(t_{i+1},t_i)$ by X_{i+1}, $\underset{\sim}{v}(t_{i+1},t_i)$ by $\underset{\sim}{v}_{i+1}$, and $\underset{\sim}{x}(t_i)$ by $\underset{\sim}{x}_i$, the conditions that $\underset{\sim}{x}(t)$ is continuous at t_i, $i = 1,2,\ldots,m$, and that it satisfy the boundary conditions give the system of equations

$$M_m \begin{bmatrix} \underset{\sim}{x}_0 \\ \\ \\ \underset{\sim}{x}_m \end{bmatrix} = \begin{bmatrix} B^0 & & & & B^1 \\ -X_1 & I & & & \\ & -X_2 & I & & \\ \cdots & \cdots & \cdots & \cdots & \cdots \\ & & & -X_m & I \end{bmatrix} \begin{bmatrix} \underset{\sim}{x}_0 \\ \\ \\ \underset{\sim}{x}_m \end{bmatrix} = \begin{bmatrix} \underset{\sim}{b} \\ \underset{\sim}{v}_1 \\ \\ \underset{\sim}{v}_m \end{bmatrix} \tag{1.10}$$

In this case, by scaling the boundary conditions so that $||B^0|| + ||B^1|| = 1$, we can always arrange to choose the points t_i to ensure that $||M_m||$ satisfy $||M_m|| \lesssim 2 + \gamma$ for arbitrary $\gamma > 0$. However, m becomes a function of γ and may have to be chosen large. It is not difficult to show that in this case we must have an inequality of the form

$$||M_m^{-1}|| \lesssim K\,m \tag{1.11}$$

It is more difficult to show that K does not become large with the unstable solutions to (1.1). However, this is so and an inequality which demonstrates this, $||M_m^{-1}|| \lesssim 2k_1 nm \quad (1 + 0\,(1/m))$, is given in [2]. This dependence on m is inevitable and does not appear to cause problems in practise. On the other hand the scaling problems which make the inversion of M_0 so difficult are avoided. Thus multiple shooting works, and partial pivoting techniques have proved completely satisfactory for the solution of (1.10) [1].

Multiple shooting turns out to provide a suitable starting point for analyzing superposition methods which do not compute a complete basis for the solution set on each subinterval but attempt to reduce the number of differential equation integrations required by carrying forward information from previous subintervals. In this case the effect of the instability of the differential equation needs to be considered. Practical experience, for example the comprehensive experiments of Scott and Watts [3], indicates that instability need not be a problem. Here we record the result that suitably engineered versions of the stabilized march will be stable if multiple shooting is stable on the same set of points.

2. THE STABILIZED MARCH

The basic idea here is that if the boundary conditions are separated by which we mean that they take the form

$$B^0 = \begin{bmatrix} B_1^0 \\ B_2^0 \end{bmatrix}, \quad B^1 = \begin{bmatrix} 0 \\ B_2^1 \end{bmatrix}, \quad \underset{\sim}{b} = \begin{bmatrix} \underset{\sim}{b}_1 \\ \underset{\sim}{b}_2 \end{bmatrix} \tag{2.1}$$

where $B_1^0 = p \times n$ and $B_2^0 = q \times n$ with $q = n - p$, then we can ask that the particular integral $\hat{\underset{\sim}{v}}(t,0)$ satisfy

$$B_1^0 \ \hat{\underset{\sim}{v}}(0,0) = \underset{\sim}{b}_1 \tag{2.2}$$

in which case we can construct $\underset{\sim}{x}(t)$ by superposition using a solution or rank q of the matrix system

$$B_2^0 \ \hat{X}(0,0) = 0 \tag{2.3}$$

as initial conditions for the complementary-function integration. Instability is again a problem. However, now the best we can do is try and repair the information on the allowable subspace of complementary functions by some such technique as reorthogonalisation at the shooting points.

It is convenient to derive the superposition methods from multiple shooting. We set

$$x_i = \left[E_1^i \mid E_2^i \right] \begin{bmatrix} \underset{\sim}{d}_1^i \\ \underset{\sim}{d}_2^i \end{bmatrix} + \underset{\sim}{w}^i, \quad i = 0,1,\dots,m \tag{2.4}$$

where E_1^i is $n \times p$, and E^i is nonsingular with inverse $(E^i)^{-1} = F^i = \begin{bmatrix} F_1^i \\ F_2^i \end{bmatrix}$. Substituting in the boundary conditions gives

$$\begin{bmatrix} B_1^0 \\ B_2^0 \end{bmatrix} \left[E_1^0 \mid E_2^0 \right] \begin{bmatrix} \underset{\sim}{d}_1^0 \\ \underset{\sim}{d}_2^0 \end{bmatrix} + \left[E_1^m \mid E_2^m \right] \begin{bmatrix} \underset{\sim}{d}_1^m \\ \underset{\sim}{d}_2^m \end{bmatrix} = \begin{bmatrix} \underset{\sim}{b}_1 \\ \underset{\sim}{b}_2 \end{bmatrix} - \begin{bmatrix} B_1^0 \\ B_2^0 \end{bmatrix} \underset{\sim}{w}^0 - \begin{bmatrix} 0 \\ B_2^1 \end{bmatrix} \underset{\sim}{w}^m \tag{2.5}$$

so that $\underset{\sim}{d}_1^0 = 0$ provided (i) $B_1^0 E_2^0 = 0$, and (2.6)

$$\text{(ii)} \quad \underset{\sim}{b}_1 - B_1^0 \underset{\sim}{w} = 0 \tag{2.7}$$

It is necessary to adjoin q further conditions to determine $\underset{\sim}{w}^0$, and it is assumed that these take the form $G^0 \underset{\sim}{w}^0 = 0$. To reduce the continuity conditions we assume that $\underset{\sim}{d}_1^j = 0$, $j=0,\ldots,i-1$, then writing $X_i E^i = \tilde{X}^i$, $\tilde{\underset{\sim}{v}}^i = \underset{\sim}{v}_i + X_i \underset{\sim}{w}^{i-1}$, we have

$$- \left[X_1^i \mid X_2^i \right] \begin{bmatrix} 0 \\ \underset{\sim}{d}_2^{i-1} \end{bmatrix} + E^i \begin{bmatrix} \underset{\sim}{d}_1^i \\ \underset{\sim}{d}_2^i \end{bmatrix} = \tilde{\underset{\sim}{v}}^i - \underset{\sim}{w}^i \tag{2.8}$$

Multiplying through by F^i gives

$$\begin{bmatrix} F_1^i & \tilde{X}_2^i \\ F_2^i & \tilde{X}_2^i \end{bmatrix} \underset{\sim}{d}_2^{i-1} + \begin{bmatrix} \underset{\sim}{d}_1^i \\ \underset{\sim}{d}_2^i \end{bmatrix} = F^i(\tilde{\underset{\sim}{v}}^i - \underset{\sim}{w}^i) \tag{2.9}$$

so that $\underset{\sim}{d}_1^i = 0$ provided (i) $F_1^i X_2^i = 0$ (2.10)

(ii) $F_1^i(\tilde{\underset{\sim}{v}}^i - \underset{\sim}{w}^i) = 0$ (2.11)

Again it is necessary to impose q additional conditions $G^i \underset{\sim}{w}^i = 0$ to determine $\underset{\sim}{w}^i$. Note that the quantities which have to be computed at each stage are $\tilde{X}_2^i$ and $\tilde{\underset{\sim}{v}}^i$. They satisfy

$$\frac{dX_2^i}{dt} = A(t)\tilde{X}_2^i , \quad X_2^i(t_{i-1}) = E_2^{i-1} \tag{2.12}$$

and

$$\frac{d\underset{\sim}{v}^i}{dt} = A(t)\underset{\sim}{v}^i + \underset{\sim}{f}(t) , \quad \underset{\sim}{v}^i(t_{i-1}) = \underset{\sim}{w}^{i-1} \tag{2.13}$$

In the Godonov-Conte algorithm considered in [3] we set $X^i = Q^i \begin{bmatrix} U^i \\ 0 \end{bmatrix}$, $Q^i = \left[Q_2^i \mid Q_1^i \right]$ and compute

$$\left[E_1^i \mid E_2^i \right] = \left[Q_1^i \mid Q_2^i \right] , \; G^i = \left[Q_2^i \right]^T , \; F_1^i X_2^i = U^i , \underset{\sim}{w}^i = (E_1^i)(E_1^i)^T \tilde{\underset{\sim}{v}}^i \tag{2.14}$$

The unknowns are the $\underset{\sim}{d}_2^i$ and these satisfy

$$\begin{bmatrix} B_2^0 E_2^0 & & & B_2^1 E_2^m \\ -U^1 & I & & \\ \cdots & \cdots & \cdots & \cdots \\ & & -U^m & I \end{bmatrix} \begin{bmatrix} \underset{\sim}{d}_2^0 \\ \vdots \\ \underset{\sim}{d}_2^m \end{bmatrix} = \begin{bmatrix} \underset{\sim}{b}_2 - B_2^0 \underset{\sim}{w}^0 - B_2^1 \underset{\sim}{w}^m \\ F_2^1 \tilde{\underset{\sim}{v}}^1 \\ F_2^m \tilde{\underset{\sim}{v}}^m \end{bmatrix} \tag{2.15}$$

If $B_2^0 = 0$ then these equations can be permuted to block upper triangular form which makes the solution very convenient.

Other possibilities can be based on an elimination factorization of X_2^i say

$$X_2^i = P_i \begin{bmatrix} L^i \\ H^i \;\; I_p \end{bmatrix} \begin{bmatrix} U^i \\ 0 \end{bmatrix} \tag{2.16}$$

where P_i is a permulation matrix specifying the row interchanges. In this case

$$E^i = P_i \begin{bmatrix} 0 & L^i \\ I_p & H^i \end{bmatrix}, \quad G^i = \begin{bmatrix} I_q & | & 0 \end{bmatrix} P_i \tag{2.17}$$

If $P_i = I$ (no interchanges) then one possibility is

$$E^i = \begin{bmatrix} 0 & I_q \\ I_p & R^i \end{bmatrix}, \; \underset{\sim}{x}^i = \begin{bmatrix} I_q \\ R^i \end{bmatrix} \underset{\sim 2}{d}^i + \begin{bmatrix} 0 \\ F_1^i \, \tilde{v}^i \end{bmatrix}, \; R^i = H^i (L^i)^{-1} \;, \tag{2.18}$$

and R^i satisfies the matrix Riccati equation of invariant imbedding

$$\frac{dR}{dt} = A_{21} - RA_{11} + A_{11}R - RA_{12}R \;. \tag{2.19}$$

3. THE ERROR ANALYSIS IN OUTLINE

It has been possible to exploit the connection between multiple shooting and the stabilized march to give what is essentially a backward error analysis which shows that the stabilized march inherits the nice properties of multiple shooting provided $||F^i||$, $||E^i||$, and $\left|\left|\begin{bmatrix} F_1^i \\ G^i \end{bmatrix}^{-1}\right|\right|$ are of moderate size [2]. The key idea is to consider the transformation $\underset{\sim}{x}_i = E^i \underset{\sim}{c}^i + \underset{\sim}{w}^i$

where the E^i , $\underset{\sim}{w}^i$ are the quantities *actually computed* in carrying out the stabilized march. Introducing permutation matrices P_{pq} we can show that

$$P_{pq}\begin{bmatrix} I & & & \\ & F^1 & & \\ & & \ddots & \\ & & & F^m \end{bmatrix} M_m \begin{bmatrix} E^0 & & & \\ & E^1 & & \\ & & \ddots & \\ & & & E^m \end{bmatrix} P_{pq}^{-1} \begin{bmatrix} \underset{\sim}{c}_1 \\ \\ \underset{\sim}{c}_2 - \underset{\sim}{d}_2 \end{bmatrix} = \begin{bmatrix} \underset{\sim}{u}_1 \\ \\ \underset{\sim}{u}_2 \end{bmatrix} \tag{3.1}$$

where the right hand side is small under reasonable assumptions. The key assumption concerns the form of the error estimate considered because these methods are typically used in situations where both truncation error and rounding error (as the instability driver) are important. We have assumed that the error in integrating (1.1) from τ to $\tau + \Delta t$, for $\Delta t < \Delta t_0$ fixed, small enough, can be expressed in the form $||\underset{\sim}{a} - \tilde{\underset{\sim}{a}}|| \leq (K_1\Delta t^\alpha + K_2\varepsilon)\chi(||\tilde{\underset{\sim}{a}}||)$ where $\underset{\sim}{a}$ is the result of the exact integration, $\tilde{\underset{\sim}{a}}$ the computed solution, $\alpha > 1$, K_1, K_2, and ε are characteristic of the problem, of the numerical procedure used, and of the rounding error, and $\chi(z)$ satisfies (for $z \gtrsim 0$) (i) $\chi(z) \gtrsim 0$, (ii) $\chi(z)$ monotone nondecreasing, and (iii) $\chi(z) \lesssim 1+z$.

In conclusion, we note that the conditions implied by this analysis are satisfied by Godonov's algorithm, by the elimination algorithm with row interchanges provided $||(L^i)^{-1}||$ does not grow too large, but not in general by the algorithm which leads to the matrix Riccati equation. Thus the problem of critical lengths is connected directly with the stability of an L - U decomposition.

REFERENCES : [1] Osborne, M.R. : ' On shooting methods for boundary value problems' J. Math. Anal. and Applic., 27(1969) , pp 417-422. [2] Osborne M.R. : 'Aspects of the numerical solution of boundary value problems with separated boundary conditions', Working Paper, Computing Research Group, Australian National University. [3] Scott, M.R. and Watts, H.A. : Computational solution of linear two point boundary value problems via orthonormalisation', SIAM J. Numer. Anal., 14 (1977), pp 40 - 70.

INITIAL-VALUE PROBLEM INTEGRATION FOR SHOOTING METHODS

Donald G.M. Anderson
Division of Applied Sciences
Harvard University

Shooting methods reduce boundary-value problems to root finding problems involving the integration of initial-value problems. A major reason for continuing interest in shooting methods is the availability of sophisticated codes for both of these subproblems. More attention has been paid to exploiting the structure of the root finding than of the initial-value problems which arise. The design of integrators has been regarded as a separable issue, and the initial-value problems dealt with simply by using the best available general purpose code. In reviewing considerations in the design of integrators, Hull [1] parenthetically raised the question whether applicability to shooting methods should be among such considerations. I argue that this question should be answered in the affirmative, and furthermore, that closer attention should be paid to this aspect of the problem when designing codes for both initial and boundary-value problems.

Diekhoff et al [2] report careful comparisons of the performance of high-quality codes representing the three principal classes of integrators on a variety of boundary-value problems solved by a shooting method. As part of a project to evaluate mathematical software for initial-value problems, I had occasion to examine the performance in a shooting method of a number of other codes, then and now among the best available. Suffice it to say that the results are consistent with the conventional wisdom derived from the work over the past decade of authors too numerous to mention individually here (see [3], and references therein). For smooth, non-stiff problems of moderate size, Runge-Kutta methods perform well when derivative evaluations are inexpensive and low to moderate accuracy is required; extrapolation methods when evaluations are inexpensive and moderate to high accuracy is required; Adams predictor-corrector methods when evaluations are expensive or when the solution must be calculated at a large number of intermediate points. The state of the art demands adaptive selection of step size, and order when feasible, with higher order methods being preferred for smooth problems and moderate to high accuracy. It is very difficult to test, compare and evaluate codes, but intuition and experience seem in accord.

The integration of the initial-value problems dominates the cost of solving a boundary-value problem by shooting methods. There is room for ingenuity in exploiting the structure of the problem; the potential gains are high. The design of most integrators does not facilitate this, but could be enhanced to make them more effective tool for this, and other, purposes. Watts, see pages 19-39, surveys existing codes for initial and boundary-value problems. My remarks are complementary, and necessarily brief. It is possible only to offer a few suggestions and examples; a more detailed discussion will be presented elsewhere.

Codes vary widely in organization, but the underlying design philosophy seems to be that an integrator should ask for little more than is required to specify the problem, and produce an approximation to the solution at a specified terminal point. Such codes are useful for naive users, or experts on routine problems. And it can be very deliterious to performance to permit the unwary user to fiddle with a complicated, carefully tuned code. But the sophisticated user can reasonably ask for a more flexible tool for nonroutine use in challenging problems, and at a minimum, for more opportunity to monitor and control the course of the calculation.

For the sake of definiteness, consider the two-point boundary value problem

$$y'(x) = f(x,y,p) \quad , \quad a \leq x \leq b \; ,$$

$$g(y(a),y(b),p) = 0 \; ,$$

where $y,f \in R^n$, $p \in R^\ell$, $g \in R^{\ell+n}$. The vector of parameters p is to be determined as part of the solution. Extension to multipoint or overdetermined side conditions is straightforward. Assume that the user will supply routines for the evaluation of f , g and their first derivatives. We are interested in an ordinary, parallel or multiple shooting method in which candidate approximate solutions are defined piecewise as solutions of initial-value problems (to be solved by some given integrator). Let s be a vector whose elements are the set of initial conditions parameterizing the approximate solution. The task of finding s and p to enforce continuity of the piecewise solution and to satisfy the boundary conditions constitutes the root finding problem. Assume some version of the Newton method is used, probably incorporating damping, continuation and secant or chord method modifications. In addition to the initial-value problems defining y , and any others defining auxiliary quantities, this involves solving a much larger set of variational equations of the form

$$z'(x) = A(x)z(x) + c(x) ,$$

with suitable initial conditions, where $z, c \in R^n$ and $A \in R^{n\times n}$. A, c and the initial conditions involve y, f, g and their first derivatives — in particular

$$A(x) = \frac{\partial f}{\partial y}(x,y,p) .$$

For present purposes, we need not be more precise; further details are to be found in survey papers in these proceedings, especially those of Daniel, Bulirsh, Deuflhard and Scott.

For the sake of definiteness, think in terms of an integrator based on a variable-step, variable-order Adams predictor-corrector method which uses a Newton or chord method in the corrector iteration. The assumed availability of $\partial f/\partial y$ makes this iteration natural; it is sufficiently advantageous so that integrator users are increasingly being asked to supply $\partial f/\partial y$ even for non-stiff problems, or it is approximated internally. Some of the remarks to follow are relevant to other classes of integrators based on Runge-Kutta or extrapolation methods, but are most easily appreciated in the Adams method context. Some are relevant in altered form in finite-difference or finite-element methods. Some make additional demands on or provide new options for the user of the boundary-value-problem code; some can be implemented by the designer of shooting-method codes, as user of the integrator; some require modifications in the design of the initial-value-problem routine.

For simplicity, suppose there are no auxiliary quantities to be calculated and that no use is made of explicit boundary conditions to reduce the number of unknowns. In ordinary shooting, there are $\ell+n$ unknowns, and $\ell+n+1$ systems of n equations are to be integrated over the interval [a,b] — either from left to right or right to left. Let the interval [a,b] be divided into $m \geq 1$ subintervals. In parallel shooting, there are $\ell+mn$ unknowns and $m(\ell+n+1)$ systems to be integrated — either from left to right or right to left. Continuity conditions are imposed at $m-1$ interfaces between subintervals, for $m > 1$. (Ordinary shooting is the special case $m=1$.) In multiple shooting, m matching points are introduced interior to the subintervals, and continuity conditions are imposed there. Integration is carried out from left to right from a , from right to left from b , and both left to right and right to left from the interfaces between subintervals. There are $\ell+(m+1)n$ unknowns and $2m(\ell+n+1)$ systems to be integrated. We shall not consider other possible configurations of shooting and matching points. Assume ℓ , m and/or n are sufficiently large so that efficiency is a factor.

Probably the worst way to deal with these initial-value problems, for $m > 1$, would be to reduce them to a standard interval, say [0,1], by affine transformations of the independent variable, combine them into a grand system

$$Y'(t) = F(t,Y) \quad , \quad 0 \leq t \leq 1 \quad ,$$

and apply the integrator to determine $Y(1)$, given $Y(0)$. While this is formally convenient in theoretical discussions, it hides the structure of the initial-value problem. Unless the shooting points are optimally chosen, it forces the integrator to work on the scale of the most nonuniform subinterval. Although this can be alleviated in part by careful programming of the F and $\partial F/\partial Y$ (which will be very spars routines, performance of integrators often degrades nonlinearly with increasing size. Moreover, for damping, output, secant and chord metho modifications and other reasons, one would like to be able to solve for y alone, without z , in many instances. We can therefore reduce consideration to the canonical task of solving for y , or y and ℓ+n z's, on a single subinterval. The y and z equations can be combined in a single system, but there is internal structure to be exploited.

The variational equations are linear. The z's are coupled to y through A and c , but not to one another. A is common to all z equations: repetitious evaluations of A and c should be avoided. Adams method integrators could avoid the corrector iteration entirely for linear problems by solving the resulting linear system directly. The LU factorization can be used repeatedly. Moreover, A is often sparse: for example, when a higher order equation is reduced to a first-order system. This kind of sparsity could be detected and exploited if the integrator could accept specification of the higher order equation directly and carry out the reduction internally. One would like to take a single step in the y integration, then advance the z's through the same step (suppressing the step adjustment mechanism) exploiting the structure of the variational equations. This calls for a more elaborate system of communication with the user than most initial-value problem codes provide for, or a special purpose code.

The sparsity of $\partial f/\partial y$ could also be used in the corrector iteration in the y equation, perhaps by means of sparse matrix routines, using a user-specified or code-inferred sparsity pattern. (The Harwell multiple shooting code uses such routines, but in the Newton-method iteration for s and p.) This is most relevant for large n: for example, in the method of lines. At a minimum, one should demand that the linear equations solver inside the integrator be modularized so it could be replaced or used independently if desirable. (I have encountered the anomalous situation of having three copies of essentially the same linear equations package in a boundary-value problem program because two were inaccessible in initial-value problem and root-finding problem codes respectively.) This requires thorough documentation.

Consider the Newton-method iteration for s and p. We shall not concern ourselves here with the structure of the linearized problems at each stage; other papers in these proceedings deal with that subject. Rather, we observe that at a stage where the error in the root is of order ε (in some norm) we neglect terms of order ε^2 in defining the underlying affine approximation, and it is consistent to evaluate the function whose zero is sought with errors of order ε^2 and its derivative with errors of order ε. This has a number of implications: It motivates the use of the chord method or secant method updates once a good approximation to the derivative has been found. It indicates that the tolerance used in integrating the initial-value problems should be varied: moderate at the outset and refined as the iteration proceeds. It means that the z equations need not be integrated as accurately as the y equations. Only the latter issue needs further discussion.

Most initial-value problem codes accept a single tolerance against which some local error measure is compared. A few permit a vector of tolerances to be specified corresponding to the components of the solution vector. But this is helpful only in assuring that the y equation controls the selection of step size and order. Some could be modified to use different orders for different components; none that I am aware of allow different step sizes. If the y equation then the z equations are advanced, the z's could be advanced on a consistent but larger mesh than the y's. A more natural approach, in my opinion, is offered by observing that by asking for $\partial f/\partial x$ as well as $\partial f/\partial y$ and $\partial f/\partial p$, which are involved in the variational equations, we can evaluate

$$y''(x) = \frac{\partial f}{\partial y}(x,y,p)y'(x) + \frac{\partial f}{\partial x}(x,y,p)$$

Most implementations of variable-step, variable-order Adams methods make it awkward to use information about y''. But there are implementations which can easily be extended to do so, though no such code now exists to the best of my knowledge. (Analogous methods for stiff systems have been implemented, and fixed-step versions have a long history.) Methods which use y'' information are known to have superior accuracy and stability properties. Given that such Adams codes now commonly ask for $\partial f/\partial y$ anyway, it is reasonable to expect that they optionally accept $\partial f/\partial x$ and use y'' information. Second derivatives of f, thence z'', are less likely to be readily available; they must be simulated when solving the corrector equations. Suppose we advance the y equation using y'' information, with errors which are $O\{h^{2k}\}$ for some representative step size h. If the z equations are advanced using the same mesh points, without using z'', the corresponding errors will be $O\{h^k\}$. Such errors are consistent with the observation above.

The use of y'' requires evaluation of $\partial f/\partial y$ at each step, but this is used thereafter in the z equations. When solving only for y, it may be preferable not to use y'' – with a smaller step size – since $\partial f/\partial y$ need then be evaluated only when a chord method proves inadequate in the corrector iteration.

The structure considered above is essentially that of the initial-value problems within a given subinterval. Two further related elements will be discussed, necessarily more briefly: segmentation and iteration. The former connotes the fact that subintervals are introduced and dealt with independently; the latter that a sequence of initial-value problems with similar solutions are to be solved during the iteration.

All adaptive integrators need an initial step size. Higher order multistep methods need starting values. It is usual now to have the routine generate these automatically. For an Adams method this involves use of a small initial step size and low order, relying on the adaptive mechanism to adjust these thereafter. A cost penalty varying from code to code is exacted by this transient behavior. For parallel and multiple shooting methods there may be many such costly transients, and if m is too large there may be a significant loss in efficiency. With fixed-order, fixed-step multistep methods, a common practice was to use a self-starting method like Runge-Kutta or extrapolation or an iterative block (or composite) method to generate starting values. For multiple shooting, one should be able to integrate in either direction from a given set of starting values. Because the initial-value problems are embedded in an iterative process, it may be useful to consider saving information. With a tentative step size and order and an initial iterant known from the previous iteration, and $\partial f/\partial y$ available to facilitate iteration, a block method might be competitive. Or a poly-algorithm offering different order Runge-Kutta methods might be used initially, or even throughout the subinterval in the early stages of the iteration when lower accuracy requirements are imposed; overhead and stability considerations may make predictor-corrector methods less cost-effective for larger tolerances.

Segmentation facilitates treatment of singularities, discontinuities or nonuniformities. It permits transformations of the independent or dependent variables in individual subintervals; we can just sketch some possibilities. A user may know the nature and location of transition layers and should be able to make use of this knowledge. Transformation to an arc length independent variable should be standard integrator option (if second derivatives are used adjustments in radius of curvature are of interest); the burden of coping with nonuniformities should not fall wholly on the adaptive step-size and order adjustment mechanism or on the selection of shooting and matching points. A magnitude-phase representation is useful for oscillatory solutions. Cogent local coordinate systems may be known a priori, or inferred from the variational equations. Multiplicative or additive decompositions to handle known asymptotic behavior can be implemented locally; the solution on some subintervals may even be represented analytically, especially in singular problems. The number and location of interfaces between subintervals can be adjusted based on the detection of pathologies by the integrator; these may move during the course of the iteration – something which is easier to cope with in shooting than in finite difference or element methods. Calculation of subsidiary quantities like global error estimates, norms or condition numbers of solutions of the original, variational or auxiliary equations, etcetera can also be useful in this regard.

Assume that to improve the robustness of the Newton method scaling, damping and continuation are used. Continuation parameters can be incorporated in p and varied automatically, but the user should be allowed to control certain elements, thereby altering the initial value problem. In some problems, $b-a$ is determined as part of the solution. Continuation in this quantity is so useful that it should be a standard option in boundary-value problem codes. Segmentation facilitates this; for example, new segments can be added as b-a increases, or existing segments can be expanded.

Such devices are easier to employ if the integrator has a built-in interpolation scheme which can be used to invert changes of variable, find locations at which side conditions are satisfied, monitor the step-size and order adjustment mechanisms for rapid variations, test for satisfaction of constraints, etcetera, and communicate such information to the user as the integration proceeds. Obviously, they make demands also on the designer and user of the shooting method code. Integrators are normally designed for one-shot problems where a priori information about global properties of the solution is unavailable, or at least not used. Some of the devices discussed above depend on such knowledge being known in advance or determined in the course of the calculation. Their use may not be helpful unless the cost can be amortized over several calculations; but we are in fact dealing with iterative processes.

In conclusion, let me reiterate that the solution of the initial-value problems lies at the heart of a shooting method. For nontrivial boundary-value problems, one should not just rely on the best available general purpose integrator to deal with them straightforwardly.

[1] Aziz, A.K. (ed.), "Numerical Solutions of Boundary-Value Problems for Ordinary Differential Equations", Academic Press, 1975.

[2] Diekhoff, H.-J., Lory, P., Oberle, H.J., Pesch, H.-J., Rentrop,P. and Seydel, R., "Comparing Routines for the Numerical Solution of Initial-Value Problems of Ordinary Differential Equations in Multiple Shooting", Numerische Mathematik 27 (1977) 449-69.

[3] Enright, W.H. and Hull, T.E., "Test Results on Initial-Value Methods for Non-Stiff Ordinary Differential Equations", SIAM J. Num. Anal. 13 (1976) 944-61.

Acknowledgment: This work was supported in part by NSF GP-34723, GJ-37362 and MPS75-15469.

WORKSHOP: Selection of Shooting Points

F. T. Krogh, D.G.M. Anderson, R. Bulirsch,
I. Gladwell, M. R. Osborne, M. Scott

F. T. Krogh

When organizing this workshop I sent to the panelist (although to the wrong address in the case of Bulirsch) the following questions.

1. Is the selection of shooting points worth doing automatically?
2. How does the selection affect convergence for nonlinear problems?
3. How does the selection affect accuracy of the parameters being determined?
4. How does the selection affect accuracy of the solution?
5. How should continuity conditions be weighted vs. boundary conditions (when solving nonlinear problems)?
6. What criteria should be used to select the shooting points?

No matter what the answer to question 1, answers for 2-5 would help to answer 6. I think it is fair to say that at this point not enough is known to give anything more than the results of some experience and some opinions as far as question 6 is concerned. Such is the purpose of this workshop. I hope the contributions here will stimulate further work on this problem.

During the summers of 1969, 72, and 74, Jim Keener and I did some (unpublished) work on multiple shooting codes. Each summer we started over with a different overall design and different supporting software. (We switched nonlinear least squares solvers once, and initial value integrators twice.) All codes did automatic selection of shooting points, allowed for nonlinear multipoint boundary conditions, had special provision for finding eigenvalues, allowed for discontinuities, and had a number of other features. Variational equations were integrated in order to generate partials, and this of course gives information of value for the automatic selection of breakpoints. We started a new shot whenever $||V|| > K$ where V is the matrix of partials of the solution with respect to the initial conditions, and K is a constant which the user could specify. We would have preferred to use instead some estimate of the condition number of V, but it didn't seem to be worth the computational cost, especially when what we were doing seemed to work quite well. One should use a smaller value for K on the initial allocation, than on later shots, since changing breakpoints on the fly significantly slows convergence. (At least it did for us.) I believe we used different norms for $||V||$ in different codes, and if the approach outlined above is used, I would recommend a still different one. Namely,

$$||V||^2 = \sum_{j=1}^{n}\sum_{i=j}^{n} |V_{ij}||V_{ji}|$$

This norm has the important advantage that the norm is independent of the choice of units for the primary system.

Our codes were set up to solve overdetermined systems in a least squares sense and because of this, item 5 seemed to be an important issue, even affecting convergence when exact solutions were possible. When approaching convergence I believe the accuracy requested on the continuity conditions should be close to the global integration error on the shot to the left of the discontinuity. This is probably too stringent when a long way from the solution, although it might well be a good strategy if the tolerances used for the initial value integration were relaxed when far from the solution. Although our codes never reached this point, I believe the boundary value code should select the size of the error tolerance used in the initial value code; the user should however select the type (default, absolute, relative, etc.) of error control used for the primary system.

D. G. M. Anderson

A basic reason for using parallel or multiple shooting in nonlinear problems is reduction of the diameter of the ball of potential Newton iterants to facilitate convergence. Subsidiary considerations, relevant also to linear problems, are control of error propagation and maintenance of a well-conditioned relationship between parameters, the latter being a rather different issue for separated and non-separated boundary conditions. Assuming that we are solving both the original differential equation and corresponding variational equations, this suggests a strategy based on monitoring norms and condition numbers, or bounds thereon, as these quantities are generated, with attempts (under user control, periodic or by thresholds) to adjust shooting and matching points to roughly equilibrate the variation. A side-effect is suppression of spurious singularities at intermediate stages of the iteration. Strategies similar to this seem to have been employed successfully by a number of codes.

Segmentation of the interval is also useful to accommodate singularities, discontinuities or nonuniformities, either known a priori or inferred from the local behavior of the solution or the variable step and/or order integrator. It permits transformations of dependent and independent variables in individual segments, adapts readily to multipoint side conditions, and facilitates continuation in interval length. It provides a concise representation of the solution (as initial value problems defined on subintervals) for subsequent manipulation or generation of output; but output considerations should be secondary and a separate issue.

For these reasons, a shooting method code should provide both automatic and user-controlled options for shooting and matching point selection, if only as a tool for solving tough problems, and other facilities to aid the user in exploiting segmentation.

R. Bulirsch

In our experience the selection of shooting points is not crucial to the convergence behavior of our routine BOUNDSOL. We do the selection "outside" the routine in order not to overload the procedure. However in the case of optimal control the distribution of the shooting points was sometimes a matter of life and death if there were discontinuities in the dependent variables. These discontinuities usually arise from constraints in the state variables which then cause discontinuities in the corresponding Lagrange multipliers. Here at least, one shooting point had to be placed between consecutive discontinuities in order to prevent the routine from diverging. We do not have an explanation for this yet.

I. Gladwell

Codes should provide a facility to decide on the direction of integration so that the user can specify the direction of decaying solutions, if any. They should also permit the user to specify integration inwards from both ends as is sometimes necessary. Codes should also permit users to specify breakpoints in the range of integration so as to treat discontinuities satisfactorily. Clearly these breakpoints might be used as multiple shooting points but must not be used in an automatic shooting point selection code. If the length of the range is to be determined as part of the boundary value problem, this should be considered in the shooting point selection process; it is far from clear how. In a driver code for inexperienced users no information should be required concerning the shooting points except possibly the direction of integration. This implies that there must be an automatic selection of shooting points, however crude.

M. R. Osborne

1. Multiple shooting is conceptually an exact procedure. The aim of distributing the shooting points is to ensure that the numerical solution of the resulting system of equations is easy. If this is equivalent to making the condition number of the multiple shooting matrix relatively well conditioned, then we need to make the individual fundamental matrices X_i approximately equal in norm. This is a test which has proved serviceable.

2. If we consider finite differences as equivalent to multiple shooting with small spacing between the shooting points (i.e., small $\Delta t_i = t_{i+1} - t_i$) then we can suggest one possible method for choosing t_i. If the differential equation is

$$\frac{d\underset{\sim}{x}}{dt} = A(t)\underset{\sim}{x} + \underset{\sim}{f}(t)$$

then we desire

$$||X_i|| = ||I + A_i\Delta t_i + O(\Delta t_i)|| = \text{const.}$$

If we write the constant in the form $1+\gamma h$, then in the maximum norm the condition becomes

$$\frac{\Delta t_i}{h} = \frac{\gamma}{\varphi(A_i)}$$

where $\varphi(A_i) = (||I + A_i \Delta t_i|| - 1) / \Delta t_i = \sum_{k \neq j} |(A_i)_{jk}| + (A_i)_{jj}$

where j is the maximizing index in the row sums. This can be viewed as a change of variables from $t \to z$ where h is thought of as a mesh spacing in z, and where γ is a scale factor so that t=1 maps into z=1. We have picked mesh points by choosing points t_i corresponding to equispaced points in z.

This method has proved very favorable for nearly singular problems -- for example

$$(\epsilon + t) \frac{d^2x}{dt^2} = f(t, x)$$

On the other hand it is not good, for example, for singular perturbation problems as it suggests a uniformly fine distribution over the interval.

Preparation of this manuscript, and Krogh's contribution were supported by the National Aeronautics and Space Administration under Contract No. NAS 7-100, at the Jet Propulsion Laboratory.

COLSYS--A Collocation Code for Boundary-Value Problems

by

U. Ascher, J. Christiansen and R. D. Russell

1. Introduction

The methods which have been implemented in general purpose codes to solve systems of boundary-value ODE's can be divided into two groups. The first is that of initial-value methods (shooting), in which most of the current working codes fall (e.g., [35], [116], [238]). The second is that of global methods--finite difference and finite elements. Finite differences with deferred corrections have been implemented by Lentini and Pereyra [167 ,170]. As far as we know, ours is the only general-purpose code of this type based on finite elements.

Finite elements have been considered to be generally slower than other methods for ODE's and therefore have been ruled out of competition despite their attractive theory. We believe that finite-element methods, other than collocation, are indeed too slow; however, collocation at Gaussian points, when implemented efficiently, is competitive with finite differences [226], [227]. At the same time, collocation's sound theoretical footing has resulted in the derivation of effective algorithms for error estimation and mesh selection (see Section 2). These aspects and the stable performance of the procedure make it very attractive.

Consider a mixed order system of d (nonlinear) differential equations of orders $m_1 \leq m_2 \quad . . . \leq m_d$,

$$(1.1) \qquad u_n^{(m_n)}(x) = F_n(x; \underset{\sim}{z}(\underset{\sim}{u})) \qquad a < x < b, \; n = 1, . . . ,d,$$

where $\underset{\sim}{u} = (u_1, . . . ,u_d)$ is the sought solution vector and

$\underset{\sim}{z}(\underset{\sim}{u}) = (u_1, u_1', \ldots, u_1^{(m_1-1)}, u_2, \ldots, u_2^{(m_2-1)}, \ldots, u_d, \ldots, u_d^{(m_d-1)})$ is the vector of unknowns that would result from converting (1.1) to a first order system. These differential equations are subject to $m^* = \sum_{n=1}^{d} m_n$ (nonlinear) multi-point separated boundary conditions

$$(1.2) \qquad g_j(\zeta_j; \underset{\sim}{z}(\underset{\sim}{u})) = 0 \qquad j = 1, \ldots, m^*$$

where ζ_j is the location of the j-th boundary or side condition, $a \le \zeta_1 \le \zeta_2 \le \ldots \le \zeta_{m^*} \le b$.

The collocation method implemented in COLSYS solves (1.1)-(1.2) directly, without converting it to a first-order system. This is in contrast to other codes. A conversion to a first-order system would increase the size of the problem and change the algebraic structure of its discretization.

Let π be a mesh on $[a,b]$,

$$(1.3) \qquad \begin{cases} \pi : a = x_1 < x_2 < \ldots < x_N < x_{N+1} = b \\ h_i = x_{i+1} - x_i \;,\; i = 1, \ldots, N; \; h = \max\limits_{1 \le i \le N} h_i \;, \end{cases}$$

and $P_{\ell,\pi} = \{v; v|_{(x_i,x_{i+1})}$ is a polynomial of degree $< \ell$, $i = 1, \ldots, N\}$. The collocation approximation is a vector $\underset{\sim}{v} = (v_1, \ldots, v_d)$ such that $v_n \in P_{k+m_n,\pi} \cap C^{(m_n-1)}[a,b]$, $n = 1, \ldots, d$, with $k \ge m_d$ being the number of collocation points per subinterval (x_i, x_{i+1}). If $\{\rho_j\}_{j=1}^{k}$ are the Gauss-Legendre points on $[-1,1]$, then the collocation points are defined by

$$(1.4) \qquad x_{ij} := \frac{x_i + x_{i+1}}{2} + \frac{1}{2} h_i \rho_j =: x_{i+1/2} + \frac{1}{2} h_i \rho_j \qquad i = 1, \ldots, N \quad j = 1, \ldots, k.$$

The collocation solution $\underset{\sim}{v}$ is determined by requiring that

$$(1.5)\qquad v_n^{(m_n)}(x_{ij}) = F_n(x_{ij};\underset{\sim}{z}(\underset{\sim}{v})) \qquad j = 1, \ldots, k,\ i = 1, \ldots, N,\quad n = 1, \ldots, d$$

and that $\underset{\sim}{v}$ satisfy (1.2). Assuming that a sufficiently smooth isolated solution u to (1.1)-(1.2) exists, Newton's method converges quadratically to $\underset{\sim}{v}$ provided the initial approximation is close enough to $\underset{\sim}{u}$, and [43]

$$(1.6)\qquad \|u_n^{(\ell)} - v_n^{(\ell)}\| = O(h^{k+m_n-\ell}) \qquad \ell = 0, \ldots, m_n,\ n = 1, \ldots, d$$

$$(1.7)\qquad |(u_n^{(\ell)} - v_n^{(\ell)}(x_i)| = O(h^{2k}) \qquad i = 1, \ldots, N,\ \ell = 0, \ldots, m_n - 1,\quad n = 1, \ldots, d,$$

$$(1.8)\qquad \|\phi\| := \sup_{a\le x\le b} |\phi(x)|, \qquad \|\phi\|_{(i)} := \sup_{x_i\le x\le x_{i+1}} |\phi(x)| .$$

When writing any finite element code, the following aspects should be considered:

1. Basis functions
2. Linear-system solution
3. Error estimation
4. Mesh selection
5. Nonlinear-problem solution.

We briefly describe the selection of basis functions and the linear-system solver here; for full details the reader is referred to [14], [73].

For reasons of stability, efficiency and flexibility in order and continuity, B-splines were chosen as the basis functions. Restricted versions of de Boor's algorithms [69] were constructed, taking into account that (i) we are solving a system of ODE's, so many repetitive calculations can be avoided, (ii) the continuity of the piecewise polynomials at the mesh points is of a special type (i.e., there are exactly k knots in each interior mesh point for any of the d piecewise polynomial spaces), and (iii) frequently we evaluate the B-splines at points which are placed in a regular fashion in each subinterval (e.g., the collocation points). Significant savings are made in the evaluation of the B-splines and the solution and their derivatives.

For the solution of the linear equations for the coefficients of the piecewise polynomials defining v, resulting from the collocation approximation to a linear (or linearized) differential problem (1.1)-(1.2), we use the code of de Boor-Weiss [73]. This is possible after ordering the coefficients such that all those associated with one subinterval (x_i, x_{i+1}) are adjacent. The resulting matrix has an "almost block diagonal" structure (see [13, §4]). Gauss elimination with scaled row pivoting is performed.

We consider the error estimation and mesh selection as implemented in COLSYS in Section 2 and the implementation in COLSYS of a nonlinear solver in Section 3.

A number of test problems are reported in Section 4. They range from mildly difficult to difficult ones. We believe that some of the reported results cannot be achieved in a comparably efficient manner by any other current code.

All the computations reported here were carried out at the University of British Columbia, using the IBM Fortran H compiler with double precision (14 hexadecimal digits). The first two examples were clocked under MTS on the Amdahl V/6-II and the last two on the IBM 370/168, which is about 1.6 times slower for our code.

2. Algorithms for error estimation and mesh selection

When the number of collocation points per subinterval, k, is made large enough so that $k > m_d$, the following local error behaviour holds [13], [228]. At $x \in [x_i, x_{i+1})$

$$\text{(2.1)} \qquad e_n^{(\ell)}(x) := u_n^{(\ell)}(x) - v_n^{(\ell)}(x) = \frac{u_n^{(k+m_n)}(x_i)}{2^{k+m_n-\ell}} P_n^{(\ell)}\left(\frac{2}{h_i}(x - x_{i+1/2})\right) h_i^{k+m_n-\ell}$$

$$+ O(h^{k+m_n+1-\ell}) \qquad \ell = 0, \ldots, m_n, \; n = 1, \ldots, d$$

where

$$\text{(2.2)} \qquad P_n(\xi) := \frac{d^{k-m_n}}{d\xi^{k-m_n}} p(\xi); \qquad p(\xi) \equiv p(k;\xi) := \frac{(\xi^2 - 1)^k}{(2k)!} \qquad -1 \le \xi \le 1.$$

The error expression (2.1) is basic to both our mesh selection and our error estimation strategies. Note that by neglecting the higher order, but global term, an a posteriori error estimate can be obtained directly from (2.1) by using the computed solution in order to approximate $u_n^{(k+m_n)}(x_i)$, as done for mesh selection later. The obtained procedure for error estimation, however, is unreliable. This is because (i) the estimate depends explicitly on the high convergence rate of $k + m_n - \ell$ which often is not achieved in practice, (ii) the approximation to the high order derivatives $u_n^{(k+m_n)}(x_i)$ may be inaccurate, and (iii) the neglected global higher order term in (2.1) is not always of negligible magnitude.

Our error estimate is obtained by halving the mesh, computing another approximate solution and comparing the two approximations [13]. Let the meshes be $\{x_i\}_{i=1}^{N+1}$ and $\{\hat{x}_i\}_{i=1}^{2N+1}$, with $\hat{x}_{2i-1} := x_i$, $\hat{x}_{2i} := x_{i+1/2}$, and let the corresponding collocation solutions be $\underset{\sim}{v}$ and $\hat{\underset{\sim}{v}}$, respectively. For fixed values of n, ℓ and i, $1 \le n \le d$, $0 \le \ell \le m_n - 1$, $1 \le i \le N$, compute the values

$$\Delta_1 := |v_n^{(\ell)}(x_{i+1/6}) - \hat{v}_n^{(\ell)}(x_{i+1/6})|; \; \Delta_2 := |v_n^{(\ell)}(x_{i+1/3}) - \hat{v}_n^{(\ell)}(x_{i+1/3})|.$$

Then (2.1) gives

$$\text{(2.3)} \qquad \max_{x\in[\hat{x}_{2i-1},\hat{x}_{2i}]} |u_n^{(\ell)}(x) - \hat{v}_n^{(\ell)}(x)| \doteq w_{k,k-m_n+\ell}(\Delta_1 + \Delta_2)$$

where $w_{k,\nu}$ are precomputed weights which are stored in COLSYS as constant data $(k = 1, \ldots, 5,\ \nu = 0, \ldots, k-1)$.

This method of computing error estimates has proved to be suitable in practice, as it is not as affected by the difficulties mentioned above. When the mesh is very inappropriate, the error estimate (2.3) tends to become less reliable, but when the mesh is adequate, even if it is highly nonuniform, the error estimate (2.3) becomes quite accurate.

The same remarks hold for the mesh-selection algorithm described below. It performs well only when the mesh to be refined sufficiently reflects the solution's behaviour. Thus, in general we only trust it to a certain extent. As a consequence, the process of halving the mesh is not just done for error estimation, but also as a complementary mesh refinement option and a useful check on the mesh selection procedure.

Consider now the problem of selecting a mesh $\{x_i^*\}_{i=1}^{N^*+1}$ in order to equidistribute the local (and hopefully dominant) term in the error expression (2.1). This is done using a previously computed solution $\underset{\sim}{v}$ on a "current mesh" $\{x_i\}_{i=1}^{N+1}$.

Given a set of tolerances tol_j and pointers $ltol_j$, $j = 1, \ldots, ntol$ $(1 \le ltol_j \le m^*; 1 \le ntol \le m^*)$, the code attempts to satisfy

$$\text{(2.4)} \qquad \|z_\nu(\underset{\sim}{u}) - z_\nu(\underset{\sim}{v})\| \le tol_j + \|z_\nu(\underset{\sim}{v})\| tol_j \qquad \nu = ltol_j\,,\quad j = 1, \ldots, ntol.$$

We aim at finding $\{x_i^*\}_{i=1}^{N^*+1}$ such that, when halved, it yields an approximate solution which satisfies (2.4) with a minimum N^*. This minimizes the computational effort involved. Thus we try to equidistribute the error.

For a given $ltol_j$, let n and ℓ be the corresponding component index and derivative index, i.e., $\sum_{\mu=1}^{n-1} m_\mu + \ell + 1 = ltol_j$. From (2.1) we have that

$$(2.5) \qquad \|e_n^{(\ell)}\|_{(i)} \doteq c_{k,k-m_n+\ell} |u_n^{(k+m_n)}(x_i)| h_i^{k+m_n-\ell} \qquad i = 1, \ldots, N$$

where the $c_{k,\nu}$ are computable constants stored in COLSYS. Letting

$$(2.6) \qquad s_j(x) := \frac{c_{k,k-m_n+\ell}}{tol_j(1 + |v_n^{(\ell)}(x)|)} |u_n^{(k+m_n)}(x)|$$

and

$$(2.7) \qquad s(x) := \max_{1 \le j \le ntol} [s_j(x)]^{1/k+m_n-\ell}$$

(for each j, n and ℓ defined as above), we get that (2.4) is approximately satisfied by requiring

$$(2.8) \qquad s(x_i^*)h_i^* \le 1 \qquad i = 1, \ldots, N^*.$$

The last requirement is approximately satisfied using the solution $\underset{\sim}{v}$ on the mesh $\{x_i\}_{i=1}^{N+1}$ to obtain an easily computed expression--see [13,§2] for full details and explanations. Here, we simply define

$$\hat{u}_n(x_{i+1}) := \frac{2|v_n^{(k+m_n-1)}(x_{i+1}) - v_n^{(k+m_n-1)}(x_i)|}{x_{i+2} - x_i} \qquad i = 1,\ldots,N-1,$$

$$\hat{u}_n(x) := \begin{cases} \hat{u}_n(x_i) & x \in [x_i, x_{i+1}) \qquad i = 2,\ldots,N \\ \hat{u}_n(x_2) & x \in [x_1, x_2) \end{cases}$$

$$\hat{v}_j(x) := v_n^{(\ell)}(x_i) \qquad x \in [x_i, x_{i+1})$$

and

$$(2.9) \qquad \hat{s}(x) := \max_{1 \le j \le ntol} \left[\frac{c_{k,k-m_n+\ell} \cdot \hat{u}_n(x)}{tol_j(1 + |\hat{v}_j(x)|)}\right]^{1/k+m_n-\ell} \qquad x \in [a,b].$$

Then $\hat{s}$ is a piecewise constant computable function and (2.4) is satisfied up to order h by requiring

$$(2.10) \qquad \int_{x_i^*}^{x_{i+1}^*} \hat{s}(x)dx = 1 \qquad\qquad i = 1, \ldots, N^*.$$

In practice, (2.10) cannot always be used to determine N^* because the collocation solution $\underset{\sim}{v}$ used to compute $\hat{s}$ may be very inaccurate and because we wish to satisfy (2.4) after halving a mesh selected by the algorithm. We therefore determine N^* first, as described below, and then use the principle of error equidistribution in order to define the mesh points x_i^* :

$$(2.11) \qquad \int_{x_i^*}^{x_{i+1}^*} \hat{s}(x)dx = \frac{1}{N^*} \sum_{\mu=1}^{N} \hat{s}(x_\mu)h_\mu , \qquad\qquad i = 1, \ldots, N^*.$$

The choice of N^* and the decision whether to select a different mesh at all, rather than just halving the current mesh $\{x_i\}_{i=1}^{N+1}$ (and obtaining an error estimate) are incorporated into the following:

<u>General algorithm for mesh selection and error estimation</u>

1. Given the current mesh $\{x_i\}_{i=1}^{N+1}$, compute a collocation solution $\underset{\sim}{v}$.

2. If the nonlinear iteration for $\underset{\sim}{v}$ does not converge, halve the current mesh. If the new mesh is larger than $\overline{N}$, the maximum allowable from storage specifications, then exit; otherwise, let the refined mesh become the current one and go to step 1.

3. If the current mesh has been obtained by halving a former one, and convergence occurred on both, then compute error estimates using (2.3) and check if (2.4) are satisfied. If yes, then exit.

4. Compute

$$r_1 := \max_i \hat{s}(x_i)h_i , \quad r_2 := \sum_{i=1}^{N} \hat{s}(x_i)h_i \quad \text{and} \quad r_3 := \frac{r_2}{N} .$$

5. If $r_1 < 2r_3$ then halve the current mesh, let the refined mesh become the current one and go to step 1.

6. Define $N^* := \min\{\frac{1}{2}\bar{N}, N, \frac{1}{2}\max\{N, r_2\}\}$, determine $\{x_i^*\}_{i=1}^{N^*+1}$ according to (2.11) and let this mesh become the current one, and go to step 1.

Remarks

1. The ratio $\frac{r_1}{r_3}$ represents the amount by which the mesh fails to be equidistributed.

2. The choice of N^* is made so that $\frac{1}{2}N \leq N^* \leq N$ and so that a subsequent halving of the mesh is possible. Also, r_2 is a prediction by the code, using (2.10), for the optimal N^*.

3. As an added measure of caution, the mesh is automatically halved if

(i) the size of the current mesh is smaller than that of the former mesh, or

(ii) there have been 3 consecutive mesh selections resulting in the current mesh size N, or

(iii) there have been 3 consecutive pairs of mesh selections followed by mesh halving, resulting in the same mesh size N.

All of the above restrictions serve as safeguards to ensure a smooth transition from the initial stage, where inadequate information is available, to an advanced stage, where the mesh selection procedure in step 6 of the algorithm is based on enough information to perform well. At that stage the meshes produced automatically by the code are usually far superior to those which human intuition would produce. This is demonstrated by examples in Section 4.

3. The nonlinear solver

For appropriate vector functions $\underset{\sim}{v} = (v_1, \ldots, v_d)$ and $\underset{\sim}{w} = (w_1, \ldots, w_d)$ consider the linearized differential operators of (1.1)-(1.2),

$$(3.1) \qquad L_n \underset{\sim}{w} \equiv L_n(\underset{\sim}{v})\underset{\sim}{w} := w_n^{(m_n)} - \sum_{\ell=1}^{m^*} \frac{\partial F_n(\cdot; \underset{\sim}{z}(\underset{\sim}{v}))}{\partial z_\ell} z_\ell(\underset{\sim}{w}) \qquad n = 1, \ldots, d,$$

$$(3.2) \qquad \beta_j \underset{\sim}{w} \equiv \beta_j(\underset{\sim}{v})\underset{\sim}{w} := \sum_{\ell=1}^{m^*} \frac{\partial g_j(\zeta_j; \underset{\sim}{z}(\underset{\sim}{v}))}{\partial z_\ell} z_\ell(\underset{\sim}{w}) \qquad j = 1, \ldots, m^*.$$

It is assumed that the Green's function exists for the problem

$$(3.3) \qquad \begin{cases} L_n(\underset{\sim}{u})\underset{\sim}{w} = 0 & n = 1, \ldots, d \\ \beta_j(\underset{\sim}{u})\underset{\sim}{w} = 0 & j = 1, \ldots, m^* \end{cases}$$

and this, together with sufficient smoothness assumptions, implies that Newton's process of quasilinearization converges quadratically if the initial approximation is sufficiently close to $\underset{\sim}{u}$ [43].

The fast convergence of Newton's method when the available approximation is close to the one sought is particularly attractive in our setting of solving on a number of meshes. After convergence for the first time (on a coarse mesh), an excellent initial approximation is available for the nonlinear iteration process on subsequent meshes. On the other hand, it is well known that if the initial approximation is far away from the solution, Newton's method tends to perform inconsistently. Thus, if we were to use "pure" Newton's method alone, we might at times not achieve convergence at all. Moreover, if the first mesh is very inadequate, we would not like to invest too much time in trying to converge to a noisy piecewise polynomial approximate solution, but rather to refine the mesh and try again.

These considerations prompt us to use a modified (or damped) Newton's method. In particular, given an approximate solution $\underset{\sim}{v}^s$, a (hopefully better) approximate solution $\underset{\sim}{v}^{s+1}$ is obtained by setting

$$(3.4) \qquad \underset{\sim}{v}^{s+1} := \underset{\sim}{v}^s + \lambda_s \underset{\sim}{w}^s$$

where $\underset{\sim}{w}^s$, the Newton correction, is the collocation solution of the linear problem

$$(3.5) \qquad \begin{cases} L_n(\underset{\sim}{v}^s)\underset{\sim}{w} = f_n & n = 1, \ldots, d \\ \beta_j(\underset{\sim}{v}^s)\underset{\sim}{w} = \gamma_j & j = 1, \ldots, m^*. \end{cases}$$

Here L_n, β_j are as defined in (3.1), (3.2) and

$$(3.6) \qquad f_n \equiv f_n(\cdot;\underset{\sim}{v}^s) := -[v_n^{(m_n),s} - F_n(\cdot;\underset{\sim}{z}(\underset{\sim}{v}^s))]$$

$$(3.7) \qquad \gamma_j \equiv \gamma_j(\underset{\sim}{v}^s) := -g_j(\zeta_j;\underset{\sim}{z}(\underset{\sim}{v}^s)).$$

The scalar λ_s, $0 < \lambda_s \leq 1$, is the relaxation factor. When $\lambda_s = 1$, the "pure" Newton step is obtained.

The important practical and theoretical questions on controlling the relaxation factor λ_s to ensure some sort of monotonic convergence have been dealt with in depth by Deuflhard [78], [79], [80]. We have adopted a version of his scheme for the case where the Jacobian is nonsingular. This scheme consists of prediction and correction (if needed) for the value of λ_s in each iteration; see [, § 2] for details. Essentially, this monitoring of λ_s involves calculating at each iteration a collocation solution, $\overline{\underset{\sim}{w}}^{s+1}$, for the problem with a fixed Jacobian

$$
(3.8)\qquad \begin{cases} L_n(\underset{\sim}{v}^s)\underset{\sim}{w} = f_n(\cdot;\underset{\sim}{v}^{s+1}) & n = 1, \ldots, d \\ \beta_j(\underset{\sim}{v}^s)\underset{\sim}{w} = \gamma_j(\underset{\sim}{v}^{s+1}) & j = 1, \ldots, m^*. \end{cases}
$$

This additional computation is much cheaper than that for (3.5) because the Jacobian collocation matrix does not have to be recreated or reinverted after solving (3.5)--only the right-hand side changes. Appropriate norms of $\underset{\sim}{w}^s$ and $\bar{\underset{\sim}{w}}^{s+1}$ and of the right-hand sides of (3.5) and (3.8) are compared in order to decide whether to accept or reject the current value of λ_s . In case of rejection, a correction is made for λ_s using $\underset{\sim}{w}^s$ and $\bar{\underset{\sim}{w}}^{s+1}$, and the process is repeated. In case of acceptance, these values are used to predict a relaxation factor λ_{s+1} for the next iteration.

If at some point in the iteration process the predicted or corrected value for λ_s becomes smaller then a tolerance λ_{min} (we take $\lambda_{min} := .01$), then the iteration process is terminated with "no convergence." The mesh is then halved (lacking reliable information for a better refinement strategy) and the nonlinear iteration procedure is initiated again with $\lambda_0 := \lambda_{min}$.

The convergence criterion we use for the nonlinear iteration process is

$$
(3.9)\qquad \|z_\ell(\underset{\sim}{v}^{s+1}) - z_\ell(\underset{\sim}{v}^s)\| \le tol_j(1 + \|z_\ell(\underset{\sim}{v}^{s+1})\|) \quad \ell = ltol_j \quad j = 1, \ldots, ntol.
$$

See [80] for more details on this point.

The above-described procedure is designed to iterate cautiously, and has proved very effective for sensitive problems. However, if the mesh is refined in order to improve the accuracy (in an attempt to satisfy the error tolerances (3.9)) after having obtained convergence on the previous mesh, then in general we have a very good initial approximation at hand. Therefore, if the problem is not very sensitive we may abandon the extra caution at this point and proceed with the "pure" Newton's method. In fact, we iterate with a fixed Jacobian as well, as long as the norm of the right-hand side in (3.5) decreases monotonically and fast enough. Often only one full Newton iteration is needed for convergence on all but the first mesh. Since the final mesh is usually significantly finer than the first one, an efficient process is obtained.

In COLSYS, the user sets a value of a flag to describe his problem as "regular" or "sensitive." The nonlinear solver has two modes of operation, "cautious" and "fast." The "cautious" mode is one described earlier, which uses the modified Newton method with the careful control of the relaxation factor. This mode is used whenever there has been no convergence on the former mesh, in particular whe the current mesh is the initial one. If the problem is "regular," when convergence on the former mesh has been achieved and the mesh is refined, then the mode switches to "fast." One then proceeds with full Newton steps and iteration with a fixed Jacobian, reinverting the Jacobian only when the right-hand side norm of (3.5) fails to decrease each iteration by a factor μ (we take $\mu := 4$). If at some stage the norm of the right-hand side increases, then the mode is switched back to "cautious" with $\lambda_0 := \lambda_{min}$. Also, if the problem is "regular" then initially $\lambda_0 := 1$. If t problem is "sensitive" then the "fast" mode is never used and for each mesh the predicted initial value for the relaxation factor is initially $\lambda_0 := \lambda_{min}$.

4. Numerical examples

In order to demonstrate the efficacy of COLSYS, selected examples are examined now. None of these examples is "easy" to solve, at least not for the most extreme parameter values reported here, and they should be interesting to try on any code.

In the examples, the following notation is used:

$u_i(x)$ - ith component of the exact solution.

$E(u_i^{(j)})$ - uniform error in $u_i^{(j)}(x)$ (available when the exact solution is known).

est $E(u_i^{(j)})$ - estimated uniform error in $u_i^{(j)}(x)$ using (2.3).

$\text{est}_1 E(u_i^{(j)})$ - (unreliable) estimated uniform error in $u_i^{(j)}(x)$ using (2.1).

$\text{tol}(u_i^{(j)})$ - combined error tolerance for the component $u_i^{(j)}(x)$. (COLSYS allows the user to specify different tolerances for different components, and the mesh selection algorithm considers only those components for which tolerances are specified, cf. §2.)

time - actual solution time in seconds, including error checking time.

$a \pm b$ - $a \cdot 10^{\pm b}$.

k - number of collocation points per subinterval.

N(I) - successive mesh sizes, i.e., numbers N of subintervals required, followed in parenthesis by the number of Newton iterations performed on each mesh for nonlinear problems.

The errors $E(u_i^{(j)})$ are approximated by measuring the error at 3 equally spaced points in each subinterval. The initial meshes are uniform unless otherwise stated. In the case of continuation, i.e., using a formerly obtained solution for the initial approximation of another problem, the new mesh is twice as coarse as the mesh on which this initial approximation is defined.

Example 1 [127]

$$\varepsilon y'' + xy' = -\ \varepsilon\pi^2\cos(\pi x) - (\pi x)\sin(\pi x) \qquad -1 \le x \le 1$$

$$y(-1) = -2, \quad y(1) = 0.$$

Solution: $u(x) = \cos(\pi x) + \text{erf}(x/\sqrt{2\varepsilon})/\text{erf}(1/\sqrt{2\varepsilon})$.

This linear problem has a turning point at $x = 0$. The transition layer is of width $O(\sqrt{\varepsilon})$. Initial value codes cannot solve this problem for small ε, as the associated initial value problem becomes extremely ill conditioned. The turning point layer also causes difficulties for finite difference or finite element general purpose codes.

We use the example to give a detailed demonstration of the mesh selection and error estimation algorithms. With $\varepsilon = 10^{-6}$, we take $k = 4$ and $\text{tol}(u) = \text{tol}(u') = 10^{-6}$. In Table 1 we list, in addition to est E and est E', the unreliable estimates $\text{est}_1 E$ and $\text{est}_1 E'$.

Table 1 - Example #1 with $\varepsilon = 10^{-6}$

N	E	est_1E	est E	E'	$\text{est}_1\text{E}'$	est E'	number of mesh points in (-.01,.01)
8	.12 + 3	.14 - 1		.12 + 5	.45		1
16	.30 + 2	.14 - 1	.36 + 1	.59 + 4	.90	.15 + 3	1
32	.74 + 1	.14 - 1	.89	.29 + 4	.17 + 1	.73 + 2	1
64	.16 + 1	.12 - 1	.21	.12 + 4	.31 + 1	.35 + 2	1
128	.21	.79 - 2	.39 - 1	.32 + 3	.40 + 1	.16 + 2	1
128	.82	.11 + 2		.77 + 3	.38 + 4		2
128	.53 - 1	.15 - 1		.15 + 3	.21 + 2		4
256	.92 - 3	.69 - 3	.17 - 2	.30 + 1	.18 + 1	.49 + 1	8
128	.59 - 4	.16 - 4		.13 + 1	.73 - 1		49
256	.13 - 5	.80 - 5	.48 - 5	.50 - 1	.72 - 1	.46 - 1	98
128	.41 - 8	.66 - 5		.20 - 4	.26 - 2		98
256	.12 - 9	.12 - 6	.86 - 10	.63 - 6	.96 - 4	.63 - 6	196

Total time = 5.55.

Note that the last mesh with 128 subintervals has the tolerances satisfied, but there is no reliable error estimate available at that point. Note also the performance of the error estimator as the meshes improve.

Comparing the errors on the second mesh of 128 subintervals and the last mesh of the same size we see that an improvement of 8 significant digits has been obtained. Almost all the points in the last two meshes are within and around the transition layer.

Example 2 [238], [89]

$$y'' = \mu \sinh(\mu y) \qquad 0 \le x \le 1$$

$$y(0) = 0, \ y(1) = 1.$$

This example, due to Troesch, has been treated extensively in the literature (see [238] and references therein). The solution rises sharply from ≈ 0 to 1 as x approaches 1, and the slope gets steeper as μ gets larger.

Actually, for global methods the problem is not so difficult from the nonlinear standpoint. The "pure" Newton method may converge even for rather inadequate meshes. However, highly nonuniform meshes are necessary to get a few digits accuracy.

We list results for $\mu = 10, 20, 30$ and 40 in Table 2. Here continuation is used for entries 2, 3, and 4 in order to save time. The final entry relates to a calculation for $\mu = 40$ without continuation. For the first and last entries, the initial approximation is $v^0(x) := x$

Table 2 - Example #2; $tol(u) = tol(u') = 10^{-5}$; $k = 4$ for final mesh

#	μ	continuation	time	est E	est E'	N(I)
1.	10	no	1.83	.16 - 7	.33 - 3	8(11),8(5),8(4),16(3), 13(2),26(2),56(2)
2.	20	(1)	5.21	.51 - 8	.14 - 1	26(13),20(6),40(4),24(3), 48(3),25(2),50(2),100(2)
3.	30	(2)	6.44	.80 - 7	.15 + 2	50(13),32(4),64(4),36(3) 72(2),37(2),74(2)
4.	40	(3)	7.76	.38 - 7	.10 + 4	37(13),37(6),37(5),74(3), 47(2),94(2),188(2)
5.	40	no	26.41	.11 - 6	.34 + 4	8(40*),16(17),11(29), 22(2*),44(20),22(24), 44(13),26(19),52(10), 32(14),64(7),38(9),76(5), 43(5),86(4),46(3),92(2), 48(2),96(2)

* - no convergence reached; mesh halved automatically

In the last mesh for $\mu = 40$, of 95 interior mesh points 42 were inside $(1 - 10^{-6},1)$, and 81 were inside $(.99,1)$.

Example 3: The dimpling of spherical shells [276]

Consider the small finite deformation of a homogeneous, isotropic, thin elastic spherical cap subject to a quadratically varying axisymmetric external pressure distribution $p_1(1 - \xi^2/\xi_0^2)$ superimposed upon a uniform internal pressure distribution $-p_0$. Here ξ is the angle between the meridional tangent at a poin of the midsurface of the shell and the base plane and ξ_0 is the value of that angl at the only edge of the shell.

The governing equations in dimensionless form are $(x := \xi/\xi_0)$

$$\lambda[\varphi'' + \frac{1}{x}\varphi' - \frac{1}{x^2}\varphi] + \psi(1 - \frac{1}{x}\varphi) - \varphi = -\gamma x(1 - \frac{1}{2}x^2)$$

$$0 < x < 1$$

$$\mu[\psi'' + \frac{1}{x}\psi' - \frac{1}{x^2}\psi] - \varphi(1 - \frac{1}{2x}\varphi) = 0,$$

where φ is the dimensionless meridional angle change of the deformed shell and ψ is a stress function. The boundary conditions are

$$\varphi = x\psi' - \nu\psi + (1 - \nu)x = 0 \quad \text{at} \quad x = 0,1.$$

In the equations above let $\nu := .3$ and $\gamma := \frac{p_1}{p_0} = 1.1$. Thus we consider the case when the external pressure is of the same order of magnitude as the internal pressure, and slightly larger. The question is, when will a dimple be formed? This depends on the ratio of μ and $\varepsilon (\mu, \varepsilon << 1)$, where

$$\mu := \frac{p_0 a^2}{4EhH}$$

a - radius of the shell

h - thickness of the shell

$$\varepsilon^4 := \frac{h^2}{48(1 - \nu^2)H^2}$$

$H := \frac{1}{2} a\xi_0{}^2$ - height of apex above the base plane

E - Young's modulus

$$\lambda := \frac{\varepsilon^4}{\mu}$$

Using asymptotic analysis, F. Wan [276] has shown that dimpling may occur only when $\mu = O(\varepsilon) << 1$. Our calculations confirm his results.

Note that this problem has singular coefficients in the differential equations, a boundary layer near $x = 1$ and, if dimpling occurs, a transition layer in the interior (approximately at $x_t := \sqrt{\frac{2(\gamma - 1)}{\gamma}}$). Our code is ideally suited to handle this type of problem because there is no need to match numerical solutions to an analytic expansion in the neighbourhood of a singularity in the coefficients and the flexibility with mesh selection can resolve the layer regions.

In order to obtain the solution for $\mu = \varepsilon = .001$, we use a chain of simple continuations, starting each time with the formerly converged solution as a first initial approximation for the next problem in the sequence. The initial guess for the first problem is $\chi^0 \equiv 0$ and the chain of (μ,λ,γ) is $(.1,.5\text{-}3,1.05) \to (.1,.5\text{-}3,1.1) \to (.01,.1\text{-}5,1.1) \to (.464\text{-}2,.1\text{-}6,1.1) \to (.21544\text{-}2,.1\text{-}7,1.1) \to (.001,.1\text{-}8,1.1)$. With $k = 4$, the total time is 17.41 seconds to satisfy $tol(\varphi) = tol(\psi) = .1 - 5$. The profile for φ is given in Figure 1. For the final mesh of 72 subintervals 37 mesh points were in the interval $(.41,.45)$ and 16 in $(.99,1]$.

When using the last obtained solution as an initial approximation for the case $\mu = \lambda = .1 - 5 = \varepsilon^2$ (keeping $\varepsilon = .001$), no convergence was obtained. However, when starting with a zero initial approximation, convergence is promptly obtained, where the solution is essentially zero throughout the domain except for a boundary layer at the right end. The final mesh of 12 subintervals has all but one of its interior points inside $(.98,1]$. Also, for the case $\mu = .31623 - 1 \approx \sqrt{\varepsilon}$, $\lambda = .31623 - 10$ $(\varepsilon \approx .001)$, when using the solution with $\varepsilon = \mu = .001$ again as an initial approximation, convergence is obtained to a solution in which the transition layer begins to disappear and the boundary layer sharpens. The slope at the boundar layer is 3 orders of magnitude larger than that of the remainder of the transition layer (see Figure 1). Here the final mesh of 58 subintervals has 5 mesh points in $(.41,.45)$ and 21 in $(.999,1]$.

Example 4 [131], [241]

The final problem is

$$G'' + \frac{3-\nu}{2} HG' + (\nu - 1)H'G - s(G - 1) = 0$$

$$H''' + \frac{3-\nu}{2} HH'' + \nu(H')^2 - 1 + G^2 - sH' = 0$$

with boundary conditions

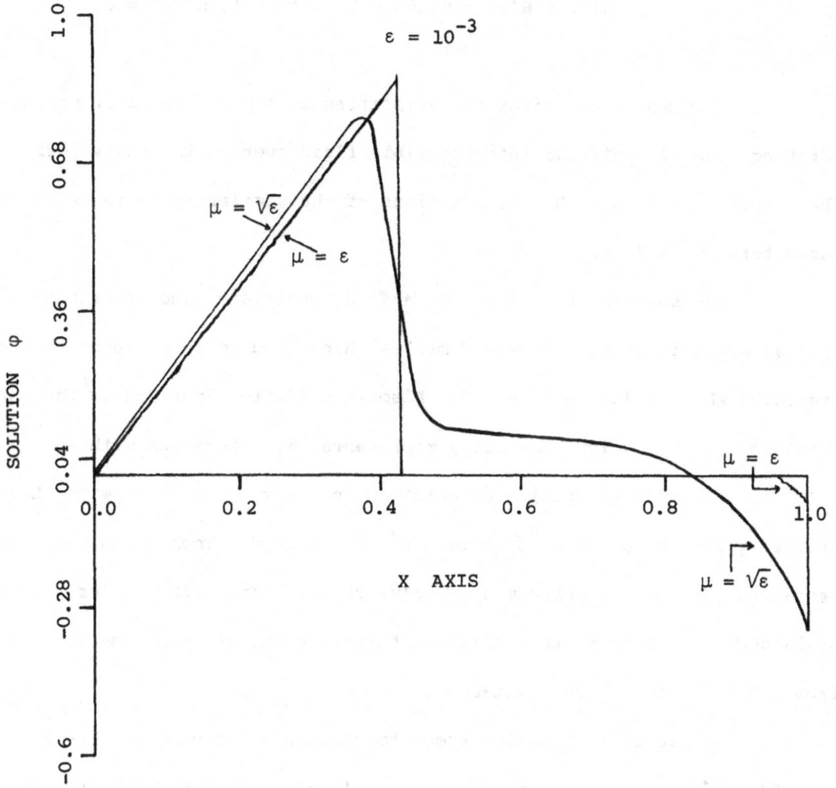
ε = 10^-3
1.0
0.68
0.36
0.04
-0.28
-0.6
SOLUTION φ
μ = √ε
μ = ε
0.0
0.2
0.4
0.6
0.8
1.0
X AXIS
μ = ε
μ = √ε

Figure 1

$$G(0) = H(0) = H'(0) = 0, \; G(\infty) = 1, \; H'(\infty) = 0.$$

This model describes the velocities in a boundary layer produced by the rotating flow of a viscous incompressible fluid over a stationary infinite disk. The velocities G and H are functions of the similarity variable x and the two parameters ν and s.

The solution functions G and H oscillate, and it is hard to find initial approximate solutions and meshes which lead to convergence of the nonlinear iteration when $\nu \uparrow 1$ and $s \downarrow 0$. Also, the finite right end of the interval of integration, L, which adequately represents ∞, increases with ν.

In order to obtain the solution for $\nu = .2$, $s = .2$ with $L = 60$, the initial guess $G := 1 - e^{-x}$, $H := - x^2 e^{-x}$ is used. Then a chain of continuations as described above is performed to solve for problems with smaller s, larger ν, or larger L. In order to facilitate this process, all problems are first mapped from $[0,L]$ onto the unit interval.

We use 2 continuation steps to get the solution for $\nu = .2$, $s = .05$, $L = 200$, and 7 more steps to get $\nu = .261$, $s = .05$, $L = 200$, in order to verify a result in [241]. The total time is approximately 2 minutes. For this value of L, however, there are still significant oscillations throughout the interval of integration, and an interval length of $L = 450$ is found more appropriate for these values of ν and s.

Increasing ν has the effect of spreading oscillations through a larger domain with a larger magnitude in H, necessitating the use of larger values of L and different meshes for adequate approximation. This also explains the need for small continuation steps for this sensitive problem (cf. [131], [241]).

In Figure 2 we plot the velocities G and H for $\nu = .3$, $s = .05$ and $L = 650$. This solution is obtained using continuation steps of $.005$ in ν and ~ 30 in L.

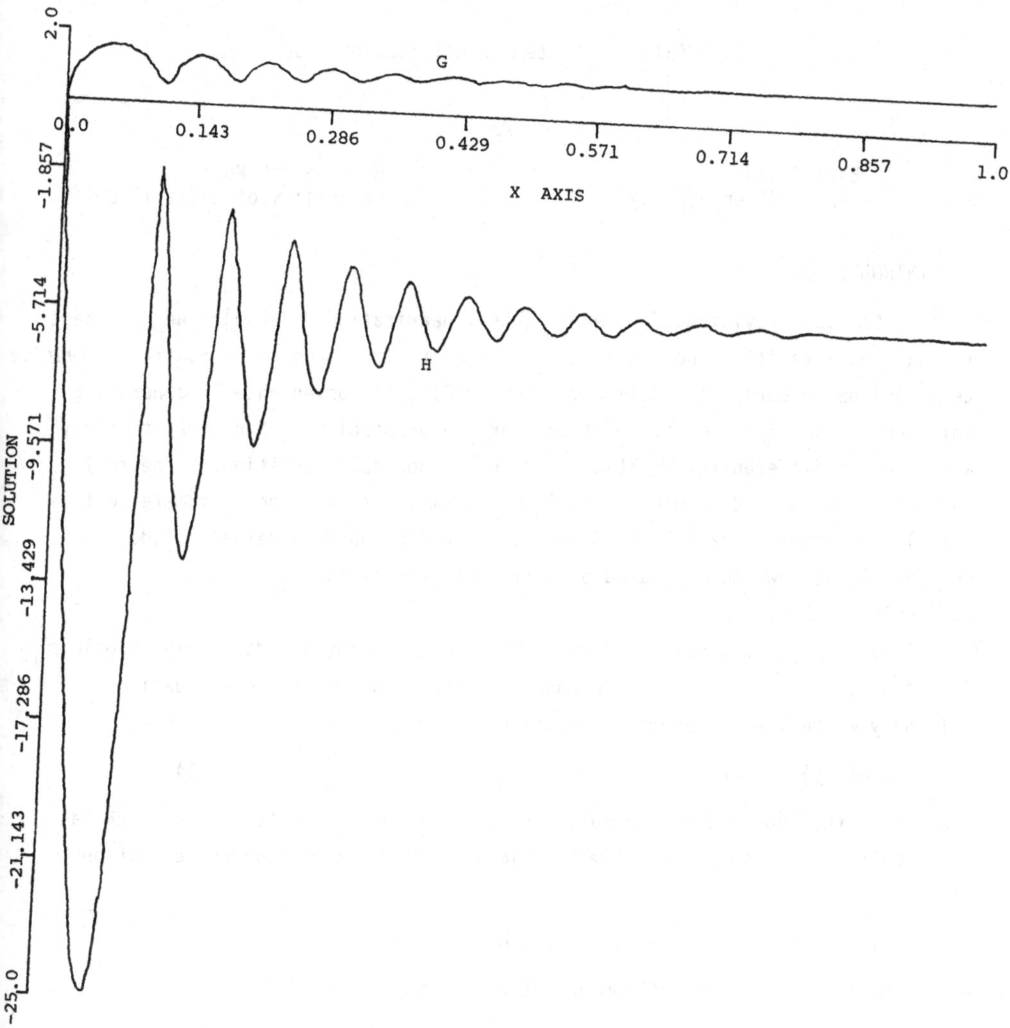
2.0
G
H
0.0
0.143
0.286
0.429
0.571
0.714
0.857
1.0
X AXIS
SOLUTION
-1.857
-5.714
-9.571
-13.429
-17.286
-21.143
-25.0

Figure 2

QUASII - A System Identification Code

by

Bart Childs
Texas A&M University

H.R. "Skip" Porter
University of Louisville

I. INTRODUCTION

QUASII is a revision of an early quasilinearization code[50]. We have kept the name because it is applicable to quasilinear first order systems (the derivative term must be linear). The design goal of QUASII was convenience in generating solutions to nonlinear multi-point boundary-value problems. Nonlinearities may arise on the differential equations and on the boundary conditions. The real-world problems we had on mind arise from system identification (parameter estimation) and generally have limited precision in the boundary values. Today's version also allows models based on difference equations.

2. GENERAL DESCRIPTION

QUASII is for the numerical solution of multi-point boundary-value problems in ordinary differential or difference equations. We write these equations (we will only write the differential equations)

$$\dot{y} = g(t,y) \qquad t \in [0, T] \tag{1}$$

where t is the independent variables and y is called the state vector which has N elements. The N equations (1) are subject to M separated boundary conditions of the form

$$q_j(y(t_j)) = b_j \qquad j = 1, 2, \ldots, M \quad (M \geq N) \tag{2}$$

We assume the boundary condition operators, q, to be like

$$y_{n_j}(t_j) = b_j \tag{3a}$$

or

$$\dot{y}_{n_j}(t_j) - b_j \tag{3b}$$

or

$$c_0 + c_1 y_1(tj) + \ldots + c_N y_N(t_j) = b_j \tag{3c}$$

or a form explicitly programmed by the user in a subroutine provided for such ad hoc procedures.

If $M > N$, then the problem is overdetermined, which is common in the problems of the design goal. Any boundary condition may be specified to be met exactly or in a least squares sense. If $M > N$, less than N boundary conditions may be met exactly.

System identification problems abound with constraints (a term which is more descriptive than boundary conditions without a boundary) of the type (3b) and (3c). In system identification problems, boundary conditions like (3b) will generally be nonlinear in terms of the state vector. If the differential equations or the boundary conditions are nonlinear, the user may supply linearizations or use automatic numerical differentiation.

The code is based on superposition of initial value solutions of the differential equation (1) (and a linearization of (1) if it is nonlinear). These methods are often called "shooting methods" which is in the same class as always calling constraints boundary conditions whether there exists a "boundary" or not.

The code is based on the superposition of particular solutions of (1) (and its linearization). The use of particular solutions reduces the effort required of the user, occasionally reduces numerical problems, and is logical. We assume

$$y(t) = P(t)a \tag{4}$$

where each column of the matrix P is a solution of (1) or the usual linearization thereof. Specifically,

$$\dot{p}^{(0)} = g(t,p^{(0)}) \tag{5}$$

where $p^{(0)}(0)$ is the best available estimate of $y(0)$ and

$$\dot{p}^{(k)} = g(t,p^{(0)}) + \left.\frac{\partial g}{\partial y}\right]_{y=p(0)} (p^{(k)} - p^{(0)}) \tag{6}$$

governs the perturbed solutions, $k = 1,2,\ldots, N$. The initial conditions $p^{(k)}(0)$ are identical to $p^{(0)}(0)$ except the kth element is perturbed by a nonzero constant. This will ensure linear independence [48].

The superscript is used to identify the vectors $p^{(k)}$. Notice the range of the columns of P and the elements of the vector of superposition constants is $k = 0, 1, 2,\ldots, n$. This convenient choice allows the zero elements to be associated with the unperturbed solution of (1) and the kth element to be associated with the particular solution of (1) or (6) obtained from perturbing the kth element of the initial value estimate. This choice makes code particularly easy to read if the supporting compiler allows zero subscripts. Fortran on many minicomputers support this and as well as the new standard Fortran.

Two straightforward proofs (or observations) are given in [48,49] which are basic to the code. The first is that the vector of superposition constants must satisfy

$$\sum_{k=0}^{n} a_k = 1 \qquad (7)$$

for the superposition of particular solutions to be a solution of (b). The second observation is that the solution (5) is a particular solution of (6) which negates the extra computations argument against the use of particular solutions given by Roberts and Shipman[221].

Each boundary condition gives an algebraic equation in terms of the superposition constant. Denoting the set of equations by

$$S\,a = d \qquad (8)$$

we again employ the null index and identify

$$S_{0,k} = 1 \qquad d_0 = 1 \qquad (9)$$

from the superposition identity. If the ith boundary condition operator is linear, then

$$S_{i,j} = q_i(p^{(j)}(t_i))$$

and (10)

$$d_i = b_i$$

If the ith operator is nonlinear, then the use of the chain rule and (4) is straightforward. Some special cases will be mentioned later.

The details of solving the overdetermined problem are a) reduce the entire set of equations (8) using pivotal elements from the equations to be met exactly (these include the superposition identity and any boundary conditions so specified b) perform the appropriate premultiplication by the transpose of the submatrix composed of rows and columns which have not furnished pivots c) complete the reduction and back substitution. See [48] for more details.

System identification is often referred to as parameter estimation. Unknown parameters are governed by the trivial differential equation of the derivative with respect to the independent variable being null. These parameters are taken to be the higher order elements of y.

3. USER REQUIREMENTS

The user must code the differential equations in a format consistent with the usual calls from initial value integrators. Specifically, the user must code a set of first order differential equations in FORTRAN like

```
DY(1) = f(Y(1), ... Y(N), T, ...)          (11)
  :
```

These statements are placed in a subroutine called RHS. If the equations (11) are nonlinear in y, then the user will also supply appropriate linearations of (11) or default to an automatic numerical differentiation. The latter will increase run time severalfold. The example presented later gives an example of (11) and its linearization.

In some cases, the user may also code particularly complex boundary conditions.

The only additional requirements is the preparation of an input data set which consists of five consecutive subsets, namely title, integer parameters, real (floating point) parameters, boundary conditions, and initial value estimates.

3.1 Title Information

The title information may be from 1 to 20 lines in length. It is printed as a heading at appropriate breaks in the output.

3.2 Integer Parameters

These include the desired level of output, a flag to indicate if the differential equations are linear, a flag to indicate automatic numerical differentiation of nonlinear differential equations, the maximum number of iterations, the number of boundary conditions, the number of differential equations (not including parameters), the number of constants or parameters on the state vector, a flag to indicate difference equations rather than differential equations, and a dozen or so more dealing with plotting, acceleration, and other routines for the experienced user.

3.3 Real Parameters

These input parameters include the nominal integration step size, a perturbation factor to ensure linear independence of the initial values, an overshoot control parameter for the nonlinear equation solver, end points of the integration range, accuracy requirements, etc.

3.4 Boundary Conditions

Each boundary condition requires the input of five parameters. Namely, the boundary value, the value of the independent variable, an index, the q operator of equation (2), and a flag specifying if the boundary condition is to be met exactly, in a least squares sense, or on a weighted least squares sense.

The q operator is taken to specify an element of the vector y if the input is positive (3 means y_3, etc), an element of $\dot{y}$ if negative (-2 means y_2, etc), or a linear combination of the elements of $\dot{y}$ if the input is zero. Large negative values cause a call to a special subroutine where the user may code the desired action.

3.5 Initial Values

The seven parameters used to define the initial value estimates are the index; a flag specifying the initial value is known and will not be allowed to change, unknown and bounded, or unknown and unbounded; the (estimated) value; the perturbation factor (which can override the one given in the Real Parameters; the upper and lower limits; and a minimum magnitude for the iterate. The last four parameters may be omitted, in most cases but this is not recommended. For example, positive parameters should be at least bounded between zero and the machine limit.

If the user wishes to stack multiple data sets, the code is structured such than only changes or added data need be input.

3.6 Typical Example

The example given in [48,49] is usually run with an input data set of 1 title cards, 5 integer parameter cards, 15 boundary value cards, and 5 initial value cards. The example is a spring-mass-dashpot with a forcing function. The differential equations may be written as

$$\dot{y}_1 = y_2 \qquad (12a)$$

$$\dot{y}_2 = -y_1y_4 - y_2y_3 + \sin(y_5\ t) \qquad (12b)$$

The parameters to be determined are the 3rd, 4th, and 5th elements of the state vector. They obey the differential equations with null right hand sides.

The boundary values at the indicated values of the independent variable are given in Table 1. These boundary values were obtained by integrating equations (12) with the initial conditions of

$$y(0) = [1.0,\ 0.5,\ 0.2,\ 1.0,\ 1.0]^T \qquad (13)$$

and then rounding to the values shown. An "estimate" of

$$y(0) = [1.2,\ 0.2,\ 0.05,\ 0.8,\ 1.2]^T \qquad (14)$$

was used to generate results, parts of which are pages 193-195.

t_i	b_i
1.0	-0.220
2.0	0.035
3.0	-0.474
4.0	-0.589
5.0	0.393
6.0	1.597
7.0	1.452
8.0	-0.388
9.0	-2.324
10.0	-2.274
11.0	0.088
12.0	2.711
13.0	2.997
14.0	0.401
15.0	-2.816

Table 1.
Boundary Values

These pages also give a brief idea of the type of interactivity which can be used with the system. Page 193 shows the first iteration with minimal output. The next page shows the linear equations (an overdetermined set) which are solved at the end of an iteration with a "high level of output. The first column of data is the boundary values which is actually the right-hand-side of the linear equation (8). It is displayed as the left most column because the first column of the coefficient matrix approaches it as convergence nears. The third page of results is typical of the output with a "low" level of output. It shows the "trace" of the solution at the boundary points is always output on the final iteration. This page of results has a typical "analysis of variance table" which is common in regression analysis. The confidence limits are estimated for the initial values and the boundary values.

4.0 QUASII versus the OTHERS

The many versions (variants might be better) of the code have been used in orbit determination, boundary layer calculation, optimal control, and parameter estimation in dynamical systems.

The primary advantages are 1.) the multipoint capabilities, 2.) each boundary condition can be met in a least squares, exact, or weighted least squares manner, 3.) statistical analysis of overdetermining boundary conditions, 4.) ease of use and 5.) quality and flexibility of output. We do not claim all these over all the others.

The disadvantages are that it uses a totally inadequate integrator as pointed out by Watts and it is not a multiple shooting code.

We are confident that our code is the worst of the general purpose codes for the plethora of boundary layer and other "stiff" problems which have been on exhibit at this conference. It is also my opinion (BC), that all these codes should include the capabilities for multipoint, least squares, and statistical analysis of the results to earn the claim of "real-world". It is not enough to be a design aid. After the hardware is built, the engineer must ascertain that the hardware built is what was designed.

5. SOME OBSERVATIONS AND OPINIONS

The current version of the code is most often run on an Amdahl 470 V6 in double precision (64 bit floating point operands). The Fortran dimension statements allow for a 20 element state vector, y, 200 boundary values-conditions, and 2,000 words of user accessable storyage for tables, etc. The run module for this version takes less than 320k bytes or approximately 40,000 64 bit words of memory. The execution time for the example in section is less than four seconds using numerical differentiation. If the user supplies the linearized differential equations, the execution time would be less than one second. The prime time costs for these runs would be approximately $6 and $1.20 respectively. These rates are comparable with those on commercial systems.

The numerical differentiation costs are worth it. Most professional analysts would spend much more (in terms of their salary) in making sure of the results of their differentiation and canceling terms. These savings are more dramatic when working with a set of 20 first order nonlinear ordinary differential equations.

The majority of the number crunching (in excess of 95% for the example) is in the numerical integration. For this reason, we see no need for concern in efficiency in the solution of equations (8), only reliability and accuracy are important.

We are usually concerned with problems where the final iteration is simply an initial value integration of the nonlinear ODEs with the "correct" initial values (this is difficult or impossible in some of the stiff problems). In each iteration we use an integration of the original ODE subject to the "best" initial value estimate available as the base solution. This gives the most straight-forward indication of convergence. That is, a "small" change in the initial value estimate or equivalently the superposition constants' approaching $[1,0,0...,0]^T$. The calculation of new estimates of the initial values is truly a Newton process. It is well known in solving nonlinear algebraic equations that an "approximate" Hessian is usually sufficient if the calculated changes in the solution are correct in the first two or three digits of the mantissa. We use this knowledge and use a larger integration step size (by a factor of 2) for the perturbed solutions than that used in the base solution.

The structure of the code would allow for easy conversion to multiple shooting. It would double the memory requirements for a 20 variable, 200 boundary condition problem if ten shooting points were allowed.

6. PLANS

The senior author will continue to maintain a working version of the current code. It is available for IBM and CDC machines. Conversion to multiple shooting or a more powerful integrator will likely not be done unless a sponsor comes forth.

A new code is in final checkout stages. It is quite similar to QUASII except it requires coding of a Frobenius-type recurrence equation for the power series of the ODE. It also requires the user to furnish analytic linearizations of the ODEs. The use of the power series integrator gives the ultimate in variable step size integration. We think this code should be of great pedagogical interest.

```
1 PARTICULAR SOLUTION PERTURBATION METHOD SYSTEM VERSION 2.4

    ************************************************************************************

    ****    THE SPRING MASS DASHPOT DATA FOR THE USUAL EXAMPLE WITH ROUNDED DATA        *

    ************************************************************************************

 INPUT DATA     1   11       LOW LEVEL OUTPUT
 NRANKC    6      NO. XCT EQ    1      NO. NXCT BVS   15
0  DO YOU WANT TO CHANGE PARAMETERS? ANSWER YES OR NO.
? NO

    ****************************************
                ITER    1  OF    7
     TIME                    SOLUTION
       0.            1.200000        .2000000        5.0000000E-02   .8000000        1.200000


 SUM OF BV DISSATISFACTIONS IS    18.83200
 0  DO YOU WANT TO CHANGE PARAMETERS? ANSWER YES OR NO.
 ? YES
   INDICATE CHANGE BY ENTERING SPECIFIED INTEGER
   INITIAL CONDITIONS =1, PERTURBATIONS=2,INTEGRATION STEP SIZE=3,FINAL TIME =4,
   NUMBER OF ITERATIONS=5, CONTINUE EXECUTING =6,STOP EXECUTION =7,OUTPUT CONTROL=8
   -OPTION?
 ? 8
   ENTER OUTPUT CONTROL PARAMETER-
 ? 1
   -OPTION?
 ? 6

     ****************************************
                 ITER    2  OF    7
      TIME                    SOLUTION
        0.            1.299948        .4493253        .1953124        .8515958        1.005050


  SUM OF BV DISSATISFACTIONS IS    5.891443
```

Figure 1 Output

Figure 2 Output

SAVE MATRIX

BOUNDARY VALUE,UNPTRBD SOLN, PTRBD SOLNS.....

1	1.00000	1.00000	1.00000	1.00000	1.00000	1.00000	1.00000
2	-.220000	-.223713	-.328772	-.292112	-.212211	-.325197	-9.500043E-02
3	3.500000E-02	7.383055E-02	.140146	1.287162E-02	7.776679E-02	.183984	8.323857E-02
4	-.474000	-.436871	-.277351	-.447804	-.436157	-.231124	-.672832
5	-.589000	-.638813	-.517521	-.600721	-.626303	-.442629	-.925958
6	.393000	.253174	.255658	.304156	.254638	.376591	.250342
7	1.59700	1.54725	1.45022	1.57211	1.49855	1.47676	1.92887
8	1.45200	1.70188	1.59288	1.68735	1.62000	1.31258	2.16579
9	-.388000	8.164415E-02	4.130642E-02	4.517948E-02	5.744474E-02	-.509196	.174784
10	-2.32400	-2.07819	-2.03299	-2.10643	-1.96943	-2.40848	-2.51077
11	-2.27400	-2.66652	-2.58352	-2.66767	-2.47731	-2.26198	-3.28169
12	8.800000E-02	-.795046	-.740732	-.773074	-.699240	.272572	-1.03036
13	2.71100	2.09547	2.08706	2.12063	1.95976	3.03402	2.49779
14	2.99700	3.37020	3.31626	3.37986	3.06746	3.24017	4.08852
15	.401000	1.65200	1.59946	1.64196	1.43875	.291118	2.04501
16	-2.81600	-1.72426	-1.73780	-1.74327	-1.61839	-3.32655	-2.03651

DET = 9.3656727E-05

CONSTANTS -1.678735 -.8784988 1.027935 1.575799 .7514389 .2020612

DOT .7451188E-01 ANORM .2872606

DIC VECTOR

-.2284005 9.2375441E-02 6.1554606E-02 .1279844 4.0616319E-02

FIGURE 3 - OUTPUT

```
*******************************************************************************
****  THE SPRING MASS DASHPOT DATA FOR THE USUAL EXAMPLE WITH ROUNDED DATA  ****
*******************************************************************************
                    ITER   7  OF   7
         TIME                 SOLUTION
        .0              1.000052   .4997831  .2000442    .9999674       1.00000
  TBV   1.000000        1.093575     -.1610852
  TBV   2.000000        .9079883     -.1673206
  TBV   3.000000        .6872255     -.3627768
  TBV   4.000000        2.794591D-02 -.9774382
  TBV   5.000000       -1.121182     -1.154340
  TBV   6.000000       -1.855145     -.1078456
  TBV   7.000000       -1.110149      1.574867
  TBV   8.000000        .9361926      2.206165
  TBV   9.000000        2.583945      .7601555
  TBV   10.00000        2.081633     -1.757615
  TBV   11.00000       -.4905672     -2.986783
  TBV   12.00000       -2.950208     -1.487206
  TBV   13.00000       -2.903213      1.630657
  TBV   14.00000       -.1126830      3.510748
  TBV   15.00000        3.023159      2.215245
SUM OF BV DISSATISFACTIONS IS    .2107574D-02
**********************************************************************
SOURCE     SUM OF SQUARES      DEG. FREEDOM      MEAN SQUARE
------     --------------      ------------      -----------
REGRESSION   40.587002               4             10.146751
RESIDUAL    -.91088663D-04          11               .82807876D-05 = S**2
TOTAL(UNC)   40.586911              15
    PER-CENT VARIATION    R**2=   99.999999     %%%%%%%%
    TEST OF OVERALL REGRESSION  FCAL=  1225336.4
 F(ALPHA)=  3.3566999          P(F(ALPHA).GT.FCAL)=   .0
    FOR RISK OF ALPHA=  .50000000D-01   ****ACCEPT REGRESSION****
    SPECIFICS OF THE BOUNDARY CONDITIONS
   T(ALPHA)=   2.2009830          ALPHA=  .50000000D-01
OBSERVATION   ESTIMATE      RESIDUAL    EST.STD.ERR.  LOWER C.L.   UPPER C.L.
 -.22000      -.21984      -.15616D-03  .14169D-03 -.22016       -.21953
  .35000D-01   .34810D-01   .18976D-03  .13285D-03  .34518D-01   .35103D-01
 -.47400      -.47351      -.48829D-03  .13067D-03 -.47380       -.47322
 -.58900      -.58922       .21665D-03  .10201D-03 -.58944       -.58899
  .39300       .39314      -.14043D-03  .91712D-04  .39294        .39334
  1.5970       1.5972      -.24249D-03  .87873D-04  1.5970        1.5974
  1.4520       1.4521      -.56599D-04  .72000D-04  1.4519        1.4522
 -.38800      -.38813       .13443D-03  .66947D-04 -.38828       -.38799
 -2.3240      -2.3238      -.19275D-03  .71603D-04 -2.3240       -2.3236
 -2.2740      -2.2740      -.14050D-04  .87304D-04 -2.2742       -2.2738
  .88000D-01   .88050D-01 -.49620D-04   .90780D-04  .87850D-01   .88249D-01
  2.7110       2.7110      -.46145D-04  .10179D-03  2.7108        2.7113
  2.9970       2.9971      -.81447D-04  .13415D-03  2.9968        2.9974
  .40100       .40098       .18035D-04  .13994D-03  .40067        .40129
 -2.8160      -2.8159      -.80717D-04  .14913D-03 -2.8162       -2.8156
        MEAN OF OBSERVATIONS=  .39266667D-01
        SUM OF THE RESIDUALS= -.98982067D-03
     SPECIFICS OF THE YI SOLUTIONS
   T(ALPHA)=   2.2009830          ALPHA=    .50000000D-01
ESTIMATED VALUE       EST VARIANCE             CONFIDENCE INTERVAL
  1.0000522          .11479856D-05       .99769396    <>   1.0024104
  .49978306          .83874584D-06       .49776733    <>    .50179879
  .20004420          .13131090D-07       .19979199    <>    .20029642
  .99996740          .11312136D-07       .99973331    <>   1.0002015
*******************************                     ***************************
```

COMPUTATIONAL METHODS IN HYDRODYNAMIC STABILITY: HYDROPACK

John M. Gersting, Jr.
Associate Professor, Computer Science and Engineering Science
Indiana University-Purdue University at Indianapolis
Indianapolis, IN 46205

Introduction

This paper presents a very brief overview of work done by the author in computational methods in the field of linear hydrodynamic stability. The paper begins with the statement of a typical eigenvalue problem, examines steps required in the solution process, and techniques that have been used to implement various steps in the solution process. The paper concludes with discussion of a software package, HYDROPACK, designed as a modular research and test mechanism for problems in hydrodynamic stability, and results for nine problems.

Problem Statement

Rather than derive a hydrodynamic stability problem from a physical situation, the reader is referred to reference [1]. As a typical linear hydrodynamic stability problem, consider the eigenvalue problem for plane Poiseuille flow. The eigensystem is

$$(1)\qquad \begin{aligned} &\phi'''' - 2\alpha^2\phi'' + \alpha^4\phi + i\alpha R((c - u)(\phi'' - \alpha^2\phi)) + u''\phi = 0 \\ &\phi(\pm 1) = \phi'(\pm 1) = 0 \end{aligned}$$

where $u = 1 - y^2$ and α is the wave number, R is the Reynolds number, $c = c_r + ic_i$ where c_r is the wave speed and c_i is the amplification factor. The eigenvalue is usually taken as c (although any two of α, R, c_r, c_i may be chosen) and the eigenfunction ϕ is complex. The Orr-Sommerfeld equation (1) is stiff in the sense that portions of the general solution grow rapidly while the parts of interest do not have a rapid growth rate.

Solution Process

The main goal of an analysis of a problem such as (1) is to obtain eigenvalues and the corresponding eigenfunctions. Two classes of techniques exist. One treats the ordinary differential equation directly and discretization is carried out within the algorithms (such as Runge-Kutta). The other technique involves discretization in advance (usually) of employing the computer by algorithms such as finite difference or method of weighted residuals; the result of these algorithms is an algebraic eigenvalue problem.

With either of the above techniques the process of determining an eigenvalue usually reduces to the following:

0. Estimation of the eigenvalue
1. Evaluation of the function

2. Evaluation of an expression to test for an eigenvalue
3. Refinement of the eigenvalue estimate

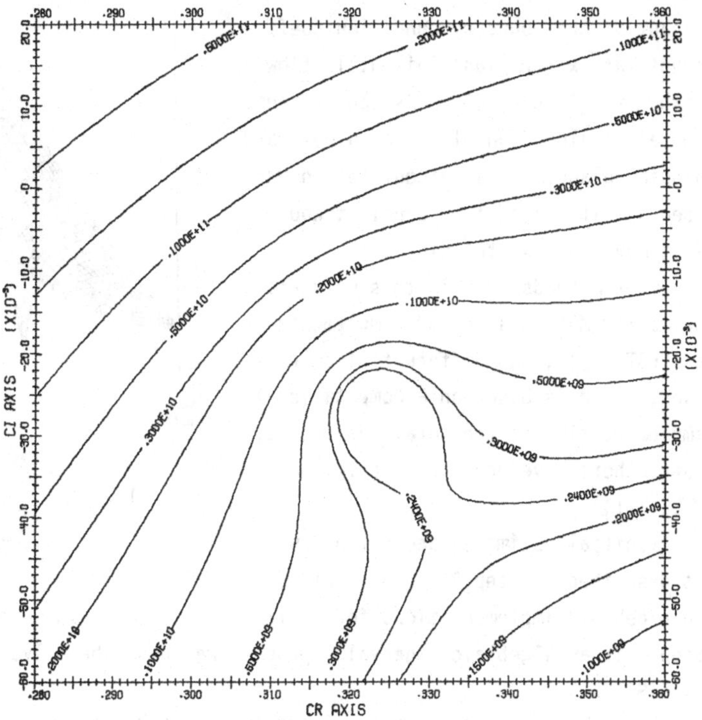

Step 0 may be the most difficult in the process. If no initial estimates are known, one way around a wild guess is to carry out steps 1 and 2 in a fashion that will produce a contour plot of the eigenvalue test condition. This plot shows such information for (1) where $|D|$, the determinant of the boundary condition coefficient matrix, has been plotted in the c_r, c_i plane with $\alpha = 1.0$, $R = 1600$. The contours do provide a good initial estimate.

Step 1, evaluation of the function, involves most of the computations in a solution so is the most expensive part of the process. Since the equations of interest are stiff, methods which avoid or control parasitic error must be used. Many computational techniques have been tried, including finite difference [2], method of weighted residuals [3], multiple shooting [4], and orthonormalized integration as described in [6] and implemented in [7] and [8].

At the end of Step 1 the process has produced a computational solution to the problem for a given estimate of the eigenvalue. The next step is to test to see if the estimate is actually an eigenvalue (except when method of weighted residuals or finite difference problems are solved directly as algebraic eigenvalue problems.)

Step 2 amounts to forming a value of some function that must be zero when an eigenvalue is located. For algebraic methods such as large finite difference or method of weighted residual problems, a determinant must be computed. For shooting methods one usually choses the 2 x 2 determinant of the coefficient matrix in the end point boundary condition equation as the test item.

Step 3 is the refinement process. The applicability of various refinement techniques is dependent on the accuracy of the estimate and the shape of the surface. This figure is a three dimensional plot of the function $\log_{10}(|D|)$ versus c_r and c_i where D is the determinant of the boundary condition coefficient matrix for plane Poiseuille flow with $\alpha = 1.0$, R = 1600. As can be seen, the eigenvalue "funnel" is on a downward sloping plane. If a descent method were used and it missed the funnel it would just move on down the slope.

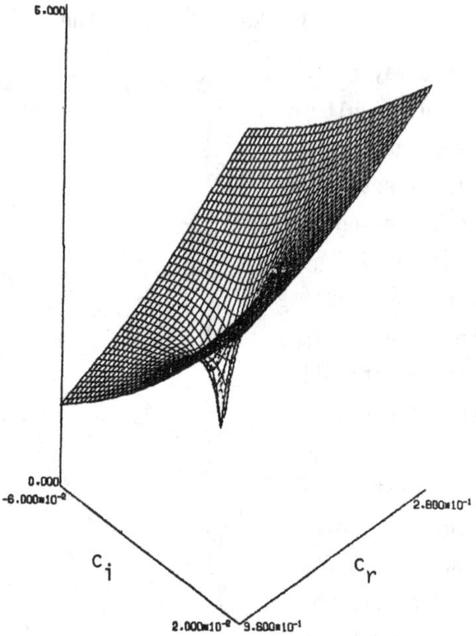

The methods used in this work are primarily Muller's method (implemented as CEST [10]), and differential correction, which is based on a computational implementation of the total derivative. Many others have been tried (e.g., MULE [11]).

Initial estimates and refinement as described in Step 3 can be avoided in algebraic implementations for small matrix sizes. In such cases the result of Step 1 is an algebraic eigenvalue problem which may be solved using routines such as EISPACK.

The process of Steps 1 through 3 is repeated until an eigenvalue is refined to a given tolerance; often a relative error of 0.1% is used.

<u>Comparison of Methods</u>

Table 1 displays results for plane Poiseuille flow for $\alpha = 1.0$, R = 2500. Except for Thomas [2] all data are from runs made on a CDC 6600. Those marked with * are original implementations from the literature, others were implemented by the author. (When estimates were required, Thomas's results for $\alpha = 1.0$, R = 1600 were used.) Each method will be described very briefly.

The method of weighted residuals implementation is a Galerkin method using polynomials that satisfy the boundary conditions as approximating and weighting functions; also see [12], [13], [14]. The method of matched initial-value problems [4] is a multiple shooting technique starting from the boundary and iterating to "match" halfway across; here initial conditions are hard to estimate, especially ϕ'' and ϕ'''. Filtered integration [5] uses the inviscid solution to the plane Poiseuille Orr-Sommerfeld equation to subtract out the parasitic error. The finite-difference implementation follows Thomas; two techniques are used, one is a refinement using Muller's method [22] which requires an initial estimate and the other is reduction to an algebraic eigenvalue problem and employing EISPACK [21].

Three sets of data are presented using orthonormalized integration using [7].

Table I

Plane Poiseuille Flow Comparisons

$\alpha = 1.0 \quad R = 2500$

Method	Ref #	Eigenvalue $c = c_r + i\,c_i$	Interval	# Nodes	Initial Estimate	Iteration Scheme	#Iter	CDC 6600 Sec./Iter	CDC 6600 Total Sec.	Notes
Finite Difference	2	0.3011 - i 0.0142	[0,1]	50						
Method of Weighted Residuals (DOUBLE)	3	0.301150 - i 0.014182	[-1,1]	14	No				2.00	Select approx. functions
Matched Initial Value Problems *	4	0.301152 - i 0.014178	[0,1]	128	Yes	Newton Raphson	20	0.32	6.40	IC's must be estimated
Filtered Integration *	5	0.301150 - i 0.014181	[0,1]	10+100	Yes	Diff. Correct.	4	0.25	1.03	Uses inviscid sol. as filter
Finite Difference	3	0.301149 - i 0.014182	[-1,1]	101	Yes	Muller	10	0.16	1.65	Uses penta-dia. array storage
Finite Difference	21	0.300701 - i 0.019737	[-1,1]	26	No				2.05	Uses EISPACK for direct sol.
Near-Ortho. Integration	7	0.301148 - i 0.014179	[-1,1]	200	Yes	Muller	10	2.15	26.05	ANG = 45° 90 orthos.
Near-Ortho. Integration	11	0.301148 - i 0.014179	[-1,1]	200	Yes	MULE	7	2.00	23.67	Initial estimate must be close
Near-Ortho. Integration	7	0.301155 - i 0.014184	[-1,1]	200	Yes	Diff. Correct.	8	6.87	59.40	Three fct. eval. per iteration
SUPORT	8	0.301150 - i 0.014199	[-1,1]	var.	Yes	Muller	15	10.60	170.40	RE=AE= 10^{-7} 2 orthos.

These differ in the refinement scheme used. Muller and MULE [11] are similar techniques. The latter uses an Atkin method to increase convergence rate. It requires fewer iterations but in general the initial estimates must be better than for Muller to guarantee convergence. Differential correction requires three functional evaluations per iteration and tends to be sensitive to initial estimates.

The final entry on the table is for the SUPORT implementation of orthonormalized integration. Although the computing time is larger, this is by far the easiest method to implement.

HYDROPACK

After carrying out comparative evaluations of techniques used on the typical and other hydrodynamic stability problems, the next step was to design and implement a software system that uses the best ideas from the various programs examined. To that end a FORTRAN control structure called HYDROPACK was designed to meet the following goals:

1. A tool for research in the field of hydrodynamic stability
2. A software package that minimizes the time to implement a new problem using either plane or axisymmetric geometries
3. A modular structure that allows for algorithm selection at each level of the solution process
4. A test mechanism for new algorithms and/or implementations

The user interface with HYDROPACK is with the control level. This level inputs and consistency checks all program data. It also prints most of the output created by the program. The user selects the algorithms to be employed at each interior level using "switch" settings in the input.

As can be seen the levels correspond to the various steps in the solution

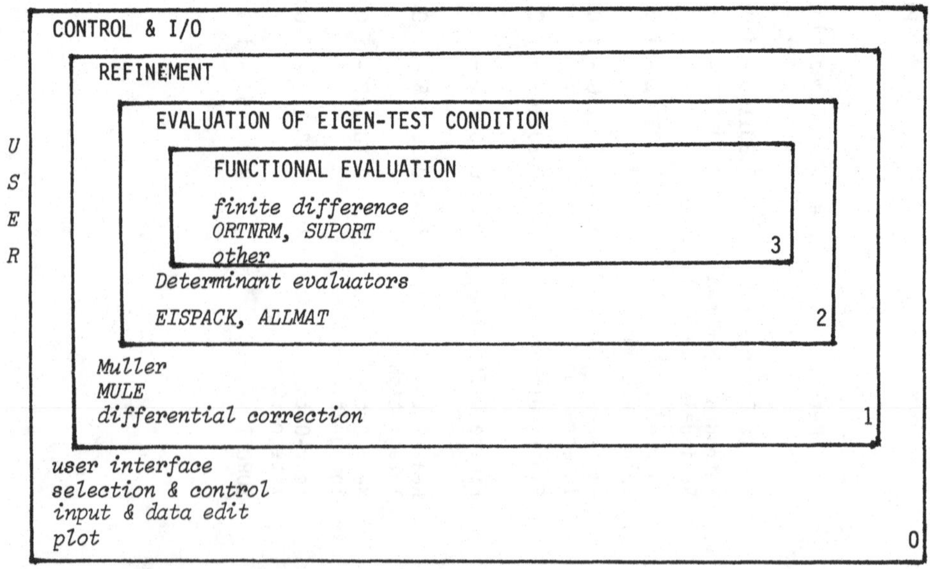

Table II Orr-Sommerfeld Problems - Neutral Stability: $c_i = 0$

Problem	Ref #	Method	α	R	c_r	β	σ	ε	k	f	SRe	Interval	#Nodes	#Iter	CDC 6600 Sec/Iter
Plane Poiseuille	1		1.02	5771	0.2639										
		O-M	1.02	5829	0.2635							[-1,1]	200	5	3.25
		O-D	1.02	5770	0.2639							[-1,1]	200	5	8.02
		F-M	1.02	5803	0.2596							[-1,1]	101	4	0.14
Couette Poiseuille	14														
	20		0.80	13900	0.2280	0.05									
		O-M	0.80	13889	0.2284	0.05						[-1,1]	200	3	3.19
		O-D	0.80	13872	0.2285	0.05						[-1,1]	200	9	7.83
		F-M	0.80	13744	0.2743	0.05						[-1,1]	101	2	0.14
Plane Porous	13		0.95	8074	0.2363		0.60								
		O-M	0.95	8052	0.2364		0.60					[-1,1]	200	5	4.36
		O-D	0.95	8039	0.2366		0.60					[-1,1]	200	5	8.40
		F-M	0.95	8090	0.2340		0.60					[-1,1]	101	5	0.13
Plane Porous with Slip	15		0.95	8184	0.2363		0.60	0.0025							
		F-M	0.95	8199	0.2347		0.60	0.0025				[-1,1]	101	7	0.14
Annulus	16		0.95	14403	0.2099				2.00						
		O-M	0.95	14503	0.2098				2.00			[2,4]	200	4	3.95
		O-D	0.95	14372	0.2097				2.00			[2,4]	200	2	9.33
		F-M	0.95	15271	0.2354				2.00			[2,4]	101	3	0.13
Annulus with Dust in Flow	17		0.95	7746	0.2423				1.10	0.05	20.0				
		O-M	0.95	7716	0.2426				1.10	0.05	20.0	[20,22]	200	7	3.93
		O-D	0.95	7863	0.2418				1.10	0.05	20.0	[20,22]	200	4	8.41
		F-M	0.95	7960	0.2541				1.10	0.05	20.0	[20,22]	200	6	0.13
Couette Annulus	18		0.95	16629	0.2084	0.01			2.00						
		O-M	0.95	16501	0.2088	0.01			2.00			[2,4]	200	9	3.90
		O-D	0.95	16661	0.2083	0.01			2.00			[2,4]	200	4	9.20
		F-M	0.95	16653	0.2154	0.01			2.00			[2,4]	101	3	0.14
Porous Annulus	18		0.95	10823	0.2208		1.00		2.00						
		O-M	0.95	10535	0.2213		1.00		2.00			[2,4]	200	3	4.06
		O-D	0.95	10450	0.2213		1.00		2.00			[2,4]	200	4	9.50
		F-M	0.95	10497	0.2226		1.00		2.00			[2,4]	101	5	0.13
Couette-Poiseu. Porous Annulus	19		0.95	14744	0.2121	0.01	0.50		2.00						
		O-M	0.95	14984	0.2101	0.01	0.50		2.00			[2,4]	200	9	4.10
		O-D	0.95	14797	0.2129	0.01	0.50		2.00			[2,4]	200	5	9.70
		F-M	0.95	17372	0.2449	0.01	0.50		2.00			[2,4]	101	5	0.14

process described earlier. Level 0 establishes the environment in which the solution is to be attempted and sets the initial eigenvalue estimates and starts up the refinement process at level 1.

It is the purpose of level 1 to control all the activities of the iteration or search such as applying Muller's method or solving a system of equations while applying differential corrections. Once the overhead in level 1 is set up a test must be made to determine if the current estimate is an acceptable eigenvalue. The need for the test initiates the test condition evaluation process which sets up its overhead and calls for a functional evaluation which initiates the process at level 3.

As the process is completed, requests from the containing level are filled. This sequence of requests, process initiation and completion continues until a properly refined estimate (or an error condition) is returned to the control level. At that point additional output is produced indicating the results of the refinement, including timings. Also, if the user has requested it, the eigenfunction is produced and tabulated or plotted.

The control program then looks for more input and the entire chain of events is repeated until the input stream is empty.

Results from HYDROPACK

The finite difference and orthonormalized integration data in Table I was produced using HYDROPACK. Table II shows results from nine problems that are part of HYDROPACK. The following key applies to the method colums: O→ orthonormalized integration, F→ finite difference, M→ Muller's method, and D→ differential correction. All refinement searches used R and c_r as the eigenvalues (with a weight of 10000 on R to scale it down to the size of c_r) while fixing α and setting $c_i = 0$ to produce neutral stability data. All the runs for a given problem started with the same estimate.

Acknowledgements

The author wishes to thank the IUPUI computer center for making the computer time for this work available and Mr. Jim Williams for his invaluable help, especially with the contour and three dimensional plots.

References

1. Lin, C.C., The Theory of Hydrodynamic Stability, Cambridge Univ. Press, 1955.
2. Thomas, L.H., "The stability of plane Poiseuille flow", Phys. Rev. 91 (1953), 780-783.
3. Gersting, J.M., and Jankowski, D.F.,"Numerical methods for Orr-Sommerfeld problems", Inter. J. for Numer. Meth. in Engr. 4 (1972), 195-206.
4. Nachtsheim, R.R., "An initial value method for the numerical treatment of the Orr-Sommerfeld equation for the case of plane Poiseuille flow", NASA TND-2414, 1964.
5. Kaplan, R.E., "The stability of laminar incompressible boundary layers in

the presence of compliant boundaries", M.I.T. Aeroelastic and Structures Laboratory Report ASRL TR 116-1 (1964), (AD 601 779).

6. Conte, S.D., "The numerical solution of linear boundary value problems", SIAM Rev., 8 (1966), 309-321.
7. Silverston, S., "ORTNRM - a FORTRAN subroutine package for the solution of linear two-point boundary value problems", Purdue Univ. Computer Sciences Dept. Report CSD TR 18, 1968.
8. Scott, M.R., and Watts, H.A., "SUPORT - a computer code for two-point boundary value problems via orthonormalization", Sandia Laboratories Report SAND 75-0198, 1975.
9. Gersting, J.M., "Numerical methods for eigensystems: the Orr-Sommerfeld problem", Comp. and Math. with Appl. 3 (1977), 47-52.
10. Funderlic, R.E., The Programmer's Handbook, Union Carbide Corp., Oak Ridge, Tenn., 1968 (AD K-1729).
11. Holt, J.G., "ASC MULE general root finding subroutine", Aerospace Corp. Report TOR-0073(9320)-8, 1973.
12. Lee, L.H., and Reynolds, W., "A variational method for investigating the stability of parallel flows", Tech. Rep. No. FM 1, Thermosciences Div., Dept. of Mech. Engr., Stanford Unov., 1964.
13. Sheppard, D.M., "The hydrodynamic stability of the flow between parallel porous walls", Phys. of Fluids, 15 (1972), 241-244.
14. Vargo, J.J., The Hydrodynamic Stability of Plane Couette-Poiseuille Flow, Masters Thesis, Arizona State Univ., Tempe, Ariz., 1969.
15. Gersting, J.M., "Hydrodynamic stability of plane porous slip flow", Phys. of Fluids, 17 (1974), 2126-2127.
16. Mott, J.E., and Joseph, D.D., "Stability of parallel flow between concentric cylinders", Phys. of Fluids, 11 (1968), 2065-2073.
17. Moorman, M.O., Jankowski, D.J., and Gersting, J.M., "Stability of parallel flows of a dusty gas in an annulus", Devel. in Mech., 7 (1973), 167-177.
18. Gersting, J. M., and Jankowski, D.F., "The hydrodynamic stability of two axisymmetric annular flows", Devel. in Mech., 6 (1971), 179-192.
19. Gersting, J.M., "The hydrodynamic stability of Couette-Poiseuille-porous annular flow", Trans. ASME - J. of Appl. Mech., 39 (1972), 840-842.
20. Potter, M. C., "Stability of plane Couette-Poiseuille flow", Phys. of Fluids, 24 (1966), 609-619.
21. Garbow, B.S., "EISPACK - a package of matrix eigensystem routines", Comp. Phys. Comm., 7 (1974), 179-184.
22. Muller, E.D., "A method for solving algebraic equations using an automatic computer", Math. of Comp., 10 (1956), 208-215.

DEMONSTRATION OF WORKING CODES

by

Bart Childs

Six codes were available for demonstration. These codes may be classified as to purpose or type: (1) Sturm-Liouville code, (2) two-point finite-difference code, (3) multipoint collocation code, (4) two-point multiple shooting code, (5) two-point multiple shooting-orthonormalization code, and (6) multipoint shooting code for system identification. A brief reference to each code follows with some elements for comparison.

SLEIGN, a Sturm-Liouville eigenvalue solver, has been prepared by Paul Bailey and Larry Shampine, see pages 274-279. This code requires the preparation of the three functional coefficients common to Sturm-Liouville definitions, six (6) parameters to define the two-point boundary conditions, the index of the desired eigenvalue, and an accuracy requirement. The primary output is the desired eigenvalue and an accuracy estimate. At user option, the solution function is output. The authors conclude "... no code can be expected to work on all problems, but this code demonstrates the feasibility of being able to solve at least the vast majority of ordinary [Sturm-Liouville] problems in a completely automatic fashion."

Victor Pereyra and Marianela Lentini are the primary architects of PASVA3 - An Adaptive Finite Difference Fortran Program for First Order Nonlinear, Ordinary Boundary Problems, see pages 67-88. This code is at least in its third generation. A discussion of this development and the availability of the code is given in the first pages of this paper by Pereyra. The user is required to input parameters describing the limits of the mesh, convergence tolerance, and the desired accuracy estimates. The user must also furnish routines that give the forms of the first order (nonlinear) differential equations and the forms of the boundary conditions. The authors report that the code is appropriate for the solution of many problems including those with "mild boundary layers." Some characteristics which should be noted include the facts that variable meshes are generated automatically and that deferred corrections are used to accelerate convergence. If some parameters and the 'initial guess solution' are not provided by the user then defaults are used or generated. Extensive checking of input and the generated solutions is carried out by the code.

COLSYS is a multipoint code for mixed orders (orders up through five) of differential equations, see pages 164-185. The collocation method makes it particularly convenient to use sets of mixed order differential equations rather than using larger sets of first order differential equations that most other codes require. Otherwise, the code is quite similar to PASVA3 in some respects. Meshes are generated automatically and approximately the same parameters as PASVA3 must be provided by the user. Both have similar dependence on an initial guess at the solution. The authors report success on many problems and suggest the code is appropriate for many 'mildly difficult to difficult' problems. The code appears particularly effective on some problems with small parameters and singularities.

Roland Bulirsch has developed a multiple shooting two-point code which has been used in many real-world applications, [35]. Stoer and Deuflhard have also contributed to the development of BOUNDSOL. This code uses predetermined shooting points, by choice of the code authors. The code appears to have a particularly effective nonlinear equation solver. The extrapolation integrator DIFSY1 is used and, according to Watts, "other one-step oriented integrators having the same argument list could easily be used."

The SUPORT code [238] and the SUPORQ code [239] are due to Scott, Watts, and others at Sandia Laboratories. SUPORT uses superposition principles coupled with an orthonormalization procedure for solving linear two-point boundary-value problems. The code allows the user to choose among the RK45, GERK, STEP, and INTRP integrators. SUPORQ combines the techniques of SUPORT with a quasilinearization process to enable solution of problems with nonlinear differential equations. It uses RKF45 and GERK integrators and Adams integrators are planned. Some shooting codes MSHOOT, SHOOT1, and SHOOT2 are under development, see pages 109-121.

QUASII is a simple shooting code for multipoint problems in system identification. Its primary purpose could be described as regression analysis with differential equation(s) models. Each boundary condition (or side condition or constraint) can be specified to be met in a least squares or exact sense. The code is based on a fixed step 4th order Runge Kutta integrator. This choice facilitates certain conveniences of desired output. Parameters are input or default values are used for: governing level, frequency and type of output; iteration limits; convergence acceleration choices; integration stepsize; accuracy; and many other user choices. The code does have some interactivity which allows for varying step sites, use of a subset of the least squares boundary conditions, varying the detail of the output and some other logical user controls to minimize the machine usage under timesharing, see pages 186-195.

Most, if not all, of the codes were operational during the conference on the CDC Cybernet service. Three of the codes were delivered in IBM Fortran. The conversion was not trivial, but it was manageable. This one workshop should not be considered as successful. A larger budget and fewer outside responsibilities on the organizing committee and code authors to have allowed at least three days prior to the conference for conversion, tuning, etc. would have made this particular workshop quite successful. We suggest this as a minimum to any future conference-workshop organizers. Further, our 10+hour/day density of conference activity did not allow us to circumvent Murphy's Law.

PROJECTION METHODS

G. W. Reddien
Mathematics Department
Vanderbilt University
Nashville, Tennessee 37235

1. Introduction. This paper is intended to be a survey of some of the theoretical developments on projection methods for the numerical solution of two-point boundary value problems, and to provide a general introduction to the major features of the theory of projection methods and the literature. Several research groups are writing general purpose codes using these methods. As examples, we cite the recent work of Ascher, Christiansen and Russell [13], Daniel and Martin [60] and deBoor [69]. An important aspect of code development and evaluation is theoretical support. Theory provides one basis for selecting the algorithms. Also, theoretical error bounds not only give the order of convergence basis for deciding among different methods, but also suggest mesh selection schemes and extrapolation procedures. We will illustrate some of these points here.

The literature on projection methods is large, particularly so since from an abstract point of view almost every numerical method is a projection method. The term includes the methods of collocation, Ritz-Galerkin, and least squares. Moreover, standard finite-difference methods in the linear case can be interpreted as projection methods applied to the dual of the given equation. See deBoor [67]. There are certain hybrid methods with attractive features that will be presented here.

Section 2 describes various examples of projection methods with references. Section 3 recalls some basic facts about projections and convergence theorems for projection methods. It is also explained there how the basic methods of section 2 fit into a general framework. Section 4 discusses superconvergence and more refined error bounds.

Many topics are ignored. We do not discuss singular problems, although there is a growing literature on them. We do not compare methods from the standpoint of operation counts or matrix bandwidths but will make mainly comparisons regarding applicability and rates of convergence. Computational considerations are vital and some work has been done. For example, see Russell and Varah [225], deBoor and Swartz [70], Sincovec [244] and Russell [227]. We also do not discuss eigenvalue problems, partial differential equations, integro-differential equations and functional differential equations.

A comprehensive survey of the literature on numerical methods for two-point boundary value problems was given by H. B. Keller [150] in June, 1974. The reader is referred there for possible references. We have made no attempt here to be inclusive.

2. Examples. Before beginning an abstract description of projection methods, indeed before even giving a definition, we consider some examples. We will, for simplicity, consider these examples as applied to the problem

(2.1) $$-y'' + a_0(x)y' + a_1(x)y = f(x), \quad 0 < x < 1$$

with Dirichlet boundary conditions

(2.2) $$y(0) = y(1) = 0.$$

We assume a_0, a_1 and f are continuous and that $f \equiv 0$ implies $y \equiv 0$.

We stress here that the problem (2.1) - (2.2) will be used as a common setting for the description of several methods. Although an important problem, projection methods are attractive because they apply to general nonlinear systems. For many projection methods, analysis and programming for nonlinear systems is not much more difficult than for (2.1) - (2.2). The smoothness conditions on a_0, a_1 and f can be easily weakened and the boundary conditions generalized. References are cited later. However, some methods have only been defined and analyzed for (2.1) - (2.2). These cases will be pointed out.

Projection methods for (2.1) - (2.2) are global function space approximation methods. That is, a function $y_n(x)$ in an approximating space is determined to approximate y for all x in [0,1]. The most used approximating spaces are polynomials and polynomial splines. The use of polynomial splines is responsible for the success of projection methods, since in addition to their excellent approximation properties, the associated matrix problems are banded and their set-up is well suited for digital computation. The emphasis here will be on projection methods with splines, although some mention will be made of polynomials.

Let $\Delta: 0 = x_0 < x_1 < \ldots < x_n = 1$ be a partition of $I \equiv [0,1]$ with $h_j = x_j - x_{j-1}$, $h = |\Delta| = \max_j h_j$, and $\underline{h} = \min_j h_j$. A family of partitions is said to be quasi-uniform if there is a constant c so that $h \leq c\underline{h}$ for all partitions in the family. Let $I_i \equiv [x_{i-1}, x_i]$.

By splines, we mean the elements of

$$S(r,k,\Delta) \equiv \{v \in C^k(I) : v \in P_r(I_i)\} .$$

Here $r \geq k \geq -1$ are integers and $P_r(I_i)$ denotes the polynomials of degree $\leq r$ over I_i. With $k = -1$, splines are simply piecewise polynomials with no continuity conditions.

2.1 Collocation. There are basically two types of collocation methods used for (2.1) - (2.2), those with smooth splines, i.e. k large, and those with k = 1. Of course, other choices are possible. Given a set of points $\{t_i\}_{i=1}^{N-2}$ where $N = \dim(S(r,k,\Delta))$, collocation methods determine approximations $y_n \in S(r,k,\Delta)$ to y by solving

$$\text{(2.1.1)} \qquad -y_n''(t_i) + a_0(t_i)y_n'(t_i) + a_1(t_i)y_n(t_i) = f(t_i) \quad i = 1,\ldots,N-2$$

$$\text{(2.1.2)} \qquad y_n(0) = y_n(1) = 0 .$$

General analyses of such methods and specific examples can be found in deBoor [67], Phillips [209], Russell and Shampine [224], Lucas and Reddien [176], deBoor and Swartz [70] and Douglas and Dupont [93]. Related references here include Ahlberg and Ito [1] and Kammerer, Reddien and Varga [143]. With $k = 1$, an effective choice for the collocation points is to let $-1 < \rho_1 < \ldots < \rho_{r-1} < 1$ be the zeros of the Legendre Polynomial of degree r-1 and define $\xi_{ij} = \frac{1}{2}(x_{i-1} + x_i + \rho_j h_i)$ to be the collocation points. With sufficient smoothness, this method which is called collocation at Gauss points achieves optimal rates of convergence in the L^∞-norm, i.e. $\|y - y_n\|_\infty = O(h^{r+1})$. Moreover, superconvergence results hold at the mesh points. We return to this later. On the other hand, smooth spline collocation methods converge at rates equal to the truncation error, namely $O(h^{r-1})$, for (2.1) - (2.2). With y_n in $S(3,2,\Delta)$ and choosing $t_i = x_i$, then convergence in the L^∞-norm is $O(h^2)$.

The convergence rate is not, of course, the sole criteria for selecting a method. Rather overall computational effort is critical. Note here that $\dim S(3,2,\Delta) = n+3$ and $\dim S(3,1,\Delta) = 2n+3$, and in general the smooth spline methods result in smaller matrices. For numerical comparisons indicating that in some cases smooth spline methods are competitive, see Sincovec [244] and Russell [227].

Smooth spline methods were given by Ahlberg and Ito [1] that replaced a few equations of the type (2.1.1) by interpolation equations for the differential equation. Let $\delta_i f \equiv f(x_i)$ and $\delta_i^1 f = f'(x_i)$. In this notation, the method $\delta_i(-y_n'' + a_0 y_n + a_1 y_n) = \delta_i f$, $i = 1, \ldots, n$, and $\delta_j^1(-y_n'' + a_0 y_n' + a_1 y)$ $= \delta_j^1 f$, $j = 0, n$, with y_n in $S(5,4,\Delta)$ was considered along with an analogue for y_n in $S(7,6,\Delta)$. Numerical comparison results are given in [1] and [79].

Collocation theory allows one to consider more general problems than (2.1) - (2.2). The papers [70], [176], [224] follow the lead of Vainikko [268] and treat nonlinear problems. Extensions to the case of nonlinear boundary conditions are given in Weiss [279], Wittenbrink [288], Reddien [214] and Voss [274]. Many of the papers on collocation assume that the lead order part of the differential equation is invertible subject to the given boundary conditions. This restriction can be easily removed as was shown by Wittenbrink [288] and Cerrutti [43]. Another approach using alternative theory is given in Reddien [215].

Collocation methods are also theoretically applicable to general vector systems. These results are described by Weiss [279], Cerrutti [43], Russell [222] and Houstis [134].

2.2. Ritz-Galerkin Method. The Galerkin method approximates the solution to (2.1) - (2.2) by solving for $y_n \in S_0(r,k,\Delta) \equiv S(r,k,\Delta) \cap \{v: v(0) = v(1) = 0\}$ the equations

$$(2.2.1) \qquad \int_0^1 (-y_n'' + a_0 y_n' + a_1 y_n) v_i(x)\, dx = \int_0^1 f v_i\, dx$$

where $\{v_i\}$ is a basis for $S_0(r,k,\Delta)$. The Ritz method chooses $y_n \in S_0(r,k,\Delta)$ so that

$$(2.2.2) \qquad \int_0^1 (y_n' v_i' + (a_0 y_n' + a_1 y_n) v_i)\, dx = \int_0^1 f v_i\, dx$$

with $\{v_i\}$ as in (2.2.1). Although there is only a small difference between (2.2.1) and (2.2.2), the difference is important. Eq. (2.2.2) allows $r = 1$. The methods are not equivalent if $k = 0$ because then (2.2.2) cannot be integrated by parts. If the integrals in (2.2.1) and (2.2.2) are done by a quadrature, then even though the continuous equations are the same, the discretized versions will not be. Moreover, different quadratures are required for the discrete methods to be well-posed. The Ritz method for (2.1) - (2.2) using C^1-cubics requires three point Gauss quadrature in each subinterval to be well-posed. See [94]. While the Galerkin method using C^1-cubics requires only two-point Gauss quadrature in each subinterval. In this case, the quadrature-Galerkin method is equivalent to collocation at Gauss points. See [227] and also section 2.6. Finally, a more subtle point concerns extension of the two methods to more general problems with more general boundary conditions. The Galerkin method can be extended in the obvious way to any problem. See Strang and Fix [260], for example. The Ritz method requires even order problems (however, see Ciarlet, Schultz and Varga [56] and Petryshyn [207]) and the approximations are taken in spaces satisfying only the essential boundary conditions [260].

General boundary conditions require the use of a modified functional or approximation space so that the Ritz method corresponds to the correct minimum principle. See, for example, Hallet, Hennart and Mund [126]. For the most part, the Galerkin method is not analyzed in the literature but rather the Ritz method is studied and for problems essentially no more general than (2.1) - (2.2). Dirichlet boundary conditions are nearly always assumed. Although it is obvious that many results extend to general even order equations, as in Natterer [190], and more general boundary conditions, as in [126], a systematic extension of all results is unavailable, e.g. superconvergence, L^∞-norm convergence, systems. It is also assumed that either the problem (2.1) - (2.2) is self-adjoint and elliptic, as in Nitsche [192], or that at least the lead order part is, as in Schatz [230]. No such assumptions are required for collocation methods. However, if a problem is self-adjoint, then (2.2.2) gives a symmetric matrix while collocation does not. This has obvious implications for computations for the associated eigenvalue problems.

Although projection methods, convergence proofs for the Ritz-Galerkin method have been somewhat different from those for collocation. The proofs follow classical lines [145] to get existence and error extimates in the usual energy norm and then use Nitsche's trick [192] to obtain optimal bounds in the L^2-norm. Important theoretical papers on existence and convergence for the Ritz-Galerkin method include Ciarlet, Schultz and Varga [53], [54], [55], [56], Perrin, Price and Varga [205], Douglas and Dupont [94], [95], Nitsche [192], Wheeler [280], Schatz [230], Blair [27], Aubin [17], Schultz [232], Urabe [265], Natterer [190] and Strang and Fix [260].

Early papers established optimal orders of convergence in the L^2-norm. With k = 0, i.e. continuous splines, Wheeler [280] established optimal rates of convergence in the L^∞-norm for (2.1) - (2.2). Partial extensions of this result are given by Natterer [190]. Blair [27] has results for the L^∞-norm but for special cases of $S(r,k,\Delta)$ with quasi-uniform assumptions on the mesh. Optimal rates in the L^∞-norm for arbitrary $S(r,k,\Delta)$ were given by Douglas, Dupont and Wahlbin [96] but with the assumption of quasi-uniform meshes. Some relaxation of this condition is given by Natterer [190]. The optimal order collocation methods given by deBoor and Swartz [70] do not require quasi-uniformity.

The influence of quadrature error on the Ritz-Galerkin method has been considered by Herbold, Schultz and Varga [129], Fix [111], Schultz [233], and Douglas and Dupont [94]. The papers [129] and [233] were concerned with the influence of quadrature error on the right hand side only while the papers [94], [111] consider setting up both the left and right hand sides by quadrature. An advantage that the Ritz method has over collocation is that less continuity for the solution is required in order to achieve best rates. For (2.1) - (2.2), collocation methods require two more continuous derivatives than the Ritz method. Moreover, from the standpoint of approximation theory, the Ritz method requires minimal smoothness. However, when the Ritz method is implemented with a quadrature scheme, this advantage is lost. See Douglas and Dupont [94].

Most of the Ritz-Galerkin papers consider linear problems only. However, see [232]. This is not always a theoretical limitation since the techniques used by deBoor and Swartz [70], H. B. Keller [151] and Vainikko [268] can be used to extend results for linear problems to nonlinear problems.

Ritz-Galerkin methods exhibit superconvergence at the mesh points, see Douglas and Dupont [94]. The Ritz-Galerkin method also has the property that after the approximation y_n has been computed, certain auxillary computations can be performed to achieve higher accuracy at selected points. See, for example, Wheeler [282], Dougles and Dupont [95], and Dupont [101]. These papers treat linear, second order problems.

2.3 Least squares. The method of least squares approximates the solution to (2.1) - (2.2) by solving for $y_n \in S_0(r,k,\Delta)$ so that

$$(2.3.1) \qquad \int_0^1 (-y_n'' + a_0 y_n' + a_1 y_n)(-v_i'' + a_0 v_i' + a_1 v_i)\, dx = \int_0^1 f(-v_i'' + a_0 v_i' + a_i v_i)\, dx$$

for all v_i as in (2.2.1). Basic references on the method of least squares are Baker [20], Russell and Varah [225], Sammon [229] and Ascher [15]. The first three of these papers treat $2m^{th}$ order linear problems with Dirichlet boundary conditions. They obtain optimal error estimates in the L^2-norm. Sammon considers the use of Gaussian quadrature to perform the integrals as does Ascher [15]. However, the paper of Ascher considers general nonlinear m^{th} order equations plus general linear boundary conditions. These two papers both require quasi-uniform meshes. Ascher establishes his error bounds for the L^∞-norm. The quasi-uniform assumption for smooth splines as given by Ascher is necessary since he relies on an interesting bound in the L^∞-norm for the orthogonal projection operator into splines established by Douglas, Dupont and Wahlbin [96]. See also deBoor [68]. Superconvergence results are also obtained in [15]. It is concluded [15] that collocation is generally superior to discrete least squares for ordinary differential equations. Computational examples are given by Serbin [242] verifying the fact that for the same order equation, the condition number for the matrix problem resulting from the method of least squares is the square of that for the Ritz-Galerkin method.

2.4 Method of Moments. There are a variety of methods that can be put in this category. The method of moments finds an approximation $y_n \in S_0(r,k,\Delta)$ so that

$$(2.4.1) \qquad \int_0^1 (-y_n'' + a_0 y_n' + a_1 y_n)\phi_i(x)\,dx = \int_0^1 f(x)\phi_i(x)\,dx$$

where $\{\phi_i(x)\}$ is a basis for $S(r',k',\Delta)$ for suitable r' and k'. In principle, there is no need for the ϕ_i's to span even a space of splines. One particular method was considered by deBoor [67] and Lucas and Reddien [177]. The integers r, k were chosen to be 3 and 2 respectively and r', k' were chosen to be 1 and 0. The paper [177] considers generalizations to general $2m^{th}$ order problems with Dirichlet boundary conditions and achieves optimal rates of convergence in the L^∞-norm with a quasi-uniform assumption on the mesh. Compared to the Ritz method, less computation is required to set up the method by quadrature. A general theory of similar methods for elliptic problems is given by Mock [189] including superconvergence results. This method has been considered in the setting of parabolic problems by Douglas, Dupont and Wheeler [97] where it is called an H^1-Galerkin procedure.

Also included in this class is the H^{-1}-Galerkin procedure of Rachford and Wheeler [213], Kendall and Wheeler [157], and Douglas, Dupont and Wheeler [98]. Write Eq. (2.1) as $Ly = f$ and let L^* denote the formal adjoint of L. This method develops approximations $y_n \in S(r,k,\Delta)$ by solving

$$(2.4.2) \qquad \int_0^1 y_n L^* v_i \, dx = \int_0^1 f v_i \, dx$$

where $\{v_i\}$ forms a basis for $S(r+2, k+2, \Delta) \cap \{v: v'(0) = v'(1) = 0\}$. Optimal rates of convergence are obtained in the L^2-norm and superconvergence results are obtained for the case $k = -1$. The analysis is restricted to second order problems but general separated boundary conditions are considered. The lead order part of the equation needs to be elliptic. The method approximates oscillatory solutions well. See [213] for numerical experiments.

2.5. Other. There are a number of other methods with attractive features that do not fit into any of the preceding categories. Indeed, some of these methods cannot properly be called projection methods but are modifications of projection methods.

One projection method is the C^0-Collocation-Finite element scheme described by Diaz [84] and Wheeler [281]. This method chooses y_n in $S_0(r,0,\Delta)$ so that

$$(2.5.1) \qquad -y_n''(\xi_{ij}) + a_0(\xi_{ij})y_n'(\xi_{ij}) + a_1(\xi_{ij})y_n(\xi_{ij}) = f(\xi_{ij})$$

and

$$(2.5.2) \qquad \int_0^1 (y_n'v_i' + a_0 y_n' v_i + a_1 y_n v_i) \, dx = \int_0^1 f v_i \, dx$$

where ξ_{ij} are the translated roots of the monic Jacobi polynomial of degree r-1, and $\{v_i\}$ spans $S_0(1,0,\Delta)$. This method achieves optimal rates of convergence in the L^∞-norm for arbitrary meshes and, in contrast to pure collocation methods, requires only minimal smoothness on the solution in order to achieve this optimal rate. Superconvergence results (better than for collocation) are obtained and extrapolation procedures as in Dupont [101] are also developed. Similar results for a combination of collocation and the H^{-1}-Galerkin method are given by Dunn and Wheeler [100].

Another method of interest is the extrapolated collocation method using C^2-cubic splines given by Fyfe [114], Archer and Diaz [11], and Daniel and Swartz [62]. This method requires uniform meshes and applies to general second-order problems. Optimal rates of convergence are obtained with a minimal set of equations, but again extra smoothness is required. The solution to (2.1) with general boundary conditions must lie in C^6. The basic idea is that equations that a cubic spline interpolant of the solution satisfies to high accuracy are derived and then solved numerically. We mention here also a related $O(h^4)$ method using C^2-cubics of Albasiny and Hoskins [3] which also requires a uniform mesh.

Finally, we mention the finite difference methods of Doedel [91], [92] and Lynch and Rice [178]. Although one approach to these methods uses ideas of classical finite differences, Doedel [92] has shown they can be interpreted as collocation methods using overlapping piecewise polynomial functions.

2.6. Interdependence. The methods cited above are in some cases closely related, and possibly identical, even though they have been derived from different starting points. In the quadrature-Galerkin method, if the total number of quadrature points used is equal to dim $S_0(r,k,\Delta)$ and the quadrature weights are nonzero, then collocation at the quadrature points is equivalent to it. Generally, however, more quadrature points are used [225]. For least squares, normally more quadrature points are used than dim $S_0(r,k,\Delta)$ and then the method can be viewed as an overdetermined collocation scheme whose equations have been scaled and solved by discrete least squares. See Russell and Varah [225] and Ascher [15].

The equivalence of the quadrature-Galerkin method when the quadrature points are chosen to be Gauss points with collocation at Gauss points has important theoretical implications. Douglas and Dupont [93] develop their proofs of convergence of collocation from the quadrature-Galerkin formulation. This approach is extendable to more general problems whereas the projection method approach is more difficult. For parabolic problems, see Douglas and Dupont [93], and for hyperbolic problems, see Houstis [133]. Hulme [137] made this observation for the initial value problem for ordinary differential equations.

2.7. Non-spline Bases. Projection methods can of course be applied to (2.1) - (2.2) without using splines. For example, one can use polynomials of degree n+2 satisfying the boundary conditions (2.2) and use collocation with collocation points chosen to be Tschebychev points translated to [0,1]. See Vainikko [267] or Kantovorich and Akilov [144]. One can also use polynomials with Galerkin's method. See, for example, Urabe [265] and Urabe and Reiter [266] and the books by Kantovorich and Krylov [145] and Mihklin [185].

3. Projection Methods. In this section we explain why the preceding methods are called projection methods and then give a few basic results that enable one to begin their analysis.

3.1. Projection Operators. Let X be a normed linear space. A projection operator P on X is a linear, idempotent ($P^2 = P$) mapping from X into itself. We will be concerned only with projections of finite rank. Let X' denote the algebraic dual of X. Then the following characterization result is known [99].

Lemma 3.1.1. Let P_n be a projection on X. Define $X_n = P_nX$. Let P_n' be the conjugate operator associated with P_n and define $X_n' = P_n'X'$. Then if x_n is in X_n,

$$x'(x_n) = 0 \tag{3.1.2}$$

for all $x' \in X'_n$ implies $x_n = 0$. Conversely, given subspaces X_n and X'_n of X and X' respectively of the same dimension and satisfying (3.1.2), then a unique projection operator P_n is defined by the relations $P_n x = x_n$ if and only if $x_n \in X_n$ and $x'(x_n) = x'(x)$ for all $x' \in X'_n$.

We have not required the linear functionals x' to be continuous. However, the following result holds [99].

Lemma 3.1.2. P_n is bounded if and only if $X'_n \subset X^*$, the dual space of continuous linear functionals on X.

The projection operators considered here will be mappings generally from $L^2[0,1]$, $C[0,1]$ or certain Sobolev spaces onto $S(r,k,\Delta)$. Given a sequence of such projections, $\{P_n\}$, one wants bounds $C(n)$ so that $\|P_n\| \leq C(n)$. It is desirable, but not necessary [267], to have sequences satisfying $C(n) \leq$ const. Suppose, for simplicity, that the sequence $\{P_n\}$ is formed by adding vectors to X_n and functionals to X'_n, i.e. $X_n = \text{span}\{\phi_1, \ldots, \phi_n\}$ and $X'_n = \text{span}\{\lambda_1, \ldots, \lambda_n\}$. Then $P_n x = \sum_{i=1}^{n} \alpha_i^{(n)} \phi_i$ and $P_n x$ satisfies

$$\sum_{i=1}^{n} \alpha_i^{(n)} \lambda_j(\phi_i) = \lambda_j(f) \ , \quad j = 1, \ldots, n.$$

Define $A_n = [a_{ij}]$ with $a_{ij} = \lambda_i(\phi_j)$. The well-posedness of P_n implies

$$\text{(3.1.3)} \qquad \begin{bmatrix} \alpha_1^{(n)} \\ \cdot \\ \cdot \\ \cdot \\ \alpha_n^{(n)} \end{bmatrix} = A_n^{-1} \begin{bmatrix} \lambda_1 f \\ \cdot \\ \cdot \\ \cdot \\ \lambda_n f \end{bmatrix} .$$

Thus bounding $\|P_n\|$ can be broken down into the following steps. First note $\|P_n x\| \leq (\max|\alpha_i^{(n)}|) \sum_{i=1}^{n} \|\phi_i\|$. A basis $\{\phi_i\}$ with $\sum_{i=1}^{n} \|\phi_i\| \leq$ const. would be convenient here. Actually, $\sum_{i=1}^{n} \phi_i \leq$ const. with $\phi_i \geq 0$ would do. Then we need to bound $\|A_n^{-1}\|_\infty$ if we know $\max|\lambda_i f| \leq$ const. $\|f\|$ in order to bound the projectors. This can be a difficult matrix problem and is dependent on a detailed knowledge of specific bases for X_n. For an excellent discussion of these matters for the case that X_n is a spline space, see deBoor [71].

Projections P_n may be thought of as general interpolation mappings since $P_n f$ interpolates f in the sense that $\lambda_i(f) = \lambda_i(P_n f)$. The following estimate of the distance between a vector and its projection is useful.

Lemma 3.1.4. $\|x - P_n x\| \leq \|I - P_n\| \operatorname{dist}(x, X_n)$.

A uniformly bounded (in norm) sequence of projections achieves best asymptotic rates of convergence. If X is a Banach space, a sequence of projections will be uniformly bounded in norm if they converge strongly to the identity operator on X.

3.2.1. Projection Methods. Let A be a linear operator with domain in a normed linear space X and range in a normed linear space Y. Let X_n be a finite dimensional subspace of X and Y_n a finite dimensional subspace of Y^* with dim X_n = dim $Y_n < \infty$. We assume $\lambda(Ax_n) = 0$ for $x_n \in X_n$ and all $\lambda \in Y^*$ implies $x_n = 0$.

Definition 3.2.1. A projection method approximates the solution x of the equation Ax = f with $x_n \in X_n$ where

(3.2.2) $$\lambda(Ax_n) = \lambda f,$$

all $\lambda \in Y_n$.

The setting for this definition can obviously be generalized. Several projection operators can be associated with Eq. (3.2.2). Using Lemma 3.2.2, define the projection P_n through AX_n and Y_n. Then Eq. (3.2.2) may be written as

(3.2.3) $$Ax_n = P_n f$$

and the representation formula

(3.2.4) $$x_n = A^{-1} P_n f$$

holds. Alternately, define the projection Q_n through X_n and $A'Y_n$. Then (3.2.2) may be written as

$$(A'\lambda)x_n = \lambda f = \lambda Ax = A'\lambda x, \tag{3.2.5}$$

or as

$$x_n = Q_n x_n = Q_n x. \tag{3.2.6}$$

If A is not bounded, then there is no guarantee that the functionals $A'\lambda$ are bounded and so P_n may be bounded while Q_n is not. Define Z_n to be any subspace of Y with dimension equal to the dimension of Y_n and so that for $z_n \in Z_n$

$$\lambda(z_n) = 0, \quad \text{all } \lambda \text{ in } Y_n$$

implies $z_n = 0$. Let Z_n and Y_n define a projection R_n. Then (3.2.2) may be written as

$$R_n A x_n = R_n f. \tag{3.2.7}$$

These projections can be related by the identities

$$P_n = (R_n|_{AX_n})^{-1} R_n \tag{3.2.8}$$

and

$$Q_n = (R_n A|_{X_n})^{-1} R_n A. \tag{3.2.9}$$

These operator formulations can be used to give an error analysis. Since

$$x - x_n = A^{-1}(f - P_n f) \tag{3.2.10}$$

then

$$(3.2.11)\qquad \begin{aligned} \|x - x_n\| &\le \|A^{-1}\|\,\|I - P_n\|\,\mathrm{dist}(f,AX_n)\\ \|Ax - Ax_n\| &\le \|I - P_n\|\,\mathrm{dist}(f,AX_n) \end{aligned}$$

and convergence results follow from the properties of the projections P_n and R_n. Also note

$$(3.2.12)\qquad \|x - x_n\| = \|x - Q_n x\| \le \|I - Q_n\|\,\mathrm{dist}(x,X_n).$$

There are many special cases of the operator A that are easy to handle. We consider two. Suppose $A = I + T$ where T is compact on $X \to X$ where X is a Banach space. Then our problem may be written as

$$(3.2.13)\qquad (I + T)v = f$$

and our numerical method may be written following (3.2.7) as

$$(3.2.14)\qquad R_n(v_n + Tv_n) = R_n f.$$

Define R_n so that it has range X_n; Eq. (3.2.14) becomes $v_n + R_n Tv_n = R_n f$. Suppose R_n converges strongly to the identity operator on X. Then $\|R_n\| \le$ const. and by Lemma 3.1.4 we have that approximation by R_n achieves best rates of convergence. With T compact and if $(I + T)^{-1}$ exists, then $(I + T)^{-1}$ is automatically bounded. It follows that

$$(3.2.15)\qquad \|R_n T - T\| \to 0 \quad \text{as } n \to \infty,$$

and so $(I + R_n T)^{-1}$ exists for n sufficiently large and $\|(I + R_n T)^{-1}\| \le$ (const.) is valid. Now operating through (3.2.13) by R_n, subtracting this from (3.2.14) and subtracting v from both sides leads to the equation

$$(3.2.16) \qquad v - v_n = (I + R_nT)^{-1}(v - R_nv).$$

We can now bound the quantities in (3.2.11) and have proved the following theorem.

Theorem 3.2.17. Let T be completely continuous mapping on a Banach space X into itself, let $(I + T)^{-1}$ exist, and let $\{R_n\}$ be a sequence of projections on X with $R_nX = X_n$ so that R_n converges strongly to the identity on X. Then for all n sufficiently large, the equation $v_n + R_nTv_n = R_nf$, with $v_n \in X_n$, has a unique solution v_n for any $f \in X$. Let v solve $v + Tv = f$. Then

$$(3.2.18) \qquad \|v - v_n\| \leq \|(I + R_n)^{-1}\| \cdot \|v - R_nv\| \leq \text{const.} \|I - R_n\| \text{dist}(v,X_n).$$

Several improvements on this basic and important theorem are immediately possible. One is by a Newton's method argument to nonlinear mappings T that are completely continuous and continuously Frèchet differentiable. We omit statements of these important nonlinear results here, but refer the reader to Vainikko [268], deBoor and Swartz [70], and Keller [151]. For the Galerkin method in the nonlinear case, analysis can be done using monotone operator theory, e.g. Ciarlet, Shultz, Varga [56].

Suppose our given equation has the form

$$(3.2.19) \qquad Ax + Bx = f$$

where A and B are mappings, possibly unbounded, from X into Y but with A^{-1} bounded and with a constant $c > 0$ so that

$$(3.2.20) \qquad \|BA^{-1}\| \leq c.$$

Assume $(A + B)^{-1}$ exists and is bounded. Given a projection method defined by X_n and Y_n, define $Z_n = AX_n$ and write the approximation equations

(3.2.21) $\lambda(Ax_n + Bx_n) = \lambda f, \quad \text{all } \lambda \in Y_n,$

as

(3.2.22) $\lambda(v_n + BA^{-1}v_n) = \lambda f, \quad v_n \in Z_n, \quad \text{all } \lambda \in Y_n.$

Defining the projection R_n by Z_n and Y_n, (3.2.22) becomes

(3.2.23) $v_n + R_n BA^{-1} v_n = R_n f.$

If BA^{-1} is compact, then we may use Theorem 3.2.17.

This analysis applies to many of the examples in section 2. Eq. (2.1.1) - (2.1.2) can be treated as follows. Define $A = D^2$, $B = a_0 D + a_1$, $Y_n = \text{span}\{\lambda_i\}$ where $\lambda_i f \equiv f(t_i)$, $X_n = S_0(r,k,\Delta)$, $Z_n = S(r-2, k-2, \Delta)$, $X = C[0,1] \cap \{v: v(0) = v(1) = 0\}$ and $Y = C[0,1]$. Assume $k \geq 2$. Convergence depends on the properties of the interpolation operator R_n on Y where $R_n f = s$ if and only if $s \in S(r-2, k-2, \Delta)$ and $\lambda_i f = \lambda_i s$, $i = 1, \ldots, N-2$. If uniformly bounded, then Theorem 3.2.17 applies.

As a consequence of formula (3.2.9) in this setting, we obtain

<u>Lemma 3.2.24.</u> $Q_n = (I + R_n BA^{-1})^{-1} R_n (I + BA^{-1}).$

This lemma is contained in deBoor and Swartz [70] and also Natterer [190]. As a consequence of it, the boundedness of Q_n can be deduced from a study of R_n. The practical implication is that one need only consider the projector associated with the lead order part of the differential operator.

Many variations on Theorem 3.2.18 and Lemma 3.2.24 are possible. We cite here Vainikko [268], Polskii [210], Petryshn [207], Browder [31], Krasnoselskii et. al. [160], and Witsch [287] as important references. Kramarz [159] replaces projections with general mappings using the theory of collectively compact operators.

Consider as another example the Ritz-Galerkin method for $(py')' = -f$,

$0 < x < 1$, $y(0) = y(1) = 0$ with $p \in C^1[0,1]$ and $p > 0$ on $[0,1]$. With $\{v_i\}$ a basis for $S_0(r,k,\Delta)$, solve

$$(3.2.25) \qquad \int_0^1 p y_n' v_i' \, dx = \int_0^1 f v_i \, dx, \quad \text{all } v_i,$$

$y_n \in S_0(r,k,\Delta)$. To put (3.2.25) in the form (3.2.2) can be done in two ways if $k \geq 1$, but only one way otherwise. The question is whether or not the left hand side of (3.2.25) can be integrated by parts without the appearance of jump terms at the mesh points. We consider (3.2.25) directly. Then the given equation is treated in weak form to find $y \in H_0^1$ so that

$$\int_0^1 p y' v' \, dx = \int_0^1 f v ,$$

for all v in H_0^1, where $H^1 \equiv \{v\colon v \text{ and } v' \text{ are in } L^2\}$ and $H_0^1 \equiv H^1 \cap \{v\colon v(0) = v(1) = 0\}$ with the Hilbert space norm [17]. Here f is considered in, say, L^2, but f could be in H^{-1}, the dual of H_0^1. Since p is positive, $\int_0^1 p y' v' \, dx$ defines a coercive bilinear form on H_0^1 and can be written for fixed y as (Ay,v) in the duality product on H^1 with A linear, A^{-1} bounded, and A mapping onto H^{-1}. See Aubin [17] or Strang and Fix [260] for details.

Define the Ritz-Galerkin projection by the subspace $AS_0(r,k,\Delta)$ and the functionals $\lambda_i(w) \equiv (w,v_i) = \int_0^1 v_i w \, dx$. Note here that the linear functionals are in the dual of H^{-1} which we identify with H_0^1. Now

$$|(Ay_n,y_n)| = |(P_n f,y_n)| = |(f,y_n)|$$

and so

$$\|y_n\|_{H^1} \leq c\|f\|_{-1}.$$

Since

$$\|Ay_n\|_{-1} = \sup_{\substack{v \\ v \in H_0^1}} \frac{|(Ay_n,v)|}{\|v\|_{H^1}} \leq c\,\|y_n\|_{H^1} ,$$

then

$$\|Ay_n\|_{-1} = \|P_n f\|_{-1} \leq \text{const.}\, \|f\|_{-1}$$

and the projections P_n are uniformly bounded. Using (3.2.11) we have

(3.2.26) $$\|y - y_n\|_{H^1} \leq \text{const.}\ \|A^{-1}\|\,\text{dist}(f, AX_n).$$

Improvements in the bound implied by (3.2.26) for both the L^2 and L^∞-norms are possible using a duality argument. See Aubin [17], Blair [27], Nitsche [192], Dupont, Douglas and Wahlbin [96], Wheeler [280] and Schultz [232]. Theoretically treating the Ritz-Galerkin method the same way as collocation leads to projections that seem impossible to bound [67].

The method of least squares can also be formulated as an operator equation with projections. Applied to (2.1) - (2.2), it can be viewed as computing $y_n \in S_0(r,k,\Delta)$ to solve

(3.2.27) $$\min_{y \in S_0(r,k,\Delta)} \|Ly - f\|_{L^2}^2$$

where $Ly \equiv -y'' + a_0 y' + a_1 y$. In the same manner as illustrated by Eq. (3.2.23), write (3.2.27) as

(3.2.28) $$\min_{v \in S(r-2,\ k-2,\ \Delta)} \|v - (f - Tv)\|_{L^2}^2 .$$

Let P_n denote the L^2-orthogonal projection operator with range $S(r-2,\ k-2,\ \Delta)$. Then (3.2.28) with $v_n = y_n''$ implies

(3.2.29) $$v_n = P_n(f - Tv_n),$$

or, finally, as

(3.2.30) $$v_n + P_n T v_n = P_n f.$$

Thus basic convergence results follow from Theorem 3.2.17. Of course,

$\|P_n\|_{L^2} = 1$. However, $\|P_n\|_{L^\infty} \leq$ const. is also known for quasi-uniform meshes and arbitrary r, k. See Douglas, Dupont and Wahlbin [96] and deBoor [68].

If one uses collocation at the Tschebychev points with polynomials as described in seciton 2.7, the projections R_n defined in analogy with spline collocation schemes satisfy on C[0,1] [267]

$$\|R_n\|_\infty \leq 8 + \frac{4}{\pi} \ln n.$$

This lack of uniform boundedness for the projections does not prevent convergence of the method. For the modification of Theorem 3.2.17 that will treat this case see [267].

4. Superconvergence. Some methods give higher order convergence rates at certain points than might be anticipated from global approximation rates. We mention here some important examples and then discuss implications of these results for more refined error estimates and the development of adaptive codes. See also the papers of Russell and Ascher in these proceedings.

4.1 Examples. For problem (2.1) - (2.2), suppose we solve for $y_n \in S_0(r,1,\Delta)$ and collocate at Gaussian points as defined in Section 2.1. Then the following theorem holds.

Theorem 4.1.1. (deBoor and Swartz). Let k be a positive integer and let r = k+1. Let the coefficients a_0 and a_1 be in C^{2k} and let y be in C^{2+2k}. Then

$$|D^i(y - y_n)(x_j)| \leq ch^{2k} = ch^{2r-2}, \quad i = 0, 1.$$

Thus, if k = 4, i.e. quintic splines are used, convergence at the mesh points is $O(h^8)$ while global convergence is $O(h^6)$. In the case k = 2, i.e. cubic splines, there is no improvement. This theorem in the quintic case requires that the solution have ten continuous derivatives.

We contrast this with the Ritz-Galerkin method. Using Eq. (2.2.2) with continuous splines, we have the next theorem.

Theorem 4.1.2. (Douglas and Dupont). Let a_0 and a_1 be in C^{r-1}, $r \geq 1$, with a_0' in L^∞ and let $f \in C$. Suppose the solution y of (2.1) - (2.2) is in $C^{r+1}(I)$ and that y_n is chosen from $S_0(r,0,\Delta)$ solving (2.2.2). Then

$$|y(x_j) - y_n(x_j)| \leq ch^{2r}.$$

Theorem 4.1.2 does not require additional smoothness to achieve superconvergence, and in the cubic spline case, $r = 3$, superconvergence occurs. However, if one implements (2.2.2) by using r-point Gauss quadrature, y is implicitly required to be in H^{2r+2}.

Both the proofs of Theorem 4.1.1 and Theorem 4.1.2 rely on the low order continuity class of the splines used in an essential way.

Other superconvergence results are known. For more facts about collocation at Gauss points, see Christiansen and Russell [52]. The C^0-collocation method of Diaz [84] and Wheeler [281] converges at the mesh of order $O(h^{2r})$ for arbitrary mesh spacings. The H^{-1} method of Rachford and Wheeler [213] and Kendall and Wheeler [157] achieves superconvergence at the Gauss points in the case $k = -1$. See Eq. (2.4.2). Convergence there is one order better than the best rate.

Dupont [101] has shown how performing certain auxiliary computations using Galerkin solutions (also H^{-1} and H^1-Galerkin) can give superconvergent approximations to the value of the solution and its derivative at any point. Arbitrary continuity classes for the splines are considered. See also Diaz [84], Wheeler [281], Kendall and Wheeler [157], and Douglas and Dupont [95].

4.2 Refined Error Bounds. If superconvergence occurs, it is possible to modify the argument that produced the superconvergence to obtain refined error bounds that indicate local dependence for the error. Suppose one uses collocation at Gauss points for (2.1) - (2.2). Then with suitable smoothness, deBoor [74] has shown (see also Christiansen and Russell [52] and Ascher, Christiansen and Russell [13]) that

$$(4.2.1) \qquad \|y - y_n\|_{L^\infty(I_i)} \le c \, \|D^{r+1} y\|_{L^\infty(I_i)} \, h_i^{r+1} + o(h^{r+1}) \; .$$

Thus to lead order the method is local and an estimate for $D^{r+1}y$ can lead to algorithms for equidistributing the error. See Pereyra and Sewell [204] and [13], [51], [52] and [74]. Similar results are known for the Galerkin method [190], for the H^{-1}-Galerkin method [213], and the C^0-collocation-Galerkin method [281].

In the case of the Galerkin method with continuous splines for (2.1) - (2.2), Natterer [190] established the bound

$$(4.2.2) \qquad \|y - y_n\|_{L^\infty(I)} \le C \max_i \, (h_i^{r+1} \, \|y^{r+1}\|_{L^\infty(I_i)}) \; .$$

Generalizations of this result to higher order equations are also given in [190]. The integrals required for the method were assumed done exactly. It was also indicated there that a bound of the form (4.2.2) does not hold for collocation at Gauss points. The existence of bounds such as (4.2.1) seems at present to be more important computationally than superconvergence, although they occur together.

Mesh Selection Methods

by Robert D. Russell

1. Introduction

The efficiency of a numerical algorithm for solving a class of problems is critically affected by its computer implementation. This is demonstrated, for example, by Shampine et al. [39], who evaluate two codes using a fourth-order Runge-Kutta-Fehlberg method to solve IVP's (initial-value problems). Their performances are quite different, a major reason being that step-size selection is done differently for each.

Once a method for solving BVP's (boundary-value problem) for ODE's (ordinary differential equations) is selected, its efficiency for solving most problems depends upon the way error estimation, mesh selection, and solution of nonlinear equations are done. Indeed, the latter two aspects affect whether difficult problems can be solved at all. Methods for solving nonlinear equations ar surveyed in [82], and here we survey mesh selection methods. Despite its importanc mesh selection is just beginning to emerge from infancy, so by necessity we shall often outline potential areas of investigation rather than give firm conclusions. W consider mesh selection for finite-element and finite-difference methods mainly. Th automatic selection of multiple shooting points is closely related and is discussed briefly (see [238] for superposition).

A number of fringe benefits have arisen from the study of mesh selection for ODE BVP's. Its overlap with the study of mesh selection for interpolation and least squares problems [90], step-size selection for IVP's, and mesh selection for PDE's (partial differential equations) has been of mutual benefit. Furthermore, mes selection considerations have precipitated a deeper investigation of error bounds fo numerical methods, viz. better understanding of a priori error estimates and more emphasis on a posteriori error estimates have resulted.

2. Preliminaries

We shall consider two basic BVP's on $[0,1]$, the scalar problem

(1a)
$$N(u) = u^{(m)}(x) - f(x,u,u', \ldots, u^{(m-1)}) = 0 \qquad 0 < x < 1,$$
$$b_i(u(0), \ldots, u^{(m-1)}(0), u(1), \ldots, u^{(m-1)}(1)) = 0 \qquad (1 \le i \le m)$$

and the dth-order problem

(1b)
$$N(u) = u'(x) - f(x,u) = 0 \qquad 0 < x < 1,$$
$$B(u(0),u(1)) = 0$$

where $u(x) = (u_1(x), \ldots, u_d(x))^T$. To treat both problems simultaneously when possible, scalar and vector functions are not distinguished. Many methods treat problems in the form (1a), while numerical methods which handle general systems usually convert to (1b). A mesh-selection approach for solving (1a) can be straightforward to generalize for solving mixed order systems, as in [13].

Using a finite element or finite difference method, an approximation $v(x)$ to the exact solution $u(x)$ is formed by solving a discrete system of equations

(1') $$N_{\pi_N}(v) = 0.$$

Here, π_N is a mesh on $[0,1]$ defined by $\pi_N : 0 = x_1 < x_2 < \ldots < x_{N+1} = 1$ with $h_i = x_{i+1} - x_i$, $h = \max h_i$, $\underline{h} = \min h_i$. The mesh-selection problem which concerns us is the following: Given a discretization method (1'), find a mesh π_N such that N is "small" but $v(x)$ computed using π_N is accurate.

Def: A family of meshes Π is quasiuniform if there exists a constant $c > 0$ such that for all $\pi \in \Pi$, $\frac{h}{\underline{h}} \le c$.* The family Π is locally quasiuniform if for all $\pi \in \Pi$, $\frac{h_i}{h_j} \le c$ whenever $|i - j| \le 1$.

Typically, the error of a numerical solution satisfies a relation like

(2a) $$|(u - v)_j| \le c \max_{1\le i\le N} \|\tau_i[u]\|_p \qquad (1 \le j \le N),$$

where $|w_j|$ is some measure of the size of $w(x)$ or its derivatives somewhere in $[x_j, x_{j+1}]$ and $\tau_i[u] = h_i{}^k T(x_i) + O(h^{k+1})$ is an expression involving high derivatives of $u(x)$. Equivalently,

(2b) $$|(u - v)_j| \le c \max_{1\le i\le N} h_i{}^k \|T(x_i)\|_p + O(h^{k+1}) \qquad 1 \le j \le N.$$

We consider this error bound as arising in the following ways:

FD For finite-difference methods

(2c) $$\|u(x_j) - v(x_j)\|_p \le c \max \|\tau_i[u]\|_p \qquad 1 \le j \le N$$

where the local truncation error $\tau_i[u] = N_\pi(u(x_i))$. Generally, this bound is derived using stability and $T(x) = u^{(\ell)}(x)$, with $\ell = k + 1$ for (1b).

FE For finite-element methods, the error for a piecewise polynomial of degree $k - 1$ on each $[x_i, x_{i+1}]$ is bounded by:

FE(1) considering a projection error, so, e.g., $\|T(x_i)\|_p = \max_{x_i\le x\le x_{i+1}} \|u^{(k)}(x)\|_p$ in (2b);

FE(2) expressing $h_i{}^k\|T(x_i)\|_p$ in terms of a residual - like $r(x) = N(u(x)) - N(v(x)) = - N(v(x))$ on (x_i, x_{i+1}).

---

* Throughout the paper, c is a generic constant.

A number of mesh-selection schemes attempt to select N such that $\max_{1\le i\le N} h_i^k \|T_i(x)\|_p$ is small, which then forces the error to become "small" for a given N, at least if the meshes are kept quasiuniform. It is particularly insightful to have certain definitions when investigating mesh selection schemes.

Def: [204] A mesh π is equidistributing wrt (with respect to) $\tau_i[u]$ if

$$(3) \qquad h_i \|\tau_i[u]\|_p^p \equiv c \qquad 1 \le i \le N,$$

where $1 < p < \infty$.* For $p = \infty$, $\|\tau_i[u]\| \equiv c$. A sequence of meshes $\{\pi_N\}$ is asymptotically equidistributing (a.e.) wrt $\tau_i[u]$ if

$$(4) \qquad h_i \|\tau_i[u]\|_p^p \equiv c \ (1 + O(h)).$$

Thus, $\{\pi_N\}$ is a.e. wrt $\tau_i[u]$ or $h_i^k \|T(x_i)\|_p$ if

$$(4') \qquad h_i \|h_i^k T(x_i)\|_p^p \equiv c, \quad \text{or} \quad h_i \|T(x_i)\|_p^\sigma \equiv c \qquad (1 \le i \le N),$$

where $\sigma = \dfrac{p}{pk+1}$. When convenient, we shall just refer to a mesh π_N being a.e. or an a.e. mesh.

In order to construct an a.e. mesh one frequently satisfies (4') for a function $m(x,u) = \|T(x)\|_p^\sigma$ by requiring

$$(4'') \qquad \int_{x_i}^{x_{i+1}} m(x,u)\,dx \equiv c \qquad (1 \le i \le N).$$

Def: [204] We call $\int_0^1 m(x,u)\,dx$ equidistributed on π_N when (4") holds.

---

* This definition arose in [204] using a slightly different error form than (2a).

This motivates the next definition, where it is important to note that $m(x,u)$ does not necessarily have any relation to the error bound (2), or even depend on $u(x)$.

Def: [283] A function $\xi(x)$ is an (admissible) monitor for (1) if

$$(5)\qquad \frac{d\xi}{dx} = m(x,u) \geq c > 0 \ \forall x \in [0,1],\ \xi(0) = 0,\ \xi(1) = 1,$$

and the partial derivatives of $m(x,w)$ are continuous $\forall x \in [0,1]$ and all $w(x)$ in a region around $u(x)$.

Note that $\int_0^1 m(x,u)dx$ is equidistributed on π_N when $\xi(x_{i+1}) - \xi(x_i) \equiv c$. If $\xi(x)$ is normalized,

$$(5')\qquad \frac{d\xi}{dx} = \frac{m(x,u)}{\int_0^1 m(x,u)dx},\quad \xi(0) = 0,$$

then $\xi(x_{i+1}) - \xi(x_i) \equiv \frac{1}{N}$ $(1 \leq i \leq N)$. When a given $m(x,u)$ is > 1 (< 1) in a region of $[0,1]$, an a.e. mesh is determined by inserting (removing) mesh points in that region. Solving elliptic PDE's, Simpson* calls $m(x,y,u(x,y))$ a concentration or density.

Motivated by the above, we consider the problem of selecting a mesh π_N to be equivalent to determining a coordinate transformation or monitor $\xi(x)$ such that equal spacing in ξ is used, i.e., the mesh π_N gives $\xi(x_{i+1}) - \xi(x_i) \equiv \frac{1}{N}$ $(1 \leq i \leq N)$. We (somewhat artificially) separate the mesh-selection methods for BVP into two categories. In the first group, either $\xi(x)$ is selected a priori or an "optimal" $\xi(x)$ is incorporated into the problem in such a way that $\xi(x)$ and $v(x)$ are calculated simultaneously. In the second group, two-cycle methods are considered, viz. one uses an iteration process where a mesh π_N (or coordinate transformation $\xi(x)$) and an approximate solution $v(x)$ are calculated alternately.

* R.B. Simpson, "Automatic local refinement for irregular meshes," Res. Rep. C5-78-1, Univ. of Waterloo, 1978.

3. Coordinate Transformations and Simultaneous Methods

For special problems, coordinate transformations or coordinate stretchings $\xi(x)$ are chosen so that boundary layers in the solution $u(x)$ disappear and a uniform mesh spacing $\xi_{i+1} - \xi_i \equiv \frac{1}{N}$ can be used. There are many examples of this in the engineering literature, e.g., see [76]. The transformation $\xi(x)$ for which $\frac{h_{i+1}}{h_i} \equiv c$ $(1 \le i \le N - 1)$ gives equal spacing in ξ is fairly simple [42] and is compared with other transformations by Blottner [28] for solving fluid flow problems. Similarly, Roberts [220] considers several choices of $\xi(x)$ for problems with end boundary layers of known thickness. The results compare favourably with using a piecewise uniform mesh, corresponding to $\xi(x)$ piecewise linear. Wilson and Schryer [285] also consider a piecewise uniform mesh for solving boundary layer problems with a Galerkin method. For general purposes, however, these a priori transformations are usually not appropriate since they require rather specific information about $u(x)$ and are complicated when nested boundary layers of different thicknesses or internal boundary layers exist.

More general approaches determine $\xi(x)$ by requiring some optimality condition to be satisfied. For example, Tang and Turcke [261] consider choosing an optimal mesh for a PDE by requiring the first variation of the potential energy to be zero. The optimal $\xi(x)$ is explicitly determined in a special case in [212].

Another possibility is to require $\xi(x)$ to be an (admissible) monitor for (1), where $\frac{d\xi}{dx} = m(x,u)$ has magnitude reflecting the behaviour of the unknown function $u(x)$. Solving the (vector) IVP

$$\frac{du}{dx} = f(x,u), \quad u(0) = u_0 ,$$

Krogh [161] suggests converting this to

$$\frac{du}{d\xi} = \frac{f(x,u)}{m(x,u)} \qquad u(0) = u_0$$

$$\frac{dx}{d\xi} = \frac{1}{m(x,u)} \qquad x(0) = 0$$

and determining $\xi(x)$ (with $\int_0^1 m(x,u)dx$ equidistributed) automatically, perhaps using local error estimates. In a stimulating paper by White [283], this basic idea is used for solving (1b), which becomes

(6a) $$\frac{du}{d\xi} = \frac{f(x,u)}{m(x,u)} \qquad B(u(0),u(1)) = 0$$

(6b) $$\frac{dx}{d\xi} = \frac{\theta}{m(x,u)} \qquad x(0) = 0$$

(6c) $$\frac{d\theta}{d\xi} = 0 \qquad x(1) = 1.$$

After $m(x,u)$ is selected, (6) is solved for an approximate solution $v(\xi)$ and mesh points $x(\xi)$ using finite differences (the trapezoid rule) and equal spacing $\xi_{i+1} - \xi_i \equiv \frac{1}{N}$. Choices of $m(x,u)$ considered include (i) arc length $\sqrt{1 + \|u'\|_2^2}$ (ii) $[1 + \|u'''\|_2^2]^{1/4}$ so that local truncation error satisfies $\|\tau_i[u]\|_2 = h_i^2\|u_i'''\|_2 \equiv c(1 + O(h))$, and (iii) $[1 + \|u'''\|_2^2]^{1/6}$ so that single-step error satisfies $h_i\|\tau_i[u]\|_2 \equiv c(1 + O(h))$. Monitors involving high derivatives of $u(x)$ can be extremely complicated to implement, and this is one reason that White recommends using arc length. However, for arc length (and presumably the other monitors?), a difficult problem transformed into (6) can still be extremely difficult to solve.* Determination of a monitor $\xi(x)$ such that both $u(\xi)$ and $x(\xi)$ have bounded derivatives for a wide class of problems could be extremely useful. Preceding White's work, Gough et al. [120] made essentially the transformation to (6) and used this approach, as we discuss in the next section.

Most of the methods in this section were originally developed for solving BVP's using finite-difference methods, but the basic approaches are usually applicable in a broader context. For example, selecting a monitor $\xi(x)$ and using Krogh's transformation of the IVP, it is straightforward to then apply multiple shooting with the shooting points equally spaced wrt $\xi(x)$.

---

* Victor Pereyra, private communication; also, see §5.

4. Two-Cycle Methods

For two-cycle methods, an approximate solution $v(x)$ is first computed on an initial mesh. A fixed $\frac{d\xi}{dx} = m(x,u)$ (whose choice is frequently motivated by (2)) is basically approximated by $m(x,v)$ and a new mesh a.e. wrt $m(x,v)$ is computed. The process is then repeated. In terms of the transformation (6), (1) is approximately solved for $v(x)$ by (1') and (6b,c) is solved for $\pi = \{x(\xi_i)\}$ alternately. Often $\int_0^1 m(x,v)dx = \theta$ is calculated directly and π_N satisfying $\int_{x_i}^{x_{i+1}} m(x,v)dx = \xi_{i+1} - \xi_i \equiv \frac{\theta}{N}$ $(1 \le i \le N)$ is solved by inverse interpolation with $x_0 = 0$. If $(x_{i+1} - x_i)m(x_i,v(x_i)) = \int_{x_i}^{x_{i+1}} m(x,v)dx$, this is equivalent to using Euler's method with equal spacing to solve (6b).

Dodson [90] uses this process to solve (1a) with a collocation method, where $m(x,u)$ involves an interpolating polynomial error bound. Taking $m(x,u)$ piecewise constant, inverting $\xi(x)$ is trivial, and fortunately this is often the natural form $m(x,v)$ takes. Dodson gives convincing arguments that a "good" mesh obtained this way is computationally more practical than obtaining an "optimal" mesh. Even if $u(x)$ is known, he demonstrates that calculating an optimal mesh involves solving difficult nonlinear equations and is often less efficient.

The major theoretical result which describes the effect of equidistributing a mesh wrt the main error bound term is a theorem of Pereyra and Sewell [204].

Theorem Suppose that (2) holds and $\int_0^1 \|T(x)\|_p^\sigma\, dx$, $\sigma = \frac{p}{kp+1}$, is equidistributed wrt π_N. If $M_L = \{x : \|T(x)\|_p^\sigma > L\}$ where L is chosen such that $\int_{M_L} \|T(x)\|_p^\sigma\, dx = \frac{1}{2}\int_0^1 \|T(x)\|_p^\sigma\, dx$, then

(7a) $$|(u - v)_j| \le \frac{c\left(\int_0^1 \|T(x)\|_p^\sigma\, dx\right)^{1/\sigma}}{N^k} + O(h^{k+1})$$

and more importantly

(7b) $$|(u - v)_j| \le c\, 2^{1/\sigma}\left(\frac{\mu(M_L)}{N}\right)^k \left(\int_0^1 \|T(x)\|_p^\rho\right)^{1/\rho} + O(h^{k+1})$$

where $\mu(M_L)$ is the measure of M_L.

If, for example, $T(x) = u^{(k)}(x)$ and $u(x)$ has a boundary layer of width ε such that $u^{(k)}(x)$ is $O(\frac{1}{\varepsilon^k})$, then the standard error bound (7a) involves a term like $(\frac{1}{N\varepsilon})^k$, but the bound (7b) is effectively reduced by ε^k if $\mu(M_L) = \varepsilon$. That is, the mesh selection effectively resolves the boundary layer independently of ε.

The two-cycle strategies, classified according to FD, FE(1), or FE(2) are now described.

FD Several mesh-selection techniques have been developed for solving (1a) with finite differences when $m = 2$. Pearson [199] attempts equidistributing $\int_0^1 |u'(x)|dx$ for singular perturbation problems. In one of the earliest papers on mesh-selection methods Brown [32] expands $\tau_i[u]$ in terms of $x(\xi) = \xi^{-1}(x)$ and attempts to solve for $\frac{1}{m(x,u)}$ such that $T(x) = 0$. Then $m(x,u)$ turns out to be a fractional derivative of $u(x)$, but not the one which arises from using (3). While Brown has the idea of equidistributing with a "two-cycle method" (a term he uses), he is unable to implement it successfully. Denny and Landis [75], also expanding $\tau_i[u]$ in terms of $x(\xi)$, attempt to set $\tau_i[u] \equiv 0$ and have mixed success [283].

Lentini and Pereyra [170], applying the midpoint rule with deferred corrections to solve (1b), approximate $T(x)$ by $\tilde{T}(x)$ and attempt equidistributing $\int_0^1 \|\tilde{T}(x)\|_p^\sigma dx$. Since the theory requires a quasiuniform mesh [148,170], a slight generalization of the theorem (as actually presented in [204]) which incorporates this modified $\tilde{T}(x)$ gives essentially (7). A central problem is that the truncation error is difficult to approximate [170,194]. In addition, the order of their acceleration method constantly changes and makes the creation of an equidistributing mesh at any stage almost impossible. An equidistributing mesh is not even attempted in practice, since once a mesh point is inserted it is not remove[d] at a later stage.

In an attempt to minimize $\tau_i[u]$ for (1b), Gough, Spiegel and Toomre [12(consider the optimal control problem of determining $\xi(x)$ in order to minimize

$$E_\ell = \int_0^1 [\sum_{i=1}^{d} \left(\frac{u_i^{(\ell)}(\xi)}{r_i}\right)^2 + w(x^{(\ell)}(\xi))^2]d\xi$$

where r_i is the oscillation of $u_i(x)$ and w is a constant. The $x^{(\ell)}(\xi)$ term is necessary since the boundary layers in $u_i(x)$ are otherwise transformed into boundary layers in $x(\xi)$. The value $w = d$ is found to make all components appear similarly smooth wrt ξ for the problems considered, while $w = 1$ makes $x'(\xi)$ change too abruptly. Since $\tau_i[u] = ch_i^2 u'''$, $\ell = 3$ is the most natural case, but only $\ell = 1$ and 2 can be conveniently handled and only for the computationally most efficient case $\ell = 1$ can they show that a minimum is obtained. For $\ell = 1$, this minimum is found by solving (6a) and modification of (6b). Significantly, the fastest and most reliable way to solve this problem is to alternately solve (6a) for $u(\xi)$ and the modification of (6b) for $x(\xi)$, using Newton's method for each.

If a finite-difference approximation $\{v(x_i)\}$ is interpolated by a spline function $w(x)$, then the interpolation error bound could be equidistributed for mesh selection,* as we do in FE(1) below. Similarly, Carey and Finlayson [40] suggest using the residual $N(w)$ for mesh selection as in FE(2). Osborne [196] constructs finite-difference methods minimizing truncation error for which an interpolant and its residual are considered. This approach could prove fruitful for certain methods, e.g., optimal methods (where the order of the method and error of an interpolant are the same) may be particularly appropriate for FE(1).

<u>FE(1)</u> The interpolation error results of Burchard [36] are used by Dodson [90] in choosing meshes a.e. wrt the dominant term in the error bound for solving (1a) with spline collocation, where a piecewise constant approximation $\bar{v}^{(k)}(x)$ to $u^{(k)}(x)$ is obtained from $v^{(k-1)}(x)$. deBoor [74] extends this to collocation with an optimal error form and for the superconvergent case, where (2b) simplifies to

$$\max_{x_j \le x \le x_{j+1}} |u(x) - v(x)| = \|u - v\|_{(j)} \le c\, h_j^k \|u^{(k)}\|_{(j)} + O(h^{k+1}) \qquad (1 \le j \le N). \tag{8}$$

---

* suggested to us by J. Christiansen.

deBoor requires (4") in the form

$$(9)\qquad \int_{x_i}^{x_{i+1}} |\overline{v}^{(k)}(x)|^{1/k}dx \equiv c \qquad (1 \le i \le N),$$

stating that no compelling reason for this mesh-selection scheme is apparent since $v^{(k-1)}(x) = u^{(k-1)}(x) + O(h)$ should imply $v^{(k)}(x) = u^{(k)}(x) + O(1)$. In fact, the $O(1)$ term can be shown to be $O(h)$ for $\overline{v}^{(k)}(x)$ [52] so that equidistribution can theoretically be expected to converge to an optimal mesh. The procedure has been extended and implemented in a computer code for solving mixed-order systems [13]. The theory of mesh selection for collocation solving (1b) is considered by van Veldhuizen [27], and his approach has the interesting difference that higher order global solutions may be utilizable.

Natterer [190] shows that when interpolation gives the error (8) without the $O(h^{k+1})$ term, certain Galerkin methods are quasi-optimal (have no $O(h^{k+1})$ term in the error bound (8)). He notes that choosing highly stretched meshes a.e. wrt $h_i^k\|u^{(k)}\|_{(i)}$ can be constructed without keeping the mesh quasiuniform, as only a local type of quasiuniformity is necessary. He shows by counterexample that collocation is not quasi-optimal, but mentions that so far experimental evidence is inconclusive. This may be because when π is a.e. wrt $h_i^k\|u^{(k)}\|_{(i)}$, the $O(h^{k+1})$ term in (8) stays small for most problems and in the limiting non-quasiuniform case, the condition of the spline matrix becomes large before the $O(h^{k+1})$ term becomes important. In addition, for many superconvergent collocation methods the error bound (8) is $\|u - v\|_{(j)} \le h_j^k\|u^{(k)}\|_{(j)} + O(h_j^{k+1}) + O(h^{k+2})$ $(1 \le j \le N)$ so that quasiuniformity is not necessary. The collocation code of [13] has had few problems in working with highly nonuniform meshes, e.g., $\frac{h_{i+1}}{h_i} \doteq 800$ and $h/\underline{h} \doteq 10^6$ have been automatically selected on real problems and created no difficulty.

Grebennikov [121] poses the problem of minimizing the error bound (8) as an optimal control problem and gives a method for finding optimal mesh points. When $u(x)$ is unknown, his approximation strategy is equivalent to (9).

FE(2) A number of authors have expressed the error for finite-element methods in terms of the residual $r(x) = N(v(x))$ [109,124,138,228] and used the residual in defining $m(x,u)$ for mesh selection [124,138,228, 40]. These methods usually redistribute the mesh reliably. It is probably best to equidistribute an $m(x,v)$ which involves $r(x)$ in the way it appears in the error bound. For superconvergent collocation methods, Russell and Christiansen give the error as an equality involving $r(x)$. In general, care should be taken to choose $m(x,v)$ independent of π_N in the limit. For example, if the dominant error term is $\max h_i^2 \|r\|_{(i)}$ where $\|r\|_{(i)} = h_i^4 \|u^{(6)}\|_{(i)} + O(h^5)$, then $m(x,v) \equiv \left(\frac{\|r\|_{(i)}}{h_i^4}\right)^{1/6}$ on $[x_i,x_{i+1}]$ approximates an $m(x,u)$ independent of π in the limit but $m(x,v) \equiv (\|r\|_{(i)})^{1/2}$ on $[x_i,x_{i+1}]$ does not.

In deciding between a derivative approximation FE(1) or a residual evaluation FE(2), one may be slightly more work than the other. It is more important to equidistribute wrt the optimal error bound. Of course, this bound in terms of the desired norm may involve derivatives, as is for example the case for Melosh and Marcal [181] who use an energy expression for monitoring. Sewell [243], who shows how ODE and PDE mesh selection can overlap, has an error bound in a Sobolev norm but assumes an L_∞ error bound holds to do mesh selection and obtains good success.

Solving (1b) by a collocation or implicit Runge-Kutta method, Weiss [279] bounds the error in terms of a truncation error. So in the sense that a finite element method is viewed as an equivalent finite-difference method, the FD approaches from before are applicable. Another possibility is to use an acceleration principle to obtain an error estimate and then equidistribute this error estimate. Robustness can be lost if this (or any other) method is used for both mesh selection and error estimation, as observed in [228].

5. Final Considerations

The way one does mesh selection obviously depends to some extent upon the context. For special classes of problems, specific a priori choices of $\xi(x)$ or reformulations incorporating $\xi(x)$ in a particular way may be appropriate. However for a general-purpose method, a broader approach such as the two-cycle method analyzed by Pereyra and Sewell [204] and implemented in [170, 13] or the transformation analyzed by White [283] is necessary. A comparison of these two general approaches with regard to their stability and efficiency would be useful. Russell and Christiansen [228] compare two-cycle methods and conclude that one shoul generally equidistribute using the dominant term $h_i^k \|T(x_i)\|_p$ in the error bound (2)--or what one suspects this term to be [243]--since it is little more effort than any other approach. The theorem then insures from (7b) that the constant for the $O(N^{-k})$ term is small for a large class of difficult problems.

The success of equidistributing with a lower order term like $h_i^{\ell} \|u^{(\ell)}\|_{(i)}$ for $\ell < k$ instead of $\ell = k$ in (8) can be very problem dependent [228]. This relates to what White does, where the reformulation favours especially simple quantities like arc length, which basically corresponds to equidistributing with $h_i \|u'\|_{(i)}$ (except an L_2 norm).

To observe the reliability of a two-cycle method versus using reformulation (6) with arc length, we solved problem 3 of [283] using a collocation code [13] several different ways. Specifically, (a) the unmodified first-order system (from a scalar second-order problem) is solved using the standard two-cycle method that this code uses; (b) the modified problem (6) is solved with equal spacing $(s_{i+1} - s_i \equiv \frac{1}{N})$ and no mesh selection; and (c) the modified problem (6) is solved with the two-cycle method as in (a). The problem, which has a boundary layer at 0 as a parameter $\varepsilon \to 0$, is solved for each of these with continuation a $\varepsilon = 1, 10^{-1}, 10^{-2}, 10^{-3}, \ldots$ until failure. Several tolerances for the code were tried, and the results for tolerance $= 10^{-2}$ are typical. We list the ε and parenthetically give the number of subintervals N used until convergence or failu

(N too large for storage).

(a) $1(5,10);10^{-1}(5,10);10^{-2}(5,10,20,10,20);10^{-3}(10,20,13,26,13,26);$
$10^{-4}(13,13,13,26,13,26);10^{-5}(13,13,13,26,26,52,28,56,28,56);$
$10^{-6}(28,14,28);10^{-7}(14,14,14,28,28,28,\ldots,\text{failure})$

(b) $1(5,10);10^{-1}(10,20);10^{-2}(10,20,\ldots,\text{failure})$

(c) $1(5,10);10^{-1}(5,10,5,10);10^{-2}(5,10,\ldots,\text{failure})$.

The modified problem (6) is more sensitive to solve by the approaches (b) and (c) than using the unmodified problem in (a), as evidenced by the early failure of continuation and by a larger number of iterations needed to solve the nonlinear problem in the successful cases ($\varepsilon = 1,.1$) than in (a). Another interesting test would be to use a two-cycle approach directly for problem (6). If the investigation of Gough et al. [120] is pertinent, one could expect it to improve the performance in (b).

Regardless of how a modified problem (6) is solved, discovery of simple monitors which generally reduce the difficulty of problems would be a significant advancement. For certain linear problems (1b), Mike Osborne* determines $m(x,t)$ involving the coefficients of the ODE when minimizing the condition number of certain matrices--an approach especially appealing for multiple shooting.

The convergence properties of methods for BVP's and IVP's are intimately related [152] and in fact the discrete equations are often identical [61]. It is interesting to compare IVP step-size selection and BVP mesh selection in such cases. If $\tau_i[u]$ is the local truncation error for a BVP method, $\tilde{\tau}_i[u] = h_i\, \tau_i[u]$ is the local truncation error for the equivalent IVP method. The merits of controlling error per unit step and error per step for the IVP are discussed in [248,172]. The equivalent strategies for the BVP are equidistributing truncation error ($\|\tau_i[u]\|_p \equiv c$) and the local step error ($h_i\|\tau_i[u]\|_p \equiv c$), respectively. White

---

* private communication; also see [197].

[283] argues that the latter is preferable; an intermediate case is $h_i \|\tau_i[u]\|_p^p \equiv c$, or $h_i^{1/p} \|\tau_i[u]\|_p \equiv c$, as used with a two-cycle method in [170].

Once a mesh-selection strategy has been selected, there are obviously many considerations still to be made for its implementation. For example, for two-cycle methods the number of allowable redistributions for a fixed N [90, 13] or the way N is increased [170, 13, 40, 138] must be dealt with, possibly to provide quasiuniformity. For certain classes of problems, the mesh selection can interact with the nonlinear iteration in an efficient fashion [40]. If a mesh is being refined without redistribution, choices other than halving may be reasonable [8]. For PDE's Brandt [30] coordinates the mesh selection and iteration method for solving the large linear systems. If the error is being accurately estimated, one can consider removing those parts of the interval on which the error is small and then re-solving on the remaining ones after obtaining new boundary conditions from the approximate solution. This method has recently been investigated for ODE's [22 and PDE's [124]. It can be especially suitable as a mesh-selection approach for equal spacing methods, although piecewise uniform meshes can be used too for difficult problems [285].

Regardless of what approach one takes, it is important to understand the performance of one's mesh-selection strategy well before it is obscured by insertin many precautionary features and sophisticated interactions. The authors of [13] have found this advice of Victor Pereyra most helpful.

Acknowledgement: I would like to express my appreciation to Uri Ascher, Jan Christiansen, and Victor Pereyra for stimulating discussions which have enhance my knowledge and appreciation of this topic.

FINITE ELEMENT MESH REFINEMENT ALGORITHM USING ELEMENT RESIDUALS

G. F. Carey[†] and D. L. Humphrey[††]

Abstract

An algorithm is formulated for automatic adaptive refinement of finite element meshes for 2-point boundary-value problems. Global *a posteriori* error bounds by the residual lead to the use of element residuals as a relative measure of solution accuracy on the elements. A statistical procedure is devised to establish the regions of refinement and the degree of refinement necessary. An associated research code has been applied to linear and nonlinear problems including applications of boundary-layer type. Numerical experiments demonstrate the effectiveness of the scheme and its value in efficient solution of nonlinear problems.

Introduction

When one is approximating the solution to 2-point boundary-value problems by finite element or finite difference methods, selection of an appropriate mesh is an important issue. There have been several mesh refinement strategies developed for finite difference solution of 2-point problems. Perhaps the earliest documented algorithm is that of Pearson [1]. In the intervening ten years, the subject has received increasing attention and a variety of methods and criteria have recently been implemented in programs. Representative bibliographies together with a detailed treatment of our analysis are reported in Reference [2]. In the following, we develop a selective mesh refinement algorithm based on element residuals in a Galerkin finite element formulation.

---

† Texas Institute for Computational Mechanics, University of Texas at Austin
††Lawrence Livermore Laboratories

Method

Element Residuals:

The analysis and algorithm we develop apply quite generally to linear and non-linear two-point boundary-value problems. In the particular class of research applications of interest, we consider non-linear differential equations of the form

$$- (p(x)u')' + q(x)u = f(x,u) \quad \text{in} \quad \Omega = (0,1) \tag{1}$$

with mixed linear boundary conditions at x = 0 and x = 1.

In a Galerkin finite element approximation to the generalized solution one considers a finite element subspace S of $H^1(\Omega)$ so that the approximation $\tilde{u}(x) \in S$ and also the test functions $v(x) \in S$. Let A denote the linear differential operator in equation (1). Then, for an approximate solution $\tilde{u}(x) \in C^0(\Omega)$, the residual $R(x) = A\tilde{u} - f$ is defined in a distributional sense by $\langle R,w \rangle$, a duality pairing on $H^{-1} \times H^1_0$. If $e(x) = u(x) - \tilde{u}(x)$ is the error in the approximate solution, then for the *linear* problem with $f(u,x) = f(x)$, the error in the H^1 norm is bounded by, [4],

$$\| e \|_1 \leq C_1 \| R \|_{-1} + C_2 \| e \|_{1/2,\partial\Omega} \tag{2}$$

where C_1 and C_2 are constants and the second term on the right arises in approximating the boundary conditions.

The induced H^{-1} norm is defined in terms of the duality pairing $\langle R,w \rangle$ and can be bounded by *computable* element residual contributions. This leads to a global residual bound of the form

$$\| e \|_{1,\Omega} \leq C_1 \; |||R|||_{\Omega} + C_2 \| e \|_{\frac{1}{2},\partial\Omega} \tag{3}$$

where

$$|||R|||_{\Omega} = \left(\sum_e \{ \| R \|_{0,\Omega_e} + \tfrac{1}{2} \left([\![pu']\!]_{\partial\Omega_e} \right) \}^2 \right)^{\frac{1}{2}} \tag{4}$$

and $[\![\ ]\!]$ denotes the jump in the integrated terms at the element boundary $\partial\Omega_e$.

If a maximum principle holds, one can also show that this bound applies on an element Ω_e. Systematic reduction of element residuals will decrease $|||R|||_\Omega$, thus reducing the H^1 norm of the solution error. To achieve this, we compute element residuals and utilize these in a statistical procedure which enriches the mesh accordingly.

Algorithm

Consider an initial mesh $M_0(\Omega)$ with local Lagrange polynomials of degree m forming the piecewise continuous basis. A finite element approximation $\tilde{u}(x)$ is computed on $M_0(\Omega)$ and the element residuals computed according to equation (4). The mean $\bar{R}(M_0)$ and standard deviation $s(M_0)$ are calculated for the set of element residuals $\{|||R_i|||\}$. This determines a distribution function for element residuals. We define refinement "intervals" on the distribution by considering the intervals

$I_1 = (-\infty,\bar{R}+ks)$, $I_2 = (\bar{R}+ks,\ \bar{R}+2ks)$, ..., $I_t = (\bar{R}+(t-1)ks,\infty)$, where k represents the fraction of a standard deviation in each interval. For example, if $k = 1$ the refinement intervals lie 1, 2, 3, ..., t standard deviations above the mean residual. Scanning the element residuals, if $|||R_i|||$ is located in refinement interval j, then element i is refined to j elements. Local interpolation determines an estimate of the nodal solution at the newly-introduced nodes. On completion of the refinement $M_0(\Omega) \to M_1(\Omega)$, a solution is computed on $M_1(\Omega)$.

Numerical Experiments

1. Linear Problem:

A linear problem with solution exhibiting interior-layer behavior for certain parameter ranges is first considered. The two point problem is to solve

$$-\ [\{\ \frac{1}{\alpha} + \alpha(x-\bar{x})^2\}u']' = 2[1 + \alpha(x-\bar{x})\tan^{-1}\alpha(x-\bar{x}) + \tan^{-1}\alpha\bar{x}] \qquad (5)$$

with $u(0) = u(1) = 0$. Here $\bar{x}$ and α are prescribed parameters. If α is large ($O(10^2)$), the solution $u(x) = (1 - x)[\tan^{-1}\alpha(x-\bar{x}) + \tan^{-1}\alpha\bar{x}]$ has an interior-layer in the neighborhood of $x = \bar{x}$. Numerical results are presented here for $\bar{x} = .36388$ and $\alpha = 100$.

In the numerical experiments quartic elements are used, beginning with an initial uniform mesh of four elements. After 8 adaptive refinements the finite element mesh consists of 29 elements with a gradual transition from either side to smaller elements within the layer [7 in (0, .25); 4 in (.25,.325); 9 in (.325,.375); 4 in (.375,.425); 5 in (.425,1.0)]. At this stage the global residual is 7.479. On subsequent refinements many elements are located in the interval (0.25,0.5), particularly at the interior layer. The "final" mesh of 74 elements yields a solution with global residual .812 and H^1 and H^0 error norms of 9.895×10^{-3} and 1.441×10^{-4}, respectively.

2. Residual and Error Correlations:

Unlike uniform meshes, non-uniform meshes generally do not have a single parameter which completely characterizes the mesh and solution quality. It is instructive to compare residual and error norms for the solution at each step in the refinement history (Figure 1).

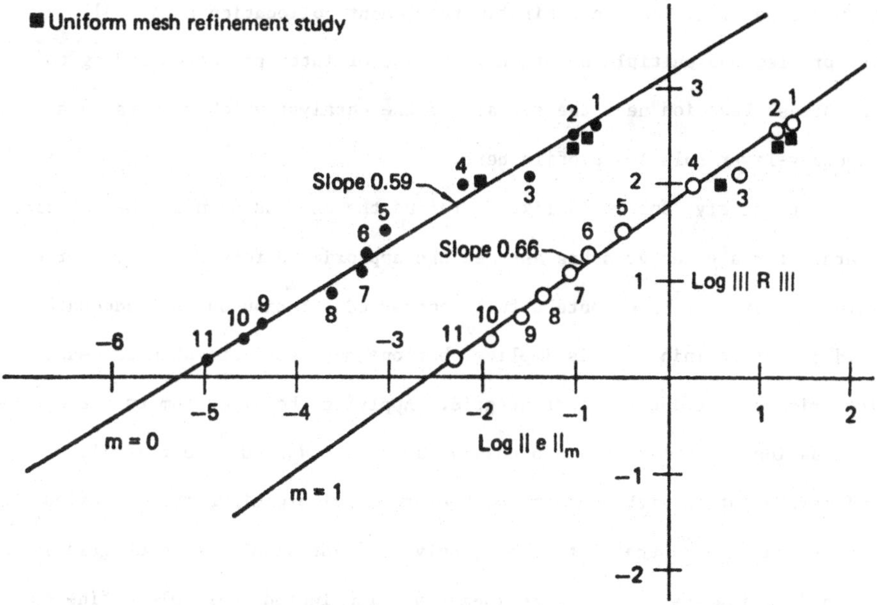

Figure 1. Log $\|e\|_m$ versus Log $|||R|||$ for D = 1.0
Numbers near data points indicate refinement level.

We deduce that our ability to compute on an adaptive non-uniform grid using the residual criterion essentially enables us to progress down the straight lines rapidly with reduced storage and computation. Note that the uniform mesh solutions also lie on the curves.

Non-Linear Boundary-Layer Problem.

We next consider a class of non-linear problems arising in heat and mass transfer studies for catalytic reactors in chemical engineering. Mass transfer for a first-order, irreversible, non-isothermal reaction in a catalyst may be described by

$$\frac{1}{s-1}(x^{s-1}u')' = \phi^2 u \exp\{\gamma(1 - \frac{1}{T(u,x)})\} \text{ in } (0,1) \tag{6}$$

with $u'(0) = 0$, $-u'(1) = B(u(1) - 1)$, and $s = 1, 2,$ or 3 for slab, cylinder or spherical catalyst geometry, respectively. The function $T(u,x) = 1 + \beta\delta + \beta(1-\delta)u(1) - \beta u(x)$ and ϕ, β, γ, δ, and B are specified reaction rate parameters. For the boundary layer problem, $\phi = 14.44$, $\beta = 0.02$, $\gamma = 20.0$, $\delta = 50.0$, and $B = 250$. This problem was investigated by Carey and Finlayson in their finite element collocation study [5]. The problem has multiple solutions, the one of interest corresponding to an intense reaction near the surface of the catalyst which results in a boundary-layer solution profile here.

Intuitively, one would like to refine the mesh as soon as the solution iterate for a given grid has assumed the approximate form of the converged solution rather than compute a fully converged solution on an inadequate grid before refining. This implies that one must estimate when to cease iteration and refine the current grid. Applying the algorithm to the problem of equation (6) which has a boundary-layer of order 10^{-3} near $x = 1$, we initiate solution with a coarse mesh of four uniform elements. Detailed inspection reveals that with $k = 1$, only the last element of each grid is refined during the first six refinements which include multiple refinements on meshes three to six when the boundary-layer is "sensed". Further refinements produce a graded mesh into the layer.

Efficient strategies for nonlinear problem may be developed in this way by interweaving mesh refinement and algebraic iteration. For this nonlinear example the most efficient strategy employed only one Newton iteration per mesh. Detailed graphs of operation counts are presented in references [2,3]. As a concluding point of interest, even if the final "near optimal" mesh is employed directly with the same starting guess, the operation count noticeably exceeds that obtained by adaptive refinement solution with no *a priori* knowledge of the solution behavior or required mesh.

References

1. Pearson, C.E., "A Numerical Method for Ordinary Differential Equations of Boundary Layer Type," J. Math. Phys., Vol. 47, pp. 134-154, 1968.

2. Humphrey, D., and Carey, G.F., "Adaptive Mesh Refinement Algorithm Using Element Residuals," TICOM Report 78-1, Texas Institute for Computational Mechanics, January, 1978.

3. Carey, G.F., and Humphrey, D., "Adaptive Refinement Using Residuals," (in preparation).

4. Oden, J.T., and Reddy, J.N., Mathematical Foundations of the Finite Element Method, Wiley Interscience, 1976.

5. Carey, G.F., and Finlayson, B.A., "Orthogonal Collocation on Finite Elements," Chemical Engineering Science, Vol. 30, pp. 587-596, 1975.

Acknowledgement

This research was supported by Grant No. N00014-78-C-0550 from the Office of Naval Research.

C^0 - Collocation - Galerkin Methods

G.F. Carey
Texas Institute for Computational Mechanics
The University of Texas at Austin

M.F. Wheeler
Mathematical Sciences Department
Rice University

Abstract

A C^0-Collocation - Galerkin (C^0-C-G) method is formulated and analyzed for finite element solution of linear and nonlinear singular boundary-value problems. Theoretical error estimates are ascertained for both the linear problems and a specific class of nonlinear problems. Convergence rates and superconvergence behavior are established and verified in numerical experiments. As a particular class of important research applications, we consider heat and mass transfer problems that arise for catalytic reactors in chemical engineering. The Jacobi points are introduced to determine optimal orders of accuracy and utilized in a new method for determining the boundary flux to optimal order. Numerical results are presented for sample problems.

Introduction

C^0-Galerkin techniques presently constitute the most widely applied class of finite element methods for boundary-value problems. A variety of special finite element methods have been proposed in recent years. The general motivation is to provide more efficient, simpler, computational techniques, as in collocation methods, or to treat discontinuities, layers, and other irregular solution behavior better, as in the H^{-1} and C^0-C-G methods [1,2].

The C^0-C-G method combines some of the features of collocation (in the element interior) with those of Galerkin projections (at the element interfaces). The theoretical foundations and error analysis of this method for linear and nonlinear two-point problems form part of this investigation. We implement the procedure in a research program designed to solve nonlinear heat and mass transfer problems for catalytic reactors in chemical engineering. These problems are characterised by nonlinear reaction rate functions and will exhibit multiple solution states, including boundary and interior-layer behavior for some parameter ranges, [3].

Method

The diffusion of mass in a catalyst pellet may be described by the nonlinear two-point boundary-value problem for concentration $y(x)$,

$$Ly \equiv xy''(x) + (s-1)y'(x) + xq(x)y = xf(x,y), \quad x \in I, \qquad (1)$$

with $y'(0) = 0$, $-y'(1) = Bi_m(y(1)-1)$ and $I = (0,1)$. Here the prime denotes differentiation, $s = 1,2$ or 3 for slab, cylindrical or spherical geometry, $f(x,y)$ is the nonlinear reaction rate term and Bi_m is a mass transfer parameter. Usually $q(x) = 0$ in these applications.

We consider the particular case of a spherical catalyst pellet $(s = 3)$ for $Bi_m \to \infty$ so that $y(1) = 1$, and a reaction rate $f(y) = \phi^2 y \exp[\gamma\,(1-1/T)]$, $T = 1 + \beta - \beta y$. This corresponds to an irreversible, first-order, non-isothermal reaction. The reaction rate parameters ϕ, γ, β characterize the nature of the nonlinear reaction involved.

Let δ be a partition of I, δ: $0 = x_0 < x_1 < x_2 \dots < x_N = 1$, $h_i = x_i - x_{i-1}$, $I_i = (x_{i-1}, x_i)$ and $P_r(I_i)$ be the set of polynomials of degree less than $(r + 1)$ on I_i. Define

$$M(r, \delta) = \{v \in C^0(I) \mid v \in P_r(I_i),\ i = 1,2,\dots, N\} \qquad (2)$$

and

$$\hat{M}(r, \delta) = M(r, \delta) \cap \{v \mid v(1) = 1\} \qquad (3)$$

Let $\{\alpha_j\}_{j=1}^{r-1}$ be the set of Jacobi points on I and $\{A_j\}_{j=1}^{r-1}$ the Jacobi weights defined by the quadrature formula

$$\int_I x(1 - x)p\,dx = \sum_{j=1}^{r-1} \alpha_j(1 - \alpha_j)\, p(\alpha_j)A_j, \quad p \in P_{2r-3}(I) \tag{4}$$

Set $\alpha_{ij} = x_{i-1} + h_i\alpha_j$, $i = 1, 2, \ldots, N$, $j = 1, 2, \ldots, r - 1$.

The C^0-collocation-Galerkin method is defined as follows: Let $Y \in M(r, \delta)$ satisfy

$$Y(1) = 1, \quad LY(\alpha_{ij}) = \alpha_{ij}\, f(\alpha_{ij}, Y(\alpha_{ij})),$$

$$-\int_0^1 x\, Y'v'dx + (s-2)\int_0^1 Y'\, v\, dx = \int_0^1 x\, f(x, Y(x))\, v\, dx, \quad v \in \hat{M}(r, \delta) \tag{5}$$

The linear operator determines a block diagonal coefficient matrix with single overlap between adjacent diagonal blocks and the nonlinear reaction rate term introduces only diagonal and perhaps single column entries in the Jacobian if a Newton iteration is applied.

In the transport application the boundary flux "links" transfer processes in the pellet and fluid phases and is of special interest. We obtain a highly accurate approximation Γ_j to the flux at x_j, $j > 0$, by the local quadrature

$$x_j\, \Gamma_j\, h_j \equiv -\int_{x_{j-1}}^{x_j} \{(s-3)\, x\, Y' + x\, q(x - x_{j-1}) + x\, f(x, Y)(x - x_{j-1})\}dx$$

$$+ x_{j-1}\, (s-2)(Y(x_j) - Y(x_{j-1})) \tag{6}$$

This equation is motivated by considering $\int_{x_{j-1}}^{x_j} Ly(x-x_{j-1})$ and integrating the first term by parts [2,3].

We can show that if $f = f(x)$, $s = 3$, $q = 0$,

$$Y(x_j) = y(x_j), \quad \Gamma_j = y'(x_j) \tag{7}$$

and

$$\| x(Y-y)^{(j)} \|_{L^2} \le Ch^{1-j} \left\{ \sum_{\ell=1}^{N} \left(h_\ell^{k-1} \| xy^{(k)} \|_{L^2} \right)^2 \right\}^{\frac{1}{2}}, \quad 2 \le k \le r+1$$

where $h = \max h_i$. In the case $q \neq 0$ the estimates $|(Y-y)(x_j)| \le Ch^{2r}$ and $|\Gamma_j - y'(x_j)| \le Ch^{2r}$ are obtained. A theoretical treatment of the equations

$$Ly = xy'' + (s-1)y' + q\,x\,y = xf(x,y)$$

and

$$y_t = Ly - f(x, y), \tag{8}$$

will appear in a later paper [4].

Results

Representative results are tabulated below for numerical experiments which explore rates of convergence and the use of Jacobi points in our C^0-collocation-Galerkin method. The linear problem on $x \in (0,1)$,

$$y'' + \frac{2}{x} y' = (\sinh 2x) / (11\, x \sinh 2), \quad y'(0) = 0, \quad y(1) = 1 \tag{9}$$

is a normalized form ($y(1) = 1$) of an example presented in reference 5. It has the exact solution $y(x) = 1/11 + 10/11 (\sinh 2x) / (x \sinh 2)$. Errors at the nodes for computations on successively refined meshes of cubic elements are presented in Table 1. The C^0-C-G solution is essentially exact at the nodes as anticipated, any discrepancy arising primarily from the quadrature. The results are markedly superior to those obtained in reference 5 using collocation.

Table 1.

Computed Nodal Errors

Node Location	$h^{-1} = 2$	$h^{-1} = 4$	$h^{-1} = 8$	$h^{-1} = 16$
0	2.59×10^{-6}	1.07×10^{-7}	9.4×10^{-9}	7×10^{-10}
$\frac{1}{4}$		2.7×10^{-7}	9.6×10^{-9}	5×10^{-10}
$\frac{1}{2}$	3.88×10^{-6}	8.9×10^{-8}	7.9×10^{-9}	4×10^{-10}
$\frac{3}{4}$		9.4×10^{-7}	3.9×10^{-9}	2×10^{-10}

In the following two tables we present results for the nonlinear mass transfer problem described by equation (1) with $f(y) = \phi^2 y \exp[\gamma/(1 - 1/T)]$, $T = 1 + \beta(1 - y)$ and with boundary conditions $y'(0) = 0, y(1) = 1$. We chose $\phi = .5$, $\gamma = 18$ and $\beta = .3$ which corresponds to a relatively uniform reaction through the pellet thickness [3].

The flux is a quantity of significant practical interest and we demonstrate the preceding theoretical results concerning both the use of Jacobi points and also our quadrature rule for optimal flux computation (Iteration tolerance 10^{-8}).

Table 2.

Mesh	Jacobi Points $\|\Gamma - y'(1)\|$	Jacobi Points $\|Y'(1) - y'(1)\|$	Gauss Points $\|Y'(1) - y'(1)\|$
$h^{-1} = 2$	2.1×10^{-8}	3.7×10^{-6}	1.0×10^{-5}
$h^{-1} = 4$	2×10^{-9}	2.2×10^{-6}	3.0×10^{-6}
$h^{-1} = 8$	3×10^{-9}	1.6×10^{-8}	8.0×10^{-7}

The predicted improvement in flux values using Jacobi points in the C^0-C-G formulation and using the quadrature form for Γ are evident.

Similar conclusions follow from Table 3. Here the convergence tolerance for the Newton iteration is 1.2×10^{-12}. Empirically, we obtain the rate estimate $|Y'(1) - y'(1)| \sim Ch^{3.36}$ and a similar asymptotic estimate for

$|\Gamma - y'(1)|$. These rates are consistent with those of the corresponding linear problem, as one would expect with this form of nonlinear reaction rate term [4].

Table 3.

Mesh	$\lvert\Gamma - Y'(1)\rvert$	$\lvert Y'(1) - y'(1)\rvert$
$h^{-1} = 2$	5.89×10^{-9}	4.3×10^{-5}
$h^{-1} = 4$	2.66×10^{-9}	3.7×10^{-6}
$h^{-1} = 8$	1.78×10^{-10}	3.8×10^{-7}
$h^{-1} = 16$	1.2×10^{-11}	3.9×10^{-8}

Conclusions

The collocation-Galerkin finite element method combines some of the efficiency of collocation with the lower continuity requirements associated with Galerkin formulations. The degree of difficulty of implementation is slightly more complex then these more standard approaches. Unlike C^1 collocation methods, flux boundary conditions may be satisfied weakly and there is no restriction on the partition. The low continuity requirements imply that the method is suited to numerical solution of problems with higher-derivative discontinuities, interior layers and boundary-layers such as those that may arise in catalytic reactor problems.

References

1. J. Diaz, "A hybrid collocation Galerkin method for the two-point boundary-value problem using continuous piecewise polynomial spaces," Ph.D. thesis, Rice University, Houston, Texas, 1975.

2. M.F. Wheeler: "A C^0-collocation finite element method for two-point boundary-value problems and one space dimensional parabolic problems," SIAM J. Numer. Anal. Vol. 14, No. 1, 1977.

3. G.F. Carey and B.A. Finlayson: "Orthogonal collocation on finite elements," J. Chem. Eng. Sci., vol. 30, pp. 587-596, 1975.

4. M.F. Wheeler and G.F. Carey: "Analysis of collocation-Galerkin methods and Superconvergence for nonlinear two-point problems" (in preparation).

5. R.D. Russell and L.F. Shampine: "Numerical methods for singular boundary-value problems," SIAM J. Numer. Anal., Vol. 12, No. 1, 1975.

Acknowledgement. This research was supported by the Office of Naval Research Grant N00014-78-C-0550.

An Extrapolation Method Based on Solving a Sequence of Collocation Problems

Steven Pruess, University of New Mexico

1. Introduction. In this paper a method based on collocation is studied for solving a scalar linear two point boundary value problem with separated end conditions. Extensions to more general problems should be straightforward. The code approximates solutions by a piecewise polynomial satisfying the boundary conditions exactly and chosen to collocate the differential equation at Gaussian points. Approximations are provided to the solution only at discrete output points specified by the user; these approximations are generated by Richardson's h^2- extrapolation process applied to a sequence of subproblems. When the accuracy requested by the user is attained at one of the interior output points x, the problem is "chopped" in the sense of [7], i.e., it is reduced to two problems, one with x as left boundary point, the other with x as right boundary point. Suitable boundary conditions are imposed at x for each subproblem.

2. Algorithm Details. The mathematical notation is similar to that in [3]: given the differential equation $Lu = f$ on $[a,b]$ where $L := D^m + a_{m-1} D^{m-1} + \cdots + a_1 D + a_0$, subject to the boundary conditions $\lambda_i u = \gamma_i \quad 1 \le i \le m$. The set $\{\lambda_i\}$ of linear functionals has the first ℓ (last $m-\ell$) involving only function and derivative values of order up to $m-1$ at $x = a$ $(x = b)$. Let $\Delta = \{a = x_1 < \cdots < x_N = b\}$ be a partition of $[a,b]$ and for some k let $P_{m+k,\Delta}$ be the space of piecewise polynomials of order $m+k$ (degree $< m+k$) over Δ. The collocation approximation u_Δ is that element of $P_{m+k,\Delta} \cap C^{m-1}[a,b]$ which satisfies the boundary conditions, and $(Lu_\Delta)(\tau_j) = f(\tau_j)$ $1 \le j \le k(N-1)$. The collocation points $\{\tau_j\}$ are chosen as in [3] to be Gaussian points relative to Δ.

Assuming the original problem has a unique solution; existence and uniqueness of U_Δ is shown in [3], as is the error estimate

$$\| D^j (u-u_\Delta) \| = O(h^s) \quad o \leq j \leq m \quad , \quad s: = k + \min(k,m-j),$$

where $h = \max_i (X_{i+1} - X_i)$ and $\| \cdot \|$ is the max-norm. More importantly, at the knots $|D^j(u-u_\Delta)(x_i)| = O(h^{2k})$ for $0 \leq j < m$. In [6] is sketched an argument that the error at knots is of the form $\alpha_1 h^{2k} + \alpha_2 h^{2k+2} + \cdots$ so Richardson's h^2- extrapolation can be used. That argument assumes equally spaced knots and is not complete, however, the details apparently can be cleaned up and, in fact, extended to the case of uniform subdivisions of a non-uniform mesh [5].

The code is given a set $\{x_i\}_{i=1}^N$ where output $U_\Delta(x_i)$ is desired, and a requested accuracy. Two tolerances AE and RE are input and the code attempts to return answers satisfying $|U(x_i) - U_\Delta(x_i)| \leq AE + RE * |U_\Delta(x_i)|$. The answer $\{U_\Delta(x_i)\}$ is actually the result of several Richardson extrapolation. The first such approximation is derived by letting $\Delta = \{X_i\}$ (assumed to include a,b). Collocation at Gaussian points over $P_{m+k,\Delta} \cap C^{m-1}[a,b]$ for some k produces $\{U_\Delta(x_i)\}$. It was intended that the code should choose k adaptively but currently this must be input. The second approximation is provided by a similar procedure based on a new partition consisting of end points and midpoints of subintervals of the previous Δ. Extrapolation provides an error estimate for each $U_\Delta(x_i)$; this process is continued (each new partition has twice the number of subintervals as the preceding one) until convergence is attained for at least one of the output points. At most four columns of the Richardson table are kept in addition to the error estimator; thus, the most accurate answer possible is $O(h^{2k+6})$. For higher order problems ($m > 2$) derivative estimates at knots are also computed and extrapolated.

As soon as the answer is sufficiently accurate at one of the output points x_i, the problem is subdivided into $Lu = f$ on $[a,x_i]$ and on $[x_i,b]$. The needed boundary conditions at x_i are of the form $(D^j u)(x_i) = (D^j u_\Delta)(x_i)$ $0 \leq j \leq J$ for appropriate J. Here $(D^j u_\Delta)(x_i)$ is the current estimate. This subdivision process is easily handled using a stack, each level of which contains the end points of the interval on which a problem is to be solved. Also, it is necessary to know how many subintervals are in the partition used for that level in the stack so that subsequent extrapolations can be done correctly.

For each collocation problem the subroutines of [2] are used to set up the linear system for the coordinate of U_Δ with respect to the standard B-spline basis. A modification of the Gauss elimination algorithm with partial pivoting for block banded matrices given in [4] was used. This modification uses no extra storage above that of the original coefficient matrix since the nonhomogeneous term is modified as elimination proceeds, avoiding the need to save multipliers.

3. Numerical Examples. The first table gives a summary of the effort required for several test problems. For $k = 1$ to 4 one-hundredth the number of multiplications required for setting up and solving the linear systems is given, as well as the number of calls to the coefficient evaluation routine. For all problems $AE = RE = 10^{-6}$ was used. The "easy" class consisted of four problems on $[0,1]$ with solutions of the form $x^i(1-x)^j e^x$ for various choices of the order m and boundary conditions. The "decaying" category is a set of seven problems which had rapidly growing or decaying solutions in certain regions:

$$u'' + (3 \cot x + 2 \tan x)\, u' + .7u = 0 \qquad u(30) = 0 \qquad u(60) = 5$$

$$u'' - (1 + x^2)u = 0 \qquad u(0) = 1 \qquad u(14) = 0$$

$$u'' + \alpha\, xu = \pi^2 \cos \pi x - \alpha \pi x \sin(\pi x) \qquad u(-1) = -2 \qquad u(1) = 0$$

For $\alpha = 10^2,\ 10^4,\ 10^6$

$$u'' + 300\, xu' + 300\, u = 0 \qquad u(0) = 1 \qquad u(1) = 0$$

$$u'' + u' - 1000u = 0 \qquad u(0) = 1 \qquad u(1) = \tfrac{1}{2}\,.$$

The final group consisted of the two problems:

$$u'' + \frac{2}{x} u' + \frac{1}{x^4} U = 0 \qquad u(1/3\pi) = 0 \qquad u(1) = \sin 1$$

$$u'' + 10u' + 1000u = 0 \qquad u(0) = 1 \qquad u(1) = 0\,.$$

All of these problems either can be solved exactly or the solutions are tabled, see [1], [8] . The choice of output points varied: for the first and last classes 4 to 9 roughly equally spaced points were used, for the second about 7 to 10 points were used with some in the boundary layers.

Although the methods using low order splines are most efficient in terms of setup and solution time they do use far more function evaluations. To make an intelligent choice for k one needs to have some estimate of the complexity of the coefficients as well as paying heed to the nature of the solution and the requested accuracy. Future experiments will also look at even larger values for k as well as letting the code make the choice of

It should be pointed out that testing was done on other problems, with other requested accuracies and other extrapolation sequences (besides doubling These results have been omitted for brevity but are not substantially differen from the ones presented.

Table 2 gives the distribution of the ratio of actual error to requested error for the problems described above. The higher order methods are quite reliable; the lower order cases could be improved with a more sophisticated algorithm which monitors ratios of corrections to the columns of the

Richardson table to determine if extrapolation should be done or not. This would also improve the performance on the oscillatory class of problems.

REFERENCES

1. U. Ascher, J. Christiansen and R. Russell, A collocation solver for mixed order systems of boundary value problems, TR 77-13, Univ. of British Columbia Computer Science Dept., 1977.

2. C. de Boor, Package for calculating with B-splines, SIAM J. Numer. Anal., 14 (1977), 441-472.

3. C. de Boor and B. Swartz, Collocation at Gaussian points, SIAM J. Numer. Anal., 10 (1973), 582-606.

4. C. de Boor and R. Weiss, SOLVEBLOK: a package for solving almost block diagonal linear systems, submitted to TOMS.

5. J. Goodman, Ph.D. thesis, in preparation.

6. R. Russell, Collocation for systems of boundary value problems. Numer. Math. 23 (1974), 119-133.

7. R. Russell and J. Christiansen, Adaptive mesh selection strategies for solving boundary value problems, SIAM J. Numer. Anal., 15 (1978), 59-80.

8. M. Scott and H. Watts, Computational solutions of linear two-point boundary value problems via orthonormalization, SIAM J. Numer. Anal., 14 (1977), 40-70.

Table 1. Efficiency

100's of * required: number of function evaluations

	k = 1	k = 2	k = 3	k = 4
Easy	32:200	55:152	88:96	173:96
Decaying	544:3400	672:1840	915:1000	994:552
Oscillatory	551:3445	284:778	419:458	421:234

Table 2. Reliability r: = actual error/error requested

number of outpoint points where

	$r \leq 1$	$1 < r \leq 2$	$2 < r \leq 5$	$5 < r \leq 10$	$10 < r \leq 100$	100
k = 1	39	3	3	2	8	
k = 2	40	7	9	2	2	
k = 3	44	4	9	2	1	
k = 4	55	3	2	0	0	

WORKSHOP ON BASIS SELECTION

reported by

S. Pruess, G. Reddien, R. Russell, R. Sincovec, M. Wheeler

The objective of the basis selection workshop was to encourage discussion of recent developments and to generate new ideas related to basis selection for people to try. This topic is still in its infancy so there probably exist many unexplored possibilities that were not mentioned during the short time for the workshop. This report is written as an account of what actually took place during the ninety minutes allowed for the workshop. The remarks at the end represent the authors' opinions of the conclusions that one might reach based on the discussions that occurred as well as recommendations based on personal experience or opinions.

R. Russell opened with a description of Carl deBoor's B-spline algorithm since many present in the audience were not familiar with B-splines. It was generally agreed upon that the flexibility, availability, and power of the B-spline codes are responsible for their widespread use. It was noted that the Lagrange basis has found widespread use on engineering problems, probably because of the ease in extracting quantities of interest.

G. Reddien commented that many of the properties of polynomial B-splines carried over to exponential, trigonometric, and fractional power splines. One analog which does not exist, unfortunately, is the recursion formula for generating higher order splines. A determinant representation must be used instead, which is perfectly adequate for many examples but troubles can arise for the exponential case.

A lengthy discussion was precipitated by M. Osborne when he asked why not use monomials as a local basis. There were responses as to their poor conditioning and their lack of continuity which results in extra work. Various people disagreed with these responses but finally, U. Ascher closed the case by reemphasizing that the availability and known reliability and efficiency of the B-spline codes were responsible for their popularity. He noted that C. deBoor had proposed several alternative bases but Ascher wanted to see good implementations before he would switch from B-splines. We make the additional remark, that perhaps a fruitful area of investigation would be to look at mesh independent bases.

S. Pruess made some comments about the large condition numbers associated with matrices arising in collocation. Some of the difficulty apparently comes from scaling problems in the boundary condition equations. However, none of the ill-conditioning appears to bother any of the quantities commonly output. It was suggested that this has to do with the fact that only linear combinations of solutions are usually observed and, with a stable algorithm, the condition number has no effect on these. Several people indicated that they did not believe this.

Related to the topic of basis selection is the question of method selection. It seems that for problems for which a uniform mesh is unsatisfactory, the low order continuity methods are most appropriate. Collocation at Gauss points has wide applicability and is computationally efficient, which are strong points in its favor. However, for second and fourth order elliptic problems, the Ritz-Galerkin method is attractive. It preserves symmetry and is readily adaptable to both the eigenvalue problems, where it is very good, and also parabolic problems.

A student of M. Wheeler, R. Malahy, showed several slides illustrating applications of polynomial splines of differing continuity classes to time dependent problems with boundary layers in the solutions. These Ritz type methods included H^{-1}-Galerkin, H^1-Galerkin, and C^0-Galerkin. These methods appear to be attractive but it was also apparent that not enough computational comparisons have been made to determine where any of these methods is best. The results presented by Malahy indicated less numerical dispersion with a discontinuous basis for boundary layer problems on uniform meshes. From a theoretical point of view, the C^1 spaces require a quasi-uniform mesh whereas no restriction is necessary with C^0 spaces. Obviously discontinuous spaces will yield best approximations results because the approximations are local. Other related matters are contained in the following remarks. Whether or not oscillations occur in the numerical solution can depend on the location of the collocation points. Investigation of both the method and the continuity to produce stability in various situations might be worthwhile.

For smooth problems for which a uniform mesh is satisfactory, many more methods become competitive. It would be useful to have a classification of two-point boundary value problems (e.g., boundary layer, singular, oscillatory) and a set of sample problems that could be used for comparison.

In conclusion, excellent codes now exist for large classes of difficult two-point boundary value problems. Further refinements of these codes probably will yield minimal improvements. However, looking at mesh independent bases might yield significant improvements. Also, additional work on basis selection for two-point boundary-value problems can give important insight for time dependent and multi-dimensional problems even though they may not be optimal for two-point boundary-value problems. More specifically, additional work needs to be done on less optimal methods, as well as interior penalty methods (e.g., those between C^0 and C^1). The question of fixed mesh, variable order splines should be examined. Superconvergence values seem to have not been used explicitly in the development of codes except by Pruess and Ascher, Russell, and Christiansen (COLSYS). COLSYS uses superconvergence in obtaining error estimates which are used for mesh selection. It seems this could be exploited more.

A final question, does the development of vector computers and parallel processors have any bearing on method or basis selection?

MESH SELECTION FOR BOUNDARY-VALUE CODES

Chairperson: Andy White, University of Texas at Austin

Panel Members: Uri Ascher, University of British Columbia
Graham F. Carey, University of Texas at Austin
Marianela Lentini, California Institute of Technology
Victor Pereyra, California Institute of Technology
Robert D. Russell, Simon Fraser University

1. Introduction

The panel members represent three working codes designed to solve boundary-value problems: COLSYS (Ascher and Russell), NONREF (Carey), and PASVA3 (Lentini and Pereyra). COLSYS is designed to approximate the solution of the general system of equations

(1a) $$y^{(m)}(t) + f(y^{(m-1)}(t),\ldots,y(t),\ t) = 0, \qquad t \in (0,1),$$

(1b) $$b(y^{(m-1)}(0),\ldots,y(0);\ y^{(m-1)}(1),\ldots,y(1)) = 0,$$

where y, f, b are n-vectors. Discretization of the differential equation is accomplished via piecewise polynomials (splines) and collocation. NONREF is constructed to calculate approximate solutions to equations of the form

(2a) $$t^{1-a}\frac{d}{dt}\left[t^{a-1}\frac{dy}{dt}\right] = g(y), \qquad t \in (0,1),$$

(2b) $$\frac{dy}{dt}(0) = 0, \quad \frac{dy}{dt}(1) = C[y(1) - 1].$$

This code employs a Galerkin finite element (spline) discretization of the differential equation (2a). PASVA3 generates an approximate solution to the first-order system of equations

(3a) $$y' = f(y,t), \qquad t \in (0,1),$$

(3b) $$b(y(0),\ y(1)) = 0,$$

where y, f, b are n-vectors. Here, the trapezoidal finite difference scheme and deferred corrections are used to discretize (3a). Each of these codes is discussed in more detail elsewhere in this volume.

One difficulty common to each of these codes is that a set of points $\{t_i\}$ must be chosen upon which to base the approximate solution. For splines, these are the breakpoints at which the polynomials are joined, and for finite difference, these are the mesh points at which the solution is approximated. One focus of this report is the placement of the knots $\{t_i\}$.

It is impossible to divorce mesh selection from other concerns of the solution of boundary-value problems. For instance, the trapezoidal rule has a truncation error of

$$(4) \qquad \tau_i[y] = -\frac{1}{12} h_i^2 y'''(t_{i-\frac{1}{2}}) + O(h_i^4),$$

where $h_i = t_i - t_{i-1}$. In many cases, the leading term in this expansion is a reasonable measure of the global error; hence, where $\|y'''(t)\|$ is large, it is natural to take h_i small. In this case, mesh selection and error estimation/control are tightly interwoven. For this reason, no attempt was made to narrow the discussion to mesh selection alone. Rather, any questions were entertained dealing with the construction or performance of boundary-value codes. The distinction was made, as throughout the conference, between implicit boundary-value codes and shooting codes.

The discussion naturally divided into two parts: first, an explanation of the techniques used to accomplish mesh selection in the codes represented on the panel; second, a general questioning of the basic motivation and direction of designers of boundary-value codes. This pattern will be followed here as well.

2. Current Mesh Selection Strategies

The basic idea behind each of the strategies discussed is the same: (1) some boundary-value problems have solutions which are more difficult to accurately approximate in one region of [0,1] than another; (2) measure the difficulty ("work" required to calculate a solution) of the solution; and (3) arrange the mesh $\{t_i\}$ such that each interval does approximately the same amount of work. That is, equally distribute (equidistribute) the difficulty of finding the solution over all the intervals $\{(t_{i-1}, t_i)\}$.

Boundary-value problems with boundary-layers (narrow regions in which the solution changes very rapidly) form a popular class exhibiting this behavior. Nearly every code written with an eye to mesh selection has been tested on problems of this type. For example, the solution of

(5a) $$\epsilon y'' - y' = 0, \qquad y(0) = 1, \quad y(1) = 2,$$

is given by

(5b) $$y(t) = 1 - \frac{\exp(-1/\epsilon)}{1-\exp(-1/\epsilon)} (1-\exp(t/\epsilon)).$$

Note that near $t = 1$ the solution rises from $y = 1$ to $y = 2$ in a region of width $O(\epsilon)$.

Perhaps one way to view all of this material is in terms of a transformed boundary-value problem. For example, a good measure of the difficulty of a particular problem is the truncation error defined in (4). Now, suppose that we take

(6) $$s(t) = \int_0^t \|- \frac{1}{12} y'''(x)\|^{1/2} dx/\theta \equiv m(y,t)/\theta$$

where $\theta = \int_0^1 \|- \frac{1}{12} y'''(x)\|^{1/2} dx$. Assuming that $\frac{ds}{dt} > 0$, we can now define a transformed problem in terms of a new independent variable, s

(7a) $$\frac{dy}{ds} = \theta \frac{f(y,t)}{m(y,t)}, \qquad s \in (0,1),$$

(7b) $$\frac{dt}{ds} = \theta \frac{1}{m(y,t)}, \qquad s \in (0,1);$$

(7c) $$b(y(0), y(1)) = 0,$$

(7d) $$t(0) = 0, \qquad t(1) = 1.$$

Now, a uniform s-mesh means

(8) $$s(t_i) - s(t_{i-1}) \equiv \Delta s = \int_{t_{i-1}}^{t_i} \|- \frac{1}{12} y'''(x)\|^{1/2} dx/\theta \approx \|\tau_i[y]\|^{1/2}/\theta, \qquad i = 1,\ldots,N.$$

Thus,

$$(\theta\Delta s)^2 \approx \|\tau_i[y]\|^{1/2}, \qquad i = 1,\ldots,N,$$

and the truncation error is nearly equal on each interval.

Although very attractive, the truncation error is not the only reasonable measure of the difficulty of a solution, $y(t)$. If we were to solve the transformed boundary-value problem (7a,b/6c,d) directly on a uniform mesh, then it would pay to define $m(y,t)$ as simply as possible. One such definition is arc-length,

$$s(t) = \int_0^t \sqrt{1 + \|f(y,x)\|_2^2}\, dx/\theta .$$

This approach has been used with good results on boundary-layer problems.

Another way to solve (7a,b/6c,d) involves a two-pass procedure. The solution is approximated on a fixed mesh, then a new mesh is calculated using this approximate solution. This procedure is repeated until the mesh and the solution converge. Each of the codes, COLSYS, NONREF, and PASVA3, uses a method of this type to find a suitable mesh on which to approximate the solution. We now discuss the specific techniques used in each code.

COLSYS calculates a global approximation, $v(t)$, of the solution of (1a/1b). This approximate solution has the properties (for collocation at Gaussian points)

(9a) $v(t)$ is a polynomial of degree $k-1$ or less on $[t_{i-1},t_i]$;

(9b) $v(t)$ is $\in C^{(m-1)}[0,1]$; and

(9c) $\|y(t) - v(t)\| = Ch_i^k \|y^{(k)}(t)\| + o(h_i^k), \qquad t \in (x_{i-1},x_i),$

provided that $v(t)$ is superconvergent at breakpoints. Now, COLSYS selects a mesh that equidistributes the dominant term in the global error, (9c).

In the guise of (7a,b/6c,d), define $s(t)$ in the following way

$$s(t) = \int_0^t \|y^{(k)}(x)\|^{1/k}\, dx/\theta .$$

If the exact solution was given, then it would be an easy matter to integrate (7b/6d) to generate an equidistributing mesh. But, of course, this is not known. The actual procedure used is the following: (1) calculate an approximate solution, $v(t)$, on a fixed mesh; (2) calculate an approximation to $y^{(k)}(t)$ using differences of $v^{(k-1)}(t)$; and (3) using the approximation of $y^{(k)}(t)$ in the previous step, integrate (6b/6d) to generate a new mesh. Repeat until the mesh has converged. This is the two-pass procedure mentioned earlier. Note that $v^{(k)}(t)$ cannot be used to approximate $y^{(k)}(t)$ because $v(t)$ is a piecewise polynomial of degree $k-1$ or less.

In NONREF, a global approximation, $w(t)$, of the solution of (2a/2b) is calculated. This approximation is also a piecewise polynomial, but the function $w(t)$ is generated via Galerkin's method. That is, define the residual associated with

(2a) by

$$(10) \qquad R(u,t) = t^{1-a} \frac{d}{dt}\left[t^{a-1} \frac{du}{dt}\right] - g(u)$$

for any function $u(t) \in \mathscr{C}^2[0,1]$. Now, if we write

$$w(t) = \sum_{k=1}^{N} \alpha_k b_k(t),$$

where $\{b_k\}$ is a basis for the piecewise polynomials desired, then Galerkin's method requires that

$$\int_0^1 R(w,t)\; b_k(t)\; t^{a-1}\; dt = 0, \qquad k = 1,\ldots,N.$$

Actually, this condition is satisfied in the weak sense.

In choosing a mesh for NONREF, the quantity of interest is the residual, $R(w,t)$, defined in (10). In certain cases, it has been shown that

$$\|y(t) - w(t)\| \leq K\|R(w,t)\|,$$

where K is a constant known independent of the exact solution. The actual procedure used is a variation of the two-pass procedure: (1) generate an approximate solution, $v(t)$, on a fixed mesh; (2) calculate some suitable measure of the residual of each element and find the mean and standard deviation of this collection; and (3) place new mesh points in (t_{i-1}, t_i) by comparing the residual on this interval to the mean. Repeat until convergence. Although this does not directly relate to (6a,b/6c,d), there is still an attempt to equalize the residual, $R(w,t)$, over the mesh.

In PASVA3, a finite difference approximation, z^h, of the solution of (3a/3b) is calculated. Here, the trapezoidal rule is used to generate moderately accurate solutions, with deferred corrections used to accelerate convergence of the discrete solution. The difference approximation has a truncation error as given in (4)

$$\tau_i[y] \equiv \frac{1}{h_i}\,[y(t_i) - y(t_{i-1})] - \frac{1}{2}[f_i + f_{i+1}] = -\frac{1}{12} h_i^2 y_i''' + o(h_i^2).$$

In choosing a mesh, the quantity of interest here is the leading term in the truncation error expansion.

The actual procedure is again the two-pass method mentioned several times before: (1) calculate an approximation to the solution of (3a/3b) using trapezoidal rule; (2) using suitable differences of $\{z_i\}$, approximate $\tau_i[y]$ on each interval; and (3) add points to intervals where $\tau_i[y]$ is larger than the desired tolerance. Repeat until the mesh converges. Note that step (3) does not allow actual equidistribution of $\tau_i[y]$ because points are only added; points are not deleted where $\tau_i[y]$ is small. This is done to avoid large changes in grid size.

In each of the mesh selection techniques discussed, the basic approach remains the same. First, points $\{t_i\}$ are chosen in such a way that a given quantity, some measure of the discretization error, is roughly equal on each interval. Second, the selection of the mesh is done alternately with calculation of an approximate solution. However, neither of these is an indispensable part of a mesh selection strategy. For instance, we might choose to solve the transformed boundary-value problem (7a,b/6c,d) with s(t) defined as the arclength of the solution.

2. General Considerations

What follows is a series of comments and questions posed during this discussion. They should serve as a guide to further research and investigation into the numerical solution of two-point boundary-value problems.

Is automatic mesh selection a good idea? Clearly, there are problems for which the mesh selection apparatus is an unnecessary expense. Codes should be written with a uniform step-size option. One prime example is the solution of the transformed boundary-value problem (7a,b/6c,d) on a uniform s-mesh.

What is the relationship between the quantities equidistributed and the actual, observed error? For problems whose solutions have large gradients this is not always clear. Take the truncation error for the trapezoidal rule as the most familiar example,

$$\tau_i[y] = -\frac{1}{12} h_i^2 y^{(3)}(t_{i-\frac{1}{2}}) - \frac{1}{480} h_i^4 y^{(5)}(t_{i-\frac{1}{2}}) + O(h_i^6). \tag{11}$$

If the solution, y(t), has an exponential boundary-layer, see (5a,b), then the leading terms in (11) are

$$\tau_i[y] \approx \left[-\frac{1}{12}\left(\frac{h_i}{\epsilon}\right)^2 - \frac{1}{480}\left(\frac{h_i}{\epsilon}\right)^4 \right] \frac{1}{\epsilon} \exp\left(\frac{t_{i-\frac{1}{2}}-1}{\epsilon}\right).$$

Thus, the first term in (11) may not be a good approximation of $\tau_i[y]$ unless $h_i = O(\epsilon)$.

Should a boundary-value code be written to solve all problems? Usually, boundary-value codes are written with the solution of a particular class of problem in mind. For example, NONREF is specifically designed to handle the singularities arising from separable geometries, and PASVA3 is recommended for problems with only "mild" boundary layers. Whether or not a code is designed in great generality, there is always a dependence on the type of problem one envisions the method being applied to. Several people expressed a desire for codes, not specifically boundary-value codes, to be labeled "Slippery when wet", or when applied to particular classes of problems.

What sort of test problems should a boundary-value code be able to solve? This is closely related to the last question. From a mesh selection viewpoint, these may run the gamut from problems whose solutions are smooth to boundary-layers to inner-layers to highly-oscillatory solutions. These are listed in order of difficulty, the last being extremely difficult for all the codes represented here. An example of this type is

$$\epsilon^2 y'' + y = 0, \quad y(0) = 1, \quad y(1) = 2,$$

where the linearly independent solutions are $\sin(t/\epsilon)$, $\cos(t/\epsilon)$.

Can a code recognize "real, physical" solutions to a boundary-value problem? That is, some numerical solutions may have no physical meaning or significance: should a good code be required to reject these extraneous solutions? For example, the Falkner-Skan equation,

$$y''' + yy'' + \beta[1 - (y')^2] = 0, \qquad t \in (0,\infty),$$

$$y(0) = 0, \quad y'(0) = 0; \quad y' \to 1 \text{ as } t \to \infty,$$

has an infinite number of solutions decaying onto $y(t) = t$ for some values of β. However, the only solution with physical significance is the critically damped solution, not overdamped or oscillatory. How can extra constraints of this sort be appended to the original boundary-value problem?

Finally, we present a comment made during the discussion as a fitting conclusion of this report.

RESOLVED: Given any boundary-value code, there exists a "solution" satisfying all stopping/convergence criteria which is not close to any real solution of the original boundary-value problem.

Automatic Solution of Sturm-Liouville Eigenvalue Problems*

Paul B. Bailey
Lawrence F. Shampine
Sandia Laboratories†
Albuquerque, New Mexico 87185

1. Introduction

We are interested in the Sturm-Liouville eigenvalue problem, which concerns a second order, linear, differential equation

$$(p\psi')' + (q+\lambda r)\psi = 0 \tag{1}$$

on some interval (a,b), with boundary conditions (in the regular, or nonsingular, case) of the form

$$A_1\psi + A_2p\psi' = 0 \quad \text{at} \quad a \tag{2a}$$

$$B_1\psi + B_2p\psi' = 0 \quad \text{at} \quad b\ . \tag{2b}$$

The coefficient functions p,q,r are continuous, p and r are positive, and A_1, A_2, B_1, B_2 are given constants.

The eigenvalue problem is to find the real numbers, λ, such that there exists a nontrivial solution, $\psi(x)$, of the differential equation satisfying the two boundary conditions. Those numbers are called eigenvalues and the solutions are called eigenfunctions.

What we have tried to do is to construct a general purpose, automatic, computer code, which can be expected to work reasonably well on most problems, and which requires no more information from the user than an adequate description of the problem.

In fact, though the above description implies that the problem is nonsingular we really intend the algorithm to be such that it works on most singular problems too. But to keep matters as simple as possible we will continue to discuss only nonsingular problems for the moment, leaving until later any discussion about how singular problems are treated.

*This work was supported by the U.S. Department of Energy (DOE) under Contract No. AT(29-1)-789.

†A U.S. Department of Energy Facility.

In any case, the user of the code needs to supply a complete description of the problem, which means:

(i) subroutines for the functions $p(x)$, $q(x)$, $r(x)$

(ii) constants a,b,A_1,A_2,B_1,B_2

(iii) n, the index of the eigenvalue, λ_n, desired

(iv) accuracy requirement, τ

He may also supply (but does not have to)

(v) an initial guess, G_n, for λ_n

Upon successful completion of the computation he receives:

(i) λ_n^*, the computed eigenvalue

(ii) accuracy estimate, τ^*

(iii) initial data for ψ_n^* at each end of the interval which is such that

$$\int_a^b \left(\psi_n^*(x)\right)^2 r(x)\,dx = 1 .$$

One other option available to a user is to request values of $\psi_n^*(x)$ at selected places. That is, he may request the values of $\psi_n^*(x)$ at $x_1,x_2,\ldots,x_m$, where the choice of the x_i, $1 \le i \le m$, is entirely his.

2. Method of Computation

Basically the computational scheme is a "shooting method," but instead of integrating the given differential equation we first transform to a kind of "polar coordinates." That is, instead of ψ and ψ' the dependent variables become ρ and θ, which are defined by the equations (a slightly modified Prufer transformation)

$$\begin{aligned} c\psi &= \rho \sin \theta \\ p\psi' &= \rho \cos \theta , \end{aligned} \qquad (3)$$

or

$$\tan \theta = \frac{c\psi}{p\psi'}$$

$$\rho = \sqrt{c^2\psi^2 + p^2\psi'^2} ,$$

where c is some suitably chosen constant depending upon the particular problem. ($c = 1$ is the usual Prüfer transformation.)

Substituting (3) into (1) gives a differential equation for θ,

$$\theta' = \frac{c}{p}\cos^2\theta + c^{-1}(q+\lambda r)\sin^2\theta \tag{4}$$

with boundary conditions of the form

$$\theta(a) = \alpha\ , \quad 0 \le \alpha < \pi$$

$$\theta(b) = \beta + n\pi\ , \quad 0 < \beta \le \pi$$

for some α and β, where n is the eigenvalue index. There is also a differential equation for determining ρ,

$$\rho'/\rho = (c/p - q/c - r/c)\sin\theta\cos\theta \tag{5}$$

(but no boundary conditions, reflecting the fact that solutions of (1) and (2) are determined only up to an arbitrary multiple.) But (5) is not needed for the determination of eigenvalues; only for the eigenfunctions.

To find an eigenvalue, λ_n, one integrates (4) for $\theta(x)$ from a to some interior point M, getting $\theta_L(M;\lambda)$, and from b to M getting $\theta_R(M;\lambda)$. Putting

$$f(\lambda) = \theta_L(M;\lambda) - \theta_R(M;\lambda)\ , \tag{6}$$

the value λ_n is the zero of $f(\lambda)$.

When also the eigenfunction, ψ_n, is wanted, one can integrate (5) along with (4). Then ψ_n and ψ_n' are obtained from formulas (3). Theoretically the solution, ψ_n^*, obtained in this way should be continuous and have continuous derivative, but since λ_n^* is not exactly λ_n, ψ_n^* can be made continuous but $\psi_n^{*\prime}$ will necessarily have a small jump discontinuity.

Basically that is the scheme. Transform to Prüfer variables ρ, θ; integrate the equation for θ from both ends, getting θ_L and θ_R (the insertion of a constant, c, in the Prüfer transformation can make the integrations very much easier for a numerical integrator than would be the case for c = 1, [1]); find the zero, λ_n^*, of the resulting function $f(\lambda)$.

But of course a number of modifications of this basic scheme are necessary when the problem is singular.

3. Singular Problems

By "singular problem" we mean that either one of the ends, a or b, is infinite, or that q is not bounded and continuous there, or that p vanishes there. (r is still supposed to be nonzero even at the ends.)

For singular problems a few changes need to be made in the basic plan so far outlined.

The first change is due to the fact that the boundary condition at a singular endpoint is no longer completely arbitrary. So we have arranged to have the code itself determine the appropriate boundary condition. Essentially what is done is to choose the value for θ at that end such that θ', given by the right hand side of (4), can be finite there. For example if

$$q(b) = +\infty$$

and

$$p(b) \neq 0 \ ,$$

then

$$\beta = \pi.$$

The other problem arising at a singular endpoint is that one or more of the functions to be evaluated is infinite there, so it is necessary to stay away from that end by at least a small distance. So, for a singular problem the modification amounts to:

(i) truncate the interval (a,b) to (a′,b′) so as to avoid any singular endpoints;

(ii) solve the resulting nonsingular problem on (a′,b′), usually using the same boundary condition prescribed for (a,b);

(iii) estimate the error in λ_n^* due to using a truncated interval and

(iv) move a′ or b′ closer to a or b if necessary.

4. Choice of c

The constant c in (3) is for the purpose of making integrations of (3) easier than would be the case if c = 1 as in the usual Prüfer transformation. The idea is to choose c so that the coefficients of $\cos^2\theta$ and $\sin^2\theta$ in (3) will be as nearly equal as possible throughout the range of integration, or at least throughout those regions where the eigenfunction oscillates (where $\lambda r + q > 0$). Locally, then, the choice would be $c = \sqrt{p(\lambda r+q)}$; so overall the best that can be done is to take for c some kind of average of the values of $\sqrt{p(\lambda r+q)}$. Actually this simple device can be surprisingly effective. (See [1] for a number of typical examples.)

5. An Initial Guess for λ_n

The fact is that sometimes one just does not happen to have a good guess for the eigenvalue, λ_n. So rather than have to try to begin the computational procedure with what might be a very bad guess, we have included an algorithm for arriving at a reasonable guess when necessary. Of course a really good guess might be available, in which case the code has been designed to make good use of it. But in the other case a guess, G_n, will be found.

Obviously any such algorithm must be very inexpensive compared to the cost of just going ahead with a bad guess, and must somehow avoid impossible regions even when close by. For example in the case p = 1, r = 1, $q = 1/x - 6/x^2$ (the "hydrogen" atom) the eigenvalues, λ_n, all are negative, and $\lambda_n \to 0-$ as $n \to \infty$. In fact the eigenvalues are

$$\lambda_n = -\frac{1}{4}(n+2)^{-2} .$$

So $\lambda_{10} = -.001736$, for instance, yet $G_{10} = .00001$ would be a very bad guess. (It would not be possible to satisfy the boundary condition at $b = +\infty$, or very large b.)

But apart from complications of this sort, the algorithm used is basically this:

(i) evaluate p,q,r at 100 places scattered throughout (a,b), and save;

(ii) find G_n such that

$$\sum \sqrt{\frac{1}{p_i}(G_n r_i + q_i)} \cdot \Delta x_i = n\pi$$

where the summation is over those i such that

$$G_n r_i + q_i \geq 0 .$$

(This has a slight resemblance to a WBK estimate.)

6. Summary

The methods outlined above have been implemented in a computer code*, SLEIGN, which has been tested on a very long list of problems reported in the literature. Naturally no code can be expected to work on all problems, but this code does demonstrate the feasibility of being able to solve at least the vast majority of ordinary problems in a completely automatic fashion. For a detailed report, including worked examples, see [2].

References

1. P. B. Bailey, "A Slightly Modified Prüfer Transformation Useful for Calculating Sturm-Liouville Eigenvalues," J. Comp. Phys. (to appear).

2. P. B. Bailey, "SLEIGN, An Eigenvalue-Eigenfunction Code for Sturm-Liouville Problems," SAND77-2044, Sandia Laboratories, Albuquerque, New Mexico, 1978.

*The code, SLEIGN, is freely available from one of the authors (P.B.B.) to any interested persons.

A SUBROUTINE FOR SOLVING A SYSTEM OF DIFFERENTIAL EQUATIONS IN CHEBYSHEV SERIES

E L Albasiny

National Physical Laboratory, Teddington, England

INTRODUCTION

Algol and Fortran versions of the subroutine SETCEB have been in use for a number of years at the National Physical Laboratory. For a full description of the Algol version see Picken [3]. The purpose of the routine is to solve, in Chebyshev series form, a system of linear or nonlinear ordinary differential equations of arbitrary order. If the equations are nonlinear the user has first to linearise them and then enter the routine iteratively. The routine is applicable to initial or boundary value problems; indeed auxiliary conditions may be prescribed at intermediate points of the range. A slightly modified version of the routine is incorporated in the Numerical Algorithms Group Library. The version described in this paper may be purchased from the National Physical Laboratory.

DESCRIPTION

Suppose there are r differential equations for the r dependent variables y_1, y_2, ..., y_r and that the ith equation is written in the form

$$F_i(x, y_1, y_1^{(1)}, \ldots, y_1^{(m_1)}, \ldots, y_r, y_r^{(1)}, \ldots, y_r^{(m_r)}) = 0 . \qquad (1)$$

We assume that the equation has been transformed so that the independent variable x lies in the range $-1 \leqslant x \leqslant 1$. The linearised form of (1) may be written as

$$\begin{aligned} & f_{1,0}y_1 + f_{1,1}y_1^{(1)} + \ldots + f_{1,m_1}y_1^{(m_1)} + \\ & f_{2,0}y_2 + f_{2,1}y_2^{(1)} + \ldots + f_{2,m_2}y_2^{(m_2)} + \\ & \ldots\ldots\ldots\ldots\ldots\ldots\ldots\ldots\ldots\ldots \\ & f_{r,0}y_r + f_{r,1}y_r^{(1)} + \ldots + f_{r,m_r}y_r^{(m_r)} = g_i \end{aligned} \qquad (2)$$

where the f and g_i are functions* of x. If the differential equations are linear

* For simplicity of notation the dependence of the $f_{j,k}$ on i is not explicitly indicated in equation (2).

they will already be in this form, otherwise the f and g will depend on approximations to the y_j and their derivatives obtained on the previous entry to SETCEB.

The recommended Newton linearisation gives

$$f_{j,k} = \frac{\partial F_i}{\partial y_j^{(k)}} (x, z_1, z_1^{(1)}, \ldots, z_1^{(m_1)}, \ldots, z_r, z_r^{(1)}, \ldots, z_r^{(m_r)}) \qquad (3)$$

$$\text{with } j = 1,2, \ldots, r; \; k = 0,1, \ldots, m_i , \qquad (4)$$

where the z's and their derivatives are the approximations to the corresponding y's and their derivatives obtained on the previous entry to SETCEB. The function g_i is now given by

$$\begin{aligned} g_i = {} & f_{1,0}z_1 + f_{1,1}z_1^{(1)} + \ldots + f_{1,m_1}z_1^{(m_1)} + \\ & f_{2,0}z_2 + f_{2,1}z_2^{(1)} + \ldots + f_{2,m_2}z_2^{(m_2)} + \\ & \ldots\ldots\ldots\ldots\ldots\ldots\ldots\ldots \\ & f_{r,0}z_r + f_{r,1}z_r^{(1)} + \ldots + f_{r,m_r}z_r^{(m_r)} - \\ & F_i(x, z_1, z_1^{(1)}, \ldots, z_1^{(m_1)}, \ldots, z_r, z_r^{(1)}, \ldots, z_r^{(m_r)}) . \end{aligned} \qquad (5)$$

The user needs to provide an auxiliary subroutine which evaluates, for each point x, the coefficients $f_{j,k}$ and g_i for each equation.

Let us suppose that the boundary conditions have been grouped so that there are b_1 associated with equation 1, b_2 with equation 2, etc. These are arranged in a form similar to the linearised differential equations, with any nonlinear boundary condition being linearised in a manner similar to the above. The coefficients corresponding to the jth boundary condition associated with the ith differential equation ($j = 1,2, \ldots, b_i$) must be provided by the user together with the values of $x_{i,R}$ ($R = 1,2, \ldots, b_i$) at which the boundary conditions hold. Note that derivatives of y_j up to and including order m_j are permitted in the boundary conditions, in accordance with the form of equation (2).

It is assumed that each function $y_j(x)$ possesses a convergent Chebyshev series expansion, for which an approximation of degree n is sought of the form

$$y_j(x) = \tfrac{1}{2}a_{j,0}T_0(x) + a_{j,1}T_1(x) + \ldots + a_{j,n}T_n(x) \qquad (6)$$

where $T_m(x)$ is the Chebyshev polynomial of degree m defined by

$$T_m(x) = \cos(m \cos^{-1}x), \quad -1 \leq x \leq 1. \qquad (7)$$

The routine assumes that the same n is used for each y_j.

The sth derivative of $y_j(x)$ has the form

$$y_j^{(s)}(x) = \tfrac{1}{2}a^s_{j,0}T_0(x) + a^s_{j,1}T_1(x) + \ldots + a^s_{j,n-s}T_{n-s}(x) \qquad (8)$$

where the relation

$$2ka^s_{j,k} = a^{s+1}_{j,k-1} - a^{s+1}_{j,k+1}, \quad k \geq 1 \qquad (9)$$

holds, with $a^{s+1}_{j,k} = 0$ for $k > n-s-1$.

The basis of the method is to substitute the expressions (6) and (8) into the differential equation (2) and the associated (linearised) boundary conditions and satisfy the resulting linear relations at selected points x. Use of (9) then enables the system of linear equations to be reduced to one of lower order by eliminating some of the variables. If, for simplicity, we consider the case $m_j = 3$, $n = 5$ we have the following diagrammatic illustration of the dependencies given by (9):

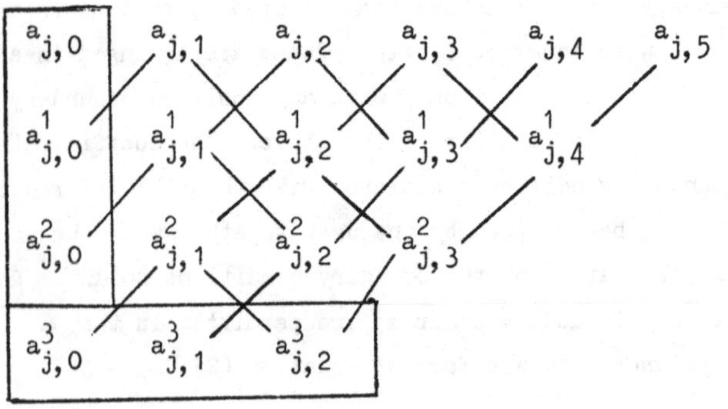

Evidently we can use the relationship (9) to eliminate all the variables in the table with the exception of those in the last row and first column. Equally we can reconstruct the table when the last row and first column are known. Proceeding in this manner, use of (9) enables the system of linear equations to be reduced to order r(n+1) in the variables

$$a^{m_j}_{j,k}\ , \quad j = 1,2,\ \ldots,\ r; \quad k = 0,1,\ \ldots,\ n-m_j \tag{10}$$

and

$$a^{s}_{j,0}\ , \quad j = 1,2,\ \ldots,\ r; \quad s = 0,1,\ \ldots,\ m_j-1\ , \tag{11}$$

the linear equations being obtained by use for the ith equation of the selected points

$$x_k = \cos\frac{\pi k}{n-b_i}\ , \quad k = 0,1,\ \ldots,\ n-b_i\ , \tag{12}$$

together with the b_i boundary conditions at the points $x_{i,R}$ $(R = 1,2,\ \ldots,\ b_i)$. Subsequent solutions of the linear equations, and integration of the series, gives Chebyshev coefficients for each $y_j(x)$ and its derivatives.

COMMENTS

The degree n of the Chebyshev series approximation has to be chosen by the user. The adequacy of the choice will normally be indicated by the rate of decrease of the Chebyshev coefficients obtained. With nonlinear equations the procedure has to be applied iteratively and an initial approximation to the solution is required. Often the simplest polynomials satisfying the boundary conditions will suffice, though any prior knowledge of the nature of the solution may be incorporated. The original differential equations have to be transformed so that the variable x lies in the range $-1 \leqslant x \leqslant 1$. Useful transformations are, for example,

(i) $x = \dfrac{2t-(b+a)}{b-a}$ if the range is originally $a \leqslant t \leqslant b$

(ii) $x = \dfrac{t-a-k}{t-a+k}$

or

$x = 1 - 2\exp\{-k(t-a)\}$

if the range is originally $a \leqslant t \leqslant \infty$.

The bulk of the time required by the routine consists in solving a dense set of linear equations of order r(n+1). Consequently the method is best suited to the case where the number r of dependent variables y_j is relatively small.

The version of the routine in the Numerical Algorithms Group Library differs from the one described here in that the user specifies the number of collocation points in the range. The routine then sets up a system of linear equations in a similar manner to that described. These may now be over-determined, in which case the boundary conditions are satisfied exactly and the remaining equations solved by a least-squares method.

EXAMPLES

An application of the use of the routine to the numerical determination of the bending of thin conical shells is described by Ferriss [2], whilst an application to the solution of van der Pol's equation has been given by Clenshaw [1].

Picken [3] quotes an application to the solution of the Falkner-Skan equation

$$\frac{d^3y}{dt^3} + y\frac{d^2y}{dt^2} = \beta\left\{\left(\frac{dy}{dt}\right)^2 - 1\right\} \tag{13}$$

with boundary conditions

$$y = \frac{dy}{dt} = 0 \quad \text{at } t = 0, \quad \frac{dy}{dt} \to 1 \quad \text{as } t \to \infty \ . \tag{14}$$

This was solved by making the transformation $x = \frac{2t}{T} - 1$ for a suitably large constant T and linearising as described to give the equation, in the form of (2),

$$z^{(2)}y - 2\beta z^{(1)}y^{(1)} + zy^{(2)} + \frac{2}{T}y^{(3)} = z^{(2)}z - \beta(z^{(1)})^2 - \beta T^2/4. \tag{15}$$

The boundary conditions associated with (15) are now

$$y(-1) = 0, \quad y^{(1)}(-1) = 0, \quad y^{(1)}(+1) = T/2 \ , \tag{16}$$

and for $\beta = 1$ ten decimal accuracy was obtained with a choice of T = 8, n = 30 after 8 iterations starting from an initial approximation of zero. The resulting Chebyshev coefficients, and the corresponding solution are given to four decimal places by

$a_{1,0}$	6.9034
$a_{1,1}$	3.8142
$a_{1,2}$	0.1505
$a_{1,3}$	-0.1051
$a_{1,4}$	0.0624
$a_{1,5}$	-0.0306
$a_{1,6}$	0.0117
$a_{1,7}$	-0.0029
$a_{1,8}$	0.0000
$a_{1,9}$	0.0004
$a_{1,10}$	-0.0002

x	t	y
-1.00	0	0
-0.75	1	0.4592
-0.50	2	1.3620
-0.25	3	2.3526
0.00	4	3.3521
0.25	5	4.3521
0.50	6	5.3521
0.75	7	6.3521
1.00	8	7.3521

The good convergence of the series is evident from the tabulated coefficients.

As a final example the equations

$$y_1^{(2)} = y_1 + y_1y_2 + y_2 - 3 + \exp(x-1)$$

$$y_2^{(2)} = y_1y_2 + 2y_2 - 6$$

with boundary conditions

$$\left.\begin{aligned} y_1^{(1)} &= y_1 + y_1y_2 + y_2 - 3 + e^{-1} \\ y_2^{(1)} &= y_1y_2 + 2y_2 - 6 \end{aligned}\right\} \quad \text{at } x = 0$$

and

$$y_1 = y_2 = 1 \quad \text{at } x = 1$$

were solved at NPL using the routine in connexion with a simplified problem concerning ion diffusion. With $n = 10$ and initial approximations of unity convergence to the solution was obtained in four iterations, the resulting first few Chebyshev coefficients being given to four decimal places by

	j = 1	j = 2
$a_{j,0}$	1.2268	2.6466
$a_{j,1}$	0.3395	-0.2862
$a_{j,2}$	0.0438	-0.0336
$a_{j,3}$	0.0034	-0.0030
$a_{j,4}$	0.0001	-0.0004

Again we observe that the series is rapidly convergent in this case.

REFERENCES

1 CLENSHAW, C W. The solution of van der Pol's equation in Chebyshev series. Numerical solution of nonlinear differential equations, edited by D Greenspan, New York, John Wiley and Sons, 1966, 55-63.

2 FERRISS, D H. A numerical determination of the bending of thin conical shells under normal loading. NPL NAC Report No 63, 1976.

3 PICKEN, S M. Algorithms for the solution of differential equations in Chebyshev series by the selected points method. NPL Maths Report No 94, 1970.

ON THE IMPLEMENTATION OF A METHOD FOR THE ESTIMATION OF GLOBAL ERRORS

PEDRO E. ZADUNAISKY*

1. INTRODUCTION

Let us consider a functional equation

(1.1.) $$T(y(x))=0$$

that we shall call the "Original Problem" and assume that it has a unique solution $y=y(x)$. Furthermore the problem is solved through a <u>convergent discretization algorithm</u>

(1.2) $$\mathfrak{T}(y_n)=0$$

on a set of grid points $x_n=x_o+n.h.(n=o,1,...)$ where the stepsize h may not be constant. The application of this algorithm produces approximations y_n to the exact solution $y(x_n)$ and our object is to obtain a good estimation of the <u>global errors</u>

(1.3) $$e_n=\bar{y}_n - y(x_n).$$

For that object we have developed a method that we have been applying in many cases, especially in several problems of Celestial Mechanics. In this field any numerical method is usually put to a rigourous test due to the high precision required in the final results.

In one of our latest papers (P.E. Zadunaisky, 1976) we have given a description of our method in full detail including numerous examples and references to our earlier work; we referred also to some recent contributions of Prof.H.J. Stetter and some of this associates on the basis of the asymptotic theory of errors and the possible application in iterative solutions of boundary value problems of O.D.E.s. More recently (P.E. Zadunaisky, 1978) we have been dealing with some cases of the N-Body Problem where, to overcome certain difficulty, we have introduced in our method a modification that opens new possibilities in its applications.

---

*Some parts of this work have been done while the author was enjoying a fellowship from the John Simon Guggenheim Foundation for the period Sept. 1977 through Aug. 1978.

Here we intend to present a short survey of the subject including some examples in order to show the advantages and limitations of the method.

2. THE METHOD AND ITS IMPLEMENTATION

2.1 - Consider a set of $\tilde{N}+1$ adjacent gridpoints $x_n, x_{n+1}, \ldots, x_{n+\tilde{N}}$ and define a suitable function $P_M(x)$ which interpolates the corresponding numerical values $\bar{y}j(j=n,\ldots,n+\tilde{N})$. In most of our applications $P_n(x)$ has been an $\tilde{N}$-th degree polynomial obtained through Newton's method of interpolation by divided differences where for convenience $\tilde{N}=10$. The whole interval of integration may then be covered piecewise by a set of sucessive polynomials that we shall call $P(x)$. Now we can form a new functional equation

(2.1) $$T(z(x))=T(P(x))$$

that we have called the "Pseudo Problem" corresponding to (1.1). The exact solution of (2.1) is evidently $z=P(x)$; by solving(2.1) numerically one obtains numbers $\bar{z}_n$ and their global errors are given exactly by

(2.2) $$w_n=\bar{z}_n-P(x_n)$$

If the right had member of (2.1) is small then the pseudo problem is close to the original problem (1.1), the numerical results will be also close and we may expect the errors to propagate approximately in the same fashion so that we can adopt w_n as a good approximation for the global errors e_n of the original problem. In the next section we shall state some sufficient conditions for the validity of this approximation. We may notice that the right hand member of 2.1) is just a function of x that we shall call $D(x)$.

2.2- Conditions of Validity

We may consider that the equation (2.1) is formed by introducing in (1.1) the perturbing term $T(P(x))=D(x)$. Then, heuristically, we may state the following criterion of validity: The estimated errors should have at least the same order of magnitude as the actual global errors provided that the order of magnitude of the function $D(x)$ is no larger than both the local truncation and round-off errors at any point of the interval of integration.

More elaborated and rigourous criteria have been established by (H.J. Stetter, 1974), (R. Frank, 1975) and ourselves (P.E. Zadunaisky, 1975) but under the hypothesis that round-off errors are negligible and imposing conditions for an asymptotic theory of truncation errors which fulfillment cannot always be assured.

2.3- A new form of the Pseudo Problem

In some cases the function $D(x)$ becomes either too large to fulfill the condition of validity or too small in which case our method is meaningless.

In this case we construct the pseudo problem in another form. To simplify our explanation let us consider the equation

(2.3) $$Ty=y'-f(x,y)=0$$

To the numerical solution we apply a Hermitian interpolation process consisting in finding polynomials that satisfy the conditions

(2.4) $$P(x_n)=\bar{y}_n \ , \ P'(x_n)=f(x_n,\bar{y}_n)$$

Now the function

$$D(x_n)=P'(x_n) - f(x_n,P(x_n))$$

becomes practically zero at the gridpoints and we modify it and the pseudo problem into the forms

(2.6) $$D(x,c)=P'(x) - f(x,(P(x)+c))$$

(2.7) $$x'=f(x,z)+D(x,c)$$

respectively where c is a conveniently chosen small constant. It is seen that the order of magnitude of D(x,c) is aproximately that of c. The exact solution of the pseudo problem is now

(2.8) $$z(x)=P(x)+c$$

and the error estimations are

(2.9) $$w_n= \bar{z}_n-(P(x)+c)$$

We have found that a convenient value of the constant c is given by

(2.10) $$c= \max(R,TR)$$

where R and TR represent a rough approximation of the average values of the local round-off and truncation errors respectively for each set of $\tilde{N}+1$ points. It is important to notice that the conditions (2.4) are fulfilled only at the gridpoints; therefore it should not be advisable to apply this form of the pseudo problem with integration methods that require calculating the functions f(x) and D(x) out of the gridpoints, like, for instance, any of the Runge Kutta type methods.

2.4- Efficiency

In the examples that will be given in the next section the analytical solution of the original problems is known and we can compare the estimated with the exact errors. We have called the Efficiency of the method the number given by the formula

$$Eff_n= -\log_{10}(|e_n - w_n|/10^{-r})$$

where r is the larger in absolute value of the two exponents of the floating forms of e_n and w_n. When $Eff_n > 0$ its integer part gives the number of figures of the r-th decimal order correctly estimated of the error.

3. EXAMPLES

The examples that follow will be described in a synthetical form; further details may be found in the especially mentioned literature.

<u>Example 1.</u>
(V. Pereyra, 1974).

Original problem: $Ty=y'' - e^y = 0$, $y(0) = y(1) = 0$

Exact solution: $y = -\ln 2 + \ln(c.\sec(1/2C(x - 1/2)))$, $c=1.33...$

Numerical solution: Störmer Formula of order p=2 applied in N=39 points; two Newton-Raphson iterations without deferred corrections.

Interpolation: Newton polynomials of 4th degree.

Pseudo Problem: $Tz = z''-e^z = P''- e^P$, $z(0) = z(1) = 0$

Maximum error: 0.5E - 5

Mean Efficiency: 2.9

<u>Example 2.</u>
(D.J. Fyfe, 1969)

Original Problem: $Ty = y'' + (4x/(1 + x^2))y' + (2/(1 + x^2))y = 0$; $y(0)=1$, $y(2)=0.2$

Exact solution: $y = 1/(1+x^2)$ (Runge's Function)

Numerical solution: A <u>collocation method</u> based on a <u>cubic spline function</u> applied in N=16 points <u>with one deferred correction.</u>

Interpolation: Newton polynomials of 4th degree.

Pseudo problem: $Tz = TP$

Maximum error: 0.4E - 4

Mean Efficiency: 2.3

<u>Examples of the N-Body Problem</u>

In the Two-Body Problem the equations of relative motion are

(3.1)
$$X'' = -M\,(x/R^3),$$
$$y'' = -M\,(y/R^3), \quad R = (x^2 + y^2)^{1/2}$$

with $M=(wk)^2(m_1+m_2)$ and where m_1 and m_2 are their masses, k^2 is the Gaussian gravitational constant and w is a convenient unit of time.

In the <u>Planar Three-Body Problem</u> the barycentric equations of motion are

$$x_i'' = (wk)^2 {}_j\, m_j(x_i - x_j)/R_{ij}^3 ,$$

(3.2)
$$y_i'' = (wk)^2 {}_j\, m_j(y_i - y_j)/R_{ij}^3 , \quad R_{ij}=((x_i-x_j)^2+(y_i-y_j)^2)^{1/2}$$
$$(i,j) = 1,2,3 \qquad j \neq i$$

By introducing generalised coordinates q_i and moments p_i and the Hamiltonian Function $H = H(q_i,p_i)$ the systems (3.1) and (3.2) can be reduced to the Hamiltonian form

(3.3)
$$q_i' = \frac{\partial H}{\partial P_i} \quad , \quad p_i' = -\frac{\partial H}{\partial q_i}$$

where $i = 1,2$ for (3.1) and $i = 1,2,\ldots,6$ for (3.2) respectively.

In the Two-Body Problem we have considered the case where the relative orbit is an ellipse which equation in polar coordinates (r, w) is

(3.4)
$$r = \frac{q(1 + e)}{1 + e.\cos w}$$

where e is the excentricity and q is the pericenter distance that corresponds to the closest approach of the two bodies. In the Three-Body Problem we have considered the classical solutions of Lagrange where the configuration of the three bodies is a periodically rotating and pulsating equilateral triangle. If at the initial time the positions of the bodies are represented by three vectors R_i°, i = 1,2,3 from the barycenter, at any other instant the vectors are $R_i = r.R_i^\circ$ where r is given by formula (3.4) corresponding to a "virtual" ellipse characterized by the parameters e and q. If e is close to 1 and q is small the bodies will come periodically to positions that are alternatively very close and very far apart; in both cases and asymptotic theory of errors may not be quite reliable because in the close positions the higher derivatives of the unknowns and the local truncation errors may be too large while in the far apart positions they may become smaller than the round-off errors. To face this difficulties we have introduced in the Pseudo Problem the modifications described in section 2.3.

From an analytic point of view it is possible to smooth out these difficulties by making a change in the independent variable in order to stabilize the system of equations and to introduce an analytic adaption of the step-size. We have used a transformation of that sort proposed by (K.Zare and V.Szebehely, 1975).

Example 3 Unperturbed orbit of Halley's comet

e = 0.97, q = 0.59, Period = 76 years

a) Original Problem: Non stabilized equations (3.1)
Exact Solution: Formula (3.4)
Numerical Solution: Cowell's Method of order p=10
Interpolation: Hermite polynomials of the 9th degree
Pseudo Problem: Modified as is section 2.3

Maximum Error: 0.3E - 10
Mean Efficiency: -0.3

b) Original Problem: Stabilized equations (3.3)
Numerical Solution: Runge-Kutta-Fehlberg Method of order p=7 (8)
Interpolation: Newton polynomials of 9th degree.
Pseudo Problem: Non modified as in section 2.1
Maximum error: 0.2E - 8
Mean Efficiency: 1.8

Example 4 Unperturbed orbit of planet Jupiter

$e = 0.05$, $q = 5.5$, Period = 11.9 years

Original Problem: Non Stabilized equations (3.3)

Exact Solution: Formula (3.4)

Numerical Solution: Rational Extrapolation (R.Bulirsch, J.Stöer,Numerische Math., 8, 1966).

Interpolation: Newton polynomials of 9th degree.

Pseudo Problem: Non modified as in section 2.1

Maximum error: 0.2E - 10

Mean Efficiency: 2.9

Example 5 Lagrangian Equilateral Solution of the Three-Body Problem

We have taken three cases as indicated in the table; the numerical solutions were obtained with Runge-Kutta-Fehlberg Method of order p=7(8); the Pseudo Problem Method was used as described in section 2,1 with Newton interpolating polynomials of 9th degree.

Case	e	q	Max. Error	Mean Eff.
Eq. (3.3), Non Stab.	0.0	1.0	1.7E-8	4.6
Eq. (3.3), Stabilized	0.1	0.9	3.3E-9	3.0
Eq. (3.3), Stabilized	0.9	0.1	5.3E-7	-0.4

REFERENCES

R. Bulirsch and J. Stoer, "Numerical Treatment of Ordinary Differential Equations by Extrapolation Methods," Num. Math., 8, 1-13, 1966.

R. Frank, J. Hertling, Ch.W. Ueberhuber, "An Extension of the Applicability of Iterated Deferred Corrections", Math. of Comp., 31, 907-915, 1977.

R. Frank, "Schatzungen des Globalen Diskretisierungfehlers by Runge-Kutta Methoden", ISNM 27, Birkhauser, 1975.

D.J. Fyfe, "The use of Cubic Splines in the Solution of Two Point Boundary Value Problems", Comp. Journal, 12, 188-192, 1969.

V. Pereyra, "Variable Order, Variable Step Finite Difference Methods for Non Linear Boundary Value Problems", Lecture Notes in Math., Springer, 363, 118-133, 1974.

H.J. Stetter, "Economical Global Error Estimation", Proc. Symp. Stiff Differential Systems, Wildbad, 1973, Plenum Publ., 1974.

P.E. Zadunaisky, "Sobre la Estimación de Errores Propagados en la Integración Numérica de Ecuaciones Diferenciales", Acta Scientífica, Obs. San Miguel, 38, 1975.

P.E. Zadunaisky, "On the Estimation of Errors Propagated in the Numerical Integration of Ordinary Differential Equations", Numer. Math., 27, 21-39, 1976.

P.E. Zadunaisky, "On the Accuracy in the Numerical Solution of the N-Body Problem", Submitted for publication in "Celestial Mechanics", D. Reidel Publ. Co, 1978.

K Zare and V. Szebehely, "Time Transformations in the Extended Phase Space", Celestial Mechanics, 11, 469-482, 1975.

AN OVERVIEW OF INVARIANT IMBEDDING ALGORITHMS AND TWO-POINT BOUNDARY-VALUE PROBLEMS

by

E. D. Denman, University of Houston

1. INTRODUCTION

Several invariant imbedding algorithms for solving two-point boundary-value problems have been published over the past twenty years. The principle of invariance was first used by Chandrasekhar [1960]. Preisendorfer [1965] based his work on radiative transfer on the concept and Redheffer [1961] analyzed scattering problems by a similar technique. The term "invariant imbedding" was first used by Bellman, Kalaba and co-workers [1963]. Numerous other workers have made contributions to the mathematical technique, among those were Wing [1962], Bellman and Wing [1975], Shimizu and Aoki [1972], Adams and Denman [1966], Denman [1970], Mingle [1973], Case and Zweifel [1967], Ribaric [1973], Scott [1973], Meyer [1973] and Casti and Kalaba [1973]. Major contributions to the application of the technique to two-point boundary-value problems have come from Bellman, Kalaba, Wing, Nelson and Scott. Co-workers of these mathematicians should be included in this list.

The technique has also been discussed in published papers. The work of Golberg [1974], Rybicki and Usher [1966], Allen and Wing [1974], Nelson and Scott [1972], and others should be recognized in any survey paper. Scott [1971] published a bibliography on invariant imbedding which still remains the most complete list of material.

Invariant imbedding is a mathematical procedure by which a particular problem is imbedded within a family of related problems. The family or related problems are initial value problems and easily solved by a digital computer.

Section 2 of this work will give the state-transition and transfer matrix algorithms which are invariant imbedding algorithms. It will be shown that these two algorithms are related. Section 3 will derive several algorithms that have been described in open literature which are special cases of the algorithms given in Section 2. The relationship to the material in Section 2 will be discussed.

Section 4 will discuss a property of the Riccati differential equation that can be used to overcome the major disadvantage of stability of the Riccati equation. Interested readers should read the report by Vandevender [1977] for more details on the technique. A similar technique was used by Yoo [1974] for decoupling of the state and costate vectors in optimal control problems.

2. STATE TRANSITION AND TRANSFER MATRICES

A large number of papers and books have been published in recent years describing the application of the state transition matrix to numerical solutions of first order differential equations. The majority of the work has been directed to the initial value problem although the state transition matrix, hereafter referred to as the STM, can easily be extended to the two-point boundary-value problem. Modified input-output matrices are the transfer matrix (TM) and the scattering matrix (SM).

Since this paper is an overview of invariant imbedding, (II) the writer feels that the development of the II algorithm should be made from a standard set of variables. The state transition matrix formulation is perhaps the most widely known formulation and will be used as a basis for the development. II algorithms have been published with little if any standardization of symbols, definitions, etc. This paper will attempt to show that variants of algorithms could be classified under a broad heading of invariant imbedding, and can be derived from the STM and TM approach. No attempt will be made to compare efficiency, accuracy or other numerical properties of the variants.

Consider a set of linear first-order differential equations of the form*

(2.1) $$\dot{x}(t) = A(t)\, x(t) + B(t)$$

where x(t) and B(t) are n x 1 vectors and A(t) is n x n. It will be assumed that A(t) and B(t) are continuous everywhere. The solution form to (2.1) is given by

(2.2) $$x(t) = \phi(t,0)\, x(o) + \int_0^t \phi(t,\tau)\, B(\tau)\, d\tau$$

where $o < \tau < t$. The matrix $\phi(t,o)$ is the STM and satisfies the equation

(2.3) $$\dot{\phi}(t,o) = A(t)\, \phi(t,o) \qquad \phi(o,o) = \phi(t,t) = I \ \ (I = \text{identity}).$$

Assuming that the integral can be defined as $\Gamma(t,o)$, then (2.2) becomes

(2.4) $$x(t) = \phi(t,o)\, x(o) + \Gamma(t,o) = o$$

where $\Gamma(t)$ must satisfy the equation

(2.5) $$\dot{\Gamma}(t,o) = A(t)\, \Gamma(t,o) + B(t) \qquad \Gamma(o,o) = \Gamma(t,t) = o$$

Recursive equations for the STM formulation can be derived and are

(2.6a) $$\phi(t,o) = \phi(t,\tau)\, \phi(\tau,o)$$

(2.6b) $$\Gamma(t,o) = \Gamma(t,\tau) + \phi(t,\tau)\, \Gamma(\tau,o).$$

The STM algorithm can be used directly for an initial value problem since x(o) is known. The boundary-value problem can be solved by the STM formulation but algebraic manipulations are required since the known variables appear on both sides of (2.4). A formulation which is more convenient is the TM approach. This model has also been referred to as the scattering model. Let $x_1(o)$ and $x_2(t)$ be specified vectors with $x_1(t)$ and $x_2(o)$ as unknowns where A(t) has been partitioned to be consistent with the dimensions of $x_1(o)$ and $x_2(t)$. Equation (2.4) can then be written as

(2.7a) $$x_1(t) = \phi_{11}(t,o)\, x_1(o) + \phi_{12}(t,o) x_2(o) + \Gamma_1(t,o)$$

(2.7b) $$x_2(t) = \phi_{21}(t,o)\, x_1(o) + \phi_{22}(t,o) x_2(o) + \Gamma_2(t,o)$$

with similar equations for interior values, $o < \tau < t$.

---

* Use of the dot will be made to denote derivatives with respect to t. Other derivatives will be fully specified.

The simple boundary-value problem has $x_1(o)$ and $x_2(t)$ specified, thus the above equations are not in the preferred forms with the specified boundary-values confined to one side of the equality. The vector $x_2(o)$ can be determined from (2.7b) and then substituted into (2.7a) to eliminate $x_2(o)$ from (2.7a). The equations then become

(2.8a) $$x_1(t) = [\phi_{11}(t,o) - \phi_{12}(t,o)\phi_{22}^{-1}(t,o)\,\phi_{21}(t,o)]x_1(o) + \phi_{12}(t,o)\phi_{11}(t,o)x_2(t) + \Gamma_1(t,o) - \phi_{22}^{-1}(t,o)\,\Gamma_2(t,o)$$

(2.8b) $$x_2(t) = -\phi_{22}^{-1}(t,o)\phi_{21}(t,o)x_1(o) + \phi_{22}^{-1}(t,o)x_2(t) - \phi_{22}^{-1}(t,o)\,\Gamma_2(t,o)$$

and can be rewritten as

(2.9a) $$x_1(t) = P_{11}(t,o)\,x_1(o) + P_{12}(t,o)\,x_2(t) + S_1(t,o)$$

(2.9b) $$x_2(o) = P_{21}(t,o)\,x_1(o) + P_{22}(t,o)\,x_2(t) + S_2(t,o)$$

where the elements $P_{ij}(t,o)$ are the transfer matrix blocks and are related to the partitioned STM blocks by

(2.10a) $$P_{11}(t,o) = \phi_{11}(t,o) - \phi_{12}(t,o)\,\phi_{22}^{-1}(t,o)\,\phi_{21}(t,o)$$

(2.10b) $$P_{12}(t,o) = \phi_{12}(t,o)\,\phi_{22}^{-1}(t,o)$$

(2.10c) $$P_{21}(t,o) = -\phi_{22}^{-1}(t,o)\,\phi_{21}(t,o)$$

(2.10d) $$P_{22}(t,o) = \phi_{22}^{-1}(t,o)$$

(2.10e) $$S_1(t,o) = \Gamma_1(t,o) - \phi_{12}(t,\overset{*}{o})\,\phi_{22}^{-1}(t,o)\,\Gamma_2(t,o)$$

(2.10f) $$S_2(t,o) = -\phi_{22}^{-1}(t,o)\,\Gamma_2(t,o).$$

It is not difficult to show, by differentiating the equations with respect to t and using (2.3), that the functions in (2.10) satisfy the equations

(2.11a) $$\dot{P}_{12}(t,o) = A_{12}(t) + A_{11}(t)\,P_{12}(t,o) - P_{12}(t,o)\,A_{22}(t) - P_{12}(t,o)\,A_{21}(t)\,P_{12}(t,o)$$

(2.11b) $$\dot{P}_{11}(t,o) = [A_{11}(t) - P_{12}(t,o)\,A_{21}(t)]\,P_{11}(t,o)$$

(2.11c) $$\dot{P}_{22}(t,o) = -P_{22}(t,o)\,[A_{22}(t) + A_{21}(t)\,P_{12}(t,o)]$$

(2.11d) $$\dot{P}_{21}(t,o) = -P_{22}(t,o)\,A_{21}(t)\,P_{11}(t,o)$$

(2.11e) $$\dot{S}_1(t,o) = [A_{11}(t) - P_{12}(t,o)\,A_{21}(t)]\,S_1(t,o) + B_1(t) - P_{12}(t,o)\,B_2(t)$$

(2.11f) $$\dot{S}_2(t,o) = -P_{22}(t,o)\,[B_2(t,) + A_{21}(t)\,S_1(t,o)].$$

The initial conditions for the functions can be determined from $\phi(o,o) = I$ and $\Gamma(o,o)$ and are

$$P_{12}(o,o) = P_{12}(t,t) = P_{21}(o,o) = P_{21}(t,t) = S_1(o,o) = S_1(t,t) = S_2(o,o)$$
$$= S_2(t,t) = o$$

$$P_{11}(o,o) = P_{11}(t,t) = P_{22}(t,t) = I.$$

A set of recursive equations can be developed for these functions by (2.6) or a signal flow graph, see Denman, [1970]. Since the functions are matrices, the order of the operation must be preserved when deriving the equations. The recursive equations are

(2.12a)

$$P_{12}(t,o) = P_{12}(t,\tau) + P_{11}(t,\tau)[I-P_{12}(\tau,o)P_{21}(t,\tau)]^{-1} P_{12}(\tau,o)P_{22}(t,\tau)$$

(2.12b) $$P_{11}(t,o) = P_{11}(t,\tau)\ [I - P_{12}(\tau,o)\ P_{21}(t,\tau)]^{-1}\ P_{11}(\tau,o)$$

(2.12c) $$P_{22}(t,o) = P_{22}(\tau,o)\ [I - P_{21}(t,\tau)\ P_{12}(\tau,o)]^{-1}\ P_{22}(t,\tau)$$

(2.12d) $$P_{21}(t,o) = P_{21}(\tau,o) + P_{22}(\tau,o)\ [I - P_{21}(t,\tau)\ P_{12}(\tau,o)]^{-1}\ P_{21}(t,\tau)\ P_{11}(\tau,o)$$

(2.12e) $$S_1(t,o) = S_1(t,\tau) + P_{11}(t,\tau)\ [I - P_{12}(\tau,o)\ P_{21}(t,\tau)]^{-1}\ [S_1(\tau,o) + P_{12}(\tau,o)\ S_2(t,\tau)]$$

(2.12f) $$S_2(t,o) = S_2(\tau,o) + P_{22}(\tau,o)\ [I - P_{21}(t,\tau)\ P_{12}(\tau,o)]^{-1}\ [S_2(t,\tau) + P_{21}(t,\tau) + P_{21}(t,\tau)\ S_1(\tau,o)]\ .$$

These recursive equations have appeared in the literature "as addition formulas," Allen and Wing [1974], and are sometimes known as the Redheffer star-products. This writer has used the equations extensively in control problems as well as in other areas, Denman [1970].

A study of the accuracy of the recursive equations was carried out by Musial [1972]. He also showed that singular values of the functions would be bypassed with little, if any, loss of accuracy. Denman and Nelson [1974] published a short paper on the singular value difficulty encountered by Tapley and Williamson in their paper [1972].

The equations given in this section will be used to derive several of the algorithms that are classified as II algorithms. It is the opinion of this writer that any algorithm which is based on the equations of this section, are II algorithms, although some workers regard specific algorithms derived from the above equation as II algorithms.

3. INVARIANT IMBEDDING AND RELATED ALGORITHMS

All of the variants of invariant imbedding algorithms known to this writer can be derived from the development given in Section 2. Algorithms useful in filtering theory, Ljung et al. [1975], Lainiotis [1974], have also been derived from these equations, thus indicating the general application of these equations to numerical methods. This section will show how the Riccati transformation, the method of superposition, the Nelson-Scott and the Kalaba algorithm can be derived from this set. The latter two algorithms will be derived in a manner consistent with the description of the algorithms given in Nelson and Scott [1972] and Scott and Vandevender [1975].

The vector solutions given in the previous section were based on the assumption that the initial value of t is zero. Thus, $x_1(t)$ and $x_2(t)$ indicate the value of these variables initialized at $t = o$. Other workers frequently define these variables with two arguments; $x_1(\tau,t)$ and $x_2(\tau,t)$. If defined with two arguments, the first argument defines the interior point τ for an interval $o < \tau < t$. This form of variables makes it possible to derive more general algorithms, ones in which the interior point τ or the end point t can be varied. The derivation will follow this manner of defining the functions with the function $\phi_{ij}(t,\tau)$, $P_{ij}(t,\tau)$ etc., retaining the previous definitions.

a) Riccati Transformation

Rybicki and Usher [1966] and their co-workers have used the Riccati transformation for the numerical solution of two-point boundary-value problems. The development will start with that algorithm.

Assume that the vectors $x_1(\tau,t)$ and $x_2(\tau,t)$ are related through the equation

(3.1) $$x_1(\tau,t) = R(\tau,o)\, x_2(\tau,t) + S(\tau,o)$$

where $R(\tau,o)$ and $S(\tau,o)$ are known or have been computed. Comparing (3.1) to (2.9a), it is seen that

(3.2a) $$R(\tau,o) = P_{12}(\tau,o)$$

(3.2b) $$S(\tau,o) = S_1(\tau,o) + P_{11}(\tau,o)\, x_1(o,t)$$

The function $R(\tau,o)$ is the function $P_{12}(\tau,o)$, thus $R(\tau,o)$ must satisfy

(3.3a) $$\frac{dR(\tau,0)}{d\tau} = A_{12}(\tau) + A_{11}(\tau)\, R(\tau,o) - R(\tau,o)\, A_{22}(\tau) - R(\tau,o)\, A_{21}(\tau)\, R(\tau,o)$$

Differentiating (3.2 b) with respect to τ and using (2.11), it is found that $S(\tau,o)$ must satisfy

(3.3b) $$\underline{dS(\tau,o)} + [A_{11}(\tau) - R(\tau,o)\, A_{21}(\tau)]\, S(\tau,o) + B_1(\tau) - R(\tau,o)\, B_2(\tau)$$

The usual initial conditions associated with (3.3a) and (3.3b) are

(3.4a) $$R(o,o) = R(\tau,\tau) = o$$

(3.4b) $$S(o,o) = x_1(o,t)$$

provided that the initial conditions are $S_1(o,o) = P_{11}(o,o) = I$. Other initial conditions may be imposed provided that the two equations of (3.2) are satisfied. It will be shown in Section 4 that the initial conditions of (3.4) may lead to numerical difficulties which can be avoided by other initial conditions.

b) Method of Superposition

An algorithm which will help in understanding the algorithms to be given later is the method of superposition. Assume that the boundary conditions for the problem are given by $x_1(o,t) = o$ and $x_2(t,t) = C_2$ with the system equations given by (2.1). The solution vectors for the interior point τ are given by

(3.5a) $$x_1(\tau,t) = \phi_{12}(\tau,o)\, x_2(o,t) + \Gamma_1(\tau,o)$$

(3.5b) $$x_2(\tau,t) = \phi_{22}(\tau,o)\, x_2(o,t) + \Gamma_2(\tau,o)$$

which follows from (2.7). The vectors at t are given by

(3.6a) $$x_1(t,t) = \phi_{12}(t,o)\, x_2(o,t) + \Gamma_1(t,o)$$

(3.6b) $$x_2(t,t) = \phi_{22}(t,o)\, x_2(o,t) + \Gamma_2(t,o)$$

The vector $x_2(o,t)$ is unknown but can be eliminated from the formulation by using (3.6b) since $x_2(t,t) = C_2$. It then follows that

(3.7a) $$x_1(\tau,t) = \phi_{12}(\tau,o)\, \phi_{22}^{-1}(t,o)\, [C_2 - \Gamma_2(t,o)] + \Gamma_1(\tau,o)$$

(3.7b) $$x_2(\tau,t) = \phi_{22}(\tau,o)\, \phi_{22}^{-1}(t,o)\, [C_2 - \Gamma_2(t,o)] + \Gamma_2(\tau,o)\ .$$

The four functions $\phi_{12}(t,o)$, $\phi_{22}(t,o)$, $\Gamma_1(t,o)$ and $\Gamma_2(t,o)$ must be known at the defined points. The algorithm is then to integrate the set of equations

(3.8)

$$\frac{d}{dt}\begin{bmatrix}\phi_{12}(t,o)\\ \\ \phi_{22}(t,o)\end{bmatrix}=\begin{bmatrix}A_{11}(t) & A_{12}(t)\\ \\ A_{21}(t) & A_{22}(t)\end{bmatrix}\begin{bmatrix}\phi_{12}(t,o)\\ \\ \phi_{22}(t,o)\end{bmatrix} \qquad \begin{matrix}\phi_{12}(o,o)=o\\ \\ \phi_{22}(o,o)=I\end{matrix}$$

(3.9) and

$$\frac{d}{dt}\begin{bmatrix}\Gamma_1(t,o)\\ \\ \Gamma_2(t,o)\end{bmatrix}=\begin{bmatrix}A_{11}(t) & A_{12}(t)\\ \\ A_{21}(t) & A_{22}(t)\end{bmatrix}\begin{bmatrix}\Gamma_1(t,o)\\ \\ \Gamma_2(t,o)\end{bmatrix}+\begin{bmatrix}B_1(t)\\ \\ B_2(t)\end{bmatrix}$$

over the interval $o < \tau < t$ with storage of the functions at τ.

This algorithm is the STM formulation where the functions $\phi_{11}(t,o)$ and $\phi_{21}(t,o)$ are not required due to the selected boundary conditions.

c) Invariant Imbedding

There are several algorithms that have appeared in the literature under the general classification of invariant imbedding algorithms. These algorithms are closely related and differ primarily in the definition of functions and the computational procedure. Rather than attempt to show all of the variants which may be in the literature, only two variants will be treated.

As before, let $x_1(\tau,t)$ and $x_2(\tau,t)$ be defined as interior variables on the interval $o < \tau < t$. Assume the general boundary conditions $x_1(o,t) = C_1$ and $x_2(t,t) = C_2$. Equation (2-9) then gives at the interval end point

(3.10a) $\qquad x_1(t,t) = P_{11}(t,o)\, C_1 + P_{12}(t,o)\, C_2 + S_1(t,o)$

(3.10b) $\qquad x_2(o,t) = P_{21}(t,o)\, C_1 + P_{22}(t,o)\, C_2 - S_2(t,o)$

and the solutions at τ are given by

(3.11a) $\qquad x_1(\tau,t) = P_{11}(\tau,o)\, C_1 + P_{12}(\tau,o)\, x_2(\tau,t) + S_1(\tau,o)$

(3.11b) $\qquad x_2(o,t) = P_{21}(\tau,o)\, C_1 + P_{22}(\tau,o)\, x_2(\tau,t) + S_2(\tau,o)$.

Equations (3.10b) and (3.11b) must be equal. Thus, these two equations can be used to find $x_2(\tau,t)$. It follows that

(3.12a) $\quad x_2(\tau,t) = P_{22}^{-1}(\tau,o)\, \{[P_{21}(t,o) - P_{21}(\tau,o)]\, C_1 + P_{22}(t,o)\, C_2$

$\qquad\qquad + [S_2(t,o) - S_2(\tau,o)]\}$.

Substituting into (3.11a), $x_1(\tau,t)$ is given by

(3.12b)

$$x_1(\tau,t) = P_{11}(\tau,o)\ C_1 + P_{12}(\tau,o)\ P_{22}^{-1}(\tau,o)\ \{[P_{21}(t,o) - P_{21}(\tau,o)]C_1 + P_{22}(t,o)\ C_2 + [S_2(t,o) - S_2(\tau,o)]\} + S_1(\tau,o).$$

The two equations given in (3.12) can be arranged by using the recursive equations of (2.12). The resulting equations are

(3.13a)

$$x_1(\tau,t) = [1 - P_{12}(\tau,o)\ P_{21}(t,\tau)]^{-1}\ \{P_{11}(\tau,o)\ C_1 + P_{12}(\tau,o)\ P_{22}(t,\tau)\ C_1 + S_1(\tau,o) + P_{12}(\tau,o)\ S_2(t,\tau)\}$$

(3.13b)

$$x_2(\tau,t) = [1 - P_{21}(t,\tau)\ P_{12}(\tau,o)]^{-1}\ \{P_{21}(t,\tau)\ P_{11}(\tau,o)\ C_1 + P_{11}(t,\theta)\ C_2 + S_2(t,\tau) + P_{21}(t,\tau)\ S_1(\tau,o)\}$$

Determination of the solution vectors requires that the P_{ij} and S_i functions in (3.13) be computed. Dividing the interval $o < \tau < t$ into the subintervals o to τ and τ to t, the functions $P_{12}(\tau,o)$, $P_{11}(\tau,o)$ and $S_1(\tau,o)$ must be computed over the first subinterval and $P_{21}(t,\tau)$, $P_{22}(t,\tau)$ and $S_2(t,\tau)$ over the second subinterval.

The functions in (3.13) must satisfy the differential equations given in (2.11) of Section 2. It is obvious from (2.11) that $P_{12}(\tau,o)$, $P_{11}(\tau,o)$ and $S_1(\tau,o)$ can be computed independently of the remaining three equations of (2.11). On the other hand, the functions $P_{21}(t,\tau)$, $P_{22}(t,\tau)$ and $S_2(t,\tau)$ cannot be computed without first computing the other three functions of (2.11) if it is assumed that (2.11) must always be satisfied. A formulation would be desired that avoids this extra computational overhead. Such a formulation would then be a variant of the general algorithm.

Rather than proceed with the general boundary conditions $x_1(o,t) = C_1$ and $x_2(t,t) = C_2$, let $C_1 = o$. Equation (3.13) then reduces to the two equations

(3.14a) $$x_1(\tau,t) = [I - P_{12}(\tau,o)\ P_{21}(t,\tau)]^{-1}\ \{P_{12}(\tau,o)\ P_{22}(t,\tau)\ C_2 + S_1(\tau,o) + P_{12}(\tau,o)\ S_2(t,\tau)\}$$

(3.14b) $$x_2(\tau,t) = [I - P_{21}(t,\tau)P_{12}(\tau,o)]^{-1}\ \{P_{22}(t,\tau)\ C_2 + S_2(t,\tau) + P_{21}(t,\tau)\ S_1(\tau,o)\}$$

when $C_1 = o$. The first term in (3.14 a) can be written as

(3.15)

$$[I - P_{12}(\tau,o)\ P_{21}(t,\tau)]^{-1}\ P_{12}(\tau,o)\ P_{22}(t,\tau) + P_{12}(\tau,o)\ [I - P_{21}(t,\tau)\ P_{12}(\tau,o)]^{-1}\ P_{22}(t,\tau) = P_{12}(\tau,o)\ P_{22}^{-1}(\tau,o) P_{22}(t,\tau) = \phi_{12}(\tau,o)\phi_{11}^{-1}(t,o)$$

by using (2.12c) and the identity

(3.16)

$$[I - P_{12}(\tau,o)\ P_{21}(t,\tau)]^{-1}\ P_{12}(\tau,o) = P_{12}(\tau,o)\ [I - P_{21}(t,\tau)\ P_{12}(\tau,o)]^{-1}.$$

The second term of (3.14a) is

$$\begin{aligned}&[I - P_{12}(\tau,o)\ P_{21}(t,\tau)]^{-1}\ [S_1(\tau,o) + P_{12}(\tau,o)\ S_2(t,\tau)]\\ &= P_{11}^{-1}(t,\tau)\ [S_1(t,o) - S_1(t,\tau)]\\ &= [\phi_{11}(t,\tau) - \phi_{12}(t,\tau)\ \phi_{22}^{-1}(t,\tau)\ \phi_{21}(t,\tau)]\ \{\Gamma_1(t,o) - \Gamma_1(t,\tau)\\ &\quad - \phi_{12}(t,o)\ \phi_{22}^{-1}(t,o)\ \Gamma_2(t,o) + \phi_{12}(t,\tau)\ \phi_{22}^{-1}(t,\tau)\ \Gamma_2(t,\tau)\end{aligned}$$

(3.17) $$= \Gamma_1(\tau,o) - \phi_{12}(\tau,o)\ \phi_{22}^{-1}(t,o)\ \Gamma_2(t,o)$$

where (2.12c), (2.10c) and (2.6b) were used to carry out the rearrangements. Equations (3.14a) then becomes

(3.18) $$x_1(\tau,t) = \phi_{12}(\tau,o)\ \phi_{22}^{-1}(t,o)\ [C_2 - \Gamma_2(t,o)] + \Gamma_1(\tau,o)$$

which is the equation of superposition, (3.7a). Equation (3.14b) can be placed in the form of (3.7b) by a similar procedure. Equation (3.14) can be used to derive the variant of II as given in the paper by Nelson and Scott, [1972]. Defining

(3.19a) $$P_{12}(\tau,o) = \phi_{12}(\tau,o)\ \phi_{22}^{-1}(\tau,o) = R(\tau)$$

(3.19b) $$P_{22}(\tau,o) = \phi_{22}^{-1}(\tau,o) = T(\tau)$$

(3.19c) $$S_1(\tau,o) = \Gamma_1(\tau,o) - \phi_{12}(\tau,o)\ \phi_{22}^{-1}(\tau,o)\ \Gamma_2(\tau,o) = e_r(\tau)$$

(3.19d) $$S_2(\tau,o) = -\ \phi_{22}^{-1}(\tau,o)\ \Gamma_2(\tau,o) = e_\ell(\tau)$$

and then using (3.14b), (2.12c) and (2.12f),

$$x_2(\tau,t) = P_{22}^{-1}(\tau,o)\ P_{22}(t,o)\ C_2 + P_{22}^{-1}(\tau,o)\ [S_2(t,o) - S_2(\tau,o)]$$

(3.20a) $$= T(\tau)\ \{T^{-1}(t)\ C_2 + e_\ell(t) - e_\ell(\tau)\}\ .$$

Equation (3.14a) can be rewritten as

(3.21) $$\begin{aligned}x_1(\tau,t) = P_{12}(\tau,o)\ \{&x_2(\tau,t) - [I - P_{21}(t,\tau)\ P_{12}(\tau,o)]^{-1}\\ &[S_2(t,\tau) + P_{21}(t,\tau)\ S_1(\tau,o)] + [I - P_{12}(\tau,o)\ P_{21}(t,\tau)]^{-1}\\ &[S_1(\tau,o) + P_{12}(\tau,o)\ S_2(t,\tau)]\}\ .\end{aligned}$$

The third and fifth term cancel, giving

(3.20b) $$x_1(\tau,t) = P_{12}(\tau,o)\ x_2(\tau,t) + [I - P_{12}(\tau,o)\ P_{21}(t,\tau)]^{-1}$$
$$[S_1(\tau,o) - P_{12}(\tau,o)\ P_{21}(t,\tau)\ S_1(\tau,o)]$$
$$= P_{12}(\tau,o)\ x_2(\tau,t) + S_1(\tau,o)$$
$$= R(\tau)\ x_2(\tau,t) + e_r(\tau)$$

which is the desired equation. Equations (3.19), and (3.20) are the equations given by Nelson and Scott, which is the variant of II used by them.

The variant that is the Kalaba and co-workers algorithm follows from (3.14), and (3.20) by introducing the functions

(3.22a) $$J(\tau,t) = \phi_{12}(\tau,o)\ \phi_{22}^{-1}(t,o)$$

(3.22b) $$K(\tau,t) = \phi_{22}(\tau,o)\ \phi_{22}^{-1}(t,o)$$

(3.22c) $$p(\tau,t) = \Gamma_1(\tau,o) - \phi_{12}(\tau,o)\ \phi_{22}^{-1}(t,o)\ \Gamma_2(t,o)$$

(3.22d) $$q(\tau,t) = \Gamma_2(\tau,o) - \phi_{22}(\tau,o)\ \phi_{22}^{-1}(t,o)\ \Gamma_2(t,o)$$

with initial conditions

$$J(o,t) = o \qquad K(t,t) = I$$
$$p(o,t) = o \qquad q(o,t) = o\ .$$

The solution vectors are then given by

(3.23a) $$x_1(\tau,t) = J(\tau,t)\ C_2 + p(\tau,t)$$

(3.23b) $$x_2(\tau,t) = K(\tau,t)\ C_2 + q(\tau,t)\ .$$

Differential equations for the four functions in (3.23) can be derived. Since two independent variables, τ and t, are involved, partial derivatives must be found. The partials for variable t are

(3.24a) $$\frac{\partial J(\tau,t)}{\partial t} = -\ J(\tau,t)\ [A_{22}(t) + A_{21}(t)\ J(t,t)]$$

(3.24b) $$\frac{\partial K(\tau,t)}{\partial t} = -\ K(\tau,t)\ [A_{22}(t) + A_{21}(t)\ J(t,t)]$$

(3.24c) $$\frac{\partial p(\tau,t)}{\mu t} = -\ J(\tau,t)\ [A_{21}(t)\ S_1(t,o) + B_2(t)]$$

(3.24d) $$\frac{\partial q(\tau,t)}{\mu t} = -\ K(\tau,t)\ [A_{21}(t)\ S_1(t,o) + B_2(t)]$$

where $S_1(t,o)$ satisfies the equation given in (2.11e).

Several variants of invariant imbedding algorithms have been derived in this section. All algorithms known to this writer that are classified as imbedding algorithms follow from the basic algorithms given in Section 2. The difference is in the definition of function and the implementation.

4. THE RICCATI DIFFERENTIAL EQUATION AND INVARIANT IMBEDDING ALGORITHMS

One of the major problems which may be encountered in the II algorithms or the Riccati transformation method is the stability of the Riccati equation, whether the equation is scalar or matrix. This problem has led to workers concluding that an algorithm which requires the solution of the Riccati equation should be avoided.

As an example, consider the equations

(4.1a) $$x_1(t) = 2x_2(t)$$

(4.1b) $$x_2(t) = -x_1(t) - 3x_2(t)$$

with boundary conditions $x_1(o) = C_1$ and $x_2(t) = C_2$. The Riccati transformation

(4.2) $$x_1(t) = R(t,o)\ x_2(t) + S(t,o)$$

leads to the Riccati equation

(4.3) $$\dot{R}(t,o) = 2 + 3\ R(t,o) + R^2(t,o)\ .$$

The solution to (4.3) is given by

(4.4) $$R(t,o) = 2\,\frac{e^{-t} - e^{-2t}}{2e^{-2t} - e^{-t}} = 2\ \frac{\exp(-5) - \exp(-2t)}{2\exp(-2t) - \exp(-t)}$$

which becomes infinite at $t = 0.693147$. A standard Runge-Kutta or Adams-Moulton algorithm would fail to find the solution for $t > 0.693147$.

The recursive algorithm given in Section 2 would avoid the problem above. If a step size of h is selected, it is necessary to compute $P_{11}(h,o)$, $P_{22}(h,o)$, $P_{12}(h,o)$, $P_{21}(h,o)$ only once since $P_{ij}(t + h,t) = P_{ij}(h,o)$ for all t and $S_1(t,o) = S_2(t,o) = o$ for this homogeneous problem. Although it appears that the computation of the six functions is inefficient, such is not the case. The two recursive equations

(4.5a) $$P_{12}(t + h,o) = P_{12}(h,o) + P_{11}(h,o)[I - P_{12}(t,o)\ P_{21}(h,o)]^{-1}\ P_{12}(t,o)\ P_{22}(h,o)$$

(4.5b) $$P_{11}(t + h,o) = P_{11}(h,o)[I - P_{12}(t,o)\ P_{21}(h,o)]^{-1}\ P_{11}(t,o)$$

provide the same information as obtained from the two differential equations of (3.3). A Runge-Kutta algorithm is used to find $P_{12}(h,o)$ and $P_{11}(h,o)$ from (3.3) at $t = o$ and is not used thereafter since (4.5) requires only algebraic operations. The only precaution required is that the term $I - P_{12}(t,o)$ $P_{21}(h,o)$ be invertible which is almost always valid because of the behavior of $P_{12}(t,o)$ and $P_{11}(t,o)$ in the vicinity of the singularity.

Scalar and matrix Riccati equations have properties that can be used to alleviate many of the numerical difficulties encountered in solving two-point boundary-value problems. Consider the simple Riccati equation given above in (4.3) which has a singularity at $t = 0.693$ when initialized to zero. The algebraic Riccati equation

$$2 + 3\,R(t,o) + R^2(t,o) = o \tag{4.6}$$

has two solutions, $R(t,o) = -1$ and $R(t,o) = -2$. If (4.3) is initialized to $R(o,o) < -1.0$, the solution will converge to $R(t,o) = -2$ for large t. Initialization of $R(o,o) > -1$ leads to a value of $R(t,o) = \infty$ at $t = t_0 + 0.693147$ where t_0 is the value of t such that $R(t_0,o) = o$.

The one solution to this scalar Riccati equation that is numerically stable and constant for all t is $R(t,o) = -2$ when integrated in a forward direction. In addition, $R(t,o) = -1$ is a stable and constant solution for integration in a negative direction.

Vandevender [1977] has described an invariant imbedding algorithm that utilizes this property of the Riccati equation. The algorithm insures boundness of the Riccati function for all t by selecting the initial condition on the Riccati equation to be the asymptotic solution. The algorithm also uses "addition formulas" or the recursive equations. A method of computing the asymptotic solution for the algebraic matrix Riccati equation has been given by Denman and Beavers, [1976]. This method is more efficient than the method used by Vandevender.

Assume that $P_{12}(\infty,o)$ is the asymptotic solution that is stable for integration in the positive direction and let $x_1(o,t) = C_1$ with $x_2(t,t) = C_2$. Equations (2.9a) and (2.9b) can then be written as

$$x_1(\tau,t) = P_{11}(\tau,o)\,x_1(o,t) + P_{12}(\infty,o)\,x_2(\tau,t) + \bar{S}_2(\tau,o) \tag{4.7a}$$

$$x_2(o,t) = P_{21}(\tau,o)\,x_1(o,t) + P_{22}(\tau,o)\,x_2(\tau,t) + \bar{S}_2(\tau,o) \tag{4.7b}$$

with

(4.8a) $x_1(t,t) = P_{11}(t,o)\, C_1 + P_{12}(\infty,o)\, C_2 + \bar{S}_1(t,o)$

(4.8b) $x_2(o,t) = P_{21}(t,o)\, C_1 + P_{22}(t,o)\, C_2 + \bar{S}_2(t,o).$

The $P_{ij}(\tau,o)$ function satisfies the usual equations but with $P_{12}(\infty,o)$ a constant for all t when $A(t) = A$. The equations are

(4.9a) $0 = A_{12} + A_{11}\, P_{12}(\infty,o) - P_{12}(\infty,o)\, A_{22} - P_{12}(\infty,o)\, A_{21}\, P_{12}(\infty,o)$

(4.9b) $$\frac{dP_{11}(\tau,o)}{d\tau} = [A_{11} - P_{12}(\infty,o)\, A_{21}]\, P_{11}(\tau,o)$$

(4.9c) $$\frac{dP_{22}(\tau,o)}{d\tau} = -P_{22}(\tau,o)\, [A_{22} + A_{21}\, P_{12}(\infty,o)]$$

$$\frac{dP_{21}(\tau,o)}{d\tau} = -P_{22}(\tau,o)\, A_{21}\, P_{11}(\tau,o)$$

(4.9e) $$\frac{dS_1(\tau,o)}{d\tau} = [A_{11} - P_{12}(\infty,o)\, A_{21}]\, S_1(\tau,o) + B_1$$

$$P_{12}(\infty,o)\, B_2$$

(4.9f) $$\frac{dS_2(\tau,o)}{d\tau} = -P_{22}(\tau,o)\, [B_2 + A_{21}\, S_1(\tau,o)].$$

The initials conditions must be modified since

(4.10a) $x_1(o,t) = P_{11}(o,o)\, x_1(o,t) + P_{12}(\infty,o)\, x_2(o,t) + \bar{S}_1(o,o)$

(4.10b) $x_2(o,t) = P_{21}(o,o)\, x_1(o,t) + P_{22}(o,o)\, x_2(o,t) + \bar{S}_2(o,o)$

If $P_{11}(o,o) = P_{22}(o,o) = I$, $P_{21}(o,o) = o$ and $\bar{S}_2(o,o) = o$, then $\bar{S}_1(o,o)$ must be initialized to

(4.11) $$\bar{S}_1(o,o) = -P_{12}(\infty,o)\, x_2(o,t).$$

The initial condition $x_2(o,t)$ is unknown for the first set of calculations. Thus $\bar{S}_1(o,o)$ cannot be found directly from (4.10). The signal flow graph is a useful mathematical tool to derive correction equations for modifying initial conditions on any one of the six transfer functions, $P_{ij}(t,o)$ and $S_i(t,o)$. It follows that if $\bar{S}_1(o,o)$ is unknown then

(4.12a) $\bar{S}_1(t,o) = S_1(t,o) + P_{11}(t,o)\, \bar{S}_1(o,o)$

(4.12b) $\bar{S}_2(t,o) = S_2(t,o) + P_{21}(t,o)\, \bar{S}_1(o,o)$

where $S_1(t,o)$ and $S_2(t,o)$ are computed with arbitrary initial conditions $S_1(oo) = S_2(o,o) = 0$. To find $\bar{S}_1(o,o)$, premultiply the equation given in (4.8) by $-P_{12}(\infty,o)$ or

(4.13)

$$-P_{12}(\infty,o)\ x_2(o,t) = -P_{12}(\infty,o)[P_{21}(t,o)\ C_1 + P_{22}(t,o)\ C_2 + \bar{S}_2(t,o)]$$

which must equal $\bar{S}_1(o,o)$ from (4.11). Substituting the $\bar{S}_2(t,o)$, and solving for $\bar{S}_1(o,o)$, one finds

(4.14) $$\bar{S}_1(o,o) = -[I + P_{12}(\infty,o)\ P_{21}(t,o)]^{-1}\ P_{12}(\infty,o)\ [P_{21}(t,o)\ C_1 + P_{22}(t,o)\ C_2 + S_2(t,o)]$$

where the "unbarred" variables are computed with the usual initial conditions.

The algorithm derived by Vandevender has more general boundary conditions and is based on the Nelson-Scott variant of invariant imbedding. The above derivation illustrates the concept of the algorithm. "Addition formulas" or recursive equations may be used if desired although the algorithm will be stable for Runge-Kutta or any other method.

5. SUMMARY

It is somewhat difficult to draw conclusions on invariant imbedding algorithms, particularly with regard to numerical accuracy and efficiency of an algorithm. The only conclusion that this writer has reached in his work with II algorithms is that no particular algorithm is ideally suited for all two-point boundary-value problems. There has not been an in-depth study of all of the algorithms such as has been carried out by Enright, Hull and Lindberg [1975] on stiff system of equations. Recent developments may modify the conclusion reached from such a study if it were carried out at this time.

REFERENCES

[1]. Chandrasekhar, S., Radiative Transfer, Dover, New York, 1960.

[2]. Preisendorfer, R. W., Radiative Transfer in Discrete Spaces, Pergamon, Oxford, 1965.

[3]. Redheffer, R. M., Difference Equations and Functional Equations in Transmission Line Theory, in Modern Mathematics for Engineers, (Beckenbach, Editor) Second Series, McGraw-Hill, New York, 1961.

[4]. Bellman, R., R. Kalaba, and M. Prestrud, Invariant Imbedding and Radiative Transfer in Slabs of Finite Thickness, American Elsevier, New York, 1963.

[5]. Wing, G. M., An Introduction to Transport Theory, John Wiley and Sons, New York, 1962.

[6]. Bellman, R. and G. M. Wing, An Introduction to Invariant Imbedding, John Wiley and Sons, New York, 1975.

[7]. Shimizu, R. and R. Aoki, Application of Invariant Imbedding to Reactor Physics, Academic, New York, 1972.

[8]. Adams, R. and E. D. Denman, Wave Propagation and Turbulent Media, American Elsevier, New York, 1966.

[9]. Denman, E. D., Coupled Modes in Plasmas, Elastic Media and Parametric Amplifiers, American Elsevier, New York, 1970.

[10]. Mingle, J. O., The Invariant Imbedding Theory of Nuclear Transport, American Elsevier, New York, 1973.

[11]. Case, K. M. and P. Zweifel, Linear Transport Problems, Addison-Wesley, Reading, Massachusetts, 1967.

[12]. Ribaric, M., Functional-Analytic Concepts and Structures of Neutron Transport Theory, Slovene Academy of Sciences and Arts, Ljublyana, Yugoslavia, 1973.

[13]. Scott, M., Invariant Imbedding and its Application to Ordinary Differential Equations, Addison-Wesley, Reading, Massachusetts, 1973.

[14]. Meyer, G. H., Initial Value Methods for Boundary Value Problems, Academic Press, New York, 1973.

[15]. Casti, J., and R. Kalaba, Imbedding Methods in Applied Mathematics, Addison-Wesley, Reading, Massachusetts, 1973.

[16]. Golberg, M. A., Some Functional Relationships for Two-Point Boundary-Value Problems, J. M. A. A., 45, 1974, 199-209.

[17]. Rybicki, G. and P. Usher, The Generalized Riccati Transformation as a Simple Alternative to Invariant Imbedding, Astrophy., 146, 1966, 871-879.

[18]. Allen, R. C. and G. M. Wing, An Invariant Imbedding Algorithm for the Solution of Inhomogeneous Two-Point Boundary-Value Problem, J. Comp. Phy., 14, 1974, 40-58.

[19]. Nelson, P., and M. Scott, The Relationship Between Two Variants of Invariant Imbedding, J. M. A. A., 37, 1972, 501-505.

[20]. Scott, M., A Bibliography on Invariant Imbedding and Related Topics, Sandia Laboratories, Rept. SC-B-71 0886, 1971.

[21]. Vandevender, W., On the Stability of an Invariant Imbedding Algorithm for the Solution of Two-Point Boundary-Value Problems, Sandia Laboratories, Rept. SAND 77-1107, 1977.

[22]. Yoo, K., Development of A Numerical Algorithm for Uncoupling of Constant Coefficient State Equations of Control Theory, Ph. D. Dissertation, University of Houston, 1974.

[23]. Musial, W. T., A Numerical Investigation of the P-Equations Relating The Matrix Riccati Equation to a Linear State Equations, M. S. Thesis, University of Houston, 1972.

[24]. Denman, E., and P. Nelson, Comment on "Comparison of Linear and Riccati Equations Used to Solve Optimal Control Problems," AIAA J., 12, 1974, 575-576.

[25]. Tapley, B. D. and W. E. Williamson, Comparison of Linear and Riccati Equations Used to Solve Optimal Control Problems, AIAA J., 10, 1972, 1154-1159.

[26]. Ljung, L., T. Kailath and B. Friedlander, Scattering Theory and Linear Least Squares Estimation, Part I: Continuous Time Problems, Proc. IEEE, 64, 131-139.

[27]. Lainiotis, D. G., Partitioned Estimation Algorithms, II: Linear Estimation, Info. Sci., 7, 1974, 317-340.

[28]. Denman, E. D. and A. N. Beavers, Jr., The Matrix Sign Function and Computations in Systems, Appl. Math and Comp., 2, 1976, 63-94.

[29]. Enright, W. H., T. E. Hull and B. Lindberg, Comparing Numerical Methods for Stiff Systems of O. D. E.'s, BIT, 15, 1975, 10-48.

[30]. Scott, M. R. and W. H. Vandevender, A Comparison of Several Invariant Imbedding Algorithms for the Solution of Two-Point Boundary-Value Problems, Appl. Math. and Comp., 1, 1975, 187-218.

Calculation of Eigenvalues of Systems of ODE's using the Riccati Transformation

by

J.S. Bramley, University of Strathclyde, Glasgow, United Kingdom.

1. Introduction

The Riccati transformation method for the computation of eigenvalues of a system of linear ODE's of even order was introduced by Scott [1]. This method is used to compute the eigenvalues of two odd ordered systems of ODE's over a semi-infinite interval; computation of eigenvalues associated with the stability of (a) perturbations of the Blasius profile [2] and (b) dual solutions in mixed convection [3]. Most of the paper is concerned with using the Riccati transformation to obtain the eigenvalues of (b) but reference will be made to the use of other methods; the compound matrix method of Gilbert and Backus [4], and orthoganisation as developed by Conte [5]. The introduction to the problems and the methods must be brief.

2. The Problems

(a) Perturbations of the Blasius profile.

The equation arising out of the perturbations of the Blasius profile is fully discussed in Wilks and Bramley [3] and is

$$y'''(z) + f_o(z)y''(z) + \sigma f_o'(z)y'(z) + (1-\sigma)f_o''(z)y(z) = 0 \qquad (1)$$

subject to homogeneous boundary conditions

$$y(0) = y'(0) = 0,\ y'(z) \to 0 \text{ exponentially as } z \to \infty \qquad (2)$$

where $f_o(z)$ is the Blasius function defined by

$$f'''_o(z) + f_o(z)f_o''(z) = 0 \qquad (3)$$

subject to boundary conditions

$$f_o(0) = f_o'(0) = 0 \text{ and } f_o'(\infty) = 1 \qquad (4)$$

It is required to calculate the eigenvalues, σ of equation (1).

(b) Mixed Convection

The equations arising out of the stability of mixed convection flow past a vertical flat plate with a uniform wall temperature are

$$M''' + \frac{3}{2} F_oM'' + (\frac{3}{2} - \lambda) F_o''M + (\lambda-2)F_o'M' + 2\gamma N = 0, \qquad (5)$$

$$N'' + P_r\left[\frac{3}{2} F_o N' + (\frac{3}{2} - \lambda)\theta_o' M + \lambda F_o' N\right] = 0, \tag{6}$$

subject to homogeneous boundary conditions

$$M(0) = M'(0) = N(0) = 0 \text{ and} \tag{7}$$

$$M' \text{ and } N \to 0 \text{ exponentially as } z \to \infty. \tag{8}$$

All the dependent variables M, N, F_o, θ_o are functions of z while Pr is the Prandtl Number fixed at 0.7, γ is a variable parameter and λ is the eigenvalue parameter. The driving equations for F_o and θ_o are

$$F_o''' + \frac{3}{2} F_o F_o'' + (1-F_o^2) + 2\gamma\theta_o = 0 \tag{9}$$

$$\theta_o'' + \frac{3}{2} \Pr F_o \theta_o' = 0 \tag{10}$$

subject to boundary conditions

$$F_o(0) = F_o'(0) = 0, \ \theta_o(0) = 1 \text{ and} \tag{11}$$

$$F_o' \text{ and } \theta_o \to 0 \text{ as } z \to \infty \tag{12}$$

With the parameter γ it is now possible to plot a graph of all eigenvalues λ against γ. In practice we are only interested in the first positive and first negative eigenvalue. The reason for this is that the flow is unstable if there are negative eigenvalues. More of the physical details of this problem are available in Wilks and Bramley [3] and Sparrow, Eichhorn and Gregg [4].

The Methods

(a) The Riccati transformation method for the computation of eigenvalues of a system of linear ODE's was introduced by Scott [1,5] and extended by Sloan and Wilks [6] and Sloan [7]. Their work considered a system of the form

$$d\underline{u}/dz = A(z,\sigma)\underline{u} + B(z,\sigma)\underline{v} \tag{13}$$

$$-d\underline{v}/dz = C(z,\sigma)\underline{u} + D(z,\sigma)\underline{v} \tag{14}$$

subject to boundary conditions

$$\alpha_1\underline{u}(0) + \beta_1 \underline{v}(0) = 0, \quad \underline{u}(x) = \underline{0}. \tag{15}$$

Here $\underline{u}$ and $\underline{v}$ are n-vectors and A, B, C, D are n x n real matrices depending on z and the eigenvalue parameter σ and $[\alpha_1, \beta_1]$ is an n x 2n matrix of rank n. Sloan and Wilks [6] transformed the dependent variables using the transformation

$$\begin{bmatrix}\underline{U}(z)\\ \underline{V}(z)\end{bmatrix} = \begin{bmatrix}\alpha_1 & \beta_1\\ \gamma_1 & \delta_1\end{bmatrix}\begin{bmatrix}\underline{u}(z)\\ \underline{v}(z)\end{bmatrix} = M\begin{bmatrix}\underline{u}(z)\\ \underline{v}(z)\end{bmatrix} \tag{16}$$

with γ_1 and δ_1 chosen such that M is nonsingular. The condition at z = 0 now takes the form $\underline{U}(0) = \underline{0}$. Relating $\underline{U}$ and $\underline{V}$ by

$$\underline{U}(z) = E(z)\underline{V}(z) \tag{17}$$

we readily derive the Riccati equation

$$E'(z) = \mathcal{B}(z,\sigma) + \mathcal{A}(z,\sigma)\, \underline{E}(z) + E(z)\, \mathcal{D}(z,\sigma) + E(z)\mathcal{C}(z,\sigma)\, E(z) \tag{18}$$

where $\mathcal{A}, \mathcal{B}, \mathcal{C}$ and $\mathcal{D}$ are coefficient matrices in the linear differential system when it is written in terms of $\underline{U}$ and $\underline{V}$. The n^2 elements of the matrix E may be calculated from the 1st order ODE (18) using the initial condition E(0) = 0.

At some point $z = \bar{z} > 0$ a switch is made from the E-system to the R-system using the transformation

$$R(z) = [\alpha_1 - E(z)\gamma_1]^{-1}\, [E(z)\delta_1 - \beta_1] \tag{19}$$

where the n x n matrix R(z) is defined by means of the transformation

$$\underline{u}(z) = R(z)\underline{v}(z). \tag{20}$$

It is readily shown that R satisfied the Riccati equation

$$R'(z) = B(z,\sigma) + A(z,\sigma)R(z) + R(z)D(z,\sigma) + R(z)C(z,\sigma)R(z) \tag{21}$$

and that the terminating condition $\underline{u}(x) = \underline{0}$ is only satisfied when

$$\det R(x) = 0. \tag{22}$$

The normal switch from the R-system to the S-system is carried out when det R(x) > 1 and vica versa. The matrix S is the inverse of the matrix R.

The above method can be used when there are n boundary conditions at each end but with both problems there is one more boundary condition at z = 0 than at z = x. Wilks and Bramley [2] discusses various ways of increasing the number of boundary conditions. The 3rd order differential equation (1) is easily converted into a system of 3 first order ODE's and a fourth equation is added to even up the system. Likewise equations (5) and (6) can be converted into a fifth order system and an additional equation added to even up the system. This method works satisfactorily in most cases but involves unnecessary work in integrating the extra equation.

Dr. David Sloan has extended his method in [6] to cover n boundary conditions at z = 0 and m boundary conditions at z = x with m+n 1st order equations. This method is described in a paper by Sloan and Bramley [8].

(b) Orthogonalisation

The method of orthogonalisation is described by Conte [9] and is inappropriat for the Blasius Problem. For the mixed convection problem two basis functions $\underline{Y}_1$ and $\underline{Y}_2$ are computed where $\underline{Y}_i = [M_i, M_i', M_i'', N_i, N_i']^T$,

$$\underline{Y}_1(0) = [0,0,1,0,0]^T \text{ and } \underline{Y}_2(0) = [0,0,0,0,1]^T.$$

After several integration steps due to the growth of rounding errors the basis vectors can cease to be independent of each other. At this point two new bases, orthogonal to each other, are calculated.

The terminating condition

$$pM_1' + q\,M_2' = 0 \text{ and } pN_1 + q\,N_2 = 0$$

implies that $$\det \begin{bmatrix} M_1' & M_2' \\ N_1 & N_2 \end{bmatrix} = 0 \tag{23}$$

(c) Compound Matrix method

Gilbert and Backus [10] introduced this method in 1966, followed recently by Ng and Reid [11]. Davey [12] has recently explained the method in terms of the Ricca transformation. Let $M = \phi_1, \phi_2$ $N = \psi_1, \psi_2$ be any two linearly independent solutio of equations (5) and (6) both of which satisfy the known initial boundary condition Then if p,q are arbitrary constants the most general solution of the linear equatio formed out of equations (5) and (6) will be

$$\left.\begin{aligned} &M = p\phi_1 + q\phi_2, \; M' = p\phi_1' + q\phi_2' \\ &M'' = p\phi_1'' + q\phi_2'', \\ &N = p\psi_1 + q\psi_2, \quad N' = p\psi_1' + q\psi_2' \end{aligned}\right\} \tag{24}$$

It is convenient to define ten new quantities

$$\left.\begin{aligned} y_1 &= \phi_1\phi_2' - \phi_1'\phi_2, & y_2 &= \phi_1\phi_2'' - \phi_1''\phi_2, \\ y_3 &= \phi_1\psi_2 - \psi_1\phi_2, & y_4 &= \phi_1\psi_2' - \psi_1'\phi_2, \\ y_5 &= \phi_1'\phi_2'' - \phi_1''\phi_2', & y_6 &= \phi_1'\psi_2 - \psi_1\phi_2', \\ y_7 &= \phi_1'\psi_2' - \psi_1'\phi_2', & y_8 &= \phi_1''\psi_2 - \psi_1\phi_2'', \\ y_9 &= \phi_1''\psi_2' - \psi_1'\phi_2'', & y_{10} &= \psi_1\psi_2' - \psi_1'\psi_2 \end{aligned}\right\} \tag{25}$$

The ten differential equations for y_i, $i = 1[1]10$ are found by differentiating equations (25) and using equations (5) and (6). These equations are

$$\left.\begin{aligned}
y_1' &= y_2 \\
y_2' &= y_5 - \frac{3}{2} F_o y_2 - (\lambda-2)F_o' Y_1 - 2\gamma\, y_3 \\
y_3' &= y_6 + y_4 \\
y_4' &= y_7 - \frac{3}{2} PrF_o y_4 - \lambda PrF_o' y_3 \\
y_5' &= (\frac{3}{2} - \lambda)F_o'' y_1 - \frac{3}{2} F_o'' y_5 - 2\gamma y_6 \\
y_6' &= y_8 + y_7 \\
y_7' &= y_9 - \frac{3}{2} PrF_o y_7 - \lambda PrF_o' y_6 + (\frac{3}{2} - \lambda)\theta_o' y_1 \\
y_8' &= y_9 - \frac{3}{2} F_o y_8 - (\lambda-2)F_o' y_6 - (\frac{3}{2} - \lambda)F_o'' y_3 \\
y_9' &= -\frac{3}{2} PrF_o y_9 - \lambda PrF_o' y_8 + Pr(\frac{3}{2} - \lambda)\theta_o' y_2 - \frac{3}{2} F_o y_9 \\
&\quad - (\lambda-2)F_o' y_7 - (\frac{3}{2} - \lambda)F_o'' y_4 - 2\gamma y_{10} \\
y_{10}' &= Pr(\frac{3}{2} - \lambda)\theta_o' y_3 - \frac{3}{2} PrF_o y_{10}
\end{aligned}\right\} \qquad (26)$$

The initial conditions at $z = 0$ are

$$y_i = 0 \quad i \neq 9 \quad \text{and} \quad y_9 = 1. \qquad (27)$$

At $z = x$, $p\phi_1' + q\phi_2' = 0$ and $p\psi_1 + q\psi_2 = 0$ implies that $y_6 = 0$.

Discussion

The boundary condition at $z = x \to \infty$ causes a little difficulty because the asymptote of the curve for eigenvalue plotted against x must be found. The method used in practice was to find a value for σ or λ above and below the asymptote and then keep halving the interval until the eigenvalue was of the required accuracy. The asymptotics of the Blasius problem are well known and can be used to improve th efficiency of this process. The asymptotics for the mixed convection problem are not known and it was thought having to derive asymptotic expansions made all the methods less attractive to use.

Of the three methods, the Riccati method is the only one that is suitable for the Blasius problem. Orthogonalisation is unappropriate because there is only a single base vector. The compound matrix method is easily adapted to the Blasius problem but the resulting equations and boundary conditions are the same as the three first order ODE's, obtained from equation (1), and boundary conditions (2).

this means that the compound matrix method is unsuitable for finding eigenvalues of the Blasius problem. Using the Riccati method Wilks and Bramley [2] have obtained the first twenty eigenvalues of the Blasius problem, and these results compare favourably with calculations of other workers. In most cases only the initial switch from the E-system to the R-system is made.

Eigenvalues of the mixed convection problem are calculated using all three methods. For most cases the Riccati method is well behaved but occasionally det R rapidly increases and the equations become unintegrable before you can switch to the S-system. This problem can be reduced by taking smaller integration steps and thus decreasing the efficiency of the method. Even though the author has discovered cases where the integration steps have to be reduced so much as to make the method use an unacceptable amount of computer time. Orthogonalisation gives satisfactory results but in this problem the rescaling is not carried out very often. The compound matrix method also gives satisfactory results. This method does not rescale the elements, and in this problem the y_i's of equations (26) do not exhibit any growth. In problems where the y's grow rapidly the compound matrix method can and does breakdown.

There is difficulty with the semi-infinite domain mostly associated with the mixed convection problem: deciding if you have integrated the differential equations out to a point at which x is large enough. The graphs of eigenvalue against z for the Blasius problem are well behaved. Figure 1 gives an example of a not so well behaved graph of eigenvalue against z for the mixed convection problem. If the integration were carried out to a larger value of x will any new eigenvalues appear? This problem is unanswered at the moment.

Table 1

Method	No. of driving equations	No. of equations	TOTAL
Riccati	5	6	11
Orthogonalisation	5	10	15
Compound Matrix	5	10	15

Graph of First Positive Eigenvalue against L for $\gamma = -0.8$.

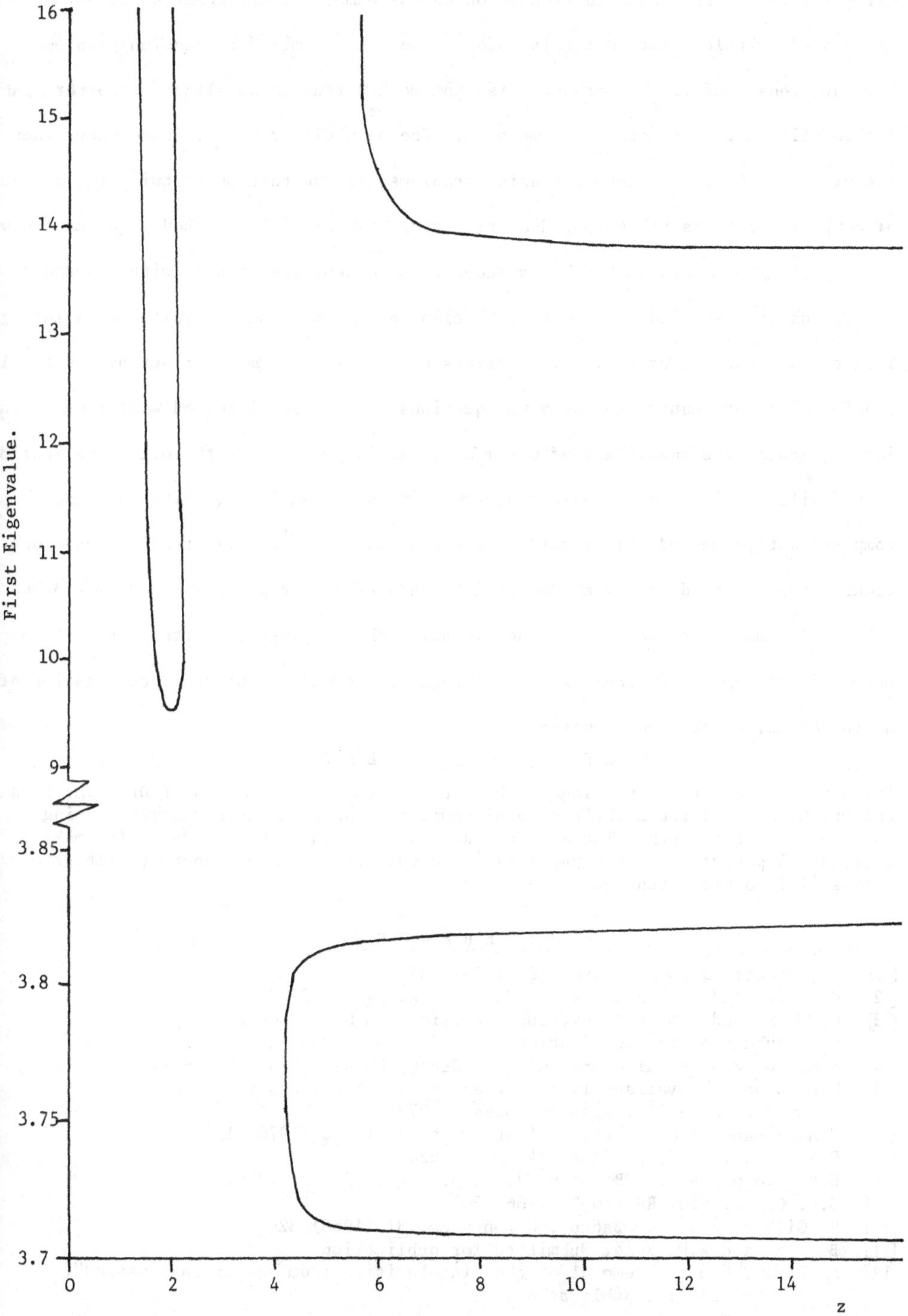

Figure 1.

In general the amount of computing time taken in computing the same problem using all three methods is in proportion to the number of differential equations integrated. Table 1 sets out this information for the mixed convection problem. The equations used in the orthogonalisation method tend to be slightly shorter than the equations from the other two methods. The main differences in time occur when the Riccati method runs into switching problems, it can take up to twice the amount of computing time as the compound matrix or orthogonalisation methods. We must now ask how all these methods may be extended to an eigenvalue problem with n boundary conditions at z = 0 and m boundary conditions at z = x (x being finite or infinite). The current problems use driving equations but we will assume that our hypothetical problem does not require any driving equations. The Riccati method will require the integration of the equivalent of n x m differential equations, the orthogonalisation method will require the equivalent of (m+n) x m differential equations and the compound matrix method will require the equivalent of $\binom{n+m}{m}$ differential equations. Clearly the compound matrix method will be unsuitable for problems where m > 3 and n > 3. The main disadvantage of the Riccati method against the orthogonalisation method is the amount of tedious algebra required before the start of computation of a problem using the Riccati method.

ACKNOWLEDGEMENTS

The author wishes to acknowledge with gratitude the contributions of Dr. D.M. Sloan and Dr. G. Wilks through their helpful comments, ideas and encouragement during the course of this work. The author also wishes to thank Dr. A. Davey for making available a preprint of his paper [12] and thus bringing the paper by Gilbert and Backus [10] to his attention.

REFERENCES

[1] M.R. Scott, J. Comp. Phys. 12 (1973) 334.
[2] G. Wilks and J.S. Bramley, J. Comp. Phys. 24 (1977) 303.
[3] G. Wilks and J.S. Bramley, Dual Solutions in Mixed Convection, submitted for publication.
[4] E.M. Sparrow, R. Eichhard and J.L. Gregg, Phys. Fluids. 2 (1959) 319.
[5] M.R. Scott, "Invariant Imbedding and its Applications to ODE's" Addison-Wesley, Reading, Mass., 1973.
[6] D.M. Sloan and G. Wilks, J. Inst. Math. Appl. 18 (1976) 117.
[7] D.M. Sloan, J. Comp. Phys. 24 (1977) 320.
[8] D.M. Sloan and J.S. Bramley, J. Comp. Phys. 1978 or 1979.
[9] S.D. Conte, Siam Review 8 (1966) 309.
[10] F. Gilbert and G.E. Backus, Geophysics, 31 (1966) 326.
[11] B.S. NG and W.H. Reid, Submitted for publication.
[12] A. Davey, "On the removal of the singularities from the Riccati method", submitted for publication.

IMPLEMENTATION OF AN ITERATIVE TECHNIQUE FOR THE SOLUTION OF GENERALIZED EMDEN-FOWLER EIGENPROBLEMS

R. C. Flagg,* C. D. Luning** and W. L. Perry*

INTRODUCTION

We consider the nonlinear eigenproblem

$$\begin{aligned} & u''(x) + \lambda a(x)u^{\nu}(x) = 0, \; 0 < x < 1, \; \nu \in \mathbb{R}, \; \nu \neq 1, \\ & \alpha u(0) - \beta u'(0) = 0, \\ & \gamma u(1) + \delta u'(1) = 0. \end{aligned} \tag{1}$$

By means of the transformation

$$u(x) = \lambda^{1/(1-\nu)} \, y(x) \tag{2}$$

this eigenproblem can be converted to the nonlinear boundary value problem

$$\begin{aligned} & y''(x) + a(x)y^{\nu}(x) = 0, \; 0 < x < 1, \\ & \alpha y(0) - \beta y'(0) = 0 \\ & \gamma y(1) + \delta y'(1) = 0. \end{aligned} \tag{3}$$

which is a model for many problems of physical significance in Newtonian and non-Newtonian fluid mechanics, as well as gas dynamics. We will refer to (1) as a generalized Emden-Fowler eigenproblem.

In this paper we relate the results of implementation of an iterative technique specific to the generalized Emden-Fowler eigenproblem for the so-called superlinear case, $\nu > 1$. The iterative technique used, based on the work in [1], was motivated by the work in [2], [3], and [4].

---

*Texas A&M University, College Station, Texas 77843
**Sam Houston State University, Huntsville, Texas 77340

THE ITERATIVE TECHNIQUE

Our assumptions concerning problem (1) are:

(i) $a(x)$ is positive and in $C(0,1) \cap L^1(0,1)$

(ii) $\gamma\beta + \gamma\alpha + \alpha\delta \neq 0$

(iii) $\alpha, \beta, \gamma, \delta \geq 0$, or

$\alpha > 0,\ \beta \geq 0,\ \delta < 0,\ 0 < \gamma < -\alpha\delta/(\alpha+\beta)$, or

$\beta < 0,\ \gamma > 0,\ \delta \geq 0,\ 0 < \alpha < -\gamma\beta/(\gamma+\delta)$

With these assumptions, the main result of [1] which contains the iterative technique is proved. It may be stated:

Let the assumptions (i), (ii), and (iii) hold. With $u_0(x) = |\alpha x + \beta|$, let $\{\lambda_k, u_k\}_{k=1}^{\infty}$ be the sequence defined inductively: λ_k is the least positive eigenvalue and u_k is the corresponding positive eigenfunction of

$$u''(x) + \lambda a(x) u_{k-1}^{\nu-1}(x) u(x) = 0, \qquad 0 < x < 1$$

$$\alpha u(0) - \beta u'(0) = 0,$$

$$\gamma u(1) + \delta u'(1) = 0,$$

normalized by

$$\beta u_k(0) + \alpha u_k'(0) = (\operatorname{sign} \beta)(\alpha^2 + \beta^2).$$

There exists a positive solution (λ, u) of (1) such that $\{\lambda_k\} \to \lambda$ and $\{u_k\} \to u$ uniformly on $[0,1]$ as $k \to +\infty$. Moreover the convergence is monotone:

$$0 < \lambda_1 < \lambda_2 < \dots < \lambda \ ;$$

$$u_0(x) > u_1(x) > u_2(x) > \dots > u(x) > 0, \quad 0 < x < 1 .$$

It may be noted that by utilizing the Green's function $K(x,t)$ for $L(u) = u''$ with the boundary conditions in (1), (4) may be rewritten

$$u(x) = \lambda\int_0^1 K(x,t)a(t)u_{k-1}^{\nu-1}(t)u(t)dt \equiv \lambda(T_{k-1}u)(x) \tag{7}$$

In fact it is this equivalent integral equation formulation of (4) that allows us to prove in [1] existence of the positive eigenpair (λ_k, u_k) at each step of the iterative procedure.

To implement the iterative technique one may use the differential equation formulation (4) or the integral equation formulation (7).

If one chooses to use (4), then at each step of the iterative procedure, a linear Sturm-Liouville problem must be solved. This solution must then be normalized according to (5) and used as part of the weight function in the next linear Sturm-Liouville problem to be solved. In our implementation using (4), we used a code called SLEIGN, developed by Bailey, Gordon, and Shampine [5]. SLEIGN is explained elsewhere in this volume.

On the other hand if one chooses to use (7), then at each step of the iterative procedure a linear integral equation eigenvalue problem must be solved. In an appropriate Hilbert space T_{k-1} from (7) is a Hilbert-Schmidt operator. Therefore Galerkin's method [6] may be used to find approximations to λ_k and u_k at each step. In our implementation we reduced the problem of solving (7) to the matrix eigenvalue problem

$$A_k V = \mu B_k V$$

where A_k is symmetric and B_k is symmetric positive definite. We used the subroutine EIGZF from the IMSL library to solve this problem.

In our implementations, we found that the first method using the differential equation (4) was the faster of the two methods. Consequently we present our results from the first method only.

IMPLEMENTATION AND EXAMPLES

At each step, SLEIGN was used to solve (4). SLEIGN returned the eigenval and initial values of the eigenfunction at both endpoints as well as informatic about accuracy. We used the three point Adams predictor formula with four poi Adams corrector formula to compute the eigenfunction across (0,1), checking th the values matched at $x = 1/2$. The initial values were then used to normaliz the eigenfunction according to (5). The eigenfunction was then approximated by a Legendre polynomial (defined on (0,1)). Then the new eigenpair (λ_k, u_k) was compared with the previous eigenpair (λ_{k-1}, u_{k-1}). If $|\lambda_k - \lambda_{k}$ and $\max_{x\in[0,1]} |u_k(x) - u_{k-1}(x)|$ were both smaller than the maximum of (a) a preassigned tolerance, and (b) the accuracy of the solution returned from SLEI the program was stopped and the final eigenpair printed. Otherwise another iterative step was taken.

All calculations were done in double precision on the Amdahl 460V/6 at Texas A&M University.

Example 1.

$$u'' + \lambda(x+1)^{-11/4} u^{5/2} = 0, \quad 0 < x < 1$$

$$u(0) - 2u'(0) = 0$$

$$u(1) - 4u'(1) = 0$$

This problem has an infinite number of solutions of the form $C(x+1)^{1/2}$ wit $\lambda^{-1} = 4C^{3/2}$. With our normalization $C = 2$. Any normalization can be used--t one chosen by us was for convenience in the presentation of the results in [1]

The computed solution and actual solution are tabulated below:

x	Computed Solution	Actual Solution
0	1.99997	2.0
.1	2.09759	2.09761
.2	2.19088	2.19089
.3	2.22803	2.28035
.4	2.36644	2.36643
.5	2.44948	2.44948
.6	2.52980	2.52982
.7	2.60767	2.60768
.8	2.68328	2.68328
.9	2.75682	2.75682
1.0	2.82839	2.82842

Computed eigenvalue .088388341 Actual eigenvalue .088388348

The computed solution was obtained in 5 iterations. Execution was halted when successive eigenvalues and maximum deviation of successive eigenfunctions was less than 10^{-5}. Total execution time was 8.65 seconds.

Example 2.

$$u''(x) + \lambda u^3(x) = 0, \quad 0 < x < 1, \qquad u(0) = u(1) = 0 \tag{8}$$

The solution of this problem involves an elliptic sine function, whose values may be calculated using tables.

The results obtained are tabulated below. Since the solution is even about $x = 1/2$, values for u are shown only up to $x = 1/2$. Symmetry was obtained in the computed solution. The eigenvalue was calculated as 95.1.

x	Computed Solution	Actual Solution
0	0	0
.1	.09637	.09961
.2	.19963	.19790
.3	.29201	.28879
.4	.35466	.35498
.5	.37677	.38025

The computed solution was obtained in eight iterations. Execution in our method was halted when successive eigenvalues and maximum deviation of successive eigenfunctions was less than 10^{-3}. We could not ask for a smaller tolerance, as SLEIGN was returning results with accuracy tolerance of 10^{-3}. Execution time was 11.27 seconds.

References

1. C. D. Luning and W. L. Perry, Solution of superlinear eigenvalue problems via a monotone iterative technique. Revision Submitted to Journal of Differential Equations.

2. C. D. Luning and W. L. Perry, Iterative solution of Hartree's equations, Journal of Mathematical Physics, 17 (1976), pp. 1156-1159.

3. C. D. Luning, An iterative technique for obtaining solutions of a Thomas-Fermi equation, To appear in SIAM J. Math. Anal., June 1978.

4. C. D. Luning and W. L. Perry, An iterative technique for solution of the Thomas-Fermi equation utilizing a nonlinear eigenvalue problem. Quarterl of Applied Mathematics, 35 (1977), pp. 257-268.

5. P. B. Bailey, M. K. Gordon, L. F. Shampine, Solving Sturm-Liouville eigen value problems, Sandia Laboratories Report SAND 76-0560, October 1976.

6. M. Krasnoselskii, Topological methods in nonlinear intergral equations, Pergamon, New York, 1964.

TEST EXAMPLES FOR COMPARISON OF CODES FOR NONLINEAR BOUNDARY VALUE PROBLEMS IN ORDINARY DIFFERENTIAL EQUATIONS

Kubíček M., Hlaváček V. and Holodniok M.*

Department of Chemical Engineering, Prague Institute of Chemical Technology, 166 28 Praha 6, Czechoslovakia

A number of nonlinear boundary value problems, arising in chemical reaction engineering, hydrodynamics, plasma physics and biology are proposed to serve as examples for testing of codes for solution of nonlinear boundary value problems. These examples cover a broad spectrum ranging from easy to extremely difficult problems.

INTRODUCTION

Nonlinear boundary value problems occur in a wide variety of physical situations, for instance, diffusion occuring in the presence of an exothermic chemical reaction, heat conduction associated with radiation effects, deformation of shells, etc. For these examples the nonlinear equations represent a true physical situation. However, there is a number of nonlinear boundary value problems which result after certain mathematical transformations. To illustrate this family of equations boundary layer problems will be presented. Though a flow of a real viscous fluid is described by rather complicated nonlinear partial differential equations (Navier-Stokes equations) certain transformations make it possible to convert them into a nonlinear boundary value problem for ordinary differential equations. Finally, nonlinear boundary value problems result after a proper discretization of nonlinear elliptic partial differential equations with two independent variables. A specific group of problems is created by the family of optimization problems which require to establish the "optimum profiles". In this paper we wish to select some typical problems which cover a broad

* Computing Centre

spectrum ranging from easy to extremely difficult problems as well as to indicate appropriate methods used for their numerical solution.

So far several techniques have been proposed for solving nonlinear boundary value problems, e.g., shooting, finite - difference methods combined with the Newton-Raphson procedure, invariant imbedding, false transient methods, continuation etc. Assessing the relative merits of different methods is not an easy task. Although good quality software for solution of nonlinear boundary value problems has been developed , a systematic comparison of relative merits of particular routines used towards solution of difficult problems is missing in the literature so far. It therefore seems appropriate at this conference to present a collection of difficult nonlinear boundary value problems which might be used in future as the test examples.

In addition we would like to stress that the examples suggested represent a live physical situation and are not artificially created. Our discussion is limited to problems which are described by a low number of differential equations.

FACTORS TO BE CONSIDERED

A number of different factors must be taken into consideration when selecting a program for handling nonlinear boundary value problems. The following is a list of some of the more important factors.

a) Shape of profiles

It is very helpful to have preliminary information on the shape of the profiles. There are problems where the shape of the profiles exhibits some pathological behavior, e.g., i) the profiles are almost discontinuous (cf. Example 3), ii) extremely steep gradients occur (cf. Example 3).

b) Multiplicity

Certain physical problems possess more than one solution. Such situation is demonstrated on Examples 2,3,4,5,6,7. For a particular problem solution at certain branch can be easily calculated by standard software while to find a solution at the other branch may represent a difficult problem, cf. Examples 2,3,5. In the vicinity of a branching point most techniques do not work too well.

c) Sparseness

Nonlinear boundary value problems of large dimension describing a physical problem are usually sparse and the numerical procedures must take advantage of it to be efficient. Such problems can arise after partial discretization of elliptic nonlinear partial differential equations or by calculation of branching points for a set of nonlinear differential equations representing a boundary value problem. Examples of large set of equations will not be presented here.

d) Stiffness

If the system to be solved by shooting is stiff it is essential to use an integration method that is capable of coping with stiffness. Examples of weakly stiff problems are presented in Example 3 and Example 4 .

e) Inherent instability of the initial value problem

Certain initial value problems may be very sensitive to guessed initial conditions or are inherently unstable. Examples of inherent instability are presented: Example 3 (integration from $\xi = 0$ to $\xi = 1$ practically impossible) and Example 5 (integration in both directions impossible). The orthogonalization algorithm for quasilinearization may cope with this difficulty [12] .

There are of course other factors to be considered, but the above list represents the major ones.

COMPARING OF ALGORITHMS

A comparison of algorithms is not an easy business. For initial value problems Partlett [1] and Scott [2] shown that slight variations in the programming on different computers or the use of a different compiler on the same computer can result in drastic changes in accuracy and computer times. Of course the same conclusions are true for nonlinear boundary value problems. Following criteria for comparison may be considered :

a) Computer time expenditure.
b) Computer storage requirements
c) Possibility of a reliable calculation of the problem

d) Complexity of the program

e) Extent of additional programming work to handle a particular problem by standard software

The test problems suggested should help in drawing some conclusions regarding the points a and c. Each problem is classified as VS (very simple), S (simple), C (complicated), D (difficult), VD (very difficult), ED (extremely difficult).

EXAMPLE 1:

Confinement of a plasma column by radiation pressure is described by so called Troesch's two-point boundary value problem e.g. [3,4,5] :

$$\frac{d^2y}{d\,z^2} = n \sinh ny \qquad y(o) = 0, \quad y(1) = 1. \tag{1-1}$$

For higher values of the parameter n this problem becomes difficult. Some results calculated by modified shooting - parameter mapping [5] are reported in Tab. 1-1.

Table 1-1 : Results for Example 1

n	Classification	Resulting $y'(o)$
5	VS	0.0457
10	S	0.358E-3
15	C	0.244E-5
20	D	0.165E-7
30	D	0.75 E-12

EXAMPLE 2:

Heat and mass transfer in a porous spherical catalyst where a first-order reaction occurs is described by a nonlinear boundary value problem [6]

$$\frac{d^2y}{d\xi^2} + \frac{a}{\xi}\,\frac{dy}{d\xi} = \phi^2\, y \exp\left[\frac{\gamma\beta\,(1-y)}{1+\beta(1-y)}\right] \tag{2-1}$$

subject to boundary conditions

$$\xi = 0 : \quad \frac{dy}{d\xi} = 0, \qquad \xi = 1 : \quad y = 1. \tag{2-2}$$

For technical purposes usually a plot "η - ϕ" is drawn, here the effectiveness factor η is defined as

$$\eta = \frac{a+1}{\phi^2} \left. \frac{dy}{d\xi} \right|_{\xi=1} . \tag{2-3}$$

It can be shown that for higher values of the parameters γ and β multiple solutions exist in a certain range of the parameter ϕ .

The problem can be solved by shooting from ξ =0 to ξ =1, an integration of the equations from ξ = 1 to ξ = 0 cannot be easily performed. Test results are reported in Table 2-1. For higher values of $\gamma\beta$ the plot "η-ϕ" is drawn in Fig. 2-1 [7]. This figure reveals that for certain values of ϕ up to 15 solutions may exist.

Table 2-1:

Numerical solution and test results for Eqs. (2-1) and (2-2)

Parameters	Number of solutions	Procedure used	Classi-fication	Results	Remarks
a=0, γ=20, β=0.1, ϕ = 1	1	shooting	S	y(o)=0.3745	
a=2 , γ=20 β=0.05, ϕ = 6	1	finite differences	S	y(o)=0.0023	
a=0, γ=20 β=0.05, ϕ = 1	1	finite differences	S	y(o)=0.5521	
a=2, γ=40 β=0.2, ϕ = 0.6	3	shooting	C	y(o)=0.9070 y(o)=0.3639 y(o)=0.000102	
a=2, γ=60 β=2.5 ϕ =0.1135	15	shooting	ED	see Fig. 2-1	Taken from Aris and Copelowitz [7]

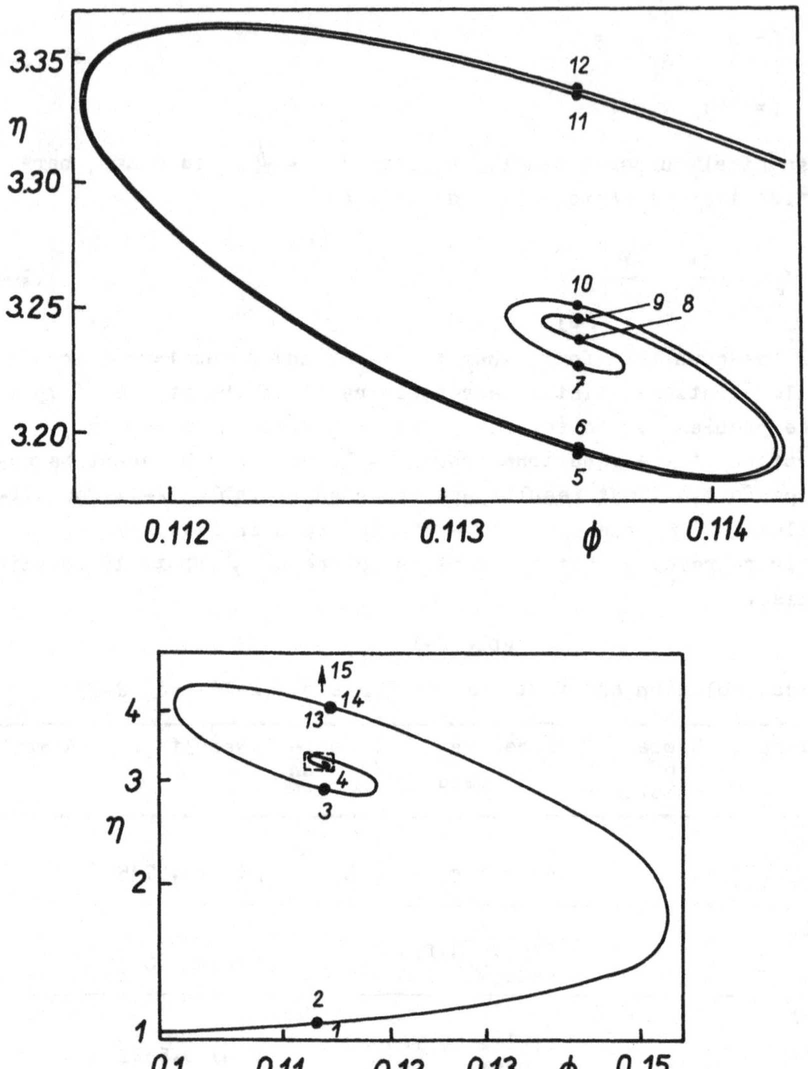

Fig.2-1: Dependence of η on ϕ for higher values of $\gamma\beta$. a=2, γ=60, β =2.5

EXAMPLE 3:

The one-phase one-dimensional dispersion model describing the steady state behavior of a tubular nonadiabatic reactor where a first-order reaction occurs may be written in a dimensionless form [9] :

$$\frac{1}{Pe_H}\,\frac{d^2\theta}{d\xi^2} - \frac{d\,\theta}{d\xi} + BDa(1-y)\exp\left(\frac{\theta}{1+\theta/\gamma}\right) - \beta(\theta-\theta_c) = 0 \qquad (3\text{-}1)$$

$$\frac{1}{Pe_M}\,\frac{d^2 y}{d\xi^2} - \frac{dy}{d\xi} + Da(1-y)\exp\left(\frac{\theta}{1+\theta/\gamma}\right) = 0\,.$$

The corresponding boundary conditions are :

$$\xi=0 : \quad Pe_H\theta = \frac{d\theta}{d\xi}, \qquad Pe_M y = \frac{dy}{d\xi} \qquad (3\text{-}2)$$

$$\xi=1 : \quad \frac{d\theta}{d\xi} = \frac{dy}{d\xi} = 0.$$

This problem for particular values of the governing parameters may cover the whole range of classification. For higher values of the parameter B multiple solutions may exist up to certain values of Pe_H and Pe_M. For fixed values of β, θ_c, $Pe_M/Pe_H = q$, and γ the parametric plane "Pe_M – Da" is shown in Figs. 3-1 and 3-2. Here the regions with one, three and five solutions of (3-1, 3-2) are drawn. For an adiabatic case (β =0) only one or three solutions of (3-1) exist. For the case $\beta = 0$ the temperature and concentration profiles may be very flat or may exhibit a small "hook" near the point ξ =1, see Fig. 3-3.

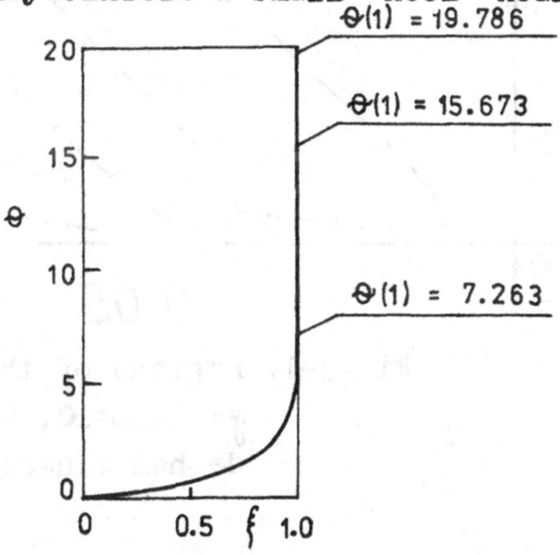

Fig. 3-3: Three solutions for adiabatic case, $y = \theta/B$. γ =20, B=20, $Pe_M = Pe_H =$ = 291.3, Da=0.05826, $\beta = 0$.

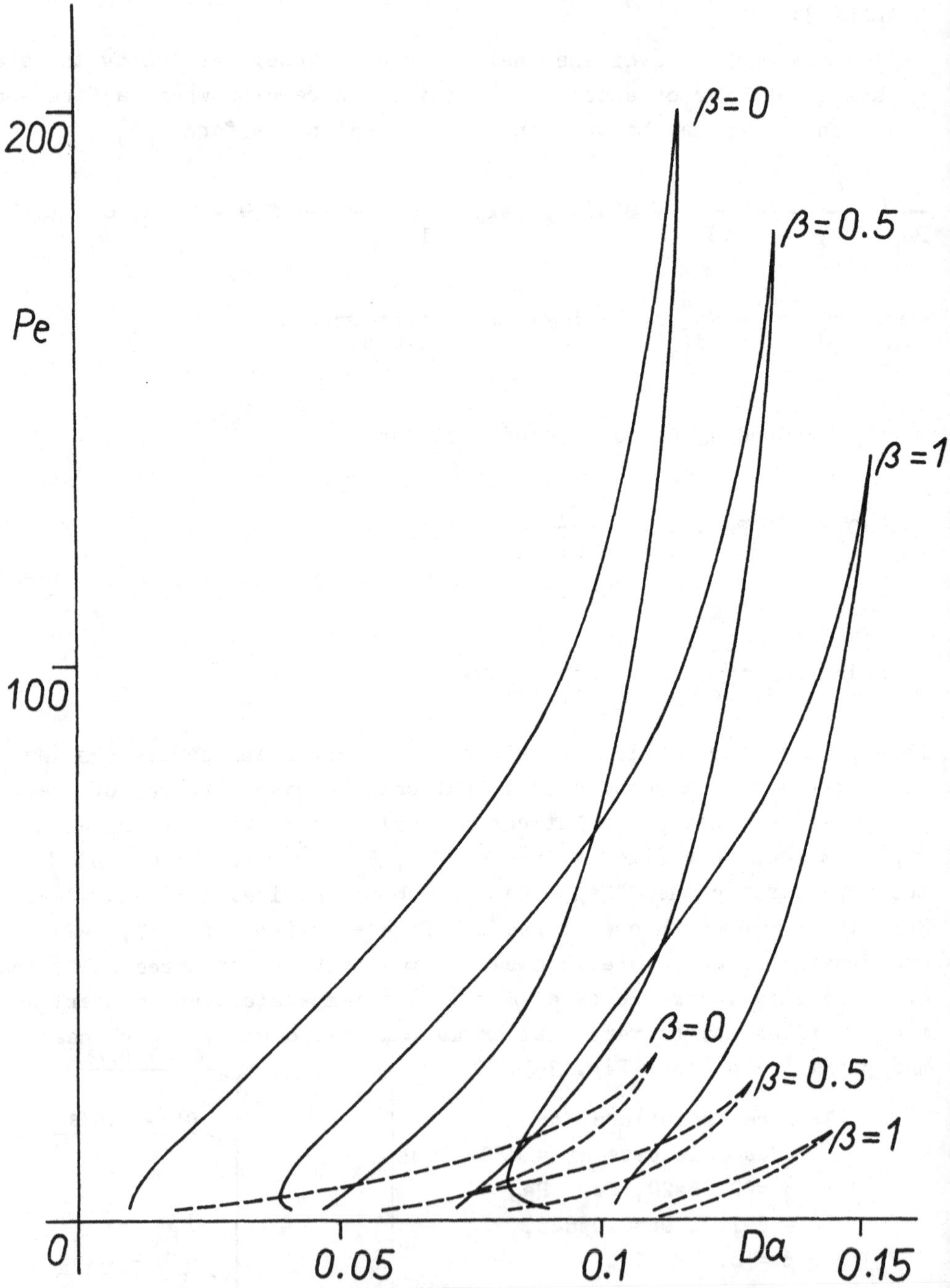

Fig.3-1: Regions of three solutions in the plane Da-Pe_M. γ=20, B=10, Θ_c=0, Pe=Pe_M. Full lines: q=4, dashed lines: q=1.

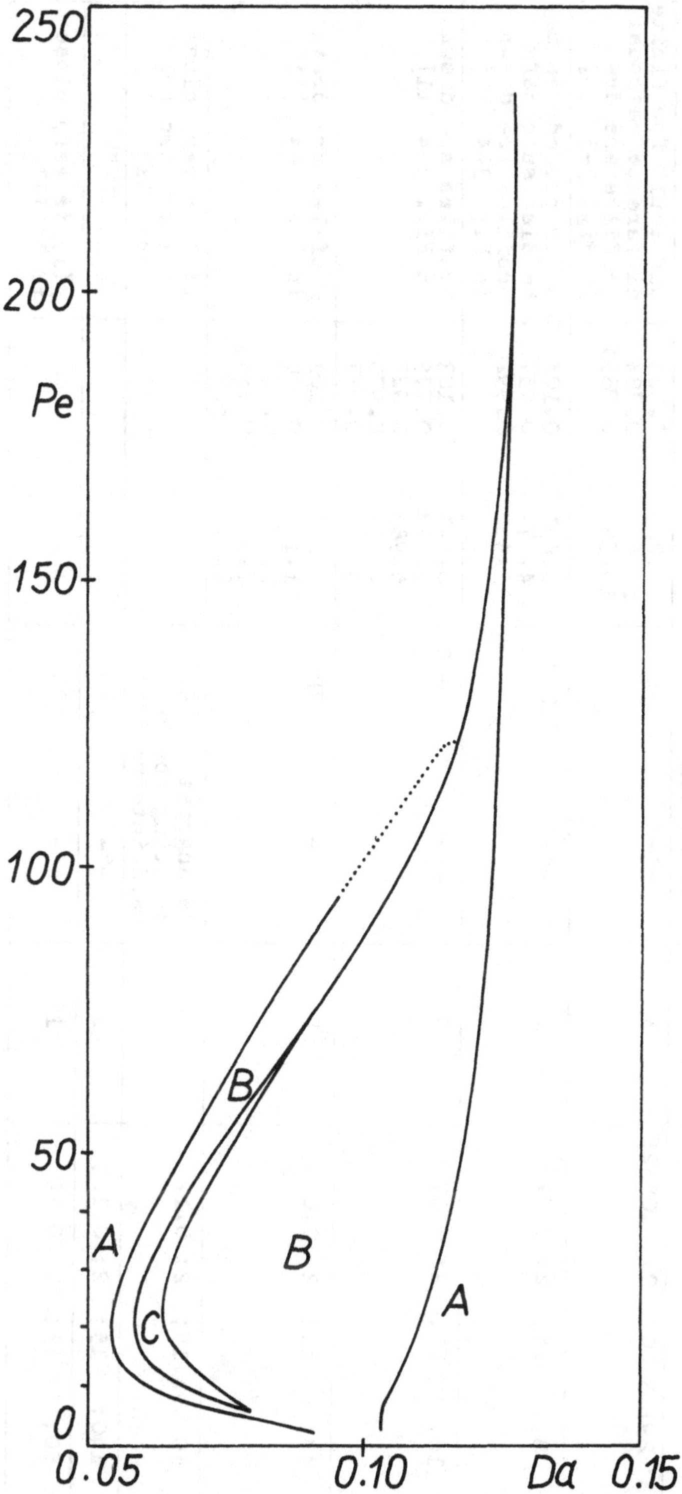

Fig.3-2: Regions of multiple solutions in the plane Da-Pe_M. γ=20, B=15, θ_c=0, β=2, q=2, Pe=Pe_M. A: one steady state, B: three steady states, C: five stedy states.

Table 3-1: Numerical solution and test results for Eqs (3-1.3-2), $\gamma = 20$, $\theta_c = 0$

Parameters Pe_H; Pe_M; B; β; Da	Number of solutions	Procedure used	Classification	Results $\theta(1)$	$y(1)$	Remarks
2.5; 5; 15; 0; 0.07	1	Shooting (backward integration)	S	0.609	0.104	Other procedure may be also successful
291.3; 291.3; 20; 0; 0.05826	3	-"-	VD	7.263 15.67 19.79	0.363 0.784 0.9895	Difficult for finite difference methods; profiles are drawn in Fig. 3-3 [10]
4; 8; 15; 2; 0.07	3	-"-	D	0.631 4.271 3.462	0.104 0.957 0.992	Other procedures may be also successful, profiles are drawn in Fig. 3-4 [11]
5; 10; 15; 2; 0.07	5	-"-	D-VD	0.641 6.684 6.983 4.566 3.222	0.103 0.779 0.925 0.970 0.977	Profiles are drawn in Fig. 3-4 [11]
22; 44; 15; 2; 0.07	5	-"-	VD	0.683 11.13 11.27 7.97 2.41	0.101 0.920 0.989 0.9999_{27} 1-10	Profiles are drawn in Fig. 3-4 [11]
50; 100; 15; 2; 0.12	3	We suggest shooting (backward integration)	ED			y(1) is very close to 1 for two solutions [11]
70; 140; 15; 2; 0.123	3	-"-	ED			-"-
25; 50; 15; 2; 0.12	1	-"-	ED			y(1) is very close to 1 [11]

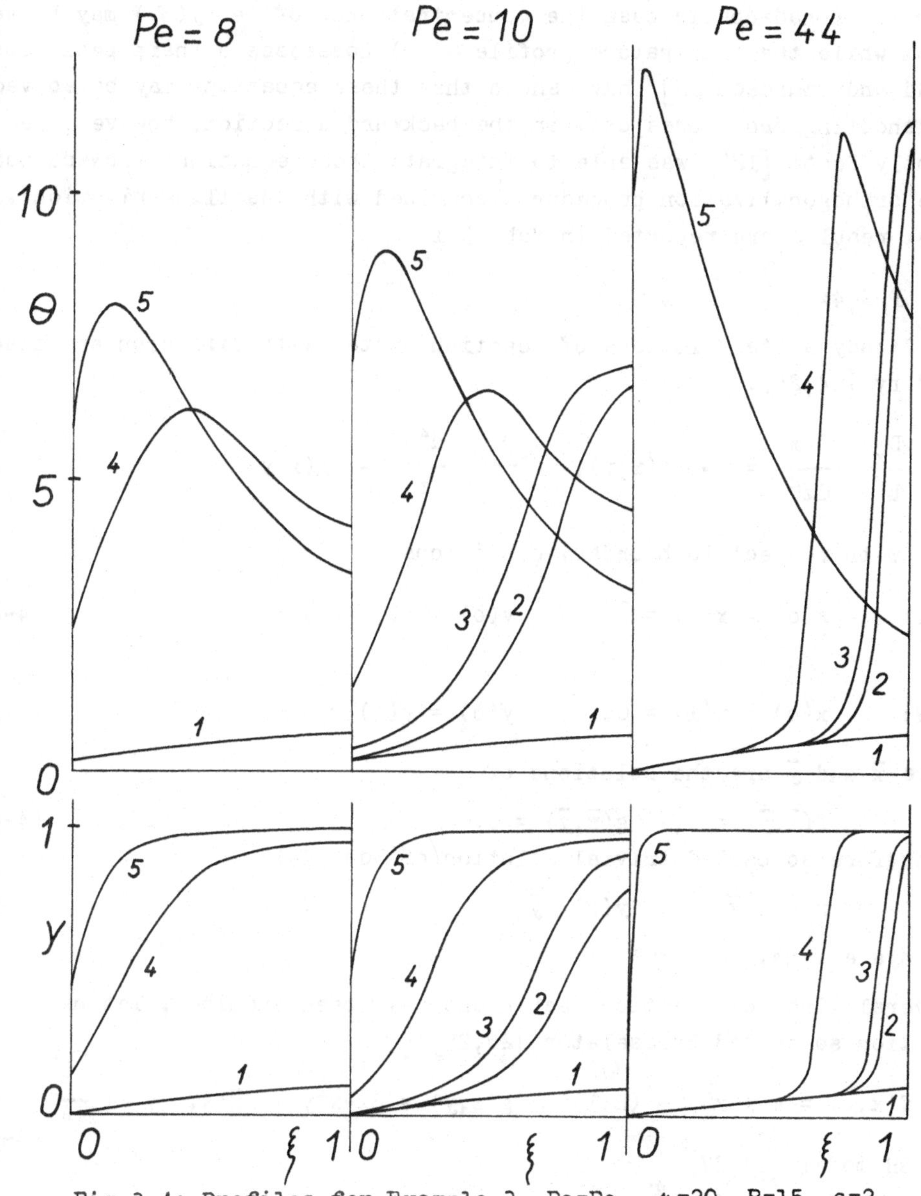

Fig.3-4: Profiles for Example 3, $Pe=Pe_M$. $\gamma=20$, B=15, q=2, $\Theta_c=0$, $\beta=2$, Da=0.07.

For the nonadiabatic case the concentration profile $y(\xi)$ may be ve flat while the temperature profile $\Theta(\xi)$ possesses a sharp peak. Cos Rudd and Amundson [9] have shown that these equations may be solved by shooting procedures only in the backward direction, however, recently Scott [12] was able to integrate these equations forward usi the orthogonalization procedure (combined with quasilinearization). Test results are reported in Tab. 3-1.

EXAMPLE 4:

Steady state solutions of reaction system with diffusion are desc bed by [24,26]:

$$\frac{D_x}{L^2}\frac{d^2x}{dz^2} = -f(x,y), \qquad \frac{D_y}{L^2}\frac{d^2y}{dz^2} = -g(x,y) \qquad (4-1$$

with respect to boundary conditions

$$\text{BC1:} \qquad x(o) = x(1) = \bar{x}, \qquad y(o) = y(1) = \bar{y} \qquad (4-2$$

or

$$\text{BC2:} \qquad x'(o) = x'(1) = 0, \qquad y'(o) = y'(1) = 0. \qquad (4-3$$

Here $\bar{x}$ and $\bar{y}$ are the solutions of

$$f(\bar{x},\bar{y}) = 0, \qquad g(\bar{x},\bar{y}) = 0. \qquad (4-4$$

Therefore so called trivial solution of Eqs (4-1)

$$x(z) \equiv \bar{x}, \qquad y(z) \equiv \bar{y} \qquad (4-5$$

always exists.

Several kinds of reaction mechanisms have been examined, let us mention so called Brusselator [26,25]

$$f(x,y) = A + x^2y - (B+1)x\,, \quad g(x,y) = Bx - x^2y\,, \quad \bar{x} = A, \quad \bar{y} = \frac{B}{A} \qquad (4-6$$

or SH model [24,27]

$$f(x,y) = \alpha\frac{\nu_o + x^\gamma}{1+x^\gamma} - x(1+y), \qquad g(x,y) = x(\beta + y) - \delta y, \qquad (4-7$$

where $\bar{x}$ and $\bar{y}$ have to be calculated iteratively from (4-4).

Results of our extensive calculation are presented in Figs. 4-1 and 4-2. It is evident that a number of solutions of governing equations may exist [24,25]. For instance for parameters presented in Fig. 4-1 the problem defined by Eqs.(4-1), (4-2) and (4-6) may posses for L = 0.1, 0.2 and 0.3 three, six and eight solutions, respectively. Fig. 4-2 displays the results for problem given by Eqs. (4-1), (4-3) and (4-7). Here the boundary conditions of second kind are considered. For L = 0.1, 0.2, 0.3 and 0.4 three, seven, nine and nine solutions exist, respectively.

EXAMPLE 5:

Steady flow of an incompressible viscous fluid between two infinite rotating disks is described by a nonlinear boundary value problem [e.g. 13-23]

$$
\begin{aligned}
F'' &= \sqrt{R}\,HF' + R\,(F^2 - G^2 + k) \\
G'' &= 2RFG + \sqrt{R}\,G'H \\
H' &= -2\sqrt{R}\,F
\end{aligned}
\qquad (5\text{-}1)
$$

subject to the boundary conditions

$$
\begin{aligned}
F(0) &= H(0) = 0, \quad G(0) = 1 \\
F(1) &= H(1) = 0, \quad G(1) = s.
\end{aligned}
\qquad (5\text{-}2)
$$

The problem is to calculate the functions $F(\xi)$, $G(\xi)$ and $H(\xi)$ and the parameter k for various values of R and s in the ranges $0 \leq R < \infty$ and $-1 \leq s \leq 1$. Notice that six boundary conditions have been formulated for a fifth order system since the parameter k is unknown.

This problem is considered in the literature, for higher values of the Reynolds number R, as a particularly difficult numerical problem. So far a number of numerical techniques have been proposed to solve it : Lance and Rogers [15] and Osborne [17] used the shooting method, Well [20] adapted the quasilinearization procedure, Greenspan [23] made use of the relaxation technique while Pearson [18] took advantage of the false transient method. Recently, Nguyen et al [16] and Holodniok, Kubíček and Hlaváček [21] have applied the Newton-Raphson approach, Kubíček, Holodniok and Hlaváček [13] and [14] differentiation with respect to an actual parameter and one-parameter imbedding technique, respectively, and Roberts and Shipman [19] a continuation method for sensitive problems.

According to Lance and Rogers and [29] the classical shooting method may be used for Reynolds numbers as high as approximately ~ 500. For higher values, unfortunately, this procedure failed. Recently

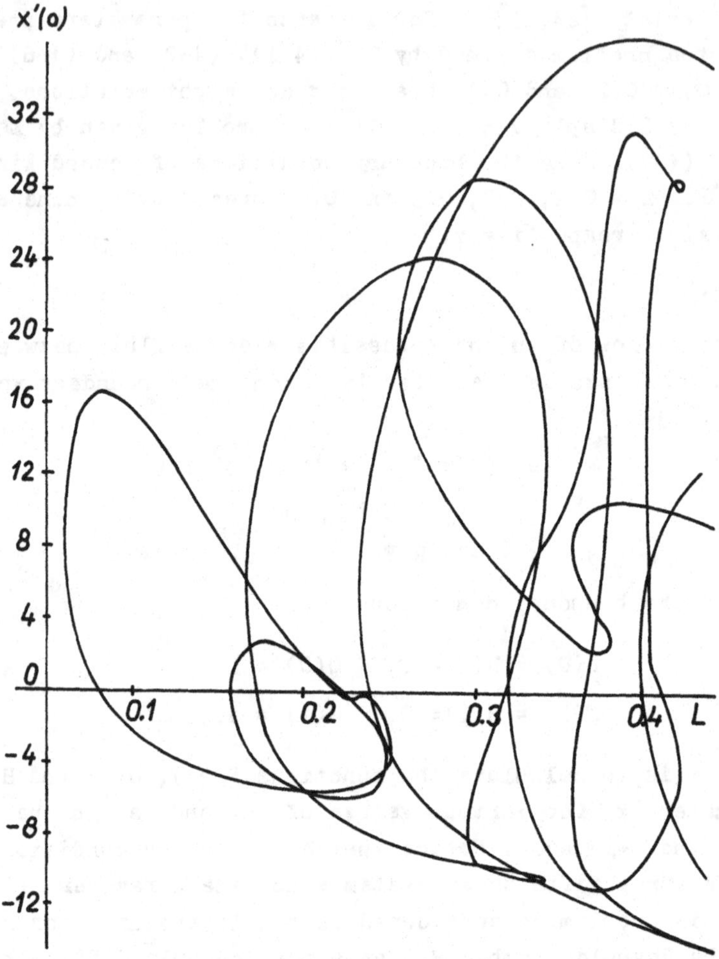

Fig.4-1 Results for Example 4,Eq.(4-6),(4-2).
A=2, B=4.6, D_x=0.0016, D_y=0.008

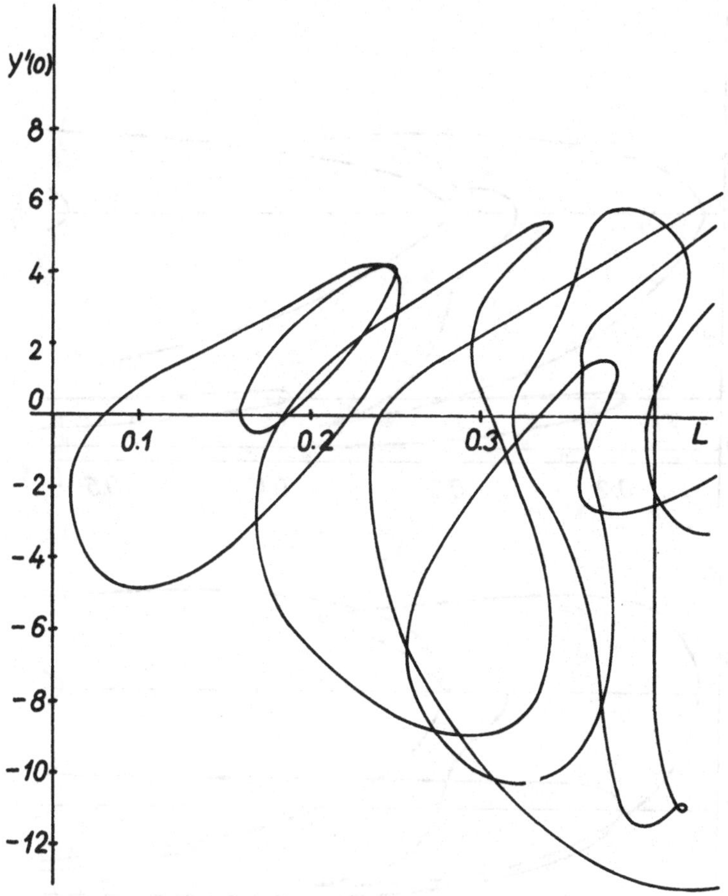

Fig.4-1: continued

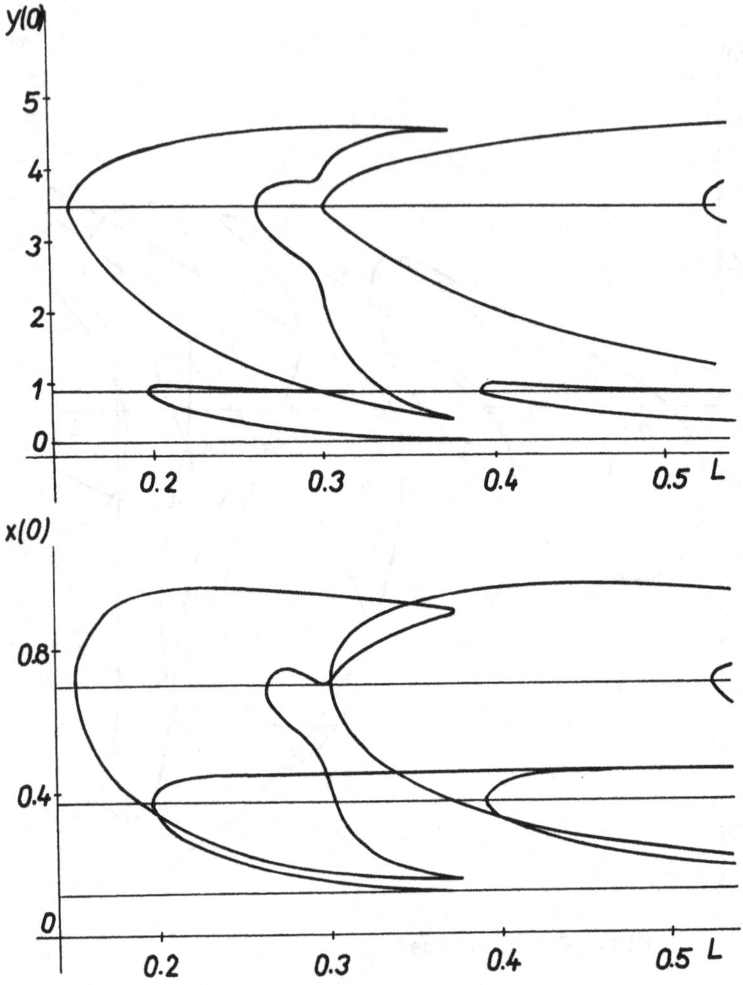

Fig.4-3 Results for Example 4, Eq.(4-7), $\alpha=12$, $\beta=1.5$, $\mu=3$, $\delta=1$, $\nu_0=0.01$, $D_x=0.008$, $D_y=0.004$.
Steady state solutions (trivial):

i	$\bar{x}_i$	$\bar{y}_i$
1	0.1157	0.1962
2	0.3728	0.8915
3	0.7006	3.5106

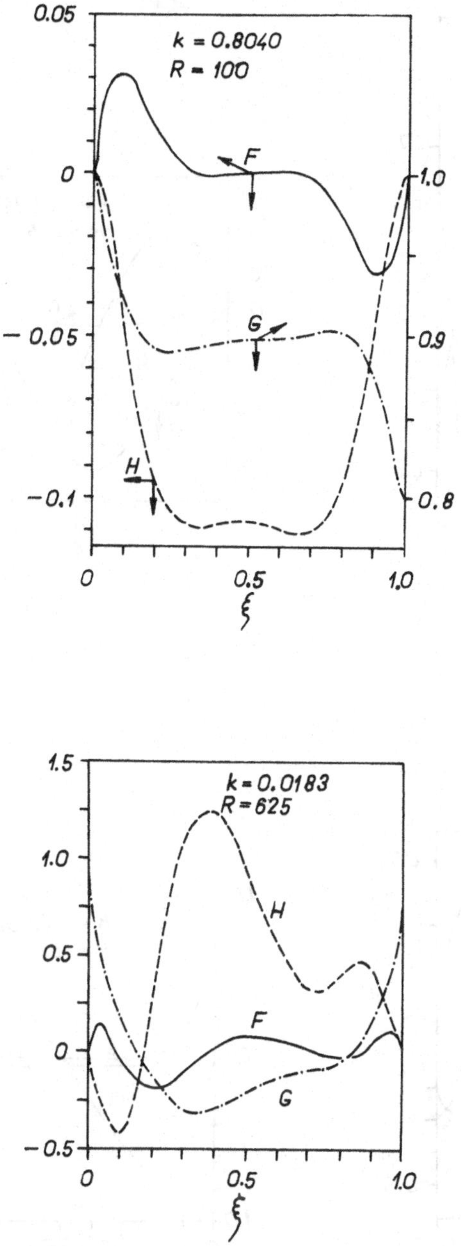

Fig.5-1: Resulting profiles for Example 5. Results have been obtained for 101 grid points used to finite difference approximation. s=0.8.

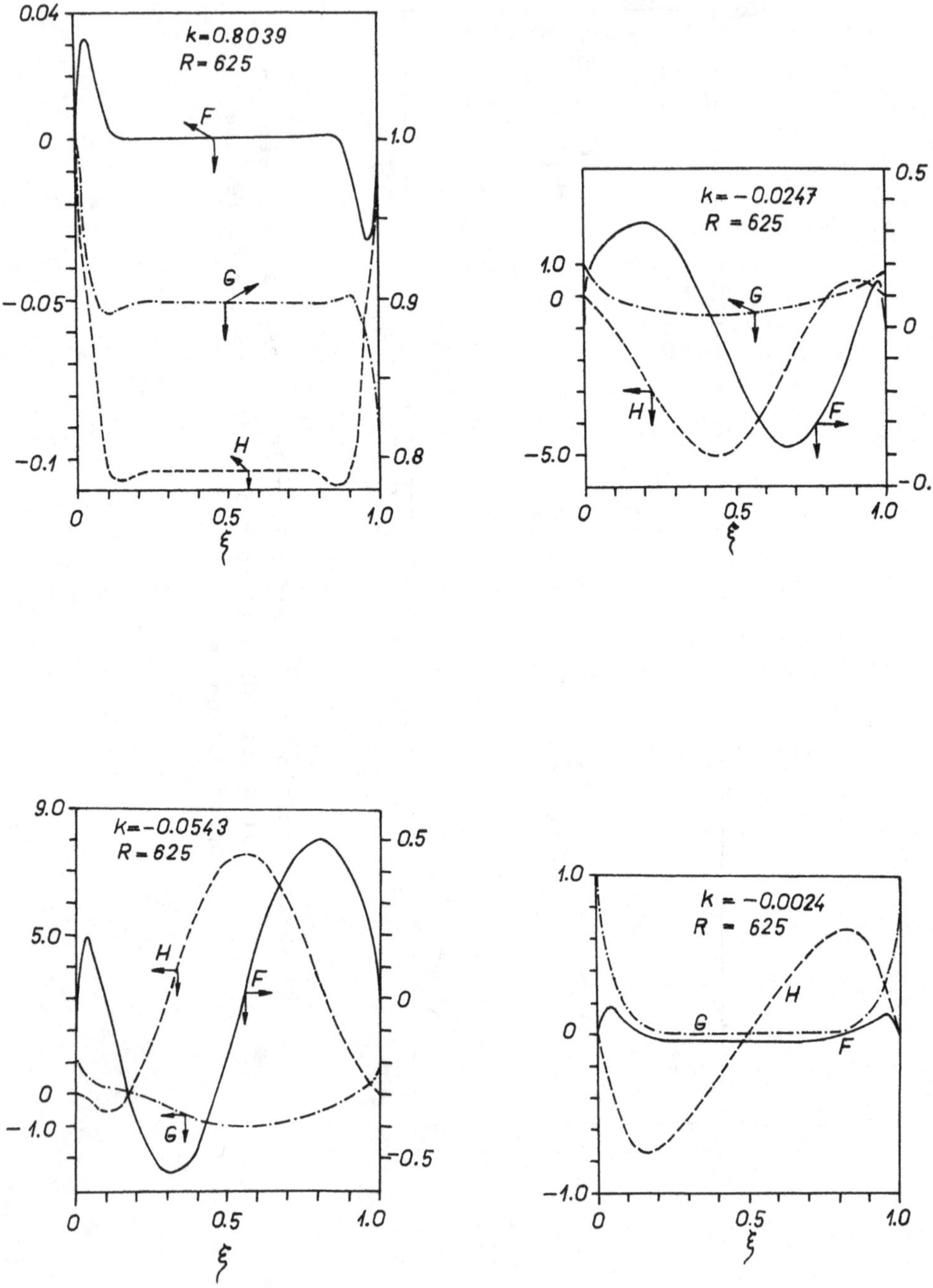
k=0.8039
R=625
F
G
H
0.04
0
−0.05
−0.1
1.0
0.9
0.8
0
0.5
1.0
ξ
k=−0.0247
R=625
1.0
0
−5.0
0.5
−0.5
k=−0.0543
R=625
9.0
5.0
−1.0
k=−0.0024
R=625

Roberts and Shipman have managed to combine the shooting method with continuation. Indeed, for the case of rotating disks they were able to calculate the solution up to $R \sim 5000$. Of course, we may expect that shooting combined with Scottś orthogonalization algorithm may be also a successful procedure. The reference results reported below have been calculated by the finite difference method. The Newton-Raphson procedure was employed to solve nonlinear finite-difference equations.

Holodniok et al [21,22] performed a detailed and systematic analysis of the problem and showed that large number of solution exists. Some profiles are very steep whilst the other are very flat. The test results are reported in Table 5-1 and Fig. 5-1.

EXAMPLE 6:

Concentration and temperature fields in a tubular reactor with recirculation are described by two differential equations

$$\frac{dy}{dz} = Da(1-y) \exp \left(\frac{\theta}{1+\theta/\gamma} \right) \tag{6-1}$$

$$\frac{d\theta}{dz} = BDa(1-y) \exp \left(\frac{\theta}{1+\theta/\gamma} \right) - \beta(\theta - \theta_c)$$

subject to mixed boundary conditions :

$$y(0) = (1-\lambda)\, y(1)$$

$$\theta(0) = (1-\lambda)\, \theta(1) \tag{6-2}$$

Some results calculated for these equations are presented in Tab. 6-1.

EXAMPLE 7:

Heat and mass transfer in a monolithic honeycomb catalyst is described by a nonlinear boundary value problem [28] :

$$\frac{dy}{d\xi} - J_D(\omega - y) = 0 \tag{7-1}$$

$$\frac{d\theta}{d\xi} - J_H(\vartheta - \theta) = 0 \tag{7-2}$$

$$\frac{1}{Pe}\frac{d^2\vartheta}{d\xi^2} - J_H(\vartheta - \theta) + BDa(1-\omega) \exp \left(\frac{\vartheta}{1+\vartheta/\gamma} \right) = 0 \tag{7-3}$$

$$J_D(\omega - y) - Da(1-\omega) \exp \left(\frac{\vartheta}{1+\vartheta/\gamma} \right) = 0 \tag{7-4}$$

Table 5-1: Numerical solution and test results for Eqs (5-1,5-2)

Parameters	Number of solutions *	Procedure used	Classification	Results $F'(0)$	$G'(0)$	k	Remarks
R = 100, s = 0.8	1	Finite-difference scheme	S	9.9E-1	-1.0E1	8.0E-1	See Fig.5-1 [21]
R = 275, s = 0.8	3	-"-	S-D	8.4E0 7.9E0 1.6E0	-1.0E1 -1.0E1 -1.7E0	-1.8E-3 1.7E-2 8.0E-1	See [21]
R = 625, s = 0.8	5	-"-	D	1.2E1 2.5E0 1.3E1 1.4E1 1.3E1	-1.4E1 -2.5E0 -1.8E1 -1.5E1 -1.5E1	1.8E-2 8.0E-1 -2.5E-2 -5.4E-2 -2.4E-3	See Fig.5-1 [21]
R = 10000, s = 0.8	5	-"-	VD				See [21]

* Recently we have found some other solutions to this problem and thus number of solutions presented has to be considered as minimum [22] .

Table 6-1: Results for Example 6. $\gamma = 20$, $\beta = 0$, $\lambda = 0.5$.

Parameters	Number of solutions	Classification	Solution $y(o)$	$\theta(o)$
B=6, Da = 0.05	1	S	0.1	0.6
B=6, Da = 0.053	3	S	0.1 0.3 0.44	0.7 1.8 2.6
B=6, Da = 0.06	1	S	0.48	2.88
B=4, Da = 0.1	1	S	0.243	0.971

$$\xi = 0 : y = 0, \quad \Theta = 0, \quad \frac{d\vartheta}{d\xi} = 0 \tag{7-5}$$

$$\xi = 1 : \quad \frac{d\vartheta}{d\xi} = 0 \, . \tag{7-6}$$

The problem can be solved by shooting or finite-difference method with the Newton-Raphson procedure, for higher values of the parameter Pe the shooting algorithm fails in both directions. Test results are reported in Tab. 7-1 .

Table 7-1: Results for Example 7

Parameters	Solution $\vartheta(0)$	Algorithm	Classification
$J_D = J_H = 28.5$, Da=0.285 B = 5, Pe=19	0.2263	shooting, finite differences	S
$J_D = J_H = 10$, Da = 0.0372, B =10, Pe = 12	0.700 0.1034 0.21	– " –	D

CONCLUSIONS

A number of difficult nonlinear boundary value problems have been presented. It is hoped that the information will prove useful to some one trying to test the methods and to improve the software for solving nonlinear boundary value problems.

REFERENCES

1. Partlett B., Wang Y.: Can you write a decent FORTRAN subroutine without knowing the computer and the compiler which will process it. SIAM 1973 National Meeting, June 18-21,1973,Hampton,Virginia.
2. Scott M.R.: On the conversion of boundary-value problems into stable initial-value problems via several invariant imbedding algorithms, in Numerical Solutions of Boundary value Problems for Ordinary Differential Equations, edited by A.K.Aziz, Academic Press, New York 1975.
3. Roberts S.M., Shipman J.S.: J. Comput. Physics 10(1972) 232
4. Jones D.J.: J.Comput. Physics 12(1973)429
5. Kubíček M., Hlaváček V.:J.Comput Physics 17(1975)95
6. Weisz P.B., Hicks J.S.: Chem.Engng.Sci. 17(1962)265
7. Aris R., Copelowitz I.: Chem.Engng.Sci. 25(1970)909
8. Kubíček M., Hlaváček V.: J.Inst.Math.Applics 12(1972)287
9. Coste P., Rudd D., Amundson N.R.: Canad.J.Chem.Engng. 39(1961)149
10. Hlaváček V., Hofmann H.: Chem.Engng.Sci. 25(1970)173

11. Kubíček M., Hofmann H.,Hlaváček V.: Chem.Engng Sci, to be publis hed
12. Scott M.R., Watts H.A.:Computational solution of nonlinear two-p boundary value problems, in Proceedings of the 5th Symposium Com puters in Chemical Engineering, Vysoké Tatry,Czechoslovakia (197 p.17
13. Kubíček M., Holodniok M., Hlaváček V.:Comp. and Fluids 4(1976)59
14. Kubíček M., Holodniok M., Hlaváček V.: Problem of a flow of an incompressible viscous fluid between two rotating disks solved b one-parameter imbedding techniques in Proceedings of the 5th Sym posium Computers in Chemical Engineering, Vysoké Tatry, Czechosl vakia (1977) 883
15. Lance G.N.,Rogers M.H.: Proc. Roy. Soc. A266 (1962)109
16. Ngueyen N.D., Ribault J.P.,Florent P.: J. Fluid Mech.68(1975)369
17. Osborne M.R.: J. Math. Anal. Appl. 27(1969)417
18. Pearson C.E.: J. Fluid Mech. 21(1965)623
19. Roberts S.M., Shipman J.S.: J.Fluid Mech. 73(1976)53
20. Well K.H.: J. Math. Anal. Appl. 40(1972)258
21. Holodniok M., Kubíček M., Hlaváček V.: J.Fluid Mech. 81(1977)689
22. Holodniok M., Kubíček M., Hlaváček V.: J.Fluid Mech., to be pub- lished
23. Greenspan D.: J.Inst. Math. Appl. 9(1972)370
24. Kubíček M., Marek M., Husták P., Rýzler V.:Bifurcation, multipli city and stability in reaction-diffusion systems in Proceedings of the 5th Symposium Computers in Chemical Engineering,Vysoké Tatry, Czechoslovakia (1977) 903
25. Kubíček M., Marek M., Rýzler P.: Bioph.Chemistry, to be publishe
26. Glansdorf P.,Prigogine I.:Thermodynamics of Structure,Stability Fluctuations. Interscience, New York 1971
27. Kubíček M., Marek M., Husták P., Rýzler V.: J.Theor.Biology in preparation
28. Votruba J. et all.: Chem.Engng Sci. 30(1975)117
29. Holodniok M.: unpublished results

Finite Deformations of Circular Arches

By Ronald S. Reagan, Getty Oil Company

Introduction

The purpose of this paper is not to discuss current or highly original research, but to present an example of a nonlinear structural mechanics problem that can be solved by the general purpose codes considered and demonstrated at this conference. The work presented herein was done as part of the author's dissertation[1]. First, the equations comprising the boundary value problem governing the finite static deformations of inextensible planar rods are derived. Next, dimensionless quantities are introduced to reduce the number of independent parameters appearing in the problem. Then, the problem is specialized to arches which are circular in the unloaded reference configuration and which are loaded by a gravity (dead) loading uniformly distributed along the arch. Next, the shooting method that was used to solve the problem is described. Finally, numerical results are presented for two equilibrium configurations of a clamped semicircular arch.

Boundary Value Problem

The example considered herein is in the class of one-dimensional elasticity problems covered by the theory of rods[2]. This theory treats bodies which are thin enough in two of their dimensions to be adequately approximated by a one-dimensional continuum. The independent variable in a rod problem can be taken as the arc distance measured along the centroidal axis from a convenient reference. The dependent variables are functions which describe the internal stress resultants and deformed geometry of the rod. The equations of the boundary value problem for the circular arch are derived below using the differential geometry of a plane curve, the equations of static equilibrium, and the constitutive (stress-strain) relationship.

Consider the configuration of a curved rod shown in Fig. 1. This configuration could be any deformed or undeformed (stress-free) state of the rod. S is the arc distance measured along the centroidal axis from some convenient origin. The plane curve described by the centroidal axis is located by the position vector $\underset{\sim}{Q}(S)$. The components of $\underset{\sim}{Q}$ with respect to the fixed cartesian coordinate system shown are denoted as X and Y so that

$$(1) \qquad \underset{\sim}{Q} = X\,\underset{\sim}{i} + Y\,\underset{\sim}{j}$$

where $\underset{\sim}{i}$ and $\underset{\sim}{j}$ are unit base vectors as shown. The unit tangent vector $\underset{\sim}{t}$ is defined as

$$(2) \qquad \underset{\sim}{t} = \frac{d\underset{\sim}{Q}}{dS} = \cos v\,\underset{\sim}{i} + \sin v\,\underset{\sim}{j}$$

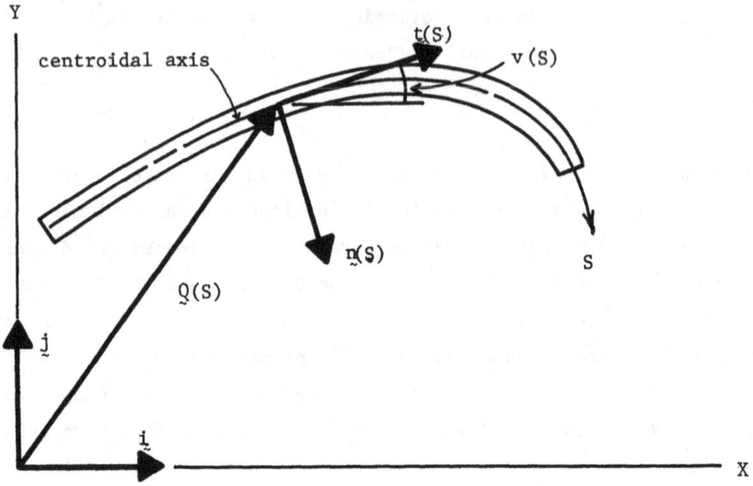

Fig. 1. Differential Geometry of Centroidal Axis

where v is the angle between $\underset{\sim}{i}$ and $\underset{\sim}{t}$ as shown. The unit normal vector $\underset{\sim}{n}$ is defined as

$$(3) \qquad \underset{\sim}{n} = \underset{\sim}{t} \times \underset{\sim}{k} = \sin v\, \underset{\sim}{i} - \cos v\, \underset{\sim}{j}$$

where $\underset{\sim}{k} = \underset{\sim}{i} \times \underset{\sim}{j}$. The curvature K is defined as

$$(4) \qquad K = -\frac{dv}{dS}$$

with the minus sign included to correspond to the related sign convention used below for the bending moment. Derivatives of $\underset{\sim}{t}$ and $\underset{\sim}{n}$ with respect to S are related to $\underset{\sim}{t}$ and $\underset{\sim}{n}$ as

$$(5) \qquad \frac{d\underset{\sim}{t}}{dS} = -\sin v \frac{dv}{dS}\, \underset{\sim}{i} + \cos v \frac{dv}{dS}\, \underset{\sim}{j} = K\, \underset{\sim}{n}$$

and

$$(6) \qquad \frac{d\underset{\sim}{n}}{dS} = \cos v \frac{dv}{dS}\, \underset{\sim}{i} + \sin v \frac{dv}{dS}\, \underset{\sim}{j} = -K\, \underset{\sim}{t}$$

The static equilibrium equations for the rod are derived from force and moment balances for the free body diagram shown in Fig. 2. This diagram shows the forces and moments acting on the portion of the rod between the cross sections at S and $S + \Delta S$. The internal stress resultants are the bending moment M and the force $\underset{\sim}{F}$. The sign convention for the internal stress resultants is indicated on the section at $S + \Delta S$. The external loading $\underset{\sim}{P}$ is a force per unit arc length. Summation of forces yields

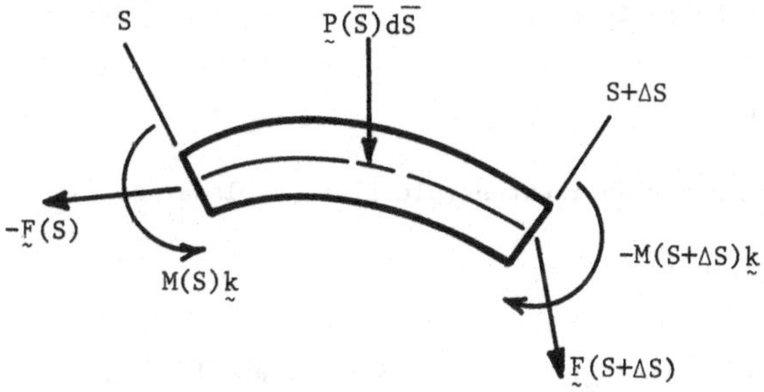

Fig. 2

Free-Body Diagram

$$(7) \qquad \underset{\sim}{F}(S + \Delta S) - \underset{\sim}{F}(S) + \int_{S}^{S+\Delta S} \underset{\sim}{P}(\bar{S})\, d\bar{S} = \underset{\sim}{0}$$

where $\bar{S}$ is a dummy variable of integration and $\underset{\sim}{0}$ is the null vector. Dividing both sides of Eq. 7 be ΔS and taking the limit as $\Delta S \to 0$ results in

$$(8) \qquad \frac{d\underset{\sim}{F}}{dS} = -\underset{\sim}{P} \quad .$$

$\underset{\sim}{F}$ can be expressed in terms of the basis vectors $\underset{\sim}{n}$ and $\underset{\sim}{t}$ as

$$(9) \qquad \underset{\sim}{F} = F_n \underset{\sim}{n} + F_t \underset{\sim}{t}$$

where F_n is the shear force and F_t is the axial force. Introducing Eq. 9 into Eq. 8 and using Eqs. 5 and 6 yields the scalar equations

$$(10) \qquad \frac{dF_n}{dS} = - K F_t - P_n$$

and

$$(11) \qquad \frac{dF_t}{dS} = K F_n - P_t$$

where P_n and P_t are the components of $\underset{\sim}{P}$ with respect to the basis vectors $\underset{\sim}{n}$ and $\underset{\sim}{t}$. Summation of moments about the left end of the free-body diagram yields

$$(12) \qquad -\underset{\sim}{k}\left[M(S+\Delta S) - M(S)\right] + \left[\underset{\sim}{Q}(S+\Delta S) - \underset{\sim}{Q}(S)\right] \times \underset{\sim}{F}(S+\Delta S) + \int_{S}^{S+\Delta S} \left\{\left[\underset{\sim}{Q}(S) - \underset{\sim}{Q}(S)\right] \times \underset{\sim}{P}(\bar{S})\right\} d\bar{S} = \underset{\sim}{0}$$

Dividing both sides of Eq. 7 by ΔS and taking the limits as $\Delta S \to 0$ yields

$$(13) \qquad -\frac{dM}{dS}\underset{\sim}{k} + \underset{\sim}{t} \times \underset{\sim}{F} = \underset{\sim}{0}.$$

Expanding the cross product results in

(14) $$\frac{dM}{dS} = -F_n \quad .$$

The constitutive equation for an inextensible elastic planar rod is

(15) $$M = EI\,(K - K_o)$$

where E is the modulus of elasticity, I is the second moment of the area of the cross section, and K_o is the curvature of the rod in the unstressed reference configuration. This reference configuration for a circular arch is shown in Fig.3. The geometry of the centroidal axis is described by the independent parameters a, which is half of the angle subtended by the arch, and L, which is half of the length of the centroidal axis. The radius R_o and the curvature K_o are given as L/a and a/L, respectively.

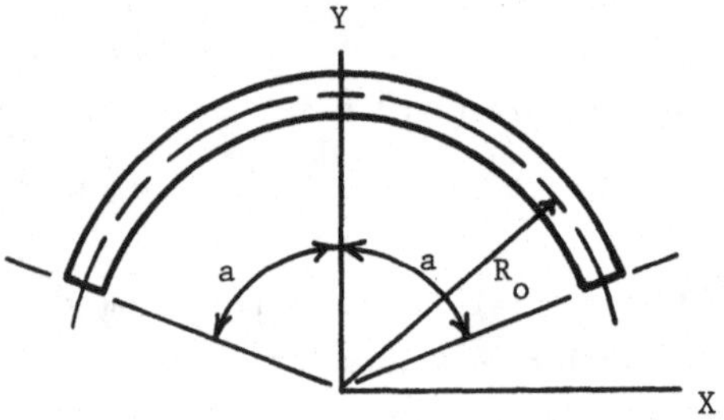

Fig. 3
Reference Configuration
For a Circular Arch

The sixth-order boundary value problem for the circular arch consists of the differential equations (Eqs. 2, 4, 10, 11, and 14), the constitutive equation (Eq. 15), and appropriate boundary conditions. The independent variable is S and the dependent variables are X, Y, v, F_n, F_t, and M. The form of the boundary conditions depends on the support conditions at the ends of the arch. The example to be discussed further is restricted to clamped, semicircular arches loaded with vertical (dead weight) loading. For this loading the vector $\underset{\sim}{P}$ is expressed as

(16) $$\underset{\sim}{P} = -P_o \underset{\sim}{j} = P_o\,(\cos v\, \underset{\sim}{n} - \sin v\, \underset{\sim}{t})$$

where P_o is the load parameter.

Dimensionless quantities are introduced to reduce the number of system parameters from three (EI, L, and a) to one (a). These quantities are defined as follow

characteristic length = L   characteristic force = EIL^{-2}

$$s = \frac{S}{L} \qquad \underset{\sim}{f} = \frac{\underset{\sim}{F} L^2}{EI}$$

$$r_o = \frac{R_o}{L} = \frac{1}{a} \qquad m = \frac{M\,L}{EI}$$

(17) $$\underset{\sim}{q} = \frac{\underset{\sim}{Q}}{L} = x\,\underset{\sim}{i} + y\,\underset{\sim}{j} \qquad \underset{\sim}{p} = \frac{\underset{\sim}{P}L^3}{EI}$$

$$k = L\,K$$

$$k_o = L\,K_o = a$$

Introducing these into the example boundary value problem and using a prime (') to denote differentiation with respect to s yields

$$k = m + a \qquad \text{Constitutive Equation}$$

(18)

Differential Equations — Geometry:

$$x' = \cos v$$
$$y' = \sin v$$
$$v' = -k$$

Differential Equations — Equilibrium:

$$f_n' = -kf_t - p_o \cos v$$
$$f_t' = kf_n + p_o \sin v$$
$$m' = -f_n$$

Boundary Conditions:

at $s = -1$: $x = -2/\pi$, $y = 0$, $v = \pi/2$

at $s = 1$: $x = 2/\pi$, $y = 0$, $v = -\pi/2$

Solution Method and Results

A shooting method was used to solve Eqs. 18 to find equilibrium configurations of the arch for various values of the load parameter p_o. The initial value solutions were calculated with the 4th order Runge-Kutta-Gill integrator RKGS from the IBM Scientific Subroutine Package. The missing boundary conditions were adjusted using Newton's Method with the Jacobian matrix computed by numerical differentiation.

The analysis results are presented in the load-displacement curve in Fig. 4, the deflected shapes in Fig. 5, and the curves in Fig. 6, which show the internal stress resultants as functions of arc distance. In Fig. 4, the load parameter

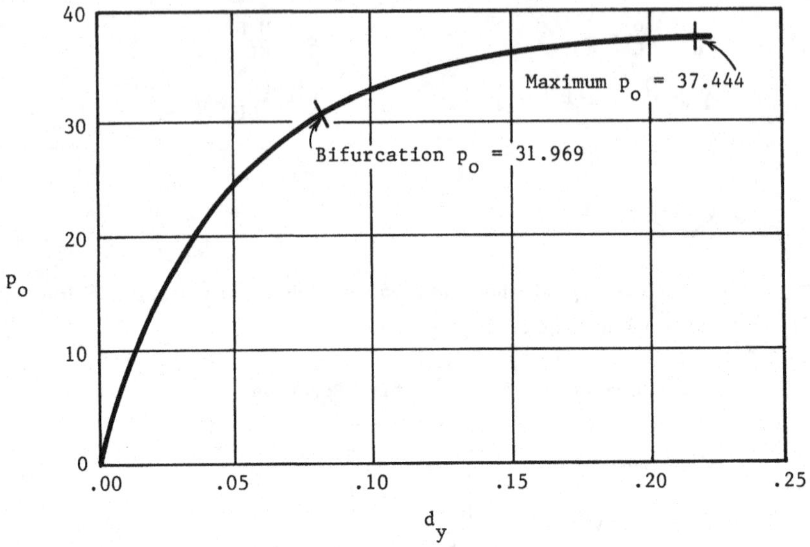

Fig. 4 Load-Displacement Curve

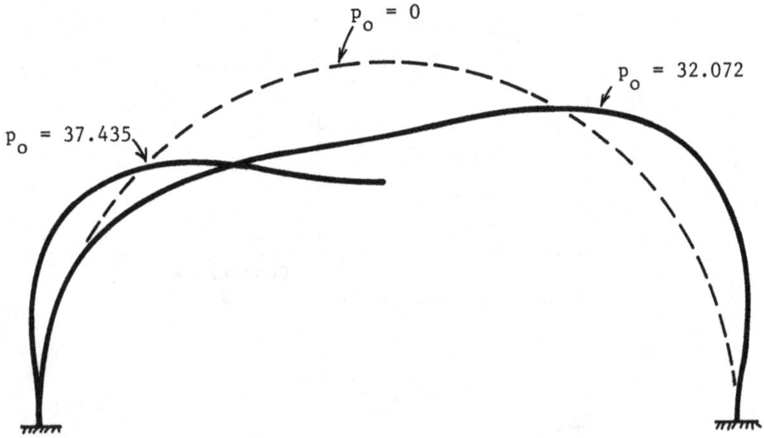

Fig. 5 Deflected Shapes

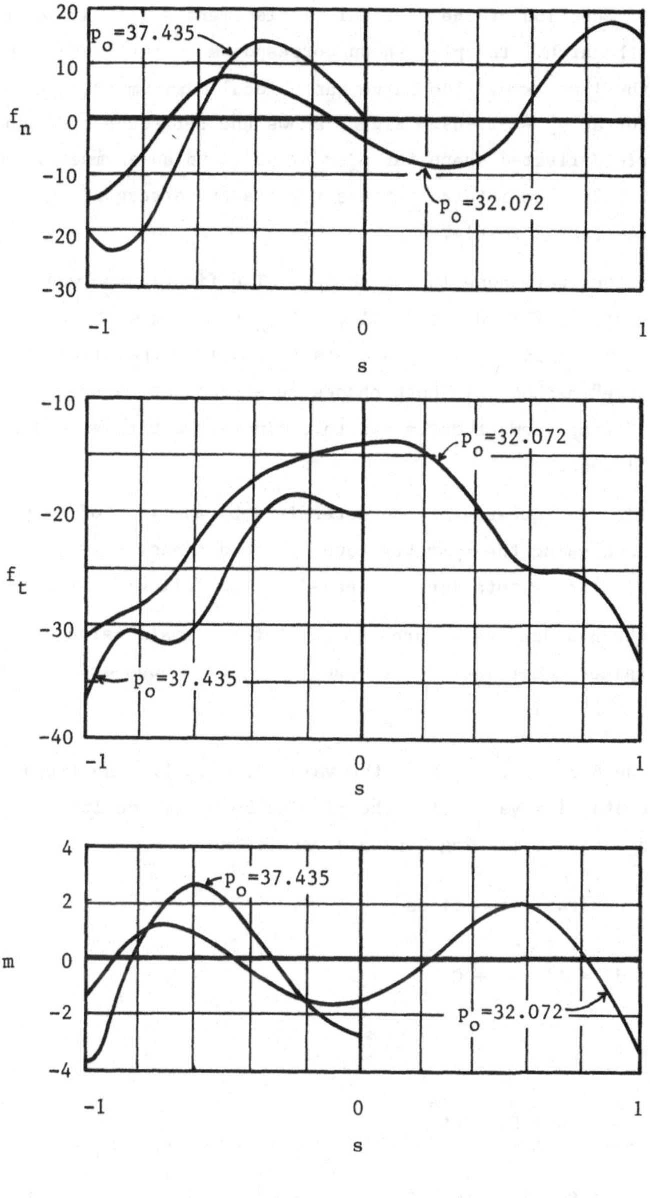

Fig. 7 Internal Stress Resultants

p_o is plotted as a function of the vertical displacement d_y (positive downward) at the center of the arch. The plot shown corresponds to configurations which are symmetric about the line $x=0$. The curve has a local maximum at $p_o = 37.444$ and a bifurcation point at $p_o = 31.969$. Fig. 5 shows the reference configuration for $p_o = 0$, a symmetric deflected shape for $p_o = 37.435$, and an asymmetric deflected shape for $p_o = 32.072$. The internal stress resultants corresponding to these configurations are plotted in Fig. 6.

The calculations were done in two phases. The first phase was to determine symmetric configurations for selected values of p_o starting with zero and ending with the local maximum. The second phase was to estimate the bifurcation point using a "brute force" method. In both phases an extrapolation technique was used to "follow" a load-displacement curve and to estimate starting values for the missing boundary conditions.

The symmetric configurations were determined by analysis of only the left half of the arch and using the symmetry boundary conditions ($f_n = x = v = 0$) at the center $x = 0$. The computations proceeded in the following steps:

1. Solve the boundary value problem (BVP) for a small value of p_o, say 5. Store the values determined for d_y and the missing boundary conditions (f_n, f_t, and m) at $s = -1$.

2. Solve the BVP for p_o = twice the value used in 1. Use linear extrapolatic to estimate starting values for the missing boundary conditions. Store the values of d_y and the missing boundary conditions.

3. Fit the quadratic functions

(19) $$d_y = A + Bt + Ct^2$$

and

(20) $$p_o = D + Et + Ft^2$$

to the last three points (d_y, p_o) calculated previously, where t is an approx- imate arc distance measured along the d_y-p_o curve. Approximate t by the chorc distances between successive points. Fit similar expressions for the missing boundary conditions. Estimate the value of p_o for t incremented by the same amount it was for the last step using extrapolation in Eq. 20. Similarly estimate the corresponding values of the missing boundary conditions. Solve the BVP for the new value of p_o.

4. If p_o decreased in the last step, estimate the maximum value of p_o as the maximum of the parabola that interpolates the last three points. Otherwise repeat step 3.

The bifurcation point and nearby equilibrium configurations were found by adding a small horizontal force at the center of the arch. A procedure similar to the one described to find the symmetric configurations was used. The full arch length and the boundary conditions in Eqs. 18 were used. The p_o-d_x curve was followed instead of p_o-d_y, where d_x is the horizontal displacement at the center of the arch. After a fixed number of load steps, the horizontal force was removed and the p_o-d_x curve was followed in the opposite direction until d_x became negative. Parabolic interpolation was used to determine the bifurcation load.

References

[1] Reagan, Ronald S., "Finite Deformations of Circular Arches," PhD Dissertation, Dept. of Engineering Science, Louisiana St. Univ., August, 1970.

[2] Antman, S. S., "The Theory of Rods," Handbuch der Physik, Vol. VIa/2, Springer-Verlag, Berlin-Heidelberg-New York, 1972.

A SEVERE TEST PROBLEM FOR TWO-POINT BOUNDARY VALUE ROUTINES

by

B. A. Troesch
University of Southern California
Los Angeles, California

1. Problem Statement

Among the problems that have been used repeatedly as test problems for two-point boundary value routines is a nonlinear problem of fifth order. It describes a mathematical model for the similarity solution of rotating flow over a stationary disk, with a magnetic field applied in the direction of the axis of rotation. The governing equations are (see [2], [6], [13])

$$f''' + \tfrac{1}{2}(3-n)ff'' + nf'^2 + g^2 - 1 - sf' = 0 \qquad (1.1a)$$

$$g'' + \tfrac{1}{2}(3-n)fg' + (n-1)gf' - s(g-1) = 0 \qquad (1.1b)$$

with the boundary conditions

$$f(0) = f'(0) = g(0) = 0, \quad f'(\infty) = 0, \quad g(\infty) = 1,$$

where the constant s measures the magnetic field strength and n the vortex behavior far away from the disk. More specifically, the azimuthal velocity behaves like r^{-n}, so that $n = -1$ corresponds to a solid body rotation and $n = 1$ corresponds to a potential vortex.

At present, the interest in this problem stems more from its mathematical and numerical aspects than from its physical significance. It represents one variant of the Falkner-Skan type systems that are still being investigated, so that a fuller understanding of the existence and uniqueness of the solutions would be desirable. As a test problem for two-point boundary value routines the system has the property that its solution becomes progressively more difficult as $n \to 1$ and $s \to 0^+$, thus providing a simple scale for the effectiveness of routines.

In the following sections we will mention existing results and also point out questions that might be answered as a by-product, if the system is used as a test problem for boundary value routines.

2. The known numerical solutions

The original solutions of Holt [4] cover a wide range of parameters, and from these the particular set $n = -0.1$, $s = -0.2$ has often been chosen as a test problem (see [8], [10], [11], [12]). The most difficult parameters for which numerical solutions have been obtained are $s = 0.05$ and $n = 0.261$ [12], and $s = 0.05$ and $n = 0.3$ [1]. These results confirm the structure of the solutions that have been derived for small s in [13], where regions of abrupt changes alternate with regions of gradual changes. The asymptotic results in [13] could best be confirmed by numerical solutions for fixed n and several s values, so that an extrapolation to $s \to 0$ would be possible. Although the ordering of terms in the asymptotic expansion in [13] changes as n increases through $n = 1/3$, it is likely that the numerical solutions for small s would experience a smooth transition.

It is generally agreed that for $s = 0$ solutions exist if $-1 \leq n < n_0$, but no solution exists if $n_0 < n \leq 1$ (see Fig. A1.3). The value of n_0 is 0.121736, but there is no simple interpretation of this value known: the azimuthal velocity of the driving vortex just decreases slowly with the distance from the axis. Although it seems unfair to require a two-point boundary value routine to compute a solution where none exists, it would be of interest to observe the reaction of a routine to parameter values $s = 0$ and n below and above n_0, and, in particular, to find out how accurately the routine could determine n_0.

Usually, the solutions f, g, and their derivatives are plotted against the independent variable. However, an attractive spiral is obtained in an f' versus g plot if s is small and $-1 < n < 1$, especially for the results in [12] and [1].

As pointed out already, the system (1.1) becomes more difficult to solve as $n \to 1^-$. For $n = 1$ there are results reported in [13] down to $s = 0.46$, which were obtained with the program described in [8]. Although the capabilities of this program were not fully used, smaller s values are expected to cause difficulties, since the analysis for small s in [13] leads to

$$f(\infty) = -c(s/2\pi)^{\frac{1}{2}} \exp((1 + \pi/2)/s),$$

so that for $s = 0.1$ we anticipate $|f(\infty)|$ to be about 10^{10}.

3. Analytical conjectures, existence and uniqueness

There are very few analytical results known about the system (1.1): for $s = 0$ the solutions exist for $n = -1$, but does not exist for $n = 1$ and $n = 3$ (only for $n = 3$ is a first integral known); furthermore, there exists an explicit lower bound for $f'(t)$. Miscellaneous integral relations are listed in Appendix 2 that might be useful to check numerical results, but none of them appears to lead to more definite conclusions.

Whereas in systems with a structure similar to eqs. (1.1) non-unique solutions have been found [7], [14], [15], no multiple solutions have been reported for eqs. (1.1) for $n > -1$ and any s. Multiple solutions could most likely be expected to appear, based on the linearized equations for large t, for parameter values $n > 3$, $s < \sqrt{2(n-1)}$ [13]. It has been suggested by K. Stewartson that elusive multiple solutions might be found by starting with the known multiple solutions of a similar system and by gradually transforming its parameters to possibly end up with multiple solutions for the system (1.1). It should be mentioned that the rather peculiar disappearance of the solution for $s = 0$, $n = n_0$ may actually indicate a multiple solution for $s = 0$, $n < n_0$.

It can be expected that the existence and uniqueness should not be affected if the infinite interval is replaced by a sufficiently large finite interval L. The boundary conditions at infinity should then be replaced by "appropriate" boundary conditions at L (see [5], [7]), even though experience shows that the conditions $f'(L) = 0$, $g(L) = 1$ distort the solution only in an insignificantly small interval near the end [11], [12].

As a last remark, we mention that the asymptotic analysis $s \to 0$ presented in [13] leads to a two-point boundary value problem for $-\infty < t < \infty$ where the solution is required to grow only algebraically with a known power. The numerical treatment of this somewhat unusual boundary value problem is described in [3].

Appendix 1. Asymptotic solution for large s

The two leading terms in the asymptotic solution for large s have been computed by Lewellen and King [9]. These results can be used in the continuation method or for comparison with the computed missing initial conditions $f''(0)$, $g'(0)$ and also with $f(\infty)$. With $y=\sqrt{s}t$, $g(t)=G(y)=G_0+G_1/s^2+\ldots$, $f(t) = s^{-3/2}F(y) = s^{-3/2}(F_0+F_1/s^2+\ldots)$ eqs. (1.1) transform to

$$F''' - F' + G^2 - 1 = -s^{-2}(\tfrac{1}{2}(3-n)FF''+n\ F'^2)$$

$$G'' - G+1 \quad = -s^{-2}(\tfrac{1}{2}(3-n)FG' +(n-1)GF').$$

The leading terms are independent of n:

$$F_0(y) = -(e^{-2y}+e^{-y}(4+6y)-5)/6, \quad G_0(y)=1-e^{-y},$$

so that the lowest order inital conditions become

$$f_0''(0) = -2/(3\sqrt{s}), \qquad g_0'(0) = \sqrt{s}.$$

The next terms are rather involved and will not be given here (there are some minor misprints in [9]); they lead to the initial conditions

$$f''(0) = -2/(3s^{\frac{1}{2}}) + (181-143n)/(4320s^{5/2})+\ldots,$$

$$g'(0) = s^{\frac{1}{2}} + (7-13n)/(144s^{3/2})+\ldots,$$

and to

$$f(\infty) = s^{-3/2}(-5/6 + (2023-4309n)/(8640\,s^2)+\ldots).$$

The solution, to any order, consists of polynomials and decaying exponentials, so that it is expected to furnish a good approximation only if the oscillations have a small amplitude (like for $n \approx -1$) or if the solutions are expected to be nonoscillatory (for $n > 1$). For instance, Fig. A1.1 shows that for $n=3.0$ the two leading terms furnish a reasonable approximation to the numerical results down to $s=3.0$, especially for small t, with $f''(0)$ and $g'(0)$ even at $s=2.1$ accurate to a fraction of a percent. Good agreement is also observed for $n=1.0$ down to $s=1.0$ (see Fig. A1.2). It is remarkable how well the product of the missing initial conditions $f''(0)\,g'(0)$ is approximated by the asymptotic value of $-2/3$, even down to small s values:

TABLE

n	s	$f''(0)g'(0)$	n	s	$f''(0)g'(0)$	n	s	$f''(0)g'(0)$
-1.0	0.0	-0.728	0.0	0.0	-0.532	1.0	2.0	-0.658
-1.0	1.0	-0.678	0.0	1.0	-0.658	3.0	2.1	-0.643
-0.5	0.0	-0.688	1.0	1.0	-0.626	3.0	3.0	-0.653

Appendix 2. Miscellaneous relations

In this appendix miscellaneous relations are listed. From eq. (1.1a) and the boundary conditions it follows that

$$f'(t) > s/2n - (1/n + s^2/4n^2)^{\frac{1}{2}}, \quad \text{or } f'(t) > -(1/n)^{\frac{1}{2}}$$

(cf. Fig. Al.2 for n = 1).

For certain parameter values, $f(\infty)$ is difficult to compute, so that

$$f(\infty) = -\frac{1}{s}\left(f''(0) + \frac{3}{2}(1-n)\int_0^\infty f'(t)^2 dt + \int_0^\infty (1-g^2)\, dt\right)$$

may be of some value as a check. For the potential vortex (n = 1) this equation simplifies, and in this case, the general behavior of g(t) is also known for t > 0:

$$g'(t) > 0, \qquad 0 < g(t) < 1.$$

Furthermore, a somewhat curious equation holds for n = 1 (and any s)

$$f''(0)^2 = 2\int_0^\infty (f f''^2 + f'' g^2) dt.$$

Numerical results indicate that $f'(t)$ never becomes positive if n = 1. From this property of the solution it would readily follow that $f'(t)$ has a single minimum, that $g''(t) < 0$, and that $f(t) > -s(1-g)/g'$.

A first integral of the eqs. (1.1) is only known for n = 3 (see [13]), which leads to

$$f''(0)^2 + g'(0)^2 = s,$$

and consequently n = 3, s = 0 does not admit a solution. For n = 3 there also exists the upper bound

$$g(t) \leq (1 + (s^2/12))^{\frac{1}{2}}.$$

The most conspicuous properties observed in the numerical solutions for $n < 1$ are: a) $g(t) \geq 0$, and hence, $g'(0) > 0$; b) $f(t) \leq 0$ and hence, $f''(0) < 0$; c) f', f'', g' oscillate with decaying amplitude, so that the first maximum is the largest; this appears to be true even for small s, and n near 1 where the oscillations are far from sinusoidal. But for the most difficult parameter values reported in [1] and [12] the behavior of the linearized solution about the asymptotic values takes over already after the first few oscillations. If the solution, say $f'(t)$ behaves locally like $\exp(\lambda_r t)\sin(\lambda_i t)$, then $\lambda = \lambda_r + i\lambda_i$ eventually satisfies

$$f(\infty) = -4(\lambda^2 - s + i\sqrt{2(1-n)})/(2(n-3)\lambda).$$

This relation between the damping λ_r, the wavelength $2\pi/\lambda_i$, and $f(\infty)$ are well approached, for instance, in the solution in [12].

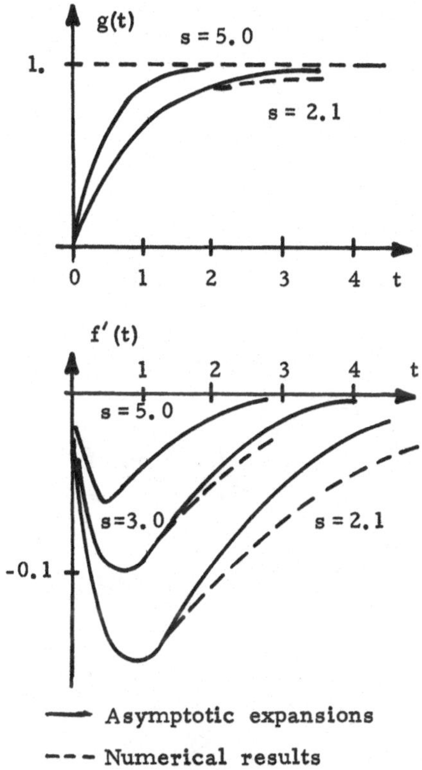

n = 3.0

Fig. A1.1

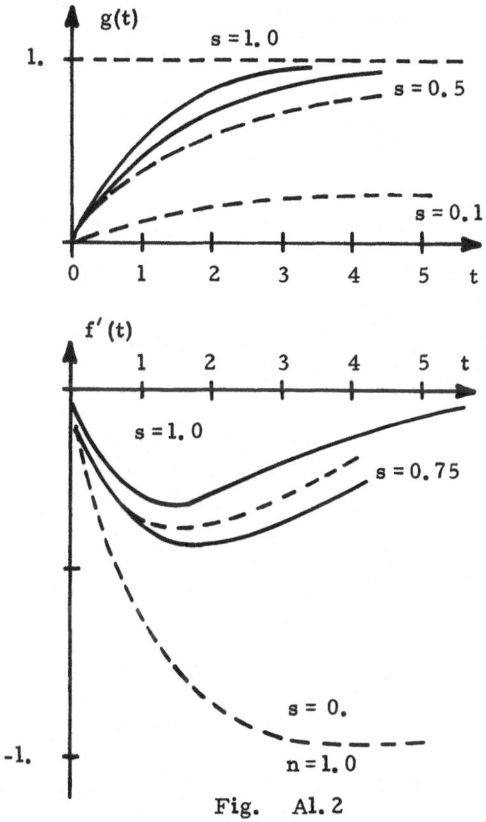

Fig. A1.2

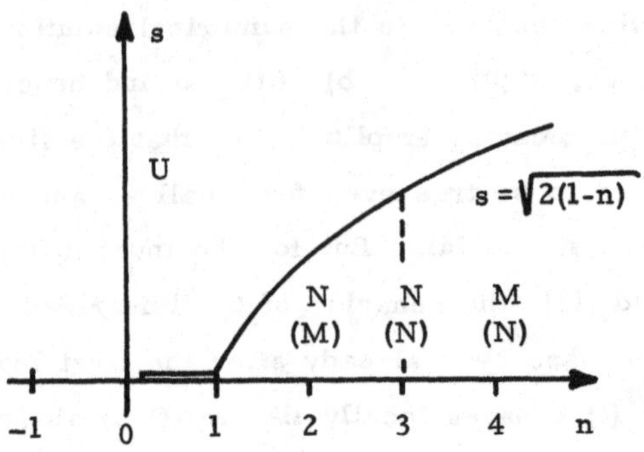

Conjectures from matching with the linearized solution [13]: U unique solution, N no solution, M multiple solutions for $f(\infty) < 0$. For $f(\infty) > 0$ the symbols are in parentheses.

Fig. A1. 3

References

1 Ascher, U., Christianson, J., and Russell, R.D. (these Proceedings)

2 Brown, S.N., and Stewartson, K. SIAM-AMS Proceedings, Vol. 10, 1976

3 Burggraf, O.R., and Stewartson, K. J. Appl. Math. Phys. (ZAMP) 26, 540-559 (1975)

4 Holt, J. Comm. ACM 7, 366-373 (1964)

5 Keller, H.B., Numerical Solution of Two-Point Boundary Value Problems, Regional Conference Series in Appl. Math. Vol. 25, SIAM, Philadelphia, Pennsylvania, 1976

6 King, W.S., and Lewellen, W.S. Physics of Fluids 7, 1674-1680 (1964)

7 Lentini, M., and Keller, H.B. (these Proceedings)

8 Lentini, M., and Pereyra, V. Math. Comp. 28, 981-1003 (1974)

9 Lewellen, W.S., and King, W.S. Report ATN-63 (9227)-1, Aerospace Corp., El Segundo, California (1962)

10 Miele, A., Aggarwal, A.K., Tietze, J.L. J. Comp. Physics 15, 117-133 (1974)

11 Roberts, S.M., and Shipman, J.S., Two-Point Boundary Value Problems: Shooting Methods, American Elsevier, New York, New York, 1972

12 Scott, M.R., and Watts, H.A. Report SAND75-0539, Sandia Laboratories, Albuquerque, New Mexico, 1975

13 Stewartson, K., and Troesch, B.A. J. Appl. Math. Phys. (ZAMP) 28, 951-963 (1977).

14 White, A.B., Jr. Report CNA-132, Center Num. Analysis, U. of Texas at Austin, 1978

15 Zandbergen, P.J., and Dijkstra, D. J. Eng. Math. 11, 167-188 (1977)

COMPUTER CODES AND OPTIMAL CONTROL THEORY

John Casti

Department of Computer Applications
and Information Systems

New York University, New York, N.Y.

1. Introduction

The majority of interesting boundary-value problems in physics and engineering arise through some variational principle. As is well known [1,2], the variational problem generates, via the Euler-Lagrange equations, a boundary-value problem whose numerical solution is the focus of this workshop. Mathematically, the foregoing set-up is essentially a classical problem in the calculus of variations. In the past two decades, an alternate point of view has arisen, whereby instead of focusing attention upon minimizing *trajectories*, we are concerned with minimizing *policies*. This is the point at which the calculus of variations parts company with modern control theory. Our goal in this short note is to characterize a few of the features of optimal control problems which distinguish their numerical treatment from the BVP of mathematical physics, and also to discuss some of the desiderata for standardized computer codes for dealing with such problems.

2. BVP and Feedback Control

The general problem we are concerned with is the minimization (over u) of

$$\int_0^T g(x,u)dt \quad ,$$

where the n- and m-dimensional vector functions x and u are related by the differential equation

$$\dot{x} = f(x,u) \quad , \quad x(0) = x_0 \quad .$$

The classical approach to the solution of this problem is to define the system Hamiltonian

$$H(x,u,\lambda) = g(x,u) + [\lambda(t),f(x,u)] \quad ,$$

and to employ the minimum principle. This leads to the BVP

$$\dot{x} = f(x,u) \quad , \qquad x(0) = x_0 \quad ,$$

$$-\dot{\lambda} = \frac{\partial g}{\partial x} + \left(\frac{\partial f}{\partial x}\right) \lambda \quad , \qquad \lambda(T) = 0 \quad ,$$

with the optimal control u* being that function of x and λ which minimizes H.

From a modern control-theoretic standpoint, the foregoing approach is deficien in that the minimizing control $u^*(t)$ is given only as a function of t, i.e. *open-loop*. For a variety of reasons, we prefer a *feedback* solution for which $u = u(x,t)$.

Since almost all effective procedures for solving the general control problem in feedback form rely upon some type of linearization, henceforth we shall discuss the problem of computer codes for the case in which g is quadratic and f is linear. Thus, we shall be concerned with efficient computer codes for solving the linear-quadratic (LQ) problem

$$\min_u \int_0^T [(x,Qx) + (u,Ru)]dt \quad ,$$

$$\dot{x} + Fx + Gu \quad , \qquad x(0) = x_0 \quad ,$$

where the matrices Q, R, F and G may be time-varying. By the above remark, it is clear that the existence of efficient codes for routinely solving LQ problems enable us to deal with the general case via successive approximations (assuming, of course, requisite smoothness of the functions of g and f).

3. LQ Problems

Since the early 1960's, it has been well known [3,4] that the above LQ problem has the feedback solution

$$u^*(x) = -R^{-1}(t)G'(t)P(t)x \quad ,$$

where P(t) is the solution of the matrix Riccati equation

$$-\dot{P}(t) = Q(t) + PF(t) + F'(t)P - PG(t)R^{-1}(t)G'(t)P \quad , \quad (*)$$

$$P(T) = 0 \quad .$$

Many more details concerning the above result and its theoretical and computational implications may be found in [4]. To avoid technical digressions, we shall assume that R is invertible on $0 \le t \le T$ and that the system is completely controllable and completely observable (see[4] for more details on these conditions).

The preceding result shows that for computational purposes, the numerical solution of optimal control problems is equivalent to the effective solution of the matrix Riccati equation (*). Thus, we examine the question of standard computer codes for the solution of (*).

4. Computer Codes for Matrix Riccati Equations

The first computational question that must be addressed in connection with the solution of (*) is that it is a *final-value* problem. Thus, it is necessary to either: (a) integrate (*) from t = T to t = 0, storing the function P(t) (off-line) or (b) perform the integration without storing P(t), determine P(0) and then re-integrate (*) in the forward direction. In either case, the accurate determination of P(t) is of prime concern, particularly in case (b) when we must re-integrate the system. The accuracy problem is especially acute when T is large, the typical case arising in practice.

Given the very specific structure of (*), it is perhaps surprising that special numerical integration schemes have not been developed to exploit the quadratic nature of the equation. However, this has not been the case. Usually, some standard integration formulas such as Runge-Kutta, Adams-Moulton, etc. are employed in the integration process. Thus, as our first step in the assembly of effective codes for control problems we state:

Problem I: Develop and implement special-purpose numerical integration schemes for the solution of (*) which take advantage of the structure of the equations to more efficiently solve the Riccati matrix equation to a specified degree of accuracy.

Since we must integrate the system dynamics in a forward direction to determine the optimal feedback control, substantial amounts of computer storage and time would be saved if we had effective procedures for determining the correct initial condition for (*) at t = 0. It can be shown that the solution of (*) is numerically stable with respect to the initial conditions. Thus, rapid techniques for estimating P(0) to a given level of accuracy is another component of good codes for LQ problems. The dependence of P(0) on the time interval T and the problem data forms our

Problem II: Determine effective extrapolation and/or estimation procedures for calculating P(0) from the problem data and the duration interval of the process.

As in many other physical problems, it is often the case that the defining data of the LQ problem (the matrices F, G, Q, R) have special structure. This is especially the case for the cost matrices Q and R, which are often diagonal or sparse due to the fact that costs are only incurred due to a small number of the state or control coordinates. For example, in a single-input system, if Q = diagonal, R = I and F = triangular, then if we choose the coordinate system in the input space so that $G = \begin{pmatrix} 0 \\ 0 \\ \vdots \\ 0 \\ 1 \end{pmatrix}$, it can be verified that P(t) is triangular for all t. The point is that the structural features of the problem data often combine to produce structural properties of the solution matrix P. The generalized X-Y functions [4], which replace (*) by a much lower-dimensional system when the number of system inputs and outputs are small relative to the dimension of the state, are another aspect of this situation. These observations lead to

> <u>Problem III</u>: Develop computer codes which take advantage of particular structures in the problem data to reduce the amount of computational work to produce P(t).

Finally, we note that in a number of interesting cases, we are concerned with the infinite-interval problem $T = \infty$. Assuming then that F, G, Q, R are constant matrices, we must solve the *algebraic* Riccati equation (ARE)

$$Q + PF + F'P - PGR^{-1}G'P = 0 \quad .$$

There are a number of connections between the ARE and the matrix Lyapunov equation

$$AX + XA' = Y \quad ,$$

a problem approachable through conventional linear algebra codes. However, the special quadratic structure of the ARE suggests that improvements over the use of standard linear codes might be possible and, indeed, in some instances this has been shown to be the case. For example, in [5] it is shown that the $n(n + 1)/2$ equations represented by the ARE can be replaced by nm for the components of the feedback law $K = -R^{-1}G'P$. If $m << n$, this represents a considerable computational reduction. Such a result suggests

> <u>Problem IV</u>: Determine special algorithms and methods for the numerical solution of the ARE, taking into account the special properties and symmetries of the problem data.

5. Some Existing Codes

We are aware of the existence of only a few formal computer packages for dealing with system-theoretic and optimal control problems. For instance, at the Institute di Automatica of Bologna University (Italy), a very extensive set of programs for dealing with linear system problems has recently been published [6]. In this set of routines, one finds a wide variety of programs for performing various matrix operations associated with tests for controllability (rank determination), realization theory (reduction to triangular form), calculation of Kronecker indices (determinations of a basis from a set of vectors) and so forth. However, no optimization components appear among these routines. Furthermore, the routines are designed only for the treatment of linear systems and, as a result, are essentially special matrix manipulation programs.

Another set of published programs which does contain primitive routines for Riccati matrix computations was assembled by a group at SMU a few years ago [7]. However, the routines given for optimal control are weak in the sense that no real effort was made to present state-of-the art procedures for integrating the relevant Riccati equation. Other codes suitable for various procedures such as system identification, distributed parameter control and stability analysis are known to be available at research centers like MIT, Lund U. (Sweden) and IRIA (France). However, since these codes have not been published, their utility for the general scientific community remains very restricted. What is needed is a widely-distributed collection of routines incorporating the best features of the above-mentioned codes, while at the same time being aware of the rapid developments taking place on the theoretical front, which have implication for numerical solution of control problems.

6. Summary

Here we have briefly sketched what, in our opinion, appears to be a program for the development of computer codes useful in optimal control theory. Taking into account the importance of feedback decisions in control, it has been shown that the methods available for solving classical variational problems and their associated BVP may not be suitable for optimal control considerations. It can only be hoped that some of the problems indicated here will soon be addressed by the computer community and that efficient, widely available codes for optimal control will soon become available.

REFERENCES

[1] Courant, R. and D. Hilbert, *Methods of Mathematical Physics*, Interscience, New York, 1953.

[2] Lanczos, C., *Variational Principles of Mechanics*, University of Toronto Press, Toronto, 1960.

[3] Kalman, R., "Contributions to the Theory of Optimal Control," *Boll. Soc. Mat. Mexicana,* 5 (1960), 102-119.

[4] Casti, J., *Dynamical Systems and their Applications: Linear Theory,* Academic Press, New York, 1977.

[5] Casti, J., "A New Equation for the Linear Regulator Problem," *Journal of Optimization Theory & Applications,* 17 (1975), 169-175.

[6] Beghelli, S. and R. Guidorzi, *Teoria dei Sistemi: Esercizi e Programmi Fortran,* Patron Editore, Bologna, Italy 1978, (Italian).

[7] Melsa, J. and D. Gibson, eds. *Computational Techniques and Fortran Programs for Linear Optimal Control Problems*, McGraw-Hill, New York, 1970.

Editor's Note: This paper was not presented at the conference due to medical problems in Dr. Casti's family. We are pleased to include the paper, list Dr. Casti as a participant, and report that Dr. Casti's family is now in good health. BC

Workshop on Benchmark Problems and Code Availability

Chaired and Summarized by

Paul Nelson*

Georgia Institute of Technology

This workshop took the form of brief presentations and general discussions concerning the title subjects, and also the problem of code transportability. It is only with considerable trepidation that I attempt to paraphrase and summarize the various views presented, because most participants are decidedly capable of expressing their views without the aid of an intermediary. I apologize and accept responsibility for any misrepresentations, and suggest that anyone interested in further details contact the participants, both for what they truly said and what they would now say, given another opportunity.

The workshop opened with a presentation by H. A. Watts of eleven test problems which have been found useful in the code development program at Sandia Laboratories. The problems were specific examples of the following general classes·

1. Problems with highly oscillatory solutions.
2. Problems with strongly exponential solutions.
3. Large systems.
4. Problems with a boundary layer (a) near an end of the internal and (b) well away form an endpoint.
5. Problems with discontinuous coefficients.
6. Problems having singular intervals or singular coefficients.
7. Eigenvalue problems.
8. Nonlinear problems
9. Problems with general (nonlinear, nonseparated) boundary conditions

---

*Permanent Address: Department of Mathematics, Texas Tech University, Lubbock, Texas 79409.

In the presentation by Watts it was suggested that preferably a benchmark problem would have a known analytic solution, although this may not always be consistent with other desiderata. Peter Deuflhard (Technical University of Munich) expressed the opinion that a better test of the merit of a code is its ability to solve "real-world" problems whose solutions are not known analytically. Several people expressed concern as to how one knows, for such problems, whether the code is producing answers or merely numbers which appear reasonable. M. R. Osborne (Australian National University) suggested using internal consistency (e.g. comparison of results with different specified error tolerances) to validate code results for such problems. The chairman suggested that this approach is valid only if it is known a priori that the problem is well-posed and the method is computationally stable for the problem. Fred Krogh (Jet Propulsion Laboratory) warned of the tendency of code developers inadvertently to "fine-tune" their code to the test problems they have selected with a consequential inadvertent unfairness in comparing the performance of other codes on this test set. It is clear that there was some considerable divergence of opinion and philosophy concerning benchmark problems, not all of which was resolved by the discussion.

Fred Krogh also briefly discussed the impact of new languages upon transportability, with the proposed new Department of Defense language as an example. John Gersting (Indiana University/Purdue University at Indianopolis) described some interesting aspects of FORTRAN 77. Bart Childs (Texas A&M) suggested that it might be some time before it was necessary to be concerned in practice with FORTRAN 77. There was some discussion of the utility of verifiers (e.g. PFORT and the IMSL verifier) in assuring that a code is written in standard FORTRAN. There was further discussion, in which Victor Pereyra (Caltech) played a significant role, of the degree to which a code developer is obligated to insure that his code is written in standard language.

The codes presented at this meeting are largely available through the authors, sometimes on payment of a nominal fee for handling.

Note: The addresses given at the end of this volume are current except for Victor Pereyra and Marinela Lentini. Their address is now

Apartado 59002
ESCUELA DE COMPUTACION - U. C. V.
CARACAS VENEZUELA 105

The PASVA3 code is available from them or through the NAG Library (in an earlier version). Messrs. Albasiny, Ascher, Bailey, Bulirsch, Childs, Gersting, Gladwell, Luning, Olson, Russell, Scott and Watts should be contacted directly. BC

Appendix

of Related Information

Working Conference On Codes
For
BVP's in ODEs

	May 14 Sunday	May 15 Monday	May 16 Tuesday	May 17 Wednesday
Chairmen:		Allen	Archer	Vandevender
8:30		IP-Bulirsch	IP-Reddien	IP-Denman
9:00	Organizing Breakfast			
9:30		IP-Scott	IP-Russell	CP-Bramley
10:00				CP-Luning-Perry
10:30		IP-Gladwell	CP-Carey-Humphey	CP-Kubicek
11:00			CP-Carey-Wheeler	CP-Sternberg[2]
11:30		CP-Osborne	CP-Kagiwada-Kalaba	CP-Reagan
12:00		CP-Anderson	CP-Preuss	CP-Troesch
12:30		LUNCH	LUNCH	LUNCH
1:00	Welcome			
Chairmen:	Meyer	Diaz	Lord	Naugle
1:30	IP-Daniel	Workshop-Krogh	Workshop-Sincovec	Workshop-Nelson
2:00		Shooting Points	Basis Selection	Benchmark Probs.
2:30	IP-Watts			Transportability
3:00		IP-Ascher	Workshop-White	Closing
3:30	IP-Deufelhard		Mesh Selection	
4:00		IP-Porter		
4:30	IP-Pereyra		CP-Bailey-Shampine	
5:00		CP-Gersting	CP-Albisany	
5:30	CP-Lentini; Keller	Workshop-Childs	Workshop-Pereyra	
6:00	CP-Olson	Working Codes	Error Estimation	
6:30	Social Workshop			

5/11/78

1. Dr. I.K. Abu-Shumays
Bettis Atomic Power Lab.
Box 79
W. Mifflin, PA 15122

2. Mr. E.L. Albasiny
Division of Numer. Anal. & Comp.
National Physical Laboratory
Teddington, Middlesex TW11 OLW
ENGLAND

3. Dr. Richard Allen
Department of Math. & Statistics
University of New Mexico
Albuquerque, NM 87131

4. Dr. Donald G.M. Anderson
Division of Applied Sciences
Harvard University
Cambridge, MA 02138

5. Dr. Uri Ascher
Department of Computer Science
University of British Columbia
2075 Westbrook Mall
Vancouver B.C. CANADA V6T 1W5

6. Dr. David Archer
Dupont-Rachford Assoc.
1201 Dairy Ashford Road
Houston, TX 77079

7. Dr. Paul B. Bailey
Applied Mathematics Div. 5121
Sandia Laboratories
Albuquerque, NM 87115

8. Dr. J. Stuart Bramley
Department of Mathematics
Livingstone Tower
26 Richmond Street
Glasgow, SCOTLAND

9. Dr. Coleman Brosilow
Case Western Reserve University
Department of Chemical Engineering
Cleveland, OH 44106

10. Dr. Roland Bulirsch
Institut fur Mathematik
Der Technischen Universitat Munchen
D-8000 Munchen 2
Postfach 202420 WEST GERMANY

11. Dr. James W. Burgmeier
Department of Mathematics
University of Vermont
Burlington, VT 05401

12. Dr. Graham F. Carey
Dept. Aerospace Engr. & Engr. Mech.
University of Texas at Austin
Austin, TX 78712

13. Dr. John Casti
Grad. School of Business Admin.
New York University
100 Trinity Place
New York, NY 10006

14. Dr. S. Bart Childs
Department of Industrial Engr.
Computer & Info. Sci. Division
Texas A & M University
College Station, TX 77843

15. Mr. Jan Christiansen
Dept. of Mathematics
Simon Fraser University
Burnaby, B.C. CANADA V5A 1S6

16. Dr. J.W. Daniel
Department of Mathematics
University of Texas at Austin
Austin, TX 78712

17. Mr. Bruce Darlow
(Rice University)
5333 Richmond # 7
Houston, TX 77056

18. Dr. Eugene Denman
Department of Electrical Engr.
University of Houston
Houston, TX 77004

19. Dr. Julio Cesar Diaz
Department of Mathematics
University of Kentucky
Lexington, KY 40506

20. Dr. Peter Deuflhard
Institut fur Mathematik
Der Technischen Universitat Munchen
D-8000 Munchen 2
Postfach 202420 WEST GERMANY

21. Mr. Thurman Elder
Department of Mathematics
Eastern New Mexico University
Portales, NM 88130

22. Mr. Larry Ellis
E.G. & G. Idaho
Computer Sci. Center Rm C-11
Idaho Falls, ID 83401

23. Mr. Milton Gentry
Department of Mathematics
University of Texas at Austin
Austin, TX 78712

24. Dr. John Gersting
Department of Mathematical Sciences
IUPUI
1201 East 38th St.
Indianapolis, IN 46205

25. Dr. Ian Gladwell
Department of Mathematics
University of Manchester
Manchester M13 9PL ENGLAND

26. Ms. Ruth Gonzalez
Applied Research Labs.
University of Texas at Austin
P.O. Box 8029
Ausitn, TX 78712

27. Dr. B. Hassard
State University of New York
Department of Mathematics
Diefendorf Hall - 5
Buffalo, NY 14216

28. Mr. Neal Hennegan
Shell Oil Company
Head Office, Civil Engr.
Box 2099
Houston, TX 77001

29. Mr. David Humphrey
Lawrence Livermore Labs.
Mail Stop L122
Livermore, CA 90034

30. Mr. Donald Jezewski
(NASA-JSC)
15318 Cobre Valley Dr.
Houston, TX 77062

31. Dr. Fred Krogh
Jet Propulsion Lab.
4800 Oak Grove Drive
Pasadena, CA 91103

32. Dr. Milan Kubicek
Department of Chemical Engr.
Prague Inst. of Chem. Technology
16628 Praha 6 CZECHOSLOVAKIA

33. Dr. Marianela Lentini
Applied Mathematics 1-1-50
Firestone Laboratory
California Institute of Technology
Pasadena, CA 91125

34. Dr. Mike Lord
(on leave-Univ. Texas-Arlington)
Dept. of Applied Mathematics 2613
Sandia Laboratories
Albuquerque, NM 87115

35. Dr. C.D. Luning
Department of Mathematics
Sam Houston State University
Huntsville, TX 77340

36. Mr. Robert Malahy
(Rice University)
8007 Mullins
Houston, TX 77036

37. Dr. Melvin J. Maron
Dept. of Appl. Math. & Comp. Sci.
Speed Scientific School
University of Louisville
Louisville, KY 40208

38. Dr. Gunter Meyer
School of Mathematics
Georgia Tech
Atlanta, GA 30332

39. Ms. Kitty Morel
Department of Mathematics
University of Texas at Arlington
Arlington, TX 7xxxx

40. Dr. Norman Naugle
Department of Mathematics
Texas A & M University
College Station, TX 77843

41. Dr. Paul Nelsen
(on leave-Texas Tech Univ.)
School of Mathematics
Georgia Tech
Atlanta, GA 30332

42. Dr. Andrew M. Olson
University of Puerto Rico
Faculty of Natural Sciences
Department of Mathematics
Rio Piedras, PR 00931

43. Dr. M.R. Osborne
Computer Centre
The Australian National University
P.O. Box 4
Canberra ACT 2600 AUSTRALIA

44. Mr. James Paget
305 Memorial Drive
Room 606C
Cambridge, MA 02139

45. Dr. Victor Pereyra
Applied Mathematics 101-50
Firestone Laboratory
California Institute of Technology
Pasadena, CA 91125

46. Dr. W.L. Perry
Department of Mathematics
Texas A & M University
College Station, TX 77843

47. Dr. Steven Pruess
Department of Math. & Stat.
University of New Mexico
Albuquerque, NM 87131

48. Dr. H.R. Porter
Institute for System Science
University of Louisville
Louisville, KY 40208

49. Dr. Ronald S. Reagan
Getty Oil Company
3903 Stoney Brook
Houston, TX 77042

50. Dr. G.W. Reddien
Department of Mathematics
Vanderbilt University
Nashville, TN 37235

51. Mr. Richard Rosencranz
NASA-JSC
Mail Code FD6
Houston, TX 77058

52. Dr. R.D. Russell
Department of Mathematics
Simon Fraser University
Burnaby, B.C. CANADA V5A 1S6

53. Dr. Melvin Scott
Dept. of Applied Mathematics 2613
Sandia Laboratories
Albuquerque, NM 87115

54. Dr. Richard Sincovec
Energy Technology Applications
Boeing Comp. Serv.- Mail Stop 9C-01
P.O. Box 24346
Seattle, WA 98124

55. Mr. Sylvester Thompson
Babcock-Wilcox
Route 5 Box 432
Madison Heights, VA 24572

56. Dr. B.A. Troesch
Department of Aerospace Engr.
University of Southern California
Los Angeles, CA 90007

57. Dr. W.H. Vandevender
Applied Math. Division 2613
Sandia Laboratories
Albuquerque, NM 87115

58. Dr. H.A. Watts
Dept. of Applied Mathematics-2613
Sandia Laboratories
Albuquerque, NM 87115

59. Dr. Klaus Well
(on leave-German Aero. Lab(DFULR))
Dept. of Aero. Engr. & Engr. Mech.
University of Texas at Austin
Austin, TX 78712

60. Dr. Mary F. Wheeler
Department of Mathematical Sci.
Rice University
Houston, TX 77002

61. Dr. Andy White
Department of Mathematics
University of Texas at Austin
Austin, TX 78712

62. Dr. Pedro E. Zadunaisky
Observ. Nacional de Fisica Cosmica
Av. Mitre 3100
San Miguel(Buenos Aires) 1663
ARGENTINA

1. J.H. Ahlberg and T. Ito, A collocation method for two-point boundary value problems, Math. Comp. 29(1975), 761-776.
2. Z. Aktas and H.J. Stetter, A classification and survey of numerical methods for boundary value problems in ordinary differential equations, Int. J. for Num. Meth. in Engr., 11(1977), 771-796.
3. E.L. Albasiny and W.D. Hoskins, Cubic spline solutions to two-point boundary value problems, Comput. J. 12(1969/70), 151-153.
4. R. Alexander, Diagonally implicit Runge-Kutta methods for stiff ODE's, SIAM J. Num. Anal. 14(1977), 1006-1021.
5. R.C. Allen, J.W. Burgmeier, P. Mundorff, and G.M. Wing, A numerical algorithm suggested by problems of transport in periodic media: the matrix case, J. Math. Anal. and Appl., 37(1972), 725-740.
6. R.C. Allen and G.M. Wing, An invariant imbedding algorithm for the solution of inhomogeneous two-point boundary value problems, J. Comp. Phys. 14(1974), 40-58.
7. R.C. Allen, Jr. and G.M. Wing, Generalized trigonometric identities and invariant imbedding, J. Math. Anal. and Appl., 42(1973), 397-408.
8. E.L. Allgower and S.F. McCormick, Newton's method with mesh refinement for numerical solution of nonlinear two-point boundary value problems, Num. Math., 29(1978), 237-260.
9. R. Alt, A-stable one-step methods with stepsize control for stiff systems of ordinary differential equations, Comp. and Appl. Math. 4(1978), 29-35.
10. U. Amdursky and A. Ziv, The numerical treatment of linear highly oscillatory ODE systems by reduction to non-oscillatory type, IBM Israel Science Center, Rep. 039, Haifa, (1976).
11. David Archer and Julio Cesar Diaz, A family of modified collocation methods for second order two-point boundary value problems, SIAM J. Num. Anal. 15(1978), 242-254.
12. Argonne Code Center, Argonne National Labs., 9700 S. Cass Ave., Argonne, Ill, 60439.
13. U. Ascher, J. Christiansen and R.D. Russell, A collocation solver for two mixed order systems of boundary value problems, Tech. Rep. 77-13, Computer Science Dept., Univ. of British Columbia, 1977.
14. U. Ascher and R.D. Russell, Evaluation of B-splines for solving systems of boundary value problems, Tech. Rep. 77-14, Computer Science Dept., Univ. of British Columbia, 1977.
15. Uri Ascher, Discrete least squares approximations for ordinary differential equations, SIAM J. Num. Anal. 15(1978) 478-496.
16. U. Ascher, J. Christiansen, and R.D. Russell, COLSYS - a collocation code for boundary value problems, these proceedings.
17. J.P. Aubin, Approximation of Elliptic Boundary-Value Problems, Wiley, New York, (1972).
18. P.B. Bailey, SLEIGN - an eigenvalue-eigenfunction code for Sturm-Liouville problems, these proceedings and SAND 77-2044, Sandia Labs., Albuquerque, (1977).
19. I. Babuska, W. Rheinbolt and C. Mesztenyi, Self-adaptive refinements in the finite element method, Tech. Rep. TR-375, Inst. for Fluid Dynamics and Appl. Math., Univ. of Maryland, May, 1975.
20. G.A. Baker, Simplified proofs of error estimates for the lease squares method for Dirichlet's problem, Math. Comp. 27(1973), 229-235.
21. R.E. Bellman and R.E. Kalaba, Quasilinearization and Nonlinear Boundary-Value Problems, American Elsevier, New York, (1965).
22. R.E. Bellman, Introduction to Matrix Analysis, 2nd Ed., McGraw Hill, New York, (1970).
23. R.E. Bellman, Stability Theory of Differential Equations, McGraw Hill, New York, (1953).
24. R.E. Bellman and G.M. Wing, An Introduction to Invariant Imbedding, John Wiley and Sons, New York, (1975).
25. E.J. Beltrami, An algorithmic approach to nonlinear analysis and Optimization, Academic Press, New York, (1970).

26. T.A. Bickart, An efficient solution process for implicit Runge-Kutta methods, SIAM J. Num. Anal. 14(1977), 1022-1027.
27. J.J. Blair, Error bounds for the solution of nonlinear two-point boundary value problems by Galerkin's method, Num. Math. 19(1972), 99-109.
28. F.G. Blottner Nonuniform grid method for turbulent boundary layers, Proc. 4th Internat. Conf. on Num. Methods in Fluid Dynamics, ed. by R.D. Richtmyer, Springer-Verlag, Berlin (1975), 91-97.
29. W.R. Boland and P. Nelson, Critical lengths by numerical integration of the associated Ricatti equation to Singularity, Appl. Math. and Comp. 1(1975), 67-82.
30. A. Brandt, Multi-level adaptive solutions to boundary value problems, Math. of Comp., 31(1977), 333-390.
31. F.E. Browder, Approximation-solvability of nonlinear functional equations in normed linear spaces, Arch. Rational Mech. Anal. 26(1967), 33-42.
32. R.R. Brown, Numerical solution of boundary value problems using non-uniform grids, SIAM J. Appl. Math. 10(1962), 475-495.
33. C.G. Broyden, A class of methods for solving nonlinear simultaneous equations, Math. Comp., 19(1965), 577-583.
34. R. Bulirsch, Die Mehrzielmethode zur numerischen Losung von nichtlinearen Randwertproblemen und Aufgaben der optimalen Steuerung, Carl-Cranz-Gesellschaft, Tech. Rep. (1971).
35. R. Bulirsch, J. Stoer and P. Deuflhard, Numerical solution of nonlinear two-point boundary value problems I, Num. Math. Handbook Series Approximation, to appear.
36. H.G. Burchard, Splines (with optimal knots) are better. J. App. Anal. 3(1974), 309-319.
37. P. Businger and G.H. Golub, Linear least squares solutions by Householder transformations, Num. Math. 7(1965), 269-276.
38. J.C. Butcher, On the implementation of implicit Runge-Kutta methods, BIT 16(1976), 237-240.
39. G.D. Byrne and A.C. Hindmarsh, A polyalgorithm for the numerical solution of ordinary differential equations, ACM TOMS 1(1975), 71-96.
40. G.F. Carey and B.A. Finlayson, Orthogonal collocation on finite elements, Chem. Engr. Sci., 30(1975), 587-596.
41. G.F. Carey, A mesh refinement scheme for finite element calculations, Comp. Meth. in Appl. Mech. and Engr. 7(1976), 93-105.
42. T. Cebeci and A.M.D. Smith, A finite difference method for calculating compressible laminar and turbulent flows, J. of Basic Engr., 92(1970), 523-535.
43. John H. Cerutti, Collocation for systems of ordinary differential equations, Comp. Sci. Tech. Rept. #230 (1974), Univ. of Wisc.-Madison.
44. L. Cesari, Functional analysis and Galerkin's method, Michigan Math. J. 2(1964), 385-418.
45. L. Cesari, Asymptotic Behavior and Stability Problems in Ordinary Differential Equations, 3rd ed., Springer-Verlag, New York, (1971).
46. F. Ceschino and J. Kuntzmann, Numerical Solution of Initial Value Problems, Prentice Hall, Englewood Cliffs, NJ, (1966).
47. S. Chandrasekhar, Radiative Transfer, Dover, (1960).
48. B. Childs, D. Luckinbill, J. Bryan and J.H. Boyd, Jr., Numerical solution of multipoint boundary value problems in linear systems, Int. J. Systems Science, 2(1971), 49-57.
49. B. Childs, H.H. Doiron and C.C. Holloway, Numerical solution of multipoint boundary value problems in nonlinear systems, Int. J. Systems Science, 2(1971), 58-66.
50. B. Childs, H. Doiron and C. Holloway, QUASI - solution of multipoint boundary value problems of quasilinear differential equations, Univ. of Houston, Themis Rep. RE7-69 , (1970).
51. J. Christiansen and R.D. Russell, Adaptive mesh selection strategies for solving boundary problems, SIAM J. Num. Anal. 15(1978), 59-80.

52. J. Christiansen and R.D. Russell, Error analysis for spline collocation methods with application to knot selection, to appear.
53. P.G. Ciarlet, M.H. Schultz and R.S. Varga, Numerical methods of high order accuracy for nonlinear boundary value problems. I. One dimensional problem, Num. Math. 9(1967), 394-430.
54. P.G. Ciarlet, M.H. Schultz and R.S. Varga, Numerical methods of high order accuracy for nonlinear boundary value problems. II. Nonlinear boundary conditions, Num. Math. 11(1968), 331-345.
55. P.G. Ciarlet, M.H. Schultz and R.S. Varga, Numerical methods of high order accuracy for nonlinear boundary value problems. IV. Periodic boundary conditions, Num. Math. 12(1968), 266-279.
56. P.G. Ciarlet, M.H. Schultz and R.S. Varga, Numerical methods of high order accuracy for nonlinear boundary value problems. V. Monotone operators, Num. Math. 13(1969), 51-77.
57. P. Concus and V. Pereyra, A software package for meniscus calculations. In preparation.
58. S.D. Conte, The numerical solution of Linear boundary value problems, SIAM Review 8(1966), 309-321.
59. James W. Daniel, Extrapolation with spline-collocation methods for two-point boundary value problems I: Proposals and justifications, Aeq. Math. 16(1977), 107-122.
60. James W. Daniel and Andrew J. Martin, Extrapolation with spline-collocation methods for two-point boundary value problems II: C-2-cubics, to appear.
61. J.W. Daniel, A road map of methods for approximating solutions of two-point boundary-value problems, these proceedings and CNA-130 Center for Numerical Analysis, The University of Texas at Austin.
62. James W. Daniel and Blair K. Swartz, Extrapolated collocation for two-point boundary value problems using cubic splines, J. Inst. Math. Appl. 16(1975), 161-174.
63. B.L. Darlow, M.R. Scott, and H.A. Watts, Modifications of SUPORT, a linear boundary value problem solver: Part I - Pre-assigning orthonormalization points, auxillary initial value problem, disk or tape storage, SAND 77-1328, Sandia Labs., Albuquerque, (1977).
64. B.L. Darlow, M.R. Scott and H.A. Watts, Modifications of SUPORT, a linear boundary-value problem solver: Part II - Inclusion of an Adams integrator SAND 77-1960, Sandia Labs., Albuquerque, (1977).
65. A. Davey, A simple numerical method for solving the Orr-Sommerfeld problems, Quart. J. Mech. Appl. Math. 26(1973), 401-411.
66. DD04AD, Program documentation. Harwell, AERE, Oxfordshire, (1978).
67. C. deBoor, The method of projections as applied to the numerical solution of two-point boundary value problems using cubic splines, Thesis, Univ. of Michigan (1966).
68. C. deBoor, A bound on the L-infinity-norm of the L-2-approximation by splines in terms of a global mesh ratio, Math. Comp. 30(1976), 765-771.
69. C. deBoor, Package for calculating with B-splines, SIAM J. Num. Anal. 14(1977), 441-472.
70. C. deBoor and B. Swartz, Collocation at Gaussian points, SIAM J. Num. Anal. 10(1973), 582-606.
71. C. deBoor, Bounding the error in spline interpolation, SIAM Review 16(1974), 531-544.
72. C. deBoor and Blair Swartz, Comments on the comparison of global methods for linear two-point boundary value problems. Math. Comp 31(1977) 916-921.
73. C. deBoor and R. Weiss, Solveblok: a package for solving almost block diagonal linear systems, with applications to spline approximation and the numerical solution of ordinary differential equations, MRC TSR #1625, (1976), Madison, Wisconsin.
74. C. deBoor, Good approximation by splines with variable knots. II, Springer Lecture Note Series 363(1973), 12-20.
75. V.E. Denny and R.B. Landis, A new method for solving two-point boundary value problems using optimal node distributions, J. Comp. Phys., 9(1972), 120-137.

76. E.M. deRivas, On the use of nonuniform grids in finite-difference equations, J. Comp. Phys. 10(1972), 202-210.
77. P. Deuflhard, Ein Newton-Verfahren bei fastsingularer Funktional-matrix zur Losung von nichtlinearen Randwertaufgaben mit der Mehrzielmethode, Universitat Koln, Mathematisches Institut: Dissertation (1972).
78. P. Deuflhard, A modified Newton method for the solution of ill conditioned systems of nonlinear equations with application to multiple shooting, Num. Math. 22(1974), 289-315.
79. P. Deuflhard, A relaxation strategy for the modified Newton method, in Conference Proceedings on Optimization and Optimal Control, ed by Bulirsch, Oettli and Stoer, Lecture Notes 477, (1975), 59-73.
80. P. Deuflhard, A stepsize control for continuation methods with special application to multiple shooting techniques. Tum. Math. 7627, Techn. Univ. Munchen, (1976).
81. P. Deuflhard, H.J. Pesch and R. Rentrop, A modified continuation method for the numerical solution of nonlinear two-point boundary value problems by shooting techniques, Num. Math. 26(1976), 327-343.
82. P. Deuflhard, Nonlinear equation solvers in boundary value problem codes, these proceedings.
83. P. Deuflhard and G. Heindl, Affine invariant convergence theorems for Newton's method and extensions to related methods, to appear SIAM J. Num. Anal.
84. J.C. Diaz, A collocation-Galerkin method for two-point boundary value problems using continuous piecewise polynomial spaces, SIAM J. Num. Anal. 14(1977), 844-858.
85. E.D. Dickmanns, Optimal control for synergetic plane change, Proc. XXth Int. Astronautical Congress, (1969), 597-631.
86. E.D. Dickmanns, Maximum range three-dimensional lifting planetary entry, NASA Tech. Rep. TR R-387 (1972).
87. E.D. Dickmanns and H.J. Pesch, Influence of a reradiative heating constraint on lifting entry trajectories for maximum lateral range, 11th Int. Symp. on Space Tech. and Sci., Tokyo (1975).
88. E.D. Dickmanns and K.H. Well, Approximate solution of optimal control problems using third order Hermite polynomial functions, Springer Lecture Notes in Comp. Sci. 27(1975), 158-166.
89. H.J. Diekoff, P. Lory, H.J. Oberle, H.J. Pesch, P. Rentrop and R. Seydel, Comparing routines for the numerical solution of initial value problems of ordinary differential equations in multiple shooting, Num. Math. 27(1977), 449-469.
90. D.S. Dodson, Optimal order approximation by polynomial spline functions, Ph.D. Thesis, Purdue Univ., Lafayette, IN, (1972).
91. E.J. Doedel, The construction of finite difference approximations to ordinary differential equations, SIAM J. Num. Anal. 15(1978), 450-465.
92. E.J. Doedel, Finite difference methods for nonlinear two-point boundary value problems, SIAM J. Num. Anal., to appear.
93. Jim Douglas, Jr. and Todd Dupont, Collocation methods for parabolic equations in a single space variable based on C-1-piecewise-polynomial spaces, Springer Lecture Note Series 385(1974), Springer-Verlag, Berlin.
94. Jim Douglas, Jr. and Todd Dupont, Galerkin approximations for the two-point boundary value problem using continuous, piecewise polynomial spaces, Num. Math. 22(1974), 99-109.
95. Jim Douglas, Jr. and Todd Dupont, Superconvergence for Galerkin methods for the two-point boundary problem via local projections, Num. Math. 21(1973), 270-278.
96. Jim Douglas, Jr., Todd Dupont and Lars Wahlbin, Optimal L-infinity error estimates for Galerkin approximations to solutions of two-point boundary value problems, Math. Comp. 29(1975), 475-483.
97. J. Douglas, Jr., T. Dupont and M.F. Wheeler, H-1-Galerkin methods for the Laplace and heat equations, in Mathematical Aspects of Finite Elements in Partial Differential Equations, ed. by C. deBoor, Academic Press, New York (1974), 353-382.

98. J. Douglas, Jr., T. Dupont and M.F. Wheeler, Some superconvergence results for an H-1-Galerkin procedure for the heat equation, Lecture Notes on Computer Science 10(1974), Springer-Verlag, New York, 288-309.
99. N. Dunford and J.T. Schwartz, Linear Operators, Part I, Wiley, New York (1958).
100. Roderick J. Dunn, Jr. and Mary Fanett Wheeler, Some collocation-Galerkin methods for two-point boundary value problems, SIAM J. Num. Anal. 13(1976), 720-733.
101. Todd Dupont, A unified theory of superconvergence for Galerkin methods for two-point boundary value problems, SIAM J. Num. Anal. 13(1976), 362-368.
102. R. England, A program for the solution of boundary value problems for systems of ordinary differential equations, Culham Laboratory, UKAEA Research Group, Tech. Rep. CLM-PDN 3/73 (1976).
103. W.H. Enright and T.E. Hull, Test results on initial value methods for non-stiff ordinary differential equations, SIAM J. Num. Anal. 13(1976), 944-961.
104. W.H. Enright, T.E. Hull and B. Lindberg, Comparing numerical methods for stiff systems of ODE's, BIT 15(1975), 10-48.
105. W.H. Enright, Improving the efficiency of matrix operations in the numerical solution of stiff ODE's, Univ. of Toronto, Dept. of Comp. Sci., Tech. Rep. 98, (1976).
106. M.A. Epton, An exponential theory of implicit Runge-Kutta processes, Boeing Computer Services Report, Seattle, WA, (1977).
107. P. Farahzad and R.P. Tewarson, An efficient numerical method for solving the differential equation of renal counterflow systems, Comp. Bio. Med. 8(1978), 57-64.
108. A.F. Fath, Computational aspects of the linear optimal regulator problem Proc. Joint Auto. Control Conf., (1969), 44-49.
109. N.B. Ferguson and B.A. Finlayson, Error bounds for approximate solutions to nonlinear ordinary differential equations, AIChE J. 18(1972) 1053-1059.
110. B.A. Finlayson, Method of Weighted Residuals and Variational Principles, Academic Press, New York, (1972).
111. George J. Fix, Effects of quadrature errors in finite element approximation of steady state, eigenvalue, and parabolic problems, in The Mathematical Foundations of the Finite Element Method with Applications to Partial Differential Equations, ed. by A.K. Aziz, Academic Press (1972), New York, 525-556.
112. G.E. Forsythe, M.A. Malcolm and C.B. Moler, Computer Methods for Mathematical Computations, Prentice Hall, Engelwood Cliffs, NJ, (1977).
113. L. Fox, The Numerical Solution of Two Point Boundary Problems in Ordinary Differential Equations, Clarendon, England, (1957). value problems, Comput. J. 12(1969), 188-192.
114. D.J. Fyffe, The use of cubic splines in the solution of two-point boundary value problems, Comp. J. 12(1969), 188-192.
115. C.W. Gear, Numerical Initial Value Problems in Ordinary Differential Equations, Prentice Hall, Engelwood Cliffs, NJ, (1971).
116. I. Gladwell, Shooting codes in the NAG library, these proceedings.
117. S. Godunov, On the numerical solution of boundary-value problems for systems of linear ordinary differential equations, Uspekhi Mat. Nauk. 16(1961), 171-174.
118. M.A. Goldberg, Some functional relationships for two-point boundary value problems, J. Math. Anal. and Appl. 45(1974), 199-209.
119. G.H. Golub and C. Reinsch, Singular value decomposition and least squares solutions, Num. Math. 14(1970), 403-420.
120. D.O. Gough, E.A. Spiegel, and J. Toomce, Highly stretched meshes as functionals of solutions, in Proc. 4th Internat. Conf. Num. Methods in Fluid Dynamics, ed. by R.D. Richtmyer, Springer-Verlag, (1975). 191-196.

121. A.I. Grebennikov, The choice of nodes in the approximation of functions by splines, USSR Comp. Math. and Math. Phys., 16(1976), 208-213.

122. S.G. Greenberg and Y. Bard, A comparison of computational methods for solving the algebraic matrix Riccati equation, Proc. IEEE Conf. Decision and Control, December 1971.

123. A.G. Greenhill, On Riccati's equation and Bessel's equation, Quart. J. of Math., 16(1879), 294-298.

124. F.M. Guerra and E.B. Becker, Finite element analysis for the adaptive method of rezoning, TICOM Rep. Univ. of Texas at Austin, (1977).

125. G. Hall and J.M. Watt, editors, Modern Numerical Methods for Ordinary Differential Equations, Clarendon Press, Oxford, (1976).

126. P. Hallet, J.P. Hennart and E.H. Mund, A Galerkin method with modified piecewise polynomials for solving a second-order boundary value problem, Num. Math. 27(1976), 11-20.

127. P. Hemker, A Numerical Study of Stiff Two-point Boundary Problems, Math. Centrum, Amsterdam, (1977).

128. P. Henrici, Discrete Variable Methods in Ordinary Differential Equations John Wiley and Sons, New York, (1962).

129. R.J. Herbold, M.H. Schultz and R.S. Varga, The effect of quadrature errors in the numerical solution of boundary value problems by variational techniques, Aeq. Math. 3(1969), 247-270.

130. A.C. Hindmarsh, GEAR: Ordinary differential equation system solver, Rep. UCID-3001, Rev. 3, Lawrence Livermore Labs., Livermore, CA, (1971).

131. J.F. Holt, Numerical solution of nonlinear two-point boundary problems by finite difference methods, Comm. ACM, I (1964), 366-373.

132. M.K. Horn, Developments in high-order Runge-Kutta-Nystrom formulas, Ph.D. Dissertation, Univ. of Texas, Austin, (1977).

133. E.N. Houstis, Application of method of collocation on lines for solving nonlinear hyperbolic problems, Math. Comp. 31(1977), 443-456.

134. Elias Houstis, A collocation method for systems of nonlinear ordinary differential equations, J. Math. Anal. Appl. 62(1978), 24-37.

135. T.E. Hull, W.H. Enright, B.M. Fellen and A.E. Sedgwick, Comparing numerical methods for ordinary differential equations, SIAM J. Num. Anal., 9(1972), 603-637.

136. T.E. Hull, W.H. Enright and K.R. Jackson, User's guide to DVERK - a subroutine for solving non-stiff ODE's, Univ. of Toronto, Dept. of Comp. Sci., Tech. Rep. 100, (1976).

137. B. Hulme, One-step piecewise polynomial Galerkin methods for initial value problems, Math. Comp. 26(1972), 415-426.

138. D. Humphrey and G.F. Carey, Adaptive mesh refinement algorithm using element residuals, these proceedings and TICOM Rep. 78-1, Univ. of Texas, Austin, 1978.

139. C.D. Hunter and B. Childs, A statistical study of numerical analysis applied to the regression of nth order differential equations, Proc. 22nd Conf. of Army Mathematicians, Army Research Office, Durham, (1976). 497-507.

140. H.G. Hussels, Schrittweitensteuerung bei der integration gewohnlicher differentialgleichungen mit extrapolationverfahren, M.Sc. Thesis, Universitat Koln, Germany, (1973).

141. IMSL - International Mathematical and Statistics Libraries, Inc., Houston, (1978).

142. K.R. Jackson, W.H. Enright and T.E. Hull, A theoretical criterion for comparing Runge-Kutta formulas, Univ. of Toronto, Dept. of Comp. Sci., Tech. Rep. 101, (1977).

143. W.J. Kammerer, G.W. Reddien and R.S. Varga, Quadratic interpolatory splines, Num. Math. 22(1974), 241-259.

144. L.V. Kantorovich and G.P. Akilov, Functional Analysis in Normed Spaces, Pergamon Press, New York, (1964).

145. L.V. Kantorovich and V.I. Krylov, Approximate Methods of Higher Analysis, Interscience, New York (1964).
146. J.P. Keener and F.T. Krogh, Jet Propulsion Lab. Computing Memoranda, Pasadena.
147. H.B. Keller, Numerical Methods for Two Point Boundary Value Problems, Blaisdell, London, (1968).
148. H.B. Keller, Accurate difference methods for linear ordinary differential systems subject to linear constraints, SIAM J. Num. Anal. 6(1969), 8-30.
149. H.B. Keller, Accurate difference methods for nonlinear two point boundary value problems, SIAM J. Num. Anal. 11(1974), 305-320.
150. H.B. Keller, Numerical solution of boundary value problems for ordinary differential equations: survey and some recent results on difference methods, in Numerical Solutions of Boundary Value Problems for Ordinary Differential Equations, ed. by A.K. Aziz, Academic Press, New York, (1975), 27-88.
151. H.B. Keller, Approximation methods for nonlinear problems with application to two-point boundary value problems, Math. Comp. 29(1975), 464-474.
152. H.B. Keller and A.B. White, Jr., Difference methods for boundary value problems in ordinary differential equations, SIAM J. Num. Anal. 12(1975), 791-801.
153. Herbert B. Keller, Numerical Solution of Two Point Boundary Value Problems, CBMS Series 24(1976), SIAM, Philadelphia.
154. H.B. Keller, Numerical solution of bifurcation and nonlinear eigenvalue problems, in Applications of Bifurcation Theory, ed. by P. Rabinowitz, Academic Press, New York, (1977), 359-384.
155. H.B. Keller, Constructive methods for bifurcation and nonlinear eigenvalue problems, in Proc. 3rd Int. Symp. on Comp. Methods in Applied Sc. and Engr., Versailles, France(1977).
156. H.B. Keller and V. Pereyra, Difference methods and deferred corrections for ordinary boundary value problems, to appear in SIAM J. Num. Anal.
157. R.P. Kendall and M.F. Wheeler, A Crank-Nicolson H-1-Galerkin procedure for parabolic problems in a single space variable, SIAM J. Num. Anal. 13(1976), 861-876.
158. J. Kowalik and M.R. Osborne, Methods for Unconstrained Optimization Problems, Amer. Elsevier Pub., New York(1978).
159. Luis Kramarz, Global approximations of solutions to initial value problems, Math. Comp. 32(1978), 35-60.
160. M.A. Krasnoselskii, G.M. Vainikko, P.P. Sabreiko, J.B. Rutizki and W.J. Stezenko, Naherungsverfahren Zur Losung von Operatorgleichungen, Akademie-Verlag (1973), Berlin.
161. F.T. Krogh, Algorithms for changing the step-size, SIAM J. Num. Anal., 10(1973), 949-965.
162. F.T. Krogh, Preliminary usage documentation for the variable order integrators SODE and DODE, Computing Memo 399, JPL, Pasadena, (1975).
163. M. Kubicek and V. Hlavacek, A review of application of shooting methods for nonlinear chemical engineering problems, Scientific Papers of the Prague Inst. of Chem. Tech. K9 (1974), 5-35.
164. J.D. Lambert, Computational Methods in Ordinary Differential Equations, John Wiley and Sons, London, (1973).
165. L. Lapidus and J.H. Seinfeld, Numerical Solution of Ordinary Differential Equations, Academic Press, New York, (1971).
166. M. Lentini, Correcciones diferidas papa problemas de contorno en sistemas de ecuaciones diferenciales de primer orden, Pub. 73-04, Depto. de Comp. Fac. Ciencias, Univ. Central de Venezuela, Caracas.
167. M. Lentini and V. Pereyra, A variable order finite difference method for nonlinear multipoint boundary value problems, Math. Comp. 28(1974), 981-1004.
168. M. Lentini and V. Pereyra, PASVA2-Two point boundary value problem solver for nonlinear first order systems, Lawrence Berkeley Lab. program documentation report, (1975).

169. M. Lentini and V. Pereyra, Boundary problem solvers for first order systems based on deferred corrections, in Numerical Solution of Boundary Value Problems for Ordinary Differential Equations, Edited by A.K. Aziz, Academic Press, New York, (1975).
170. M. Lentini and V. Pereyra, An adaptive finite difference solver for nonlinear two point boundary problems with mild boundary layers, SIAM J. Num. Anal. 14(1977), 91-111 also STAN-CS-75-530, Comp. Sci. Dept., Stanford Univ. 1975.
171. M. Lentini, Boundary Value Problems over Semi-Infinite Intervals, Ph.D. Thesis, Cal. Inst. of Tech., (1978).
172. B. Lindbergh, Characterization of optimal stepsize sequences for methods for stiff differential equations, SIAM J. Num. Anal., 14(1977), 859-887.
173. O.V. Lokutsyevsku, Numerical methods for the solution of partial differential equations(in Russian)(All-union conf. on functional analysis and its applications), Uspekhi Mat. Nauk 11(1956), 224.
174. M.E. Lord and H.E. Watts, Modifications of SUPORT, a linear boundary-value problem solver: Part III - Orthonormalization Improvements, SAND 78-0522, Sandia Labs., Albuquerque, (1978).
175. P. Lory, Homotopieverfahren und Anwendung der Mehrzielmethode auf mathematische Modelle aus der Physiologie, Work done in preparation of a dissertation (Technische Universitat Munchen, Institut fur Mathematik).
176. T.R. Lucas and G.W. Reddien, Some collocation methods for nonlinear boundary value problems, SIAM J. Num. Anal. 9(1972), 341-356.
177. T.R. Lucas and G.W. Reddien, A high order projection method for nonlinear two-point boundary value problems, Num. Math. 20(1973), 257-270.
178. R.E. Lynch and J.R. Rice, A higher order difference method for differential equations, CSD-TR 244, Math. Sci. (1977), Purdue University West Lafayette, Indiana.
179. G.I. Marchuk, Numerical methods for nuclear reactor calculations(in Russian), M. Atomizdat, 1958.
180. K. Martensson, On the matrix Riccati equation, Information Sciences, 3(1971), 17-49.
181. R.J. Melosh and P.V. Marcal, An energy basis for mesh refinement of structural continua, Int. J. Num. Meth. Engr., 11(1977), 1083-1091.
182. P. Merluzzi and C. Brosilow, Runge-Kutta integration algorithms with built-in estimates of the accumulated truncation error, Computing 20(1978) 1-16.
183. G.H. Meyer, Initial Value Methods for Boundary Value Problems, Academic Press, New York, (1973).
184. G.H. Meyer, The method of lines for Poisson's equation with nonlinear or free boundary conditions, Num. Math. 29(1978), 329-344.
185. S.G. Mikhlin, The Numerical Performance of Variational Methods, Wolters-Noordhoff (1971), The Netherlands.
186. W.E. Milne, Numerical Solution of Differential Equations, John Wiley and Sons, New York, (1953).
187. P. Nelson, Jr. and I.T. Elder, Calculation of eigenfunctions in the context of integration-to-blowup, SIAM J. Num. Anal. 14(1977), 124-136.
188. W.L. Miranker and G. Wahba, An averaging method for the stiff oscillatory problem, Math. Comp., 30(1976), 383-399.
189. M.S. Mock, Projection methods with different trial and test spaces, Math. Comp. 30(1976), 400-416.
190. Frank Natterer, Uniform convergence of Galerkin's method for splines on highly nonuniform meshes, Math. Comp. 31(1977), 457-468.
191. A.W. Naylor and G.R. Sell, Linear Operator Theory in Engineering and Science, Holt, Rinehart, and Winston, New York, (1971).
192. J. Nitsche, Ein Kriterium fur die Quasi-Optimalitat des Ritzschen Verfahrens, Num. Math. 11(1968), 346-348.
193. S.P. Norsett, Semi-explicit Runge-Kutta methods, The Univ. of Trondheim, Mathematics and Computation Rep. 6/74, Trondheim, Norway.
194. J. Oliger, Approximate methods for atmospheric and oceanographic circulation problems, in Proc. 3rd Int. Symp. on Comp. Meth. in Appl. Sci. and Engr., Springer-Verlag, (1978).

195. J.M. Ortega and W.C. Rheinboldt, Iterative Solution of Nonlinear Equations in Several Variables, Academic Press, New York, (1970).

196. M.R. Osborne, Minimizing truncation error in finite difference approximations to ordinary differential equations, Math. of Comp., 21 (1967), 133-145.

197. M.R. Osborne, On shooting methods for boundary value problems, J. Math. Anal. and Appl. 27(1969), 417-433.

198. W.R. Paterson and D.L. Cresswell, A simple method for the calculation of effectiveness factors, Chem. Engr. Sci. 26(1971), 605-616.

199. C.E. Pearson, A numerical method for ordinary differential equations of boundary-layer type, J. Math. Phys., 47(1968), 134-154.
C.E. Pearson, On a differential equation of boundary layer type, J. Math. and Phys., 47(1968), 351-358.

200. V. Pereyra, The difference correction method for nonlinear two point boundary value problems of class M, Rev. Union Mat., Argentina 22(1965), 184-201.

201. V. Pereyra, Iterated deferred corrections for nonlinear operator equations, Num. Math. 10(1967), 316-323.

202. V. Pereyra, Iterated deferred corrections for nonlinear boundary value problems, Num. Math. 11(1968), 111-125.

203. V. Pereyra, High order finite difference solution of differential equations, Comp. Sci. Dept., Stanford Univ. Report STAN-CS-73-348.

204. V. Pereyra and E.G. Sewell, Mesh selection for discrete solution of boundary value problems in ordinary differential equations, Num. Math. 23(1975), 261-268.

205. F.M. Perrin, H.S. Price and R.S. Varga, On higher-order methods for nonlinear two-point boundary value problems, Num. Math. 13(1969), 180-198.

206. G. Peters and J.H. Wilkinson, The least squares problem and pseudoinverses, Comp. J. 13(1970), 309-316.

207. W.V. Petryshyn, Direct and iterative methods for the solution of linear operator equations in Hilbert space, Trans. Amer. Math. Soc. 105(1962), 136-175.

208. L. Petzold and C.W. Gear, Methods for oscillating problems, Univ. of Illinois, Dept. of Comp. Sci., Rep. UILU-ENG-77-1752.

209. James L. Phillips, The use of collocation as a projection method for solving linear operator equations, SIAM J. Num. Anal. 9(1972), 14-28.

210. N.I. Polskii, Projection methods in applied mathematics, Soviet Math. Dokl. 3(1962), 228-242.

211. J.E. Potter, Matrix Riccati solutions, SIAM J. Appl. Math. 14(1966), 496-501.

212. W. Prager, A note on the optimal choice of finite element grids, Comp. Meth. Appl. Mech. Engr., 6(1975), 363-366.

213. H.H. Rachford, Jr. and Mary F. Wheeler, An H-1-Galerkin procedure for the two-point boundary value problem, in Mathematical Aspects of Finite Elements in Partial Differential Equations, ed. by Carl deBoor, Academic Press (1974), 353-382.

214. G.W. Reddien, Approximation methods for two-point boundary value problems with nonlinear boundary conditions, SIAM J. Num. Anal. 13(1976), 405-411.

215. G.W. Reddien, Approximation methods and alternative problems, J. Math. Anal. Appl. 60(1977), 139-149.

216. J.K. Reid, Fortran subroutines for the solution of sparse systems of nonlinear equations, Harwell UKAEA Research Group, Theoretical Physics Division, Tech. Rep. AERE-R7293 (1972).

217. P. Rentrop, Numerical solution of the singular Ginzburg-Landau equations by multiple shooting, Computing 16(1976), 61-67.

218. P. Rentrop, Eine Taylorreihenmethode zur numerischen Losung von Zwei-Punkt-Randwertproblemen mit Anwendung auf singulare Probleme der nichtlinearen Schalentheorie, Tech. Univ. Munchen, Inst. fur Mathematik, Dissertation (1977).

219. W.T. Reid, Riccati Differential Equations, Academic Press, New York (1972)
220. G.O. Roberts, Computational meshes for boundary value problems, in Proc. 2nd Int. Conf. Num. Meth. Fluid Dyn., ed. M. Holt, Springer-Verlag, (1970), 171-178.
221. S.M. Roberts and J.S. Shipman, Two-Point Boundary Value Problems: Shooting Methods, Elsevier, New York, (1972).
222. R.D. Russell, Collocation for systems of boundary value problems, Num. Math. 23(1974), 119-133.
223. R.D. Russell, A comparison of collocation and finite differences for two-point boundary value problems, SIAM J. Num. Anal. 14(1977), 19-39.
224. R.D. Russell and L.F. Shampine, A collocation method for boundary value problems, Num. Math. 19(1972), 1-28.
225. R.D. Russell and J.M. Varah, A comparison of global methods for two-point boundary value problems, Math. Comp. 29(1975), 1007-1019.
226. R.D. Russell, Efficiencies of B-splines methods for solving differential equations, Proc. Fifth Conference on Numerical Mathematics, Manitoba (1975), 599-617.
227. R.D. Russell, A comparison of collocation and finite differences for two-point boundary value problems, SIAM J. Num. Anal. 14(1977), 19-39.
228. R.D. Russell and J. Christiansen, Adaptive mesh selection strategies for solving boundary value problems, SIAM J. Num. Anal., 15(1978), 59-80.
229. Peter H. Sammon, A discrete least squares method, Math. Comp. 31(1977) 60-65.
230. A. Schatz, An observation concerning Ritz-Galerkin methods with indefinite bilinear forms, Math. Comp. 28(1974), 959-962.
231. L.K. Schubert, Modifications of a quasi-Newton method for nonlinear equations with a sparse Jacobian, Math. Comp. 24(1970), 27-30.
232. M.H. Schultz, Spline Analysis, Prentice-Hall, Englewood Cliffs, NJ (1973)
233. M.H. Schultz, Quadrature-Galerkin approximations to solutions of elliptic differential equations, Proc. A.M.S. 33(1972), 511-515.
234. M.R. Scott, A bibliography on invariant imbedding and related topics, SLA-74-0284, Sandia Labs., Albuquerque, NM, (1974).
235. M.R. Scott and W.H. Vandevender, A comparison of several invariant imbedding algorithms for the solution of two-point boundary-value problems Appl. Math. and Comp., 1(1975), 187-218.
236. M.R. Scott, On the conversion of boundary value problems into stable initial value problems via several invariant imbedding algorithms, in Numerical Solutions of Boundary Value Problems for Ordinary Differential Equations, edited by A.K. Aziz, Academic Press, New York, (1975).
237. M.R. Scott, Invariant Imbedding and Its Applications to Ordinary Differential Equations, An Introduction, Addison-Wesley, Reading, MA, 1973
238. M.R. Scott and H.A. Watts, Computational solution of linear two-point boundary value problems via orthonormalization, SIAM J. Num. Anal. 14 (1977), 40-70.
239. M.R. Scott and H.R. Watts, Computational solution of nonlinear two-point boundary value problems, SAND 77-0091, Sandia Labs., Albuquerque, (1977), also in Proc. of 5th Symp. of Comp. in Chem. Engr. (1977).
240. M.R. Scott and H.A. Watts, SUPORT - a computer code for two-point boundary-value problems via orthonormalization, SAND 75-0198, Sandia Labs. Albuquerque, (1975).
241. M.R. Scott and H.A. Watts, A systematized collection of codes for solving two-point boundary-value problems, in Numerical Methods for Differential Systems, ed. by A.K. Aziz, Academic Press (1976), 197-227.
242. S.M. Serbin, Computational investigations of least-squares type methods for the approximate solution of boundary value problems, Math. Comp. 29(1975), 777-793.
243. G. Sewell, An adaptive computer program for the solution of DIV(P(X,Y)GRAD U) = F(X,Y,U) on a polygonal region, in Math. of Fin. Elt. and Appl. II, MAFELAP 1974, ed. J.R. Whiteman, Academic Press, New York and London, (1976).

244. Richard F. Sincovec, On the relative efficiency of higher order collocation methods for solving two-point boundary value problems, SIAM J. Num. Anal. 14(1977), 112-123.

245. L.F. Shampine and M.K. Gordon, Computer Solution of Ordinary Differential Equations: The Initial Value Problem, Freeman, (1975).

246. L.F. Shampine and C.W. Gear, A user's view of solving stiff ordinary differential equations, Univ. of Illinois, Dept. of Comp. Sci., Report UIUCDCS-R-76-829 (to appear in SIAM Review).

247. L.F. Shampine and H.A. Watts, Practical solution of ordinary differential equations by Runge-Kutta methods, SAND 76-0585, Sandia Labs., Albuquerque (1976).

248. L.F. Shampine and H.A. Watts, Global error estimation for ordinary differential equations, ACM TOMS, 2(1976), 172-186.

249. L.F. Shampine and H.A. Watts, Solving nonstiff ordinary differential equations-The state of the art, SIAM Review, 18(1976), 376-411.

250. L.F. Shampine and H.A. Watts, The art of writing a Runge-Kutta code, part I, in Mathematical Software III, ed. by J.R. Rice, Academic Press, London, (1977), 257-275.

251. L.F. Shampine, Cheaper integration of linear systems, SIMULATION 20(1973) p. 17.

252. D.D. Siljak, Non-Linear Systems, John Wiley and sons, New York, (1972).

253. S. Silverston, QSLIN - a Fortran subroutine package for the solution of nonlinear two-point boundary value problems, Purdue Univ., Comp. Sci. Dept. Rep. SCD TR 17, (1968).

254. R.D. Skeel and A.K. Kong, Blended linear multi-step methods, ACM TOMS 3(1977), 326-345.

255. S. Skelboe, The control of order and steplength for backward differentiation methods, BIT 17(1977), 91-107.

256. H. Spreuer and E. Adams, Pathologische Beispiele von Differenzenverfahren bei nichtlinearen gewohnlichen Randwertaufgaben, ZAMM 57(1977), 304-305.

257. J.L. Stephenson, R.P. Tewarson and R. Meija, Quantative analysis of mass and energy balance in non-ideal models of renal counterflow systems, Proc. Nat. Acad. Sci. USA 71(1974), 1618-1622.

258. J. Stoer and R. Bulirsch, Einfuhrung in die Numerische Mathematik II, Springer, Berlin, Heidelberg, New York, (1973).

259. H.J. Stetter, Analysis of Discretization Methods for Ordinary Differential Equations, Springer-Verlag, Berlin, (1973).

260. Gilbert Strang and George J. Fix, An Analysis of the Finit Element Method Prentice-Hall, Englewood Cliffs, NJ (1973).

261. J.W. Tang and D.J. Turcke, Characteristics of optimal grids, Comp. Meth. Appl. Mech. Engr., 11(1977), 31-37.

262. B.D. Tapley and W.E. Williamson, Comparison of linear and Riccati equations used to solve optimal control problems, AIAA J. 10(1972), 1154-1159.

263. L.K. Timothy and B.E. Bona, State Space Analysis, an Introduction, McGraw Hill, New York, (1968).

264. B.A. Troesch, Intrinsic difficulties in the numerical solution of a boundary value problem, Space Tech. Labs., Tech. Note NN-142(1960).

265. M. Urabe, Numerical solution of multi-point boundary value problems in Chebychev series. Theory and method, Num. Math. 9(1967), 341-366.

266. M. Urabe and A. Reiter, Numerical computation of nonlinear forced oscillations by Galerkin's procedure, J. Math. Anal. Appl. 14(1966), 107-140.

267. G.M. Vainikko, Convergence of the collocation method for nonlinear differential equations, USSR Comp. Math. and Math. Phys. 6(1966), 47-58.

268. G.M. Vainikko, Galerkin's perturbation method and the general theory of approximate methods for nonlinear equations, USSR Comp. Math. and Math. Phys., 7(1967), 1-41.